# BUILDING

A

# WORLD

# COMMUNITY

# BUILDING

## A

# WORLD

## COMMUNITY

### HUMANISM IN THE 21ST CENTURY

EDITED BY

## PAUL KURTZ

IN COOPERATION WITH

## LEVI FRAGELL & ROB TIELMAN

PROMETHEUS BOOKS • BUFFALO, NEW YORK

*BL*
*2747.6*
*.B85*
*1989*

Library of Congress Cataloging-in-Publication Data

Humanist World Congress (10th : Buffalo, N.Y.)
        Building a world community : humanism in the twenty-first century
    : papers delivered at the Tenth Humanist World Congress / sponsored
    by the International Humanist and Ethical Union (IHEU) : edited by
    Paul Kurtz with the cooperation of Levi Fragell and Rob Tielman.
            p.      cm.
        The congress was held in Buffalo, N.Y., in August 1988.
        ISBN 0-87975-538-5
        1. Humanism—20th century—Congresses. I. Kurtz, Paul W., 1925-
    II. Fragell, Levi. III. Tielman, Rob, 1946-      .
    IV. International Humanist and Ethical Union. V. Title.
    BL2747.6.H86      1988
    144—dc20                                                    89-36948
                                                                    CIP

# Contents

## IX. Bringing Up Children/Moral Education

## X. Future Issues and Trends: Biomedical Ethics

## XI. The Future of the Humanist Movement

# Introduction

How can we develop a new global ethics for humankind and what would it entail? What is the role of humanism in the world of the future?

Humanism traces its heritage back to the classical cultures of Greece and Rome, China, Africa, and Asia. It is expressed in the great literature of the ages, in philosophy, the sciences, and the arts. The humanist tradition came to fruition during the Renaissance and the Enlightenment and has continued to blossom with the emergence of modern science and modern secular democratic institutions.

Today, as our globe continues to shrink and our mutual dependence becomes apparent, humanism becomes all the more relevant to the survival of our species and of other forms of life on this planet—and humanists are in the forefront in suggesting daring new ideals for humanity.

What are some of the basic principles of the humanist outlook?

First, we are committed to free inquiry and to the free mind. We believe in the use of reason and evidence to evaluate claims to truth, and we believe in testing these claims by examining their consequences in experience. Thus we wish to encourage the use of the scientific method because of its demonstrated ability to discover the truth and to provide great benefit for humankind.

Second, we are skeptical of transcendental claims of a reality that cannot be evaluated by human reason or tested by experience. We are dubious of all the forms of superstition, whether ancient or modern, though we are open to the possibility of uncovering new dimensions in nature.

Third, we wish to use reason to help solve social and ethical problems, applying the skills of critical intelligence and a maximum of good will.

Fourth, we are deeply concerned about enhancing human values and encouraging the moral life.

Fifth, our ethical concern emphasizes the centrality of personal human happiness. We wish to foster free societies, where individuals can fulfill their own unique conceptions of the good life, consonant, of course, with the general good; societies in which individuals are entrusted with autonomy over their own lives, are able to exercise responsible choices, can lead lives of excellence and enjoyment, and can contribute to the community. We wish to tap the vast reservoirs of human creativity—intellectual, moral, and aesthetic.

Sixth, we are committed to the democratic way of life, with its ideals of freedom and equality. We are opposed to the evil of discrimination on any grounds. Tolerance is a key humanist virtue. We desire to live in peace with those of differing viewpoints; neither they nor we should be immune to criticism, but we will seek to negotiate our differences by rational dialogue and mutual understanding.

Seventh, we wish to draw upon the ethical wisdom of the past and to transmit cherished values to our children by means of moral education. But we recognize that the world is changing rapidly and that we need to discover new ethical solutions for the new social realities.

We are often asked, "Is humanism a religion? Is it simply one faith among many others?" There are some humanists who call humanism religious because it expresses high ideals and seeks to arouse passionate devotion to these ideals. Humanists differ on this point. I profoundly believe that humanism is *not* a religion in the accepted meaning of the term. It expresses, rather, a scientific, philosophical, and ethical point of view. The best term to describe humanism is *eupraxophy,* which means, literally, "good wisdom in the conduct of life." *Eupraxophy* has Greek roots: *eu,* meaning "good"; *praxis,* meaning "conduct" or "action"; and *sophia,* referring to the "wisdom" drawn from philosophy and science. *Eupraxophy* is a term that combines science, philosophy, and ethics to express a positive cosmic outlook and life-stance.

As eupraxophers, humanists are concerned with using science and philosophy to understand nature—including human nature. This concern does not stem from mere idle intellectual curiosity; we wish to apply this wisdom to the practical guidance of life.

Humanists do not have an apocalyptic vision of Armageddon. Although we appreciate the serious problems that must be met, we also have a sense of a unique opportunity for creating a better, more humanistic world as we enter the twenty-first century.

It is dramatically clear today that the nation-states comprising our world are interdependent: Whatever happens on one part of the planet affects all the rest. Whenever human rights are violated, all of humanity suffers.

The world is divided into diverse ethnic and national communities; each of us has specific moral obligations incumbent on his or her role in these communities. There are, however, basic moral decencies that are commonly recognized as binding in virtually all communities of the world. These ethical principles embody the collective heritage of humankind, and have been tested in the crucible of human experience by their consequences for human good. They include the need to be truthful; to keep our promises; to act with good will; to forbear from injuring other persons or their property; to be beneficent, compassionate, and fair; to show gratitude; to be just, tolerant, and cooperative; and to use peaceful methods to negotiate differences.

These ethical principles all too often have been applied only to the members of one's own cohesive group—whether tribal, ethnic, national, racial, or religious. Moreover, competition between different groups has often engendered animosity and hatred. The time has come for us to clearly enunciate these ethical principles so that they may be extended to *all* members of the human family.

The great religions of the past have often preached universal brotherhood. Unfortunately, intolerant or divisive faiths have helped to make this moral ideal almost impossible to implement. Narrow parochial doctrines of salvation have made it difficult for those outside of particular denominations to be fully entitled to moral consideration from those within. Secular political ideologies have likewise asserted the universality of their ideals, yet they have often resorted to force to impose their views on those who differ with them.

Regrettably, many nation-states have violated the rights of their citizens or have resorted to violence to achieve their national purposes; the bloody wars of history demonstrate that the "rule of the jungle" often prevails on the international level. There does not as yet exist a body of world law that is universally recognized and respected by all countries of the globe and supported on a transnational level.

Economic rivalries between nation-states, regional blocs, and multinational corporations dominate the world scene. National budgets, taxation, trade, commerce, and economic-development policies are made in haughty isolation, without concern for their effect on the global community.

Fortunately, there have been efforts at economic and political regional cooperation. There have been pacts and treaties between countries and religions. Rules of civilized behavior have emerged to govern these interactions, recognizing mutual interests. Unfortunately, they do not go far enough. The negative consequences of nationalistic chauvinism have been vividly demonstrated, and include nationalistic power politics, economic exploitation, racial strife, religious bigotry, hatred, and violence.

There is an urgent need to develop new political, economic, cultural, and social institutions that will make possible the peaceful coexistence and cooperation of the various regions of the globe. Before this can be fully achieved, however, it is essential that we reach a genuine worldwide ethical consensus that recognizes our duties to the world community.

Implicit in this consensus would be the recognition that each individual has responsibilities to the world community, for each of us is a member of the human species, a resident of the planet Earth, and an integral part of the global society.

As we approach the twenty-first century, we need to ask: How can we work cooperativly to create a peaceful and prosperous world where combative national allegiances are transcended? How can we confer dignity upon all human beings? What will be the roles of science and technology in the twenty-first century and what will be their impact on ethics? How do we deal with problems of sex and gender, population and ecology? What is the role of religion in the future? How shall we develop moral education? How can we ensure world peace and the survival of humankind?

The papers collected in this volume seek to answer these compelling questions, which were raised at the Tenth Humanist World Congress. The congress was sponsored by the International Humanist and Ethical Union (IHEU) and convened at the State University of New York at Buffalo in August 1988; it was the largest such meeting ever held, with more than 1,300 participants from some twenty-nine nations.

The IHEU is a coalition of more than sixty-seven humanist, secular, rationalist, free thought, skeptical, and atheist organizations in twenty-five countries throughout the world. Founded in 1952, its early officers included Sir Julian Huxley, the first president of UNESCO; Lord Boyd Orr, the first director of the United Nations Food and Agriculture Organization; and Brock Chisholm, the first head of the World Health Organization.

Headquartered in the Netherlands, the IHEU publisheds the *International Humanist* magazine, sponsors World Congresses, and has convened humanist dialogues with the Vatican and with Soviet-bloc Marxist humanists. It also maintains an active office of the Commissioner of Human Rights, which defends the right of conscience and unbelief worldwide. The IHEU is committed to the ideals of secularism, science, humanistic ethics, and democracy.

The authors of the papers in this volume hail from all parts of the globe, and are concerned with building a world community and with developing humanist institutions for the twenty-first century and beyond.

# I.

# Science, Technology, and Ethics in the Twenty-First Century

Sponsored by the Academy of Humanism

# The Responsibilities of Scientists in the Twenty-First Century

## Herbert Hauptman
### (United States)

Yuri Ovchinnikov, the former director of the Shemyakin Institute of Bio-organic Chemistry of the Academy of Sciences of the Soviet Union and the youngest person ever to be appointed vice-president of the Academy of Sciences, died recently of leukemia at the age of fifty-three. I had known him only slightly, and regret now that I did not know him better. I recently ran across an article of his entitled "Science and Morality," which appeared a number of years ago in an English language newspaper published in Moscow. It contains the following passage:

> The penetration of science into the mysteries of matter has now reached a point where it is extremely dangerous for the whole planet to orient new discoveries towards military goals. The scientist must be well versed in the ideological problems of his age. Without this commitment, the definitions of what is true and what is false, what is ethical and what is not, lose all sense, all meaning.

In a similar vein François Rabelais, the celebrated author of *Pantagruel,* wrote almost five centuries ago: "Science without conscience spells the ruin of the soul."

What were these two men, one an eminent scientist of the twentieth century, the other an equally renowned author of the early sixteenth century, trying to tell us? Let me try to explain.

We should perhaps first distinguish between science and technology. Science is the discipline that attempts to describe the reality of the world around us, including the nature of living organisms, by rational means. Technology, on the other hand, attempts to exploit the fruits of science in order to attain human goals. In short, science is to be thought of as related to knowledge, while technology is concerned with the utilization of knowledge for, one hopes, the betterment of the human condition.

Four hundred years ago no one could possibly have anticipated the enormous strides that science and technology were destined to make in the ensuing centuries. Even as recently as one hundred years ago, who would have predicted the great revolutions in these two areas that the twentieth century held in store for us? Thus the theories of relativity and quantum mechanics, the nature of the structure of matter, molecular biology, and our new understanding of life processes have changed forever the way we look at the world around us, and at the same time have irrevocably established the rational mode of inquiry, the quintessential element of the scientific method, as preferred above all others.

Technological applications, a mixed blessing at best, followed quickly on the heels of the more basic scientific discoveries; the fruits of technology then fed back into and facilitated the increasingly rapid advance of science, so that today we are racing ahead at breakneck speed to a future filled with uncertainty. Among the notable accomplishments of the past century were the invention and rapid development of the digital computer; our remarkable progress in communications, transportation, space exploration, and electronics; improved methods for the diagnosis and treatment of disease; and the use of the atom as the source of limitless amounts of energy. On the dark side, however, were the development and perfection of intercontinental missiles armed with nuclear warheads; atomic, chemical, and biological means of mass destruction; and the pollution of the environment. These were only a few of the consequences—not all inevitable—of the scientific revolutions of the twentieth century.

Thus it is clear that the spectacular advances of science and technology in this century and the current trends hold enormous promise for good and an equally great threat to our very survival. The promise is that the fruits of science will be used for the benefit and well-being of mankind, leading to never-ending improvement in the quality of life for everyone; the threat is that the fruits of science will be used for destructive purposes, leading to consequences ranging from devastating pollution of the environment to the destruction of human life by nuclear holocaust.

The threat arises from the crisis produced by the lightning advances of science and technology on the one hand and the glacial evolution of mental attitudes and modes of behavior, measured in periods of centuries, on the other. This conflict, between science and conscience, between technology and ethical behavior, has now reached the point where it threatens the destruction of humankind, if not of the planet itself, unless it is resolved on favorable terms, and resolved soon.

It is of course in some measure the responsibility of all of us to ensure that the fruits of science are used for good, not destructive, purposes. However, scientists, technicians, and engineers bear a special responsibility in this respect because, after all, it is a direct consequence of their work that we find ourselves in the predicament we face today; but the problem is made more difficult by the fact that one and the same scientific discovery may find application in different ways, some good and some bad. Thus the energy of the atom may be used to generate useful power, to treat disease, or to destroy life. What is the scientist to do? It seems to me that the scientist must be prepared to accept the challenge that Ovchinnikov and Rabelais lay before us—because not accepting it will surely invite the most disastrous consequences, perhaps including the destruction of humankind itself. This is a responsibility we must assume, and we can no longer be indifferent to the consequences of our work.

I don't pretend to know all the answers, but some hopeful developments have taken place recently.

The first is an outgrowth of a meeting of Argentinian scientists, mostly astrophysicists, held earlier this year at the University of Buenos Aires. An account of this meeting was given by Jeremy Stone in a recent issue of the *Journal of the Federation of American Scientists.* The conference topic was "Scientists, Disarmament, and Peace." Invited lecturers came from all over and included two from the Soviet Union, one each from Chile, France, Venezuela, Italy, and Poland, as well as several from Brazil and Argentina. About a hundred students were in attendance, and the conference lasted a week. The topics discussed included nuclear winter, seismic monitoring of underground testing, "Star Wars," Latin American nuclear questions, the INF treaty, economic implications of the arms race, science and ethics, the need for scientists to organize, and related questions. However, the most important consequence of the conference was undoubtedly the adoption of the Buenos Aires Oath, a sort of Hippocratic oath for scientists.

It turned out that a number of the participants had wanted such an oath from the beginning, and their presentations at the conference were oriented toward this goal and contained information designed to nudge others in that direction. They noted, for example, that almost two-billion hours are spent every year by scientists working on the planet's destruction, and that 30 percent of scientists, engineers, and technicians in the world are working on research and development for military purposes. They urged the establishment of an oath that would ethically bind scientists upon graduation to use their knowledge only for the perceived benefit of mankind. After much discussion those attending the conference approved and adopted the Buenos Aires Oath:

> Aware that, in the absence of ethical control, science and its products can damage society and its future, I pledge that my own scientific capabilities will never be employed merely for remuneration or prestige or on instruction of employers or political leaders only, but solely on my personal belief and social responsibility—based on my own knowledge and on consideration of the circumstances and the possible consequences of my work—that the scientific or technical research I undertake is truly in the best interest of society and peace.

I believe that the adoption of this oath, which by itself is not likely to make a significant impact on the problems I've described, is nevertheless a major initial step in the right direction. We need to take more such steps.

Another development that I believe shows great promise in responding to the challenge presented by Ovchinnikov and Rabelais is the recent founding of the Universal Movement for Scientific Responsibility, an independent organization without governmental, political, ethnic, or religious affiliation and based on the premise that humanity should no longer passively accept its fate, for it is now able to direct its destiny toward change based on rational processes. More specifically, the movement postulates as self-evident that humanity must seek common solutions to the problems determining the fate of the human species, tacit recognition that we're all in the same boat and that we sink or survive together. Furthermore, the group asserts that our problems can be resolved only by finding a balance between humanity's greatly increased knowledge of the universe and its proper understanding of itself, recognition that in the latter areas our knowledge is still woefully inadequate. Next, it is stated that scientific advances proceed by observation, hypothesis, and experiment, followed by a theoretical structure having logical consequences, and that these advances result in fundamental changes in nature and have an impact on the social and inner life of humanity as well, and determine its future. It is believed too that scientists representing the entire spectrum of disciplines—the natural, social, and human sciences—conscious of their responsibility and the universal nature of their mission, should be concerned with the consequences of their work. Finally, it is unequivocably asserted that it is the obligation of scientists to contribute means appropriate to the expression and satisfaction of the needs and interests of society, to the education of public opinion, and to the formulation and elaboration of decisions concerning the world community.

In order to address these issues, the Universal Movement for Scientific Responsibility proposes first to establish a permanent forum where interested persons can meet and join with others to focus attention on the problems that arise from the development of science and its applications. Its members believe as well that it is essential to promote a general awareness of the questions facing society and individuals, and that this is best done by comparing the potential benefits and risks resulting from such increased awareness. Next, the movement proposes to serve as a platform where debates on the issues can take place; it seeks to inform the public of the results of these discussions, and to formulate options to be considered by decision-makers. Finally, its members would seek to stimulate reflection on the future of man and the planet, as well as on measures urgently necessary for the safeguarding of that future.

In order to achieve these objectives the movement proposes first to hold colloquia, conferences, and seminars, the conclusions of which would be expressed as resolutions. Its members would seek to conduct or participate in activities and investigations necessary to study the problems cited by the movement and to further its aims. They would, in addition, publish the proceedings of its meetings and the results of its investigations. Finally, the movement is prepared to provide advice to international organizations and governmental and nongovernmental bodies if requested.

Finally, membership in the movement is open to all individuals, institutions, and bodies that are in accord with its ideals and principles and who pledge to assist in the realization of its aims.

In summary then, the Universal Movement for Scientific Responsibility asserts that mankind must search for solutions to problems as required by the destiny of the human species, that the only guarantor of wisdom is a public opinion that is well-informed and dedicated, and that using knowledge and rational processes, humanity should be able to reach a new level in its evolution. The movement aims to help each of us to understand the problems raised by the rapid development of science and to exploit these same scientific advances to suggest solutions to these problems. Finally, it proposes to achieve these aims by stimulating dialogue among scientists, decision makers, and the lay public by means of more colloquia, conferences, and study groups.

It seems to me that a great virtue of this organization is not only that it describes clearly our present dilemma and the desired goal, but also that it spells out in great detail the concrete steps to be taken in order to achieve its aims.

Earlier this year a conference of Nobel laureates convened at the Elysée Palace in Paris at the invitation of François Mitterrand, the President of the French Republic, and Elie Wiesel, the 1986 Nobel laureate in peace. The title of the conference was "Facing the Twenty-First Century: Threats and Promises." Not surprisingly, many of the issues discussed by the participants at that meeting were closely related to those noted here; some conclusions, most of which are self-evident, were reached at that conference.

First, it was affirmed that all forms of life must be considered to be humanity's essential heritage; destroying the ecological balance is to be regarded as a crime against the future. Next, humanity's wealth stems from its diversity, which must be protected in all its aspects—cultural, biological, philosophical, and spiritual. To this end, the virtues of tolerance, listening to others, and refusing ultimate truths must be reiterated continually. Third, the most important problems humanity faces today are both universal and interdependent. Again, science is a form of power, and access to science must therefore be equitably shared among all individuals and peoples. The gaps that in many countries separate the intellectual community from the political establishment and the lay public must be bridged; each must acknowledge the roles of the others. Education must become the absolute priority in all budgets and must help to enhance all aspects of human creativity. Science and technology must be made available to developing countries in particular, in order to help them gain control over their own future and to define the knowledge they deem necessary to their development. On the assumption that television and the news media are essential means of education for the future, education must contribute to the development of critical attitudes toward what the media cover. Education, food, and preventive health care are essential tools for population policy and the reduction of infant mortality. In particular, the more widespread use of existing vaccines and the development of new ones must be the common task of scientists and politicians.

Research into the prevention and treatment of AIDS must be pooled and encouraged, rather than slowed and over-partitioned. The cooperation of the pharmaceutical industry is essential, and governmental support and endorsement must be ensured as well. Molecular biology, which has, through its recent remarkable development, given rise to new insights and hopes in the field of medical science and helped to determine the genetic dimension of some diseases, must be encouraged and supported in order to help foresee and perhaps cure these diseases. Disarmament would give economic and social development significant impetus, because the limited resources of our planet are presently being drained by the arms industry. The Nobel laureates will convene again in two years to reconsider these problems. In the meantime, whenever crises are perceived as requiring urgent action, on-site visits will be made by a number of Nobel laureates.

It may seem that little of a concrete or lasting nature was accomplished by the conference in Paris, but I believe it was an important event nevertheless because it focused attention on some of the problems that mankind will have to address in the near future—if in fact it is to have a future. This conference, the Universal Movement for Scientific Responsibility, and the Buenos Aires Oath are among the first steps on the long road that humanity must travel if it is to secure the great benefits that science and technology promise. While these steps are small, they are significant and a hopeful sign. I believe also that if Ovchinnikov and Rabelais were alive today, they would agree.

# Human Rights and the Demographic Menace of the Twenty-First Century

## Jean-Claude Pecker

(France)

Every five seconds ten babies are born somewhere in the world. Despite the Universal Declaration of Human Rights, these babies are not all born equal. Some will live in ghettos with many sisters and brothers, and will die young from hunger, violence, illness, or sheer poverty. Some will grow up comfortably in cozy homes with few inhabitants; they will sit in front of television sets, and will eat plenty—perhaps too much—and live long. Most of these babies will live to see the middle of the next century. What kind of challenge will they have to face in our increasingly large and divided world?

It is clear enough that the time is now to face this question for tomorrow. This, of course, is more or less obvious. At the present rate of population expansion, one might predict that the population density of what are currently the most populated countries on earth—say the Netherlands or Bangladesh, with about four hundred to five hundred inhabitants per square kilometer—will be reached *in any habitable place* on earth in about four centuries. This in itself means saturation. Of course, hypothetical linear extrapolations often do not hold true; predictions of this sort are quite difficult to make and must therefore be considered provisory.

Demography is not an exact science; nor is economics. But what about meteorology? All the processes that command the motion of masses of air and changes in pressure, temperature, and humidity are indeed well known; ordinary physics, chemistry, and mathematics are sufficient tools for predicting weather. We can even model in a reasonable way the influence of the changing activities of the sun, as well as effects of volcanoes and of human activity.

Still, our meteorological predictions are only valid for, say, one week. Beyond that, they come closer to being random predictions than to being scientific ones. The reason for this is simple. We have on earth a large but finite number of meteorological observatories, and we observe the earth at various wavelengths in visible or infrared light with the aid of satellites. The wealth of data is enormous but insufficient. And still, the enormous number of parameters entering in equations as boundary conditions with limited accuracy makes the solutions valid only for a few million steps of iteration covering a few days.

Reaching billions of steps without losing accuracy would require computers that we do not have at our disposal. Even the most complex machines in use are far from sufficient. Moreover, it is known that such a large number of parameters can lead to undetermination, that is, to the chaotic behavior of the mathematical solutions. The smallest local errors are dramatically amplified and diffused over large areas, and the modeling requires that we take into account many physical phenomena, some of which are not well understood.

Still, meteorology is a relatively simple thing in comparison to the human brain and to societies. Linear extrapolation is difficult; elaborate prediction is impossible.

And here we are, trying to face the twenty-first century with our worries, our hopes, and our present knowledge of the solutions, in a time when we know by experience that knowledge is changing very quickly in all fields of human activity.

So as we examine the present trends of evolution, we must keep in mind that they may change rapidly, and that we shall have to change our policies accordingly. Nevertheless, certain trends are foreseeable. The population of the world is unmistakably increasing; perhaps it has a natural limit, but we have little idea what that might be. And even worse, the disparity between the rich and the poor is also increasing, and is likely to continue to do so.

In itself, the rapid demographic explosion will create immense danger in the future. I remember a splendid cartoon by Steve Brodner. In a series of successive panels, the earth, at first quite recognizable with its continents and oceans, was progressively covered with men and women until it became, in the last drawing, a dark-eyed, terrifying skull.

Let us look at the facts.

The total population of the world—one billion in 1850, two billion in 1930, more than five billion now—is likely to reach ten billion by 2070, and may stabilize only in the twenty-second century. This prediction is based on the average hypothesis of the United Nations: quick increase in life-expectancy, gradual and differentiated decrease in the fecundity of developing countries, and moderate increase in the fecundity of industrialized countries until we achieve stabilization in the level of replacement of successive generations. The United Nations postulates that this will happen around the year 2010; other hypotheses lead to different estimations.

Of course, all of these hypotheses assume quasi-political decisions; a decrease in fecundity, now four times in East Africa what it is in Europe and North America, has to be "decided," and that may be done only in a nondemocratic way.

However, this still means that the demographic weight of Asia, Africa, and Latin America will largely exceed that of the industrialized countries of Europe and North America. Of course, the distribution of wealth will follow quite a different trend, and we shall have to face this. One of the more visible effects of the increase of population is a concomitant increase in the size of large metropolises: the phenomenon of urbanization. Between 1950 and 2000, the number of people living in cities of more than five million inhabitants will grow from 9 percent to 16 percent in industrialized countries, and from 2 percent to 24 percent in developing countries. In the year 2000, the largest metropolises will be Mexico City, with twenty-six million; Sao Paulo, with 24 million; Tokyo and Yokohama, with seventeen million each; and New York, Calcutta, and Bombay, with fifteen million each. Paris, London, and Los Angeles lag far behind Seoul, Rio de Janeiro, Delhi, Buenos Aires, Cairo, Djakarta, Bagdad, and Teheran. It is obvious that the highest populations will be in the poorest countries.

An interesting and worrisome consequence of these demographic trends is the average age of the inhabitants of each area, or the "pyramid of ages." At the present time, for instance, Algeria, Brazil, and India have comparatively youthful populations, while the populations of Europe and North America are aging.

The economic gap is large between the developed and underdeveloped nations. The gross national product (GNP) of the richest 15 percent of the world's population is 60 percent of the total; the GNP of the poorest 20 percent is 2 percent of the total. In Bhutan, the per capita income is $80; in the United Arab Emirates, it is $4,800. What a contrast! And one can see that today's enormous gap continues to increase. The average growth of the GNP is about 2.5 percent, but that growth is unequally distributed; it is relatively large in China (4.5 percent), Brazil (4.6 percent), and South Korea (6.6 percent), but is actually decreasing in Ghana (by 2 percent), and Zaire (by 1 percent); intermediate countries such as India have a slow growth rate of 1.5 percent. Altogether, the Food and Agricultural Organization (FAO) estimates that forty out of ninety-nine developing countries are currently experiencing a lowering in their consumption per individual.

One should not schematize these distortions by limiting them to large areas or to the "average inhabitant." For example, within the European community, the GNP is five times larger in Denmark than in Portugal, whose GNP is twenty times that of Ethiopia.

The influence of the GNP upon life expectancy is important, and must be taken into account in any estimation of population growth. If one seeks to improve the GNP of developing countries, one must remember that the population growth might well be more severe in these areas than elsewhere.

The disparity of GNP around the world obviously creates hunger in many portions of the globe. An average of 3,000 calories a person is consumed daily in few countries, notably the United States and Canada, while less than 2,000 on average are consumed in India, Ethiopia, or Chad; perhaps more important, inhabitants of Zaire, the Congo, and other areas consume only 30 grams of protein a day, while in Western Europe, the Soviet Union, the United States, and Argentina, that figure is more than three times as high. Let us recall that normal alimentation requires daily from 2,500 to 3,500 calories, and at least 70 grams of protein. Again, this distorted situation is not improving. In 1965, India was saved from starvation by Canadian and American wheat cargoes. The FAO estimates that between 1961 and 1975, forty-five out of ninety-five developing countries experienced a decrease in the individual average consumption of food. In 1976, the average level of food consumption in these countries had decreased to what it was just fifteen years earlier. Fifty percent of the world's products come from the United States; this creates a dangerous world dependence on the U.S. economy and on U.S. responsibility.

In order to normalize within reason the diet of the world's population, global production of meat, milk, fish, and eggs must increase on the average by 300 to 500 percent in the developing countries, while the developed nations need increase by just 50 percent. But this is quite unlikely to occur: between 1940 and 1980, food productivity increased by 109 percent in the United States, and by only 7 to 8 percent in the Third World. Dependence on the United States and on a few other rich countries will be great for a long time to come.

One may conclude from this brief survey that such disparities must account for tensions of all kinds, besides being in themselves quite contrary, in many places, to human rights. Rich, relatively unpopulated countries such as Saudi Arabia, Oman, and Australia, and poor, densely populated areas like India and Central America are under the menace of increasing stresses that first appear in the poor suburbs of very large cities, where misery goes in hand in hand with crime and insecurity. One cannot blind oneself to the human crisis we now face, which will likely increase in the coming decades.

What is perhaps most troublesome is that our governments may wish to maintain, through what can be called a new form of colonialism, the dependence of Third World nations on the rich Western world, in order to avoid a global political crisis. Not only is this unjust, it may help to increase the disparity and bring the world to still more explosive situations. Despair is often stronger than starvation.

The world I have just described is not what I would call a human or humane world. The traditional humanistic views of the French Revolution—*liberté, egalité, fraternité*—are everywhere violated. Not only are they violated, but it seems that there is no immediate hope of improvement.

We have seen that equality is out of reach, even within any given country.

Freedom may be strongly damaged by some of the possible solutions to this unbalanced situation. Let us examine this point carefully.

One obvious solution to the population explosion is the legal enforcement of birth control. But could this not be against the consciences of the people in consideration? Would it not thus limit their freedom? Maybe so, but we must consider the question.

Another way to solve some problems is through the forced migration of large parts of some populations. The story of humanity is indeed a story of migrations. The early history of humanity seems to indicate that all men and women came from no more than two (more likely only one) centers of dispersion.

The observable distribution of physical characteristics such as size, skin color, and so on indeed follows a continuum. The historical differentiation can be followed through the science of genetics, from a very simple origin 200,000 to 300,000 years ago, to today's extreme diversity.

Obviously, millennia ago, migrations due to climatological pressures were the dominant cause of this early evolution. But migrations exist in the modern world as well. Some are well-known and historically understood; for example, political events in Europe have been the source of small and large migrations, such as those of the French Huguenots after the persecutions during the reign of Louis XIV, of the Alsatians after the Franco-Prussian War in 1871, of the Ukrainian Jews after the pogroms during the latter years of the nineteenth century, and of the White Russians later on. Even these were by far superseded by the Armenian diaspora and by the thirty million people who had to emigrate as a result of World War II.

Another type of migration is linked to economic conditions, and hence is more voluntary in nature; it is linked with employment or lack of it. This is particularly true in Europe, where "neighbors are neighbors," but it can also be seen in the United States, where many foreign minorities can hope to find work.

This situation brings many problems. On the one hand, migrants often keep their traditions and have much difficulty integrating into a new community, which they may consider to be provisional. On the other hand, the number of immigrants is large, and during periods of unemployment, the receiving countries develop, here and there, aggressive feelings of rejection and xenophobia. Laws against immigration are developed almost everywhere; but, almost everywhere, more and more clandestine migrants succeed in breaking through the barriers. How could the present world-mentality accept massive voluntary migrations? How could it accept massive forced migrations? It cannot even accept the present moderate rate of migration across the borders of rich countries!

One might still think that millions of Ethiopians could help to develop the Sahara, that millions of Indians or Indonesians could help to develop central Australia. But none of the parties involved would readily accept these solutions.

And still the present situation is explosive. At some borders (Mexico/United States, Iran/Soviet Union, and Indonesia/Australia, for instance) there is a direct connection between population growth and wealth: If nothing happens to correct the stark contrasts apparent at these borders, pressures and conflicts may ensue.

Will we be able to help humanity to survive? If we do, might it not be with the "help" of some dictatorial violations of human rights such as enforcing by law strict rules of birth control or, even more difficult, forcing millions of people to move, whether or not they wish to do so?

For people on both sides who are genuinely worried, a natural reaction to this state of affairs is recourse to philosophies of exclusion or to religious fanaticisms—some to "protect the Western World," some to "conquer the empty lands." Irrational attitudes, easily built up by sorcerer apprentices, televangelists of all kinds, ayatollahs, and more, are feeding fear, aggressivity or passivity, and hatred; these become motivations for entire populations. Because of this, we must continue to fight the everlasting battle for reason—and it is an everlasting battle indeed, against all kinds of false last resorts.

I worry, and I cannot stop worrying. One thing at least is necessary, and we must employ whatever practical means may be found to put it into practice: it is the feeling that we are all on the same spaceship, the earth—different, but in solidarity with one another. We are not equal, we are not free. But at least the feeling of solidarity—of *fraternité*—is one that should command international politics and economics from now on. I hope our governments will be able to hear such a plea; if they do not, it may mean for humanity the beginning of a very dark period indeed.

# Neurobiology and Future Values

## José M. R. Delgado
### (Spain)

During the next century, spectacular advances in science and technology will no doubt continue at an even faster pace. We can expect great improvements in outer-space exploration, industrial development, microelectronics, informatics, agriculture, health care, and other fields. There are, however, many unsolved problems, including the detrimental consequences to our ecology, the potential for misuse of some new technologies, persistent hostilities among different groups, the increasing poverty in many countries, and widespread social injustice.

Perhaps the main problem is the orientation of present civilization, which is devoted primarily to industrial and military development, concentrating on missiles instead of human beings. We may be losing, instead of gaining, control of human life because of the imbalance between our material and mental evolution and the subsequent perversion of ethics and social values. We need a new approach in order to solve new problems. Traditional philosophies and political theories are inadequate today and will not be suitable for the next century.

One urgent task is to evaluate the motivations and necessities that are shared by all of humanity instead of accepting as inevitable the disunifying elements that lead to human conflict. One approach can be to use our recently acquired understanding of neurobiology to identify common factors and improve social relations. Biology is similar in people of all races and cultures: blacks and whites, Jews and Christians, rich and poor. Our basic unity is divided by political and religious dogmas that excuse and encourage antagonism.

In an attempt to understand ourselves, we must investigate the elements that structure our identity and face the options and consequences of our behavior. Today the brain can look at the brain. We can learn to influence more intelligently our brain functions, and this new potential represents one of the most important accomplishments of natural evolution. Awareness of our increasing capacity to understand and modify man's behavior and environment are human qualities not shared with the rest of the universe. They are the result of a very slow process of phylogenetic evolution that is repeated at a much faster pace in ontogenic development. The value of human existence and the possibilities to enhance its individual and social qualities depend on analyzable neurobiological factors.

In biology, "development" may be defined as the sequential changes that continuously transform any biological system of relatively simple organization into one of increasing complexity and differentiation until a final stable stage is reached. Understanding and the establishment of values are necessarily related to the evolution of the human brain, which is the only organ capable of processing, experiencing, and reacting to the codes of information originating in the external world in light of the meaning added by values and emotions.

We are surrounded by material elements of earth, water, and air, which we may interpret and appreciate as beautiful cliffs, ocean waves, and sunsets. These elements do not have sensors for the perception of their existence or for the evaluation of their aesthetic qualities, which are of course human interpretations. Appreciation is not intrinsic to the inorganic world; it is not shared by bees or frogs because their little-developed nervous systems lack the necessary neuronal complexity and capacity to understand values. A rock or tree has identity as a material structure with a variety of physical, chemical, and functional properties that are integral parts of it, independent of their possible recognition by an observer. Each stone is different from every other, but the value of this diversity depends on human appreciation.

Spermatozoa, ovae, gastrula, and early stages of human embryonic development possess a specific identity but have no nervous system and therefore lack awareness of it. Evaluation of the neuronal activities necessary for the awareness of values are matters of definition and investigation, but we may state that they are not a sudden phenomenon. The many neurobiological factors that intervene in the development of values appear and evolve rather slowly, being related to genetic factors, nutrition, neuronal maturation, sensory inputs, cultural codes, and other elements that can and should be investigated.

## Some Neurobiological Data

There are numerous studies relating brain mechanisms and behavior in adult organisms, contributed in part by such illustrious pioneers as Pavlov, Sherrington, Lashley, Luria, and Hess. Extensive investigations have been performed in early infant behavior and development. Few attempts, however, have been made to analyze early behavior from a neurological perspective. What are the correlations between the appearance of organized movements and neuronal development? Which areas of the brain are related to the onset of mother-child communication? Where are traces of early imprinting stored? What are the neuronal bases of symbolic behavior? These and many other questions remain to be determined.

Animal research has provided some important clues. In sheep, cats, rabbits, and guinea pigs the development of excitatory and inhibitory synaptic mechanisms in the spinal cord and cortex have been studied during prenatal and postnatal periods. Maturation of the nervous system has been monitored using evoked-potential techniques. Unitary recording from immature brain cells, including spontaneous activity, interval distribution, and interdependence, has produced information about the codes used by growing brains for early communication among different structures. Research on the brain's sensory systems, including receptors, pathways, receiving areas, and processing mechanisms has yielded fundamental data for our understanding of the decisive roles of the environment and coded inputs in the neurochemical and neuroanatomical development of neurons.

Work on the human fetus by Minkowski, Hooker, Humphrey, and others has demonstrated the importance of fetal and postnatal reflexes for the development of certain brain structures and their connections. Behavioral observations of babies born before full term have allowed the extrauterine study of the prenatal organization of brain mechanisms. Unfortunately, correlative studies on postnatal brain structure and behavior are almost completely lacking. Also, little is known about the underlying cellular events that give rise to specific brain areas and their interconnections.

According to Cowen, eight major stages can be identified in the development of any part of the brain: (*a*) induction of the neural plate, (*b*) localized proliferation of cells, (*c*) migration of cells from the region where they originate to the place where they finally reside, (*d*) aggregation of cells to form identifiable parts of the brain, (*e*) differentiation of immature neurons, (*f*) establishment of connections with other neurons, (*g*) selective death of certain cells, and (*h*) elimination of some initial connections and stabilization of others.

Through a process called "neural induction," some cells in the ectodermic tissue of the developing embryo become irreversibly transformed into specialized tissue from which the spinal cord and brain will evolve. For a limited period the ectoderm is able to respond to relevant inductive signals for neural development.

The proliferative mechanisms of embryonic cells have a timing rigidly determined by genetic organization, providing cells with a "birth date," a definitive "address" of the brain area to which to migrate, and the pattern of connections to establish. Cell migration is a slow process; cells move only about a tenth of a millimeter a day, and some neurons must travel for considerable distances from their starting point in the neural tube. During this long journey, some cells are misdirected and end up in distinctly abnormal positions. Most of them are subsequently eliminated, but others produce gross disorders in brain development and future brain activities.

During the development of neurons, there is progressive elaboration of their processes and adoption of specific modes of electrical and chemical transmission. Under the influence of certain environmental factors, some neurons can switch from one chemical transmitter to another; for example, from norepinephrine to acetylcholine.

The information required for neurons to generate their distinctive pattern of dentritic branching seems genetically determined because it appears even in in vitro tissue culture. During normal brain growth, however, most neurons may be influenced by local mechnical factors, functional elements, and codes of sensory inputs. The highly programmed phases of cell death represent another important factor. In many cerebral areas, the number of neurons originally generated greatly exceeds the number that survive, and the final neuronal population may consist of only 15 percent of the initial group.

There is also a mechanism for the elimination of synaptic connections, as demonstrated in young rats: At birth, about five or six axons innervate each muscle fiber, but during the subsequent two or three weeks, these axons are progressively eliminated until only one survives.

The developing brain is an extremely plastic structure. While many regions are "hard wired" under rigidly determined genetic organs, other regions, especially the cerebral cortex, are open to a variety of influences both intrinsic and environmental. In addition, brain growth involves a variety of errors in migration, connections, and functional mechanisms.

## Appearance of Mental Functions and Values

When a lamb is born, its motor functions are well established and the animal is immediately able to walk, approach its mother, and avoid dangers. This capacity is shared by some other mammals. The reason is that the cerebral cortex, cerebellum, pyramidal tract, and other parts of the sensory-motor system are already well enough developed to allow adequately coordinated voluntary movements.

The situation in a newborn human baby is very different: Cerebral neurons are immature, motor functions are not yet established, and movements are disorganized and inefficient. The pyramidal tract will take months to acquire myelin. Human beings are born with such cerebral immaturity that their very survival depends completely on exterior help. Their behavior is similar to that of a purely spinal being or at most a midbrain preparation. Neurologists generally agree that the neonate is a noncortical being. After birth there is a transitional period during which the cerebral cortex begins to function and its activities gradually increase until a reciprocal functional correlation is established with the rest of the brain.

Experiences provided by sensory inputs from the environment decisively influence the number as well as the structural connections of postnatal cells. As long ago as 1911, Cajal suggested that the microneurons of the cerebellum, which serve as association elements, develop after birth under the influence of the infant's behavioral activities. Neurochemical processes in the brain, including the presence and functions of neurotransmitters, also require the reception of information from the outside world. In the absence of sensory stimuli, neurons will remain in an infantile stage. Codes from the environment are absorbed as a structural part of the neurons in the developing brain.

This lack of maturity explains why newborn humans cannot sit up, control their bladders, or even focus their eyes, much less walk, talk, read, or use computers. Babies are born, however, with anatomical and functional systems indispensible for survival, including regulation of heart rate, respiration, blood pressure, temperature, and urinary excretion. These systems are ready to start two or three months before birth, as demonstrated by the survival of many premature babies. Nothing is preestablished, however, concerning recognizable mental activities.

While fragile and immature at birth, all babies have a particular identity: they are recognized by their parents and have a unique store of fetal structuring and genetic determinants. Within their limited repertoire of behavior, babies display individual patterns of feeding, sleep-wakefulness, elimination, and sensory reactivity. The term "personality," which is often equated with intelligence, is generally tested with questionnaires, instrumental methods, rating scales, and interviews in an attempt to predict children's reactivity and future behavior. Theories of personality discuss sexuality, motivation, conditioning, learning, psychoanalysis, and social determinants that can be tested in adults but not in newborn infants. The concept of personality should be reserved for the period when the brain is reaching maturity, as shown by the presence of detectable mental characteristics. With this approach we may analyze the necessary elements for the appearance of personality and values.

## The Fallacy of Potentiality

In the development of the brain there is tremendous complexity, a series of sequential events, and genetic determinism. We should emphasize that genes are only triggers of cellular evolution and that during prenatal growth, many variables are present including biochemical elements from the mother and embryo that may influence and even misdirect neuronal changes and migrations.

There is no doubt that a fertilized egg has the potential to become a zygote containing all of the essential factors for the development of a new individual. The zygote subdivides into blastomeres while it is still high in the uterine tube. These cell multiplications produce a cluster of twelve blastomeres, which passes to the uterus where twelve to sixteen blastomeres form the morula. Then the blastocyte appears, which has a diameter of 0.2 millimeters and will be implanted as a parasite in the uterine wall. During the fourth week of pregnancy, the essential arrangements have been made for physiological exchange between mother and fetus. At the end of the second month, the embryo measures about 30 millimeters and from this time until birth is called a fetus. During the third month, the young fetus clearly resembles a tiny human being with a large head.

Human embryos are subject to disease, abnormal development, and abnormal growth. One infant in fourteen that survives the neonatal period carries some type of congenital abnormality. Disturbances may be induced by gene mutation, sex-linked factors, abnormal distribution of chromosomes during cell division, irradiation, chemical teratogenic agents (remember the thalidomide babies), deficiency of fetal hormones, and a variety of other elements. Thus, fertilization of an ovum is not necessarily followed by the development of a human being. There is a potentiality, but not necessarily a reality, which requires time and the supply of many elements not present in the fertilized egg.

The newborn human has the potential to become a child, an adolescent, an adult, and an old person, but is none of them. The newborn has the potential to walk, to speak any language, to acquire many skills and values, but in reality has nothing—only the capacity to learn what a particular culture may provide. The many possibilities for development will result in a comparatively limited reality. It is not who a baby is at the moment of birth but what he or she is taught that can make or destroy potential.

Parents are naturally full of expectations, hoping that their baby will have a happy, healthy, and successful life, developing a loving and wonderful personality; but in reality they have only a little baby without detectable intelligence. During the initial weeks and months, personality traits will gradually appear and genetic elements carried in the newborn will be important for shaping an evolving personality. The task of scientific research is to evaluate the contributions of the many elements that play a role in the formation of personality and values. We may say that millions of spermatozoa and ovae are potentially human beings. It is true that a block of marble may become a beautiful creation, but in the absence of chisels and hammers, and especially in the absence of the skills and talents of a sculptor, the potential may persist, but the work of art will never be created.

## Values and Human Rights

The basic principle that inspired the French Revolution was the declaration that "all men are born free and equal in rights," specifying the rights of liberty, private property, inviolability of the person, and resistance to oppression. In the words of the nineteenth-century historian Jules Michelet, this was the "credo of the new age." In 1948 the United Nations supported another collection of rights, including universal education and a minimum standard of living. These rights are suppose to be "inalienable" and to belong to the individual under natural law as a consequence of being human.

As a symbolic expression of principles these declarations are certainly commendable, but their practicality and particularly the invocation of natural law are debatable. Simply belonging to the human race does not automatically convey privileges. According to the biological "law" of a few centuries ago, pestilence desolated mankind, insects spread infections, more than half the newborns died before the age of three, old age began at thirty or forty, and only a minority survived to the age of fifty. The spectacular improvements of the modern age are not due to nature but to the intelligence of humankind, which has provided better diet, hygienic practices, and medical therapies. In a similar way, existing values and the "rights of man" are not related to natural laws, which are rather neutral about humanity's supremacy on earth, but to human agreements and moral sense. We should remember that in the time of Columbus, the Indian race of Caribes stated that "only the Caribes are human beings," and therefore members of any other group were deemed suitable flesh to be devoured in their anthropophagous festivities. Many of today's interracial and religious struggles inflict cruelties reflecting a similar underlying belief that those who differ should be eliminated.

The "natural" rights of embryos and newborn babies are even more debatable. In modern times, the legislation of several countries permits the abortion of embryos. In old China it was acceptable to kill female babies. In ancient Greece, the handicapped were destroyed. Only two hundred years ago in the United States, slaves were imported for forced labor and their children were raised as slaves. History shows that the decision to bestow values and rights on embryos, newborn babies, and adults does not depend on biological considerations but reflects only cultural and legal agreements.

Freedom, which is such a cherished goal in democratic societies, is from the biological point of view only wishful thinking at birth. During childhood and adolescence, yearning for independence causes many conflicts. In adult behavior, the reality of biological dependence and early imprinting is compounded by the demands and restrictions of society. Freedom is not a natural, inborn characteristic of mankind but the result of awareness and intelligent thinking, which must be learned by conscious individual and collective efforts. Civilization has increased many human potentials, including the possibility of greater freedom, but its fulfillment requires concerted efforts to escape from the countless elements of behavioral determination.

Heredity, representing the potential to become an idiot or a genius, is established by pure chance: It is not chosen by parents or their offspring. Newborns lack the capacity to select the sensory inputs that will be decisive for their neuronal structuring and mental activities. Intelligent planning of education by parents and society should be superior to blind chance. The elements to be decided are: Who is going to provide the necessary information and training? What and how much will be provided, and with what techniques? What should be the personal and social purpose of this cerebral planning?

The rights of human beings are not intrinsic to their existence but depend upon the moral values and circumstances of each cultural environment. Only greater individual education and cooperation between sectors of societies may in the future ensure that human rights become not promises but realities.

## Biological Unity of Humankind

The attempt to estimate the percentages of genetic and environmental elements that structure the personality of each individual is an old and unproductive dilemma: Are they perhaps fifty-fifty in importance? In reality both elements are basic because without genes or sensory inputs, mental activities cannot appear. Genes have no dormant skill. They are partial determinants of the very complex chain of reactions leading to specific cellular architectonics and functions. In forming individual minds, some elements, such as consciousness, are essential to enable the processing of information and the structuring of frames of reference somehow anatomically related to the hypothalamus, reticular formation, and several other cerebral areas. Other elements are accessory, such as the refined organization of the motor cortex necessary for playing the piano.

The physiology of humankind has many properties that are shared by other animals. Many functions of neural transmission have been investigated in frogs and lobsters with results directly applicable to human beings. The recent discoveries of neuropeptides were based on studies in mammals. The liver of a chimpanzee has proved able to take over most metabolic activities in a human patient. The heart of a baboon has been implanted in a human baby. Despite certain immunological problems, individuals of different races can exchange blood, hearts, skin, kidneys, and other organs, demonstating their functional similarity.

There is an urgent need to search for the elements that unify human beings, including many cerebral functions and basic motivations like the search for pleasure and the avoidance of pain. Surgery, medicine, and pharmacology have similar scientific and technical benefits wherever they are available. Machinery for industrial, agricultural, and domestic use can raise both living standards and productivity around the world. Mass communications are uniting the expectations of people, all of whom have similar objectives to achieve healthy, comfortable, happy, and useful lives. If we are to be spared atomic destruction or the increasing deteriorations of our natural resources and ecological system, these goals must be recognized as primary. The survival and evolution of the human species depends on the formulation and activation of plans acceptable to and beneficial for all humanity, based on our biological unity and needs, and respect for individual and cultural diversity. A common destiny, without ideological, racial, or economic descrimination, should be promulgated and potentiated through appropriate education.

An immediate objective should be to improve our understanding of personal mental functions and their biological, educational, and cultural determinants. In this way individuals would have greater awareness and therefore greater control over their personal destiny, exercising their rights in a realistic manner while decreasing their manipulation by elites who now monopolize knowledge and power. Democratization of scientific information and teaching of freedom could contribute to greater personal happiness and to reinforcing consciousness, responsibility, and identity, and also could clarify the social interdependence of all human beings.

# References

Cajal, S. Ramon y. *Histologie du Systeme Nerveux de L'homme et des Vertébrés,* vols. I and II (Paris: Maloris, 1909–1911.)

Cowan, W. M. "The Development of the Brain," *Progress in Neuroscience* (New York: W. H. Freeman, 1986).

Delgado, J. M. R. *Physical Control of the Mind: Toward a Psychocivilized Society.* World Perspectives Series, vol. XLI (New York: Harper & Row, 1969).

Maslow, A. *Toward a Psychology of Being* (Princeton, N.J.: Van Nostrand, 1968).

Prechtl, H. F. R. "The Problems for Study." *Brain and Early Behavior,* R. J. Robinson, ed. (New York: Academic Press, 1969).

# Toward a Survival Morality

## Mario Bunge
### (Canada)

## The Problem

It is becoming clearer every day that humankind is facing the most severe crisis in its history, and that it won't make it through the next millennium unless a handful of radical measures are taken worldwide. In fact, the arms race, environmental degradation, the rapid depletion of nonrenewable resources, overpopulation, unemployment, poverty, sickness, oppression, ignorance, and corruption are no longer the privilege of the very rich or the very poor societies: they affect us all.

The mad arms race may end up in a nuclear war that would destroy the entire biosphere. And even if the current unstable equilibrium were to last, the race is impoverishing all of us and is militarizing governments, industry, and even scientists. The environment is being exploited at such a reckless rate that, by mid-twenty-first century, most of our nest may have become uninhabitable, and most mineral resources will have gone. Overpopulation is overtaxing the world's economic and cultural resources to the point where entire continents may be depopulated by famine or reduced to cultural indigence. Today poverty is the lot of most human beings, and it is bound to become even more severe. Most peoples suffer under dictatorships, many of them military. Ignorance and superstition threaten to become chronic in the Third World, and to grow worse in the industrialized nations as a result of lack of faith in the future and the neglect of research and education in favor of militarization. Corruption, demoralization, and escapism are so widespread and serious among both the rulers and the underdogs that they are hitting the headlines everywhere.[1]

We have been drawn into this maelstrom for having endorsed the wrong values and the wrong morals attached to them, but we may pull through if we reconsider these guides—or, rather, misguides. Humankind may survive only by replacing profit and power with the meeting of basic needs and legitimate aspirations. The accompanying moral code is summed up in the principle *enjoy life and help to live*. This norm belongs in the secular humanistic tradition from Lucretius onward, but it can be shared by all who are sincerely concerned not only with their own survival but also with that of their posterity.[2]

## Wrong Values and Morals

The explicit or tacit moral and social philosophies underlying our present societies are either individualistic or holistic. Individualistic philosophies preach that the individual is supremely valuable and should be left free to do what he or she wants. Holism or collectivism holds that only society is valuable, and that the individual should be its servant. Individualism and its accompanying social philosophy can lead either to political liberalism or to pseudodemocratic neo-conservatism, where individuals only are free to choose who is going to exploit or betray them. Holism and the accompanying social philosophy leads either to fascism or to classical (pre-Gorbachev) communism.

Democracy is obviously incompatible with holism. However, individualism constrains democracy to the political sphere: Obsessed as it is with protecting the economic and civil rights of those who have the means to exert them, it does not enshrine the right to well-being of the greater number. By extolling those rights, classical liberalism can end up, at best, in the so-called welfare state, which is actually a relief state.

But the relief state is currently under attack not only by right-wingers but also by those who think that relief should be offered only in cases of personal tragedy or collective catastrophe caused by natural calamity or war. We should aim at a society where all able-bodied individuals have the right and the duty to earn a living for themselves and their dependents by doing socially useful work, rather than by begging, stealing, preparing for war, or soldiering. In short, we should aim at full employment in peace rather than at relief in a state of hot or cold war. Democracy should be expanded to cover access to all resources and participation in all the major decisions affecting our lives. Integral democracy should substitute political democracy.

Both individualism and holism have a list of good points and bad points, and of dos and don'ts, but neither has an objective criterion to determine what is good or bad, right or wrong. In individualism what is good for me (or for General Motors) is good for all; in holism, what is good for the State (or for the Cause) is good for all. Either way, wants are given precedence over needs. So we reach for what we (or our rulers) desire rather than for what we need to survive. We do not desire what is objectively valuable but, on the contrary, we value what we (or our rulers) desire.

The consequences for morality of such value systems are obvious. In one case we are told that we may do as we please, in the other that we may do only what the authorities want. Between the two extremes of the spoiled brat and the serf, there is no room for the responsible individual who not only enjoys living but also helps others to enjoy life. Obviously, we need a *tertium quid* between the playboy and the kamikaze moral philosophies, between the morality of pleasure (hedonism) and that of sacrifice (deontologism). We need it for humankind to survive.

Individualism fosters consumerism, which is fouling our nest, depleting nonrenewable resources, exploiting the Third World, and breeding the obsession with national security. This obsession is a major cause of the growing militarism and authoritarianism all over the world. The tragedy of the Near East should have taught us that national security cannot be bought or imposed by the force of arms: It can only be earned via negotiations on the basis of mutual respect and mutual help. Weapons buy instability, not security. Nuclear weapons buy more than instability; they buy the risk of total annihilation, and in the meantime they waste huge natural and human resources.

Thus, the root of the global crisis is a wrong valuation: one that identifies the good with whatever may bring profit or power.

## A Transvaluation of the Prevailing Values

To find a way out of any crisis one must examine its sources. If the sources of the current global crisis are the profit and power motives, let us replace these with more rational ones. What is more rational than to ask, particularly at a time of increasing uncertainty and scarcity, what we really need and want, and what we can realistically expect to attain? In short, let us go back to basics.

Everyone knows what the basic human needs are, particularly as a result of a number of studies by such international bodies as the International Labor Organization (ILO) and the Organization for Economic Cooperation and Development (OECD). All human beings have needs of three kinds: physical, such as clean air, adequate nutrition, and safety; mental, such as being loved, feeling needed, and learning; and social, such as company, peace, and participation. We also have some idea of what a legitimate want, desire, or aspiration is in a given society: It is a desire that can be satisfied, in that society, without hindering the satisfaction of any basic need of other members of the society, and without jeopardizing the integrity of the society itself.

Accordingly we attribute an item a primary value if, and only if, it contributes to keeping people alive; a secondary value if, and only if, it contributes to keeping people in good health; a tertiary value if, and only if, it contributes to meeting a legitimate want; and a quaternary value if, and only if, it contributes to meeting a fancy (that is, a desire that, in the given society, is not a legitimate want because not everyone can afford it).

We are now able to define the concepts of well-being and happiness. An animal (in particular a human being) will be said to be in a state of *well-being* if, and only if, it has met all of its basic needs; that is, it has realized all of its primary and secondary values. And an animal will be said to feel *completely happy* if, and only if, it believes it has the ability and opportunity of meeting all of its needs and wants, whether legitimate or not.

If we wish to secure a future for mankind we cannot adopt the utilitarian principle according to which one should aim at maximizing the happiness of the greatest number. In a world of increasing uncertainty and scarcity we must settle for a more modest aim—namely *reasonable happiness,* which consists of being in a state of well-being, and of being free and able to work toward the fulfillment of legitimate wants.

If this be accepted, we must agree to change our priorities: We must not allow wants to dominate needs—ours or others'. Primary values should precede secondary values. In short, we must adopt a value system rooted in basic needs and legitimate wants. Such a reform entails a moral reform.

## A Morality for Survival

Morality is about moral rights and duties, whatever the law may say. We have a *basic moral right* to an item if, and only if, it contributes to our well-being without preventing anyone from having items of the same kind. We have a *secondary moral right* to an item if, and only if, it contributes to our reasonable happiness without interfering with the exercise of the primary rights of anyone else. Thus, whereas everyone is entitled to well-being, not everyone is entitled to happiness, for getting the required means may involve competition, and in all competitions there are losers as well as winners. But of course everyone should be entitled to the pursuit of reasonable happiness.

In a society heading toward disaster there are rights without duties and duties without rights. In a viable society every right generates a duty and, conversely, every duty generates a right. For example, we have the right to enjoy nature and the duty to protect it: if we did not have the former we might not be motivated to do the latter, and if we failed to do our duty, very soon there would be no enjoyable nature left.

As with rights, we distinguish primary from secondary duties, and define these as follows. If X and Y are members of a given society, and Z is an action that X can perform without jeopardizing X's own well being, then (1) if Y has a basic moral right to Z or to an outcome of Z, then X has the *primary moral duty* to do Z for Y if, and only if, X alone in the given society can help Y exercise his or her basic moral right to Z; (2) if Y has a secondary moral right to Z or to an outcome of Z, then X has a *secondary moral duty* to do Z for Y if, and only if, X alone in the given society can help Y exercise his or her secondary moral right to Z or to an outcome of Z.

Rights and duties can be grouped into five categories: environmental, bio-psychological, cultural, economic, and political. Examples of right–duty pairs: Clean environment and environmental protection, well-being and helping others to attain well-being, access to information and diffusion of information, work and workmanship, liberty and popular participation.

Because of the way they are defined, duties and rights are ordered along the lines of values. Primary rights ought to take precedence over secondary rights. Duties are parallel; moreover, primary duties ought to take precedence over secondary rights. And an individual faced with a conflict between a right and a duty is morally free to choose either, subject only to the preceding condition. In other words, survival of self and others comes first. This is why the two main principles of public morality ought to be *universal nuclear disarmament* and *protection of the environment*. These two duties have absolute priority because the nuclear arms race and the continued deterioration and depletion of the environment, each by itself, is bound to lead to the extinction of the human species.

As for the code of personal morality based on the substitution of needs and legitimate wants for profit and power, it boils down to the maxim *enjoy life and help to live*. The first conjunct of this principle points to rights, the second to duties. And rights as well as duties can be environmental, bio-psychological, cultural, economic, and political. And, far from being mutually independent, they form a system: Indeed, the exercise of every one of them calls for rights and duties of other kinds.

The structure of our system of values and norms is shown in the following diagram:

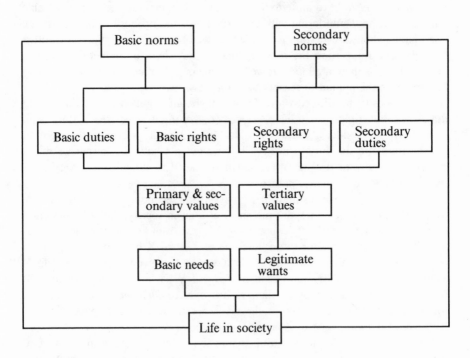

## Summary

If humankind is to survive, it will have to alter the value system and the moral code prevailing in modern societies. The pursuit of profit or power will have to be replaced with the pursuit of reasonable happiness for the greatest number, where "reasonable happiness" is defined as the satisfaction of basic needs and legitimate wants. The supreme moral principle should be to enjoy life and help to live. But in the present state of the world this principle of personal morality can only be observed if nuclear war is averted and the further deterioration of the environment brought to a halt. Hence peace and environmental protection should be the overriding principles of the morality for survival of humankind. The following diagram summarizes this morality:

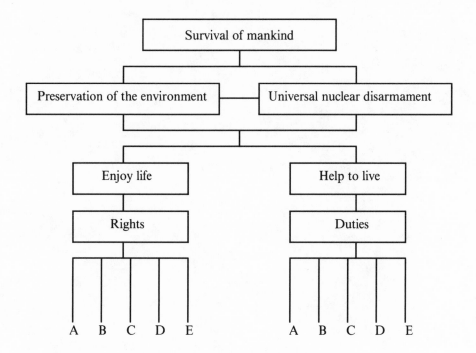

A=environmental, B=biopsychological, C=cultural, D=political, E=economic

## Notes

1. For statistics about some of the components of the current planetary crisis, see the almanacs *State of the World,* published by the Worldwatch Institute, and *World Military and Social Expenditures,* compiled by Ruth Leger Sivard.

2. For details see the author's *Treatise on Basic Philosophy,* vol. 8: *Ethics* (Dordrecht-Boston: Reidel, 1989).

# II.

# Ethics of Global Cooperation

# The Human Environment and the Challenge of Global Change

## Noel Brown
### (Jamaica)

It is only through persistent public efforts that we can hope to help society at large to understand our changing environmental situation and the new responsibilities that are inherent in our profoundly altered relations to the earth.

If scientists are to be believed, humankind has become a force almost equal to nature in affecting the environnment. If present trends continue, we will change the global environment more radically in the next century than at any time since the last Ice Age. And according to the World Commission Report on Environment and Development, the so-called Brundtland Report, many such changes are accompanied by life-threatening hazards. If we do not learn to recognize and manage these dangers, we will be leaving the consequences of our actions, and with them the future habitability of the planet, to chance—an option clearly unworthy of a civilization capable of contemplating the mysteries of the universe and the meaning of life.

But perhaps the late 1980s will prove to be a turning point. The summer of 1988 may yet become known as the "Environment Awareness Summer," when nature began in earnest to define social and developmental agendas and to demonstrate the limits of our ability to control certain natural processes vital to our economic stability and well-being. It may also be remembered for its dramatic revelations of scientific uncertainty about the state of our environment and the unpredicted consequences of human activities on the ecosystem's stability. Several indications lead to such an observation. I shall cite only two.

The first was "Drought Shock," or the "Harvest of Dust": The drought that for weeks had swept the Midwestern United States, leaving in its wake losses estimated at more than two billion dollars, established beyond doubt the relationship between the environment and the economy, or, to be more precise, between economics and climate.

Clearly, Wall Street recognized this, if the major U.S. dailies are to be believed. One headline put it this way: "Drought Sends Seed, Fertilizer Stocks Soaring." The article that followed reported that

> The drought is whetting Wall Street's thirst for companies that can reap fat profits for a long hot summer in the U.S.A. farm belt. But it is also dampening prospects for farms that would like some rain. Shares of Pioneer Hibred Inc. climbed 1¾ to 36½ Thursday, near its 1988 high, on speculation that the Des Moines–based seed corn breeders sales will grow as farmers boost next year's acreage to compensate for this year's expected poor harvest. Another big seed producer, Dekalb Corp., rose 1⅛ to 33⅛. The same rationale pushed IMC Fertilizer group 2 to 39 Wednesday.

The author went on to say that these companies are all making pure market-plays on the belief that as the droughts continue they will slash grain inventories and result in more acreage being planted. Clearly, gains are being made from fluctuations in weather conditions, but these may only be short-term gains in the grand scheme of the fundamental changes in global climate patterns. Nowhere in this report was there even the slightest hint that agriculture is a climate-dependent activity and that as a result of human intervention we are on the threshold of significant climate change.

The New York *Times* was perhaps more sensitive to these broader global implications in its report titled "Drought Brings Spectre of Major Price Increases," which warned that "natural forces that are beginning to influence production could be grave." It cited, for example, the situation in Indonesia, where harvests have not been so plentiful as they were in the early 1980s. China's grain harvests are reportedly lower than they were in the mid-1980s, possibly by as much as twenty-five million tons, or more than 5 percent of that country's annual production. And in India the situation was hardly any better, as "bad weather" ruined crops in 1987 and brought concerns about 1988's harvest. The importance of the rains was perhaps best summed up by a senior aide to Rajiv Gandhi, who admitted that "this year the monsoon will be the political event of the year."

Is this drought simply a prelude to the phenomenon of global warming yet to come? Is it a signal that unless we take changing environmental conditions more fully into account in our calculations and strategies, *nature, not humankind, could define the development agenda?*

Alvin Toffler defined future shock as the premature arrival of a future for which we are unprepared. Drought shock may one day come to be seen as the premature arrival of serious environmental stresses for which we are equally unprepared. And the responses to the U.S. drought offer some interesting lessons—not on the arrogance of power, but in a curious way, on powerlessness.

In one state, for example, the governor declared Sunday, July 3, as a "day of prayer for rain," though this invocation of divine intervention was strenuously objected to by those who would prefer the absolute separation of church and state even in a time of crisis. One group called in rain-dancers to do their thing. Strangely enough, they didn't call in scientists, with their cloud-seeding and precipitation-inducing technologies. Perhaps they sensed that we had done enough technological tampering with the atmosphere to leave bad enough alone. Another group called in the goats—five hundred, in fact—to create fire breaks with their heavy grazing, since the combination of heat and drought provide a formidable prescription for forest fires. On July 12, NBC's weather forecaster Willard Scott referred to the precipitation in some parts of the Midwest as "beautiful rain." In another instance, when the rains began in the middle of a baseball game in the Midwest, the crowd actually stood up and applauded.

Somehow, weather has arrived; it has taken center stage. A dramatic media consensus during the first week in July, 1988 clearly attests to this, as the major news weeklies—including, I might add, *Fortune* magazine—elevated the question of climate change to the status of cover stories. Finally, the time seems to have arrived for society to begin to pay serious attention. And none too soon, since time is not on our side.

For years scientists have been signaling society about the spectre of global warming, noting that if present trends continue in deforestation, the use of fossil fuels, and the buildup of greenhouses gases, then we will likely increase temperatures worldwide by 1 to 4 degrees centigrade during the next fifty years. Though the scope of such changes might appear to be insignificant, it is in fact of such import that we must call for the most urgent discussions at the highest policy levels if the adjustments and adaptations that are required are to take place in a timely fashion—especially since there are no known natural limits to the warming. And the projected implications are as unpredictable as they may be unmanageable, ranging from rising sea levels and altered precipitation patterns to changing frequency of climatic extremes induced by the heat-trap effects of greenhouse gases.

Thus far, not a single government has adjusted any of its policies to take global warming into account. But drought shock may change this.

Perhaps it was prophetic that the drought coincided with the Global Conference on the Changing Atmosphere: Implications for Global Security, held in Toronto June 28 to 30, 1988. This international meeting, perhaps the most broadly based and authoritative of its kind, not only reinforced the warnings of scientists but also issued a call to action to governments, the United Nations, nongovernmental organizations, industry, educational institutions, and the individual—in a word, to all of us—to work to counter the degradation of the atmosphere.

Foremost among the actions proposed was the reduction of emissions of $CO_2$ and other greenhouse gases, improvements in energy efficiency, and the reduction of deforestation. The conference also called for a comprehensive global convention as a framework for protocols on the protection of the atmosphere, and spelled out a rough timetable for it.

Now humanity has an agenda for managing its atmospheric resources. But does it have the will? And will it have the time?

My own belief is that the 1990s may provide us with the last window of opportunity for taking effective measures to stabilize the global climate. If we elect not to do so, we will in effect be abdicating our management responsibility and leaving the future to chance.

The second indicator of our impact on the environment was 1988's "Harvest of Sludge." The drought was only half the equation—the atmospheric half. The oceans conveyed another message to society, with their harvest of sludge and debris that washed up on the shores of New York and New Jersey, rendering these beaches unfit for use at the very time when the temperatures would have made them one of the principal sources of relief for large numbers of city dwellers. Instead, many people stayed inside their air-conditioned hives, thereby putting more pressure on power sources.

Again, the experts were confounded; many were obliged to confess that they did not know the source of these wastes. Uncertainty prevailed as the coastal managers waited for the "second wave," that is, the second cycle of tides, to ensure that the waters were fit for swimming. Perhaps the oceans' yield of unwanted debris was simply a metaphor for the global waste explosion and management issues that remain to be faced.

Someone once remarked that human societies create wealth very slowly but waste it very rapidly. If the growing volume of waste on all fronts is any indication, then this is more than an adage—it is a fact. For example, the global waste budget is astronomical and continues to increase, with exponential growth occurring on almost all fronts—municipal and household, industrial and chemical—to the point where it is now estimated at one billion tons. It was recently reported that the amount of hazardous waste being produced in the United States annually rose from 9 million metric tons in 1970 to at least 247 million in 1984. Other experts place the current figure close to 400 million metric tons a year, or 10 pounds per person per day.

The issue of waste disposal, especially urban and municipal waste, is approaching critical proportions in some developed countries, as well as posing new and ominous challenges to the Third World. Perhaps the dilemma inherent in this situation was best reflected in the spring of 1987 when the "garbage barge" made headlines as it floated for several days in the Gulf of Mexico with 3,100 tons of garbage from Long Island.

The problem was how and where to legally dispose of it. North Carolina didn't want it; Louisiana didn't want it. Dumping it in the ocean would have violated U.S. law. So for months it drifted in the Caribbean in search of a destination. Finally, this putrid mess was returned to New York, where I believe it was later incinerated, and this somewhat amusing episode closed.

Unfortunately, disposal of this particular cargo did not end the story, and in effect, waste disposal is becoming increasingly internationalized as many developing nations are being increasingly tempted to become dump sites for municipal wastes from industrialized countries. Recently there have been a number of disclosures that developing countries in the Caribbean and Africa have been approached with lucrative offers to provide facilities for the disposal of toxic and hazardous wastes from industrialized countries. In one African nation, for example, it was reported recently that the government was about to conclude a deal under which it would receive $120 million a year for five years to allow the disposal of a total of fifteen million tons of waste. In another deal, $1.6 million a year for ten years was offered in exchange for large quantities of waste containing very toxic substances—and the brokers arranging this deal would reportedly receive $1 billion.

These disclosures so outraged a number of countries, both developed and developing, that both the Organization of African Unity and the European Parliament expressed strong condemnation at this practice and urged the offending parties to refrain from carrying out their plans. Nigeria went even further by asking the United Nations to place the issue of the dumping of wastes in Africa on the agenda of its forty-third session, and a number of West African countries have banded together in what they call a "dump watch," to monitor the so-called waste trade and to prevent their territories from becoming the world's new dump sites. One group called the practice "toxic imperialism."

This is a major concern of the United Nations Environment Programme (UNEP), which has taken this question very seriously and for a number of years has been exploring ways to ensure the environmentally sound management of hazardous wastes. It recently adopted guidelines to this effect. Currently it is working on regulations for the transfrontier movement of such wastes, which governments would be required to follow.

But even if we were to stem the growing anarchy in the waste trade, society may yet be faced with another, more ominous disposal issue—that of the new but growing spectre of genetic junk, if you will, that results from biotechnology and genetic-engineering experiments. We might appropriately ask what happens to the by-products of such experiments. What are the requirements for their disposal, and what mechanisms exist for monitoring and implementing these requirements? Societies have a right to know about the waste-disposal policies of each center for genetic experimentation.

Unfortunately, given the potential dangers to health and the environment, wastes can no longer be allowed to fend for themselves, nor in desperation to surreptitiously seek safe haven. Moreover, with an expanding population and shrinking resource base, a rational world may yet be forced to consider "waste" a resource of the future. That is why UNEP strongly advocates what might be called the "four Rs": reduction, reuse, recovery, and recycling.

But global warming and ocean debris are only two of the management challenges facing humanity as it moves toward the end of the millennium. There are other equally urgent responsibilities that call for nothing less than a new covenant with the earth if indeed we are to secure our common future. These become especially compelling as we read what the environmentalist Lester Brown has so aptly called "the earth's vital signs." The indicators include:

- the loss of genetic diversity through uncontrolled development pressures, with a loss of species estimated at 10,000 a year, or one every hour. Lamentably, the extinction tragedy is compounded by the fact that we do not know what we are losing, since we do not know what we have; scientists tell us that less than 10 percent of the earth's five to thirty million species have been identified. Moreover, it would take some 25,000 professional lifetimes to accurately inventory the earth.

- the loss of productive soils through desertification, approximating 20 million acres a year in both developed and developing countries.

- deforestation, where the loss rate averages 27 million acres a year, or 50 acres a minute—a rate expected to be aggravated by the fuel-wood deficit among the world's poor, which by the year 2000 is expected to approximate 900 million cubic meters. And the implications of this are likely to be staggering, especially when it is considered that the forests, while only covering 6 percent of the earth's surface, support more than 50 percent of all plant and animal life—whereas the oceans, on the other hand, cover 70 percent of the earth's surface and have nowhere near as large a percentage of life forms.

- indoor air pollution, which is often worse than outdoor air pollution. The range of hazards includes cigarette smoke, formaldehydes used in furniture and other products, asbestos, carbon monoxide from stoves and other combustion, household pesticides, household solvents such as paint strippers, and some biological pollutants, including various bacteria.

These are but a few of the indications that an increasing amount of chemicals and other toxic substances never before encountered in nature are now being introduced into the atmosphere and oceans. It also reveals how poorly we understand the manner in which these substances interact. These problems have been heavily documented and together reveal what some have termed the "sick-earth syndrome." The challenge now is how to restore the earth's health and vitality.

And yet in a paradoxical way the timing may be right. Perhaps it was prophetic that World Environment Day 1988 coincided with the conclusion of the superpowers' summit and the exchange of the instruments for ratification of the INF Treaty.

Now for the first time we have reason to hope that, finally, one of earth's man-made scourges—the arms race—is winding down, and that the cold warriors are trading not insults and threats of the Armageddon variety, but compliments about each other's commitment to a better life for their people and a better future for humanity. Perhaps—just perhaps—we have finally reached a point where, after forty years, our vision might at last be freed to look beyond the paralyzing manias of the Cold War to the life-enhancing responsibility for the care and maintenance of this small planet humanity calls its home.

Perhaps the environment will then find its rightful place on the summit agendas of the superpowers. As we all know, one of the prerogatives of the superpowers is that when they define an issue as being important, it becomes important. Therefore, when the environment is elevated to summit-issue status, we know it has arrived.

At least a start was made—at the 1988 Toronto conference, the question of sustainable development for the first time received serious attention, and eventually summit endorsement. But we need to accelerate the process. In this connection I have three suggestions:

First, we need a new global vision and supporting institutions; a vision that, in the words of the Stockholm Declaration, encompasses each human right to freedom, equality, and conditions of life in an environment that promises a life of dignity and well-being. Only in this way can we achieve humanity's goal of protecting and managing the earth.

Second, we need an ethical perspective enabling us to perceive the world as a whole in space and time. We need to accurately perceive the nature of the facts and the pattern of their interactions if the people who make decisions are to be able to manage their consequences. Otherwise it would be morally irresponsible to decide on a course of action whose consequences cannot be anticipated, let alone managed.

Third, we need new metaphors—improved mental constructs that evoke images to guide our actions, since in the final analysis it is the way in which we respond to crises that holds the key to the solution of our dilemmas. As those with the wisdom to know have said, "However the human mind imagines the world, that is how the world tends to become," and this is where we need to mobilize all of our intellectual resources, including those expresssed through the arts, to help us to see our way more clearly. Each era creates its own metaphors, some more important than others. Today's need is for a new metaphor that touches upon many aspects of human endeavors and norms traditionally attached to familiar institutions.

In searching for metaphors, consideration might be given to the concept that we need to restore a covenant with the earth. This suggests a body of principles that would help us to learn the business of living in a manner that would be harmonious with the natural order. A number of elements for this new covenant are already in place. For example:

1. *The Declaration of Stockholm* (1972) outlines the principles of action and basic codes of environmental conduct.

2. *The World Conservation Strategy* (1980) calls for a more focused approach to the management of resources and provides policy guidelines on how this can be carried out by governments, policymakers, advisers, conservationists, and practitioners.

3. *The Declaration of Nairobi* (1982) reaffirms commitment to the Stockholm Declaration and Action Plan, and further strengthens and expands national efforts and international cooperation in the field of environmental protection. It emphasizes the need for international cooperation to ensure the future dignity of life on the planet.

4. *The Charter of Nature* (1983) underlines the importance of ensuring the proper functioning of natural systems and reaffirms the fundamental purposes of the United Nations—in particular in the maintenance of international peace and security, in the development of friendly relations

among nations, and in the achievement of international cooperation in solving problems of an economic, social, cultural, technical, intellectual, or humanitarian character.

5. *The Law of the Sea Convention* (1984) contains the principles of environmental conduct to guide contingent states in the conservation and harmonious utilization of natural resources of the sea.

6. *The Ozone Convention and Montreal Protocol* (1982 and 1987) is a detailed legal document for the protection of the ozone layer from modification due to human activity, and for the development of a protocol to control equitably global production, emission, and use of chlorofluorocarbons. It shows the need for further research and observations and calls for the adoption of appropriate legislative or administrative measures to cooperate in harmonizing appropriate policies to control, limit, reduce, or prevent human activities under their jurisdiction or control so as to prevent the likely modification of the ozone layer.

When all is said and done, however, we may need to turn our attention to the arts and literature for appropriate metaphors.

Joseph Meeker's *Comedy of Survival* may provide a useful example regarding the role of literature in our quest. As Meeker sees it, human beings are the earth's only literary creatures; he argues that if the creation of literature is an important characteristic of the human species, it should be examined carefully and honestly to discover its influences upon human behavior and the material environment—to determine what role, if any, it plays in the welfare and survival of mankind, and what insight it offers into relationships with other species and to the world around us.

In a very perceptive exercise Meeker applies his literary ecology to Dante's *Divine Comedy,* demonstrating Dante's vision that *human actions build their appropriate environment.* In this connection he talks about the pollution of Hell:

Hell is the meeting place of moral and biological pollution. The air is so bad everyone squints, the water is undrinkable, the flora dead or maimed. Sinners are likened to birds whose wings are glued. Overpopulation is a further punishment—everyone in Hell is crowded, spaceless, jammed together with others from whom there is no escape. Trapped togetherness is one of Hell's most characteristic images, repeated on many levels among sinners whose torment is to share a small space with one another.

To Meeker, our only path to salvation is to use our unique talent to understand where humanity belongs in relation to the rest of creation and to discover our appropriate role. Spiritual and artistic creativity are not special powers provided so that human beings can transcend the natural world, but features of human biological development useful for connecting humanity more deeply and fully to its planetary home. Misusing this talent could give humankind the singular distinction of being the first species to understand its own extinction.

Fortunately, doomsday is not inevitable, for we have it in our power to survive and prosper. We have the creative genius to design a future that is both environmentally enhancing and economically sustainable. As every "despairing optimist" knows, trend is not destiny.

As the scientist René Dubos was to remind us in one of his last public statements, "In human affairs, the logical future is less important than the willed future, which is largely brought about by deliberate choices—made by free will." He went on to remind us that our associates have a good chance of remaining prosperous because we are learning to anticipate the dangers we might experience in the future if we do not take technologically sound preventive measures.

And, concluding on an encouraging note, he expressed the confidence that "Homo sapiens could create humanized environments that are stable, profitable, pleasurable, and favorable to the health of the earth and the growth of civilization."

# The Inevitability of Global Cooperation

## Rodrigo Carazo
### (Costa Rica)

We live in a time in which the world has been shrinking before our eyes. We can now easily reach the most remote places of the planet, and can establish a personal conversation with people of the most diverse nationalities. Technology has set the foundations for a real rapprochement among all the inhabitants of the planet. In just a few hours, the modern means of transportation can take us to places that, while "unthinkable" a short time ago, are becoming more familiar each day.

California, until recently considered a sort of confine, is now the gateway to the Pacific, the sea of the immediate future that has surpassed all others with its fantastic commercial network. Bordered by North and South America, the Soviet Union, China, Japan, Eastern Asia, the Phillipines, Indonesia, Australia, and New Zealand, it also contains multiple islands that spread from north to south with a focal center—Hawaii—where the cultures, investments, and technology of East and West blend into an admirable composition of color, languages, and tradition.

We have recently seen the birth and development of regional efforts that anxiously search for the integration of peoples and cultures: the European Economic Community (EEC), the Association of South East Asian Nations (ASEAN), and South America's Mar del Plata, just to mention three examples.

Humankind is experiencing fundamental changes in that we may call the traditional formula of supremacy: force. The very development of nuclear weapons has shown us the impossibility of their use. Error or accident aside, it seems that the powerful ones are unwilling to destroy the planet through what would amount to a monumental suicide.

Traditional armies are incapable of "winning" wars; they have proved incompetent, on every side of the existing military spectrum, of defeating small groups of armed guerrillas. The Soviet Union was not able to dominate Afghanistan, and neither has it been possible for the United States to impose its power in Central America; Vietnam, of course, remains a classic example.

Economically speaking, it seems that the outcome has not been what was expected. The concentration of wealth in the United States, far from increasing the might of the most powerful nation on the planet, has begun to affect it in such a way that it has become the most indebted nation of the world, burdened by an unprecedented fiscal deficit and a trade deficit of astronomical proportions. Japan, West Germany, and other countries that are normally considered "well off" depend on the economic health of the United States. External debt overwhelms poor countries and threatens the stability of the financial institutions of rich countries. The Soviet Union is attempting to ease its economic woes through perestroika, which seems to be advancing very slowly. In the Third World, despair, poverty, and hunger are the permanent way of life.

Human masses move in all directions. Miserable hordes leave their places of origin in search of food and shelter whenever possible, invading—unarmed but undetainable—the rich countries of the planet. They move in constant search of the paths that have always been covered in the bounties of material riches taken from their countries.

Drugs and disease (AIDS, for example) destroy young people and nations; narcotics traffickers have become a power of such magnitude and importance that the governments of the small countries are constantly threatened, sometimes even condemned to inaction and defeat, and the strength of the rich and powerful nations sometimes seems diminished to unbelievable extent.

Today, more than ever, the environment is suffering from the exploitation of the rich to satisfy consumption and waste, and from the abuse of a population that grows without limit all over the globe. We deplete everything, whether due to disproportionate use, as with the tropical rain forest, or to irresponsible abuse, as in the case of acid rain and the destruction of the ozone layer. There is enough to satisfy the needs of everyone in this world, but not to satisfy greed, waste, and abuse.

There is no doubt, however, that we are facing a situation of change. The great powers have begun new practices of central–peripheral domination, as it has become especially difficult for them to maintain the obsolete imperial systems; neo-colonialism is an example. The use of economic might to police the world has overtaken military power, which is increasingly inoperative, much more expensive, and less productive. It seems more and more difficult to dominate an empire militarily and empires as such tend to weaken and disappear. The developed countries cannot maintain control in their traditional areas of influence, and even their own cities have become chaotic.

The end of the century brings with it the moment of change. The law of force must give way to the force of law. Law is increasingly understood as something that is conceived not in power itself, but in the overwhelming inspiration of ethics and morals.

Our current difficulties are precipitating a revitalization of values, which, due to circumstances, cannot be limited to a localistic approach and application. The time for globalization of values has arrived; it is the only way to guarantee peace, order, and the preservation of humankind. The mere proclamation of the rights to life, development, and peace constitutes an irrefutable proof that people have begun to question their future as citizens of the world, rather than of a specific country.

The need to determine global goals becomes more evident every day. A feeling of planetary responsibility must be grounded in the human aspiration to live a happy existence, and cannot be realized unless there is a repudiation of selfishness. Happiness rests on three pillars: seeing all of life as a gift, having the opportunity to live a meaningful life, and having the responsibility of sharing the gift of life, with all its richness and meaning, with other members of the human community.

We have to be clear—indeed, *convinced*—about the kind of world community in which we want to live. Each day we have a better understanding that it is not possible to live isolated in a world that is increasingly interdependent. Morality demands that we be concerned about one another; ethics demands that we behave in accordance with our feelings. If the good things of life are a gift, they are a gift for everyone, a divine gift that necessarily deserves to be shared. Those who want a rich and safe world must now realize that there is no richness or security in chaos, and that chaos is approaching through the destruction of natural resources and the threat of a morally degenerating population infected by the misery that builds up in the cities.

We can no longer protect a country by sending its troops to other regions or to other nations. Today the problem lies inside, and it is produced by a combination of prevailing local and worldwide problems.

We are used to speaking about the First World and the Third World, but the latter actually constitutes two-thirds of the world. Wealth and its exploitation cannot continue to be at the sole disposal of those who enjoy the possibility of creating more wealth, simply because they obtained it first. The truth is that there will be neither peace nor harmony in the First World if the conditions of misery prevailing today in the "Two-Thirds World" remain. Those who hold the wealth and the military and technological power are responsible for promoting the globalization of progress and development so that human, economic, and social pressures emanating from the rest of the world do not turn against them.

Our intelligence should allow us to understand the urgency of global action. Our ethics should show us the way—through solidarity, not through exploitation. The First World and the Third World can only advance toward the future if they do it together.

Solidarity must be based on realities—not just good feelings. It comes in the form of fair prices for the exports of the poor countries and in an analysis of the problem of external debt, which is an evil affecting us all, not only the indebted countries. We may apply solidarity to economic measures, so as to stop the flight of capital from the poor to the rich countries. We need solidarity to stop the arms race, which has no use at all and is wearing out the limited resources of the poor countries as well as those of the rich ones. We may also express global solidarity by curbing excessive consumption and waste in the First World nations.

Let us start with the external debt by modifying the policies of the international financial organizations. This problem is a product of excessive credit to the countries that need resources to promote their development, to compensate for increasing interest rates, and to cover the cost of their imports, which were affected by the prices of oil and manufactured goods while their exports were decreasing due to low prices. The payment of the external debt will be impossible if the global economic conditions that limit the potential of the indebted countries prevail.

Let us put an end to the complicity of the rich countries in promoting the flight of much-needed capital from the poor nations. Let us use all the payments of interest and capital made by the indebted countries to strengthen the regional-development banks such as the Interamerican Development Bank and the Asian Development Bank. In this way they be entrusted with the funds produced by the service of the debt, the responsiblity to negotiate with the creditor banks reasonable formulas of payment, and the obligation to provide credit free from any and all political conditions for investment in the poor countries.

Let us change the pernicious approaches applied by the International Monetary Fund, in order to reach goals that consider human needs more urgent than the specific financial needs of the creditors.

The humanist ethics of international solidarity and responsibility we seek are urgently required in our increasingly integrated world. However, we need an effective and immediate change of attitudes in the relationships between peoples and nations to encourage the formulation of a new global behavior for individuals as well as countries.

A good starting point in this process of change would be the elimination of that which is useless and superfluous—an effective disarmament would definitely be a positive step. The poor—those in the Third World as well as the many millions that proliferate in the world of the rich—demand the elimination of the instruments of death as a first step, without even aspiring that the rich make any sacrifice in their standard of living. The twenty-first century must be the beginning of our efforts to act as a unified whole.

# The Need for Global Political Cooperation

## Indumati Parikh

### (India)

We live in a world divided not only by the age-old loyalties of nation, race, and religion, but also by power blocs and political ideologies. To overcome these, we must stress the abiding truth that we belong to the same species of animal—we are all Homo sapiens. Our humanness unites us, and the survival of the species is our most compelling incentive to start our search for a global ethics. We are slowly becoming aware that the earth is an organic whole and that what happens on one part of it affects all of the rest. Thus we are almost obliged to develop ethical norms to guide our behavior.

Homo sapiens everywhere have had to struggle to survive, struggle for freedom from the atrocities of nature. To do this, human beings have had to use perhaps the only organ that has helped them to survive—their brains. Thought preceded action and led to knowledge, the store of which helped the species to progress, overcome difficulties, and form early societies. Ethical values were necessary for interpersonal relations and, later on, for social relations. By that time humankind had realized the value of freedom, and knowledge and truth had become the mainstays for acquiring new knowledge. Even today these are the most important values for social conduct. The Indian philosopher M. N. Roy writes, "Freedom, knowledge, and truth form the hierarchy of humanist axiology. They are interrelated logically, as well as ontologically."[1] That should be the basis of our ethics of global cooperation.

Humanity's struggle for existence made it imperative to form societies and also to develop ethical values; every society develops its own ethical norms for healthy social relations according to its own needs. It is clear that though some values are abiding and almost eternal, ethical values evolve according to the developmental stage of a particular society. Early societies had amazingly similar values, as they were fighting similar battles for survival against a very hostile environment. Humanity's beliefs and way of life changed according to its social organizations and modes of production. Primitive democratic societies worshiped "a galaxy of gods all equally powerful. But with the evolution of Monarchical society the concept of Super God came into existence."[2] Different societies in different parts of the world developed their own religions, whose moral codes would govern the society.

In India, against the background of a decaying pantheistic Hindu religion, Buddhism arose as a reaction to Brahmanical domination. According to the philosopher Tarkateerth Laxman Shastri Joshi, this was perhaps humanity's first attempt to evolve a global ethics and was based on a faith in humanity's capacity to be good on its own: "It [Buddhism] could cross the deep seas and mighty Himalayas without sword, authority of a supernatural power or resort to atrocities. No doubt the Buddhists were excellent organizers, devoted propagandists, but their greatest weapon was their objective of helping ordinary people to realize their capacity to do good to themselves."[3] Yet "Buddhism also was a product of social conditions of the epoch. Buddha secured adhesion of a rising class of traders who rejected the dogma of other-worldliness and Brahmanical rituals."[4] Buddhism was defeated by the priestly class in collaboration with the feudal lords of the land. It had an inherent weakness due to the lack of knowledge of nature and of humanity; mysteries of the universe were as yet unsolved. Thus humanity's first attempt to build a global community based on secular ethics failed.

The Renaissance marked the assertion of the individual during a period of revolt against the established church. Human creativity and a spirit of inquiry led to knowledge about humanity and nature. Europeans realized that they should try to enrich their lives on this earth and to be the makers of their own destiny. The growth of the basic sciences helped in the development of technology, which ultimately brought about Industrial Revolution. The printing press and the steam engine expanded our universe and also made it smaller.

The Renaissance ushered in the modern age, and the hunt began for markets and raw materials to feed the growing industries. The emergence of nation-states and competition among them led to the building of mighty empires. Large-scale exploitation of undeveloped nations began, and scientific knowledge percolated to the Third World—not in the form of science or scientific thought, but in the form of technology. Unfortunately, a much-needed revolution in the thinking of Third World peoples did not take place, and they were left in the backwaters of civilization. Racial discrimination became widespread, as did the economic exploitation of poor and vanquished Third World nations. Two different sets of ethical values—one for the conqueror and the other for the conquered—evolved and strengthened and remain in vogue even today.

In the meantime, Charles Darwin heralded a revolution by delving into the secret of the birth of humankind. It was proved beyond a doubt that human beings are made of the same matter as the rest of the universe. The biological sciences also provided a basis for secular morality, tracing it to the struggle for the existence of Homo sapiens. As Julian Huxley writes, "We are animals with a difference, a unique kind of organism with new capacities of reason, creative imagination, conceptual thought, and communication by speech symbols. And these have given man a second method of evolution, by means of cumulative transmission of relevant experience, and have made him the latest dominant type on earth. No other type of animal can possibly make any major evolutionary advance so long as man is there."[5]

The revolution that began with the propagation of the theory of evolution still is not complete and appears to be a continuing process. More and more information about humankind is being unearthed that could be helpful in making the future of evolution our conscious decision. The French and Russian Revolutions appear very tame affairs in the face of the potentials of this biological revolution, which has the capacity to turn our social institutions and personal relationships topsy-turvy. The challenge of such knowledge is great, but we must accept it and need fear only what will happen if it is used in a thoughtless manner.

In no period of human history has knowledge grown so fast and put such tremendous constructive as well as destructive power in the hands of mankind. The latter half of the twentieth century marked the beginning of the atomic age.

> The secret of atomic energy has suddenly been put into our human hands; and this fact has forced upon us a hasty revaluation of many of our ethical principles and their concrete application. . . . The atomic bomb has thus brought to a head the trend towards the contraction of our world . . . the separate regions of the world have, for the first time in history, shrunk politically into a single unit, though so far not an orderly but a chaotic one: and now the atomic bomb hangs with equal grimness over all parts of this infant commonwealth of man. . . . Human civilization has already been given a moral precept: nations must combine if man wishes truly to achieve the good. . . . The threat of the atomic bomb is simple—unite or perish.

Thomas H. and Julian Huxley have warned us in no uncertain terms about our fate. We must evolve ethical values fast enough to avoid a catastrophe. It is heartening that a politician of the stature of Mikhail Gorbachev has expressed the same thought: "For all the contradictions of the present-day world, for all the diversity of social and political systems in it, and for all the choices made by nations in different times, this world is nevertheless one whole. We are passengers aboard one ship, the *Earth,* and we must not allow it to be wrecked. There will be no second Noah's Ark."[7] These two stalwart men in very different but perhaps equally vital fields have given us guidance to develop our ethical values. Each one of us must understand that we need such guidance, and be ready to develop new ethical values suitable to the conditions under which we are now forced to live. Humankind has done that before. But are the common man and woman ready to march ahead?

Even in developed nations, we seem to still be living in the nineteenth century. Alexis de Tocqueville perhaps said it best:

> The first thing that strikes the observer is an innumerable multitude of men all equal and alike, incessantly endeavoring to procure the petty and paltry pleasures

with which they glut their lives. Each of them living apart is a stranger to the fate of all the rest of his kind. As for the rest of his fellow-citizens, he is close to them, but he sees them not; he touches them, but feels them not; he exists but in himself and for himself alone. . . . Above this race of men stands an immense and tutelary power, which takes upon itself alone to secure their gratifications and to watch over their fate. The power is absolute, minute, regular, provident, and mild. It would be like an authority of a parent, if, like that authority, its object was to prepare men for manhood, but it seeks on the contrary to keep them in perpetual childhood; it is well content that people should rejoice, provided they think of nothing but rejoice—it provides for their security, manages their principal concerns—but spares them all the care of thinking and all the trouble of living.[8]

This is an apt description of all people in the world today, educated and illiterate, black and white, rich and poor. The Third World nations that think their progress will echo that of the developed world behave exactly as de Tocqueville's men and the powers that rule them are no different.

On top of indifference and apathy, human beings are inclined to discriminate between the rich and the poor, the black and the white, the men and the women. Racial discrimination and religious fundamentalism are growing and so is blind faith in the supernatural, in godmen, and in religious rituals. It is strange and unfortunate that in an age when human beings are on the verge of achieving the power to shape the destiny of this planet, they seem to be reverting to primitive ways of thinking and behaving. Similarly, scientific knowledge and technology have made it possible to provide every individual on this earth with enough to satisfy his or her basic needs and even to progress; yet more than half of the world's population is starving, while in many nations food is destroyed or given to animals. Some countries are in the grip of perpetual famine caused by the vagaries of nature, the pressure of enormous population growth, poverty, and other factors. No doubt all of this is destroying the ecological balance; humanity's greed on one hand and the paucity of the means of survival on the other are dangerously eroding nature.

Population in the Third World is still uncontrolled, upsetting every plan for the future. Housing, sanitation, and a clean water supply remain a cry in the wilderness. Infant and maternal mortality—the indices of progress—are not under control in most of the Third World. How can we shape the world's future when we cannot set right its present? We cannot satisfy the needs of a major portion of the population despite the potential we have to do so. Something is wrong when the power structure does not want to set the world right for one reason or another. Corruption on a large scale is increasing all over. Life in many big cities is not safe. Easy money seems to be the fashion. Countries with tremendous technological know-how prevent unemployment by producing dangerous armaments and selling them to underdeveloped nations that can ill afford to spend on them. Hostilities are deliberately instigated between nations without any rhyme or reason.

This is a dangerous game. The people who wield power in these countries are not always sensible. They are guided by a thirst for power that is often strengthened by religious fundamentalism, and they are quite capable of using nuclear weapons if the developed nations put them into their hands. The developed nations must stop toying with dangerous weapons and using the underdeveloped world as their playground for power.

We must face the fact that powerful economic and political groups have joined hands to exploit the common people, who appear to have lost their instincts for self-preservation, no matter to what race, religion, or country they belong. In countries like India, the fatalistic outlook can explain many things. It is easy to make the common people believe that it is their fate to suffer because they did something very wrong in their past lives. This belief is still very strong and what is most disturbing is that it is on the increase. The situation in other parts of the world is not very different. Religious fundamentalism is gaining strength, fed by the rich from the Middle East as well as those from the West. Indian godmen are gaining more and more disciples in the West and often they are the financial as well as the spiritual power behind many corrupt and even dangerously criminal deeds, including selling drugs, racketeering, and smuggling.

Why is this happening? Why have the common people lost their self-confidence? Why are they allowing themselves to be used as cogs in the wheel? Why do they look to religion and the supernatural for their salvation? These are the some of the questions we must answer when we speak of an ethics of global cooperation. After all, cooperation must be between individuals, and unless individuals act as thinking beings, they will not be able to take initiative. Today man is made to "lose his power to make use of all these capacities which make him truly human, his reason ceases to operate, he accepts as truth that which those who have power over him call the truth. He loses his power to love, for his emotions are tied to those upon whom he depends. He loses his moral sense, for his inability to question and criticize those in power stultifies his moral judgment with regard to anybody and anything. He is prey to prejudice and superstition."[9] A large number of such individuals together become the masses, and the masses empower their rulers. State-controlled mass media are used to present to these unthinking masses only what the rulers want them to know and to perpetuate their ignorance, their blind faith, and their superstitious and fatalistic outlook. Are we ready to do anything about it? Are we ready to make thinking individuals out of the masses?

As humanists we accept that each individual is the "archetype of society." We believe that cooperative social relationships contribute to develop individual potentialities. But the development of the individual is the measure of social progress.[10] Ethical values must be accepted by individuals and they must be conducive to the growth of individuals as human beings—only this will guarantee that ethical values will be respected and will guide human behavior. Ours is a liberating social philosophy that believes we are the makers of our world. Roy writes, "An increasingly large number of men, conscious of their creative power, motivated by the indomitable will to remake the world, moved by the adventure of ideas, and fired with the ideal of a free society of free men, can create these conditions" under which global cooperation will be possible.[11]

If each nation were to commit itself to the ideal of freedom—that is, to the removal of all impediments to the unfolding of every individual's potential—the development of global cooperation would be possible. The world has to become a commonwealth of free individuals, and this can only be brought about by "the collective efforts of spiritually free men united in the determination of creating a world of freedom."[12]

Freedom is the driving force of human life, and it must be felt during every moment of life. Therefore, unless the atmosphere in which one lives is conducive to freedom, one cannot be free. To fight for the freedom of others becomes a fight for the extension of one's own freedom. To my mind, that is a very strong inducement.

But how do we bring about this ideal society in which each person is free to develop without fear or fetters? Perhaps no humanist has given more thought to the practical aspects of bringing about a more humanistic world than M. N. Roy. He did not want the Radical Humanist philosophy to end up being a dogma: "To consolidate the intellectual basis of the movement, Radicals will continue to submit their philosophy to constant research, examine it in the light of modern scientific knowledge and experience, and extend its application to all social sciences."[14] This clearly shows how open the Radical Humanist philosophy is and how responsible each humanist has to be. He further writes that Radical Humanists "will make the people conscious of the urge for freedom, encourage their self-reliance, and awaken in them the sense of individual dignity, inculcate the values of rationalism and secular morality, and spread the spirit of cosmopolite Humanism. By showing the people the way to solve their daily problems by popular initiative, the Radicals will combat ignorance, fatalism, blind faith, and the sense of individual helplessness, which are the basis of authoritarianism. They will put all the social traditions and institutions to the test of the humanist outlook."[14]

Roy described the humanist society in all its aspects. He had great faith in democracy as a way of life; not formal democracy or even parliamentary democracy, but democracy based on individual freedom and the decentralization of power. He visualized a pyramidal structure of the state composed of a countrywide network of peoples' committees. These committees would be the local functioning democracies and schools for training in democracy. Again, this would not be an easy task. In most countries a social, intellectual, and attitudinal revolution would have to precede the revolution that would become the new renaissance. In economic reorganization, the potential for exploitation would have to be eliminated. Such a society would need to create opportunities for the unfoldment of the intellectual and other finer human potentialities of every citizen. This can only be attained through the collective efforts of spiritually free men and women.

Unfortunately, however, today the common people everywhere seem to have lost faith in themselves. There could be several reasons for this. Two world wars, along with the threat of a third one that could destroy the world, have made people helpless spectators of events over which they have no control. There is a strong possibility that we will witness the holocaust of our civilization. But it is only the common men and women who can prevent this. The present leadership has failed miserably, so we must create a new one: "Leadership with integrity, wisdom, and moral excellence."[15] We have no time to lose. Roy warns us that already "we see a new religion rising in the world. Masses are the gods of this vulgar and secular religion and political party is the new priesthood. They have no faith in the individual, but they believe that when thousands and thousands of helpless individuals come together to follow the party leaders, an irresistible power is generated."[16]

All over the world, party politics has become the politics of power: Nothing matters but the pursuit of power. Therefore, Roy advocated a partyless democracy, where the decision-making power would increasingly belong to, and remain with, the people. Thus Roy has spelled out a broad outline of a feasible human society. Each community, each nation, may adopt its own pattern of ruling itself. As humanists we must only insist that no matter what form of government the community accepts, it must be based on human freedom—freedom for each individual to develop his or her personality economically, socially, and culturally to the fullest extent.

An ethics of global cooperation must allow each individual the freedom to take his or her rightful place in a commonwealth of nations. There can be no conflict between the requirements of social ethics and individual ethics; increasingly large numbers of people have to accept and respect global ethical values and behave accordingly. That is the only guarantee that, unlike earlier efforts, today's efforts will succeed. This time we must succeed: We are striving for the very survival of mankind. Efforts made earlier in the twentieth century failed because some nations wanted to be more equal than others. The League of Nations failed because economic competition among developed nations became sharper. The United Nations has had limited success: It could not prevent the polarization of political forces in the world, nor could it guide the newly freed nations to become developing democracies; instead, they were made to take sides, and got involved in the politics of power.

This time we must not fail. Too much is at stake. Nobody is safe on this globe when nuclear war and major nuclear accidents threaten. We have developed the broad principles of an ethics of global cooperation. As humanists we must accept and work toward them. The question is how to put them into practice; how to work toward social, economic, and political change in all parts of the world until the ethical values we evolve are accepted and practiced by an increasingly large portion of the population. We are a small group that is aware of the dangerous situation in which we have placed ourselves. We humanists believe we have evolved a suitable philosophical ideology practical enough to get us out of this impasse. If we do not exert ourselves, we will be guilty of not acting when action was necessary and perhaps would have helped.

We must work on two fronts. The masses of the Third World must be helped to reach an acceptable level of human existence. We cannot teach them ethical values and ask them to work toward a global ethics when they do not have enough food to survive. To help them to survive we must enlist the common men and women at a grass-roots level. We must do it for our own survival, because unless increasingly large numbers of people develop as human beings and become aware of human values, our world is in danger. This is an uphill task and we need all the help we can get, both moral and physical.

In addition to feeding the hungry, we must educate the uneducated. Our main tasks must be to disseminate scientific knowledge and to encourage critical thinking and the scientific attitude. There are people all over the world doing this type of work; many are not humanists in the formal sense. We should become more aware of them, explain our philosophy to them, and draw strength from them.

There is much work to be done on another front: that of the elite, the "educated" both in the developed nations and in the Third World. Often it seems that the elite are the least concerned about what happens to the world. They are de Tocqueville's men among the ruled and the rulers. We have to shake them into action to save themselves and the world.

Our problems are formidable, and we must put our heads and hearts together to find solutions to them. We must work with a missionary zeal and get everyone involved in this massive undertaking, regardless of race, religion, color, or wealth. If we do not, we will not be able to survive. We know that there are richer and better possibilities for human life, that there is the potential for a great degree of fulfillment for ourselves and for the evolutionary process of which humankind has become the spearhead. To shape the future is our privilege and also our responsibility. By evolving an ethics for global cooperation, let us be worthy of our human heritage and begin to undertake the herculean task of shaping our destiny.

## Notes

1. M. N. Roy, "Metaphysics of Morals and Social Philosophy," *Humanist Way,* Spring 1952.

2. M. N. Roy, *Fragments of a Prisoner's Diary: India's Message* (Delhi: Ajanta Publications, 1982; first published 1950), p. 74.

3. Tarkateerth Laxman Shastri Joshi, *Vaidik Samskrutiche Vikas* (Marathi), p. 386.

4. M. N. Roy, *Materialism* (Delhi: Ajanta Publications, 1940), p. 140.

5. Julian Huxley, quoted in *Two Cultures: and A Second Look,* edited by C. P. Snow (New York: Cambridge University Press, 1969), p. 74.

6. Thomas H. Huxley and Julian Huxley, *Touchstone for Ethics* (New York and London: Harper & Brothers, 1947), pp. 196–97.

7. Mikhail Gorbachev, *Peristroika* (New York: Harper, 1987), p. 22.

8. Alexis de Tocqueville quoted in H. J. Blackham, *Political Discipline in a Free Society* (London: Allen & Unwin, 1961), p. 579.

9. Erich Fromm, *Man for Himself* (New York: Fawcett, 1978), pp. 246–47.

10. M. N. Roy, *Anthology,* Thesis No. 1 (New Delhi: South Asian Publications,

1979), p. 285.

   11. Ibid., Thesis No. 15, p. 289.

   12. Ibid., Thesis No. 19, p. 290.

   13. M. N. Roy, quoted in M. Shiriah, *New Humanism and Democratic Politics: A Study of M. N. Roy's Theory of State* (New Delhi: South Asian Publications, 1979), pp. 76–77.

   14. Ibid.

   15. *Anthology,* p. 43.

   16. *New Humanism,* p. 101.

# Together, We Can Have a Future

## Victor Garadja
### translated by Victor Timofeyev
#### (Soviet Union)

The main task of the Soviet Union today is to make life more democratic and more communistic, in the best sense of the word. The new political thinking initiated by Mikhail Gorbachev is rooted in the values that all of humanity cherishes, and it emphasizes that we must think not only in political or economic terms, but also in terms of ethical and moral imperatives.

The global problems we face as we enter the twenty-first century remind us that we are at a crucial juncture in the history of society and in the evolution of nature. Quality of life is controlled by humanity and by nature, and nature, it seems, is increasingly controlled by humanity, much to its detriment. The action that we take now shall become the most important factor in the future of the earth, which is an extremely fragile habitat.

Since the middle of the twentieth century, humanity has had the power for the wholesale destruction of civilization, as well as virtually the entire environment, through nuclear holocaust. Before the atomic age, we had always believed that humanity as a whole would exist forever, though each individual would certainly die and entire civilizations might perish. Indeed, the feeling that individual death was separate and distinct from the eternal existence of humanity no doubt contributed to the development of religious tenets regarding life after death; our ancestors developed an ethics that embodied the concept of immortality because it appeared that humanity was forever.

Suddenly we encountered a new situation; we now understand that humanity as a whole may not exist forever. We have the potential to completely destroy all civilization. Previously we asked how we could make our lives better; now the most important question is whether we can save our lives after all. The danger is not our influence on nature in itself, but how we use this influence; it is imperative that we realize that the evolution of our globe rests on our shoulders. Consequently, all societies must be ruled by reason, and we must each do our part to see that reason triumphs.

We must realize, too, that the relation of society to nature depends very strongly upon the relations among peoples. We experience constant strife between nations, between classes, between religions, between races—but the problems we face now are global ones; they affect all of humanity. We must realize that we hold in common human life, and that the social relations, political views, and ethical stances that were constructed in previous times are no longer in accordance with the state of today's world.

One of the biggest difficulties simply lies in the differences of our respective aims. Today each nation seems to have its own system and its own world view; too often, these differences lead to a conflict of interest. However, global problems themselves stem from all of these conflicting interests; they are relevant to each of today's civilizations at the same time that they deal with the future of all humanity. Perhaps we shall understand the problems these conflicts have created, now that we have reached a crisis in which we all must work together simply to survive. We must unite and put our common problems first. But the question remains: Can each nation and each individual put common humanity before parochial loyalties?

History has been the test of our ethical values. Experience has proved that the voices of reason and fear are not enough to stop us from careening in a direction that is deadly dangerous. Is our fear powerful enough to prevent a nuclear war? Do we understand how real the danger is as we venture forth into the twenty-first century? Do we truly realize that if such an event occurs, there will be no winner and we all will die?

Our instinct to do right is important; but it is not necessarily enough. The problem of the future is a problem of ethics, and the meaning of ethics grows in each new historical situation because the solving of global problems demands searching and collaboration among peoples. It does not matter how we do it, as long as all peoples cooperate—this applies not only to nations but to individuals as well. Since this collaboration is increasingly important, it is imperative that we develop a global ethics that can help us to organize.

We shall survive only if we work together—more than ever before we must become our brothers' keepers. We must strive to increase ethical awareness. Politics that would be free of ethical norms today becomes not only inhuman but deadly. Politicians must learn to listen not only to words of reason but to words of conscience. Each of us now has a connection with every other human being on this planet. Only together can we decide on answers to the problem of saving the world. To do this, however, we must use reason—not the reason of a god but the reason of humanity. If humanity dies it will be because higher reason was not employed, ethical lessons were not learned, and morality stagnated.

Though the future of humanity holds many dangers, it also holds many possibilities for making the world more humanistic. We must make the most of these possibilities, and we must take action today. Together we can have a future.

# Efforts at a Global Community

## Hope N. Tawiah
### (Ghana)

I shall not belabor the history of the suppression and savage persecution of the first humanists by the powers that be of their times, for ends well known to us all. Happily, recent scientific achievements and exploits have, more than expected, vindicated the truths expounded by those who were clearly ahead of their time. Today, the achievements of the electronic age, which have contributed to the betterment of the human race more than at any time since the Renaissance, not only provide a fitting tribute to those people but are also sounding the humanist message louder, clearer, and farther.

But despite all these breakthroughs in science that have laid bare the hypocrisy, deceit, and ineffectiveness of dogma and ideology to the benefit of free thought, can it be said that humanism has achieved the aspirations of the first humanists? The answer is no; much more remains to be done.

Humanism has sought throughout the ages to evolve appropriate ethical values that will enable humankind to live together in harmony and enhanced conditions in a world unfettered by tribal, racial, and nationalistic loyalties. It is the wish of the humanist that humankind live in a world without a conception of nation-states and without conflicting religious faiths—in a world where each and every one will be his brother's keeper. Yet the most vital ingredient for the achievement of this lofty ideal continues to elude us.

Our world today is threatened by such burning issues as famine caused by the vagaries of the weather, the mind-boggling refugee problem, the ecological question, shelter for the world's poor, drug abuse, the unfortunate desire of the stronger nations to dominate and strangulate the weaker nations, and the disturbing questions of education and health, particularly the problem of infant mortality, to name just a few.

These are just some of the challenges that face humankind and the humanist movement today.

It is strange, if not sad, that in the twentieth century some nations burn and bury grains while other nations starve to death, simply because of ideological considerations. It may be worthwhile to ask whether some peoples should prosper at the expense of others, leaving them in abject poverty and misery. Should the minority deprive the majority simply because of the color of their skin? Such situations must be reversed for the betterment of the whole human race.

We need not lose sight of the efforts being made by certain agencies, organizations, and individuals to help solve some of these nagging problems. Many of these efforts would never have been possible without the acceptance of the humanist call, which gained a lot of momentum during the postwar era. The United Nations was conceived by people who were motivated by the humanist message of peace on earth and a world without wars. It was with sheer humanist values that Bob Geldof organized the "Live Aid" concert to help save the lives of millions in Ethiopia. The deprived people of the Third World need amenities like schools, clinics, and even literature that will liberate their minds from dogma. Though the humanist movement is not wanting in strengthening these areas, ironically, religious organizations have taken the lead and have, through the provisions of such amenities, indoctrinated a great number of people. We must act positively in this direction, but must also be aware of the dangers of having to rely entirely on the generosity of a few agencies and individuals for the survival of the whole world. It would be equally dangerous to put all our hopes on treaties, such as the recent INF Treaty signed between the United States and the Soviet Union, which is but a step toward peace.

Many authorities on psychology and the humanities have defined thought as the product of mind, a mental vibration that can penetrate the physical body and shape the affairs of humanity and of the world. The careful articulation of thought and proper concentration have allowed us to make our lives better, safer, and more comfortable through inventions and improvements, and arguably through deterrent armaments; but a few misdirected thoughts have plunged the world into fatricidal wars that have cost millions of lives. Can't it thus be rightfully argued that the solution to our problems lies in education? It is known that throughout history, scientific studies have revealed that only a fraction of our mind potential has been used; can't we therefore imagine the future of the human race if we maximize the use of our brains?

I believe it is now time to come to terms with the aspirations of the humanist movement if we are to achieve the peace we envisage. Never before has the rationalistic movement been so well equipped, especially in the area of information dissemination. Frequent gatherings like the Tenth Humanist World Congress are vital to plan and coordinate strategies to propagate the humanist message.

It is important that our youth be prepared for the coming century through a well-planned curriculum properly geared toward a determined course. This generation must be cultured to harness all of its energies toward its own advancement. After all, the comforts of today were once merely the thoughts of men and women who were committed to leaving this world a better place than it was when they entered it.

Efforts should be made to rid from the minds of today all negative thoughts, doubts, and dogmas that inhibit and confuse, and to nurture the Great Gospel of Optimism and Self-Confidence. Our minds, which have lain fallow for a long time, are now fertile for cultivation.

We also have to our advantage the blow dealt to organized religion by science, which has exposed its hypocrisy and other questionable aspects, leaving millions of people frustrated with the church. We must reach these people before they nurture the ugly habit of ignorance to their detriment. We must safeguard them against the destructive and negative ideas of the modern-day primitive fools who refuse to broaden their horizons toward the peaceful world we envisage for humankind, and would rather inundate the world of tomorrow with fears.

The twenty-first century poses a challenge, and now is the time to act if we are to effectively meet it. Our duty is to the whole world. Parochial nationalistic feelings are dangerous, creating chaos instead of order. We must strive ever harder for peace and for a truly global community.

# Social and Economic Development in China

## Lin Zixin
### (China)

Though China is a large country whose population constitutes 21 percent of the world's total, it is also a small country in terms of gross national product (GNP), which accounts for only 2.1 percent of the world's total. The simultaneous greatness and smallness of the country make the Chinese keenly aware of the responsibility they bear in building a world community in the twenty-first century.

The usual label applied to current Chinese economic policies is the "Four Modernizations." The government intends to turn China into a modern state by the year 2000 through the modernization of industry, agriculture, defense, and science. To achieve this goal, which includes quadrupled production and nearly tripled annual income, the national economy is being increasingly decentralized and the country is turning away from the narrow path of self-reliance that characterized the Maoist era.

After twenty years (1957–1977) of economic and social stagnation, China is ushering in a new period by concentrating on economic development and advancing all-around reform and more open policies.

Reform and openness have not only broken down the rigid economic structure and revitalized the economy, they have also battered down many concepts that have long stifled thinking, emancipating the minds of the people.

Between 1979 and 1987, the GNP, state revenues, and the average income of both urban and rural residents approximately doubled. The overwhelming majority of China's one billion people now have enough food and clothing; jobs have been created on an extensive scale in both urban and rural areas; and the acute and long-lasting shortages of consumer goods have abated.

It appears that China's per capita GNP will surely reach $1,000 (indexed in 1980) by the end of this century, thus enabling its people to lead fairly comfortable lives. Though it will be more difficult to reach the per capita GNP level of moderately developed nations (about $4,000) by the middle of the next century, the Chinese have begun to enjoy relative affluence, and modernization is moving along apace.

The Chinese are looking toward the future, and are determined to venture forth boldly to solve the crucial problems that will inevitably arise. Recently, some Chinese scholars have suggested that the "modernization of concepts" must be added to the Four Modernizations, since the old concepts have become a serious obstacle to reform and open policy.

For example, looking down on commerce and business has been a tradition in China for thousands of years. Many great advances in scientific and technological research have remained on paper or in exhibits; they are not developed into products to meet the market demand simply because people respect the work of academics but belittle efforts to solve specific problems in production and marketing.

It is increasingly necessary to introduce new concepts from abroad. But again, a serious problem arises in that the understanding of foreign societies comes largely from books and from contact with tourists. Blind opposition to everything foreign and the simple-minded labeling of foreign economies as "decaying capitalist ideas" or "bourgeois ways of life" is widespread.

The development of scientific concepts of time, communication, ecology, and so forth must become a priority in China; we must begin science education in childhood. To eliminate poverty we must first eliminate ignorance. Fighting against ignorance, backwardness, and superstition is still our essential task.

Thus, many new policies have to be adopted. But perhaps most important, a new ethics must evolve. People's concepts must change.

For thousands of years, the Chinese have invariably believed that their "Middle Kingdom" is a vast territory richly endowed by nature with abundant resources, that productive forces can be developed rapidly once the superiority of the socialist system is brought into full play, and that the time lag between China's science and technology levels and those of more advanced nations is only ten to thirty years.

Recent studies belie these assumptions. China's cultivated land, forest, grasslands, and water resources per capita are below the world's average levels, and 60 percent of China's territory consists of mountain and highland areas. China is still in the primary stage of socialism, which will last at least a hundred years. At present, China's productive forces lag far behind those of the developed capitalist countries. For example, a comparison of the ten indices of development—the average number of persons supported by each farmworker, the illiteracy rate, the per capita production of steel, railway and highway mileage, electric energy production, the number of telephones per 1,000 people, the labor distribution between urban and rural areas, and the per capita GNP—show that China is actually about a century behind the United States. Simply acknowledging this backwardness and the difficulties associated with it is a step in the right direction.

For a long time in China, many "socialist principles" believed to be beneficial have actually fettered the growth of production and are not in fact inherently socialist, or are applicable only under certain historical conditions. Conversely, many policies condemned as the "restoration of capitalism" are, under socialist conditions, favorable to the growth of production, commoditization, socialization, and modernization. As a result, a structure of ownership evolved in which undue emphasis was placed on a single form of ownership, and a rigid economic structure took shape, along with a corresponding political structure based on the over-concentration of power. All of this seriously hampered the development of the productive forces and of the socialist commodity economy.

People are now realizing that a fully developed commodity economy is an unavoidable stage in the development of the society, that it is not true that a broader scale and a higher level of socialist ownership is better, that the principal form of distribution according to work performed can be complemented with diverse forms of distribution, and that it is not peculiar to capitalism to expand markets for funds and labor service and to issue stocks and bonds, which can and should be used by socialist economies.

In short, whether or not the expansion of the productive forces is served should become the basic criteria for judging all of our work, and the historical idealism should be discarded that deals with socialism in abstract terms without any consideration of actual outcome.

During the period of social and economic stagnation, Chinese leaders advanced many impractical slogans: "We can surpass the U.K. and catch up with the U.S. in fifteen years"; "We can catch up with the world's advanced science and technology in a short time"; "Within this century we can accomplish overall modernization in agriculture, industry, national defense, science, and technology so that our national economy will stand in the forefront of the world."

One slogan they forgot, however, was "Haste makes waste."

The consequence of impatience led to the economic catastrophe of Mao's "Great Leap Forward," an ambitious plan embarked upon in the 1950s to transform China into a developed nation practically overnight. Moreover, this splendid long-range plan greatly enhanced people's expectations and its failure caused widespread lack of faith in the government.

In the 1970s Chairman Deng Xiaoping set more realistic goals for China to achieve by the end of this century and by the middle of the next century. This has had a sobering effect on the Chinese people. However, great efforts must still be made to reverse the trend of impatience for quick results and of excessive expectations for the improvement of the standard of life.

The Chinese practice of "eating in the canteen the same as everyone else" has brought up many sluggards; moreover, the "extensive employment" that distributes the work of three people among five or even ten allows many to idle away their time. The resulting low grade of service and poor quality of workmanship have aroused widespread dissatisfaction. The long-term emphasis on "class struggle as the key link" has terribly impaired the mutual trust, aid, and unity of the people. Although we often call an organization "one big family," it becomes a knotty problem to maintain this atmosphere and still foster hard work and professional ethics. It would be helpful to introduce the concept of competition and to reform the personnel system in China.

Mutual aid has been a traditional moral excellence of the Chinese. But for a period of time even this humanitarianism posed an unexpected problem. Now people are beginning to realize that without humanitarianism we cannot begin to develop a working concept of socialism.

There are 40 to 50 million handicapped people throughout China. In the past decade, the Chinese Association for the Deaf, Mutes, and the Blind (CADMB) has been allowed to resume its activities, and the Chinese Fund for the Handicapped (CFH) and the Chinese Association for the Handicapped (CAH) have been set up as well. The employment, education, and rehabilitation of the handicapped have been expanded with the support of the government and of other social organizations. International contacts among organizations of the handicapped have also increased.

All this shows that socialism has opened up the way to a bright future for humanitarianism—for the socialist system requires that people understand, respect, care for, and help others, and consider them equals in the struggle for social progress.

# Beyond Statism

Svetozar Stojanović

(Yugoslavia)

Anthropologically, ontologically, historically, morally, and theologically speaking, we have been in an absolutely new situation since 1945. If we start counting from that year, we are now in our forty-fifth year.

Mention should be made, in this context, of the obsolescent problem of human evil. The accent should be shifted now from the topic of evil to the unconcern, indifference, nonchalance, and carelessness of humankind. Confronting us is a new, most dangerous form of collective self-delusion. Because the human race's self-destruction can happen quite by chance, one can easily be a fatalist and say that in the final analysis there is nothing effective that can be done to save us from doom.

But the problem needs to be posed differently. It is ironic but true that the most radical utopia proposed right now is the survival of humankind. Is there any utopia more minimal than that? A negative utopia—a *dystopia*—would be an earth from which people had eliminated themselves.

What is the purpose of politics today and in the future? Traditionally speaking, politics concerns power over people, society, and nature. Now, as I said, politics is confronted with man's powerlessness in the face of chance. The legitimacy of governments, authorities, states, and politics appears quite different in this light. A policy that is not preoccupied with the question of humanity's survival cannot be legitimate. Moreover, the philosophical dispute between existentialism and essentialism is largely passé. In our day and age humanity's existence and essence are open to the whims of contingency.

I call for a new, transpolitical philosophy: *contingentialism*. There is the real possibility and even probability that the circle of human contingency will close once and for all: from humankind's biological contingency in the universe to the contingency of human survival.

Christians who are nonchalant about the real danger of the human race's self-destruction are no better than irresponsible atheists on the other side of the ideological divide. We do not need a Strategic Defense Initiative but a *Strategic Historical Initiative* for the salvation of humankind.

Atheists should give deep thought to whether the notion of a completely profane world gives us any chance at all of avoiding the apocalypse. Is it possible to have an atheism for which the continuation of the human species would be a sacred cause?

The world today is dominated by two systems with gigantic concentrations of power: democratic capitalism and communist statism. The latter is inferior (except in the military sense), and it feels itself to be so deep inside. In communist statism one group, the statist ruling class, has structural monopolistic control over the state and, through the state, over the means of production. If the statist ruling class would lose monopoly-ruling status in politics, it would not be in the position (like the bourgeoisie) to dominate politically through the economy, because in the statist system there is no real division between politics and the economy.

Would it be accurate, however, to evaluate communist statism as "the dead end of history"? Communist states in Europe (excepting Albania) have successfully carried out industrialization and modernization; so we cannot speak of a "dead end" in that sense. Of course, the price paid for such industrialization and modernization has to be assessed, taking primarily into account the enormous human sacrifices ("pyramids of sacrifices," as the sociologist Peter Berger would say).

The basic question to be asked now is the following: Having completed industrialization and modernization, has the statist system become the impediment to further economic and social development? Can it be seriously reformed? One thing is already clear: Statism is not as dynamic as democratic capitalism. The latter is more quickly and successfully heading toward the postindustrial information age.

We have already witnessed that statism is feasible. Its continued viability, however, depends on its ability to radically transform itself. We could call such reformed statism "statism with a civil and bourgeois face." Admittedly, a comprehensive civil society calls for a completely pluralistic state. However, by definition statism in self-transformation could not go that far. That would be revolution, not reform.

The statist class is now at a historical turning point: In order to preserve selective stategic control over the state and the means of production, it will ultimately have to sacrifice total, supercentralized, detailed control. This liberalization would be in the objective interest of a good part of the ruling class, not to mention the general population of the communist statist countries. I expect that by the end of our century the struggle for the liberalization of statism will be completed in Eastern Europe and the Soviet Union. On the agenda at the beginning of the next century, then, will be the transition from liberalized statism to democratic socialism. However, that cannot happen without great social conflicts.

# III.

# Ecology and Population

# Ecology and Environment: Our Responsibility in the Twenty-First Century

## Armin Rieser
### (West Germany)

Eighteen years ago my wife and I made our first trip to the United States. We spent four wonderful, exciting days in Manhattan with friends from the humanist societies. During one of our trips downtown, a friend made a passing remark that became a key experience in my life and helped to shape my attitude on ecology and environment. As we stepped off the bus, I threw my ticket on the street. When my friend saw this she looked at me and said very sincerely, "And you will be an ecologist?" She knew that I had just finished my Ph.D. and that I was engaged in that field, mainly in water resources.

What did I learn from that very short moment? That each individual has a responsibility for our common environment and its ecology, and can act on that. Each of us is responsible and can contribute to the future of our world; therefore we all are obligated to take part.

But in the foreword for the theme of the Tenth Humanist World Congress, I found a phrase with which I don't fully agree: "We have the ethical obligation to humankind as a whole, including a responsibility to generations yet unborn."

For me as a free-religious humanist, that cannot be the final meaning; can the survival of humankind, the human species, really be the final aim?

There is more than the obligation to humankind; there is the objective to "foster the attitude that we are all part of a world community." But what is the meaning of "world community"? To me, the community of our earth includes the lifeless as well as the living nature. It consists of animals, plants, air, soil, stones, and water: the so-called natural resources. Between all of these there exist interlinkages, interdependencies, and feedbacks. It's a very complicated and complex system.

Our planet earth is over five billion years old. The evolution of life started two billion years ago. Today we are standing on a kind of doorstep; this moment is not comparable with any other time in human history: Human beings are able to bring biological and, linked together with it, intellectual and cultural evolution to an end. Thus there is an urgent need for a global ethics.

The German physical scientist and philosopher Carl-Friedrich von Weizsäcker said in a television discussion with our former chancellor Helmut Schmidt, "A species can only survive if the mistakes it makes are not harmful for its further development. A mistake with atomic weapons can be deadly."

But there are more other—more subtle, but no less deadly—mistakes. The exhausting of available natural resources, the abuse of water and soil, the despoiling of mineral deposits, and reckless deforestation—not only in Germany and the United States, but all over the world, including the countries of the Third World—all these can accelerate the end. We must campaign against such irresponsibility. Furthermore, we must continuously point out the unnessary contamination of our environment, the water, the air, the soil. The drinking-water supply of millions of human beings is endangered not only by industry, but by agriculture and by each of us individually as well. Ground-water contamination by pesticides and fertilizers in regions of western Europe has reached levels harmful to human beings and other animals. Then of course there is the artificially increasing radioactive burden on our environment by nuclear power plants, quite apart from the madness of some military power considering a limited nuclear war.

All are abuses we cannot afford to continue in the future as we have done in the past. A change in our thinking is unconditionally necessary. For me that means to search for a healed world not through the mystical worship of nature or supernature—but through an active and engaged life.

Fortunately we have increasing millions of fellow citizens not only entering the peace movement, but entering the environmental and ecology movement as well. Included are well-known scientists, even Nobel prize–winners, such as Ilya Prigogine and Jonas Salk. Only through the activities of responsible human beings, through self-organization and autonomy, can real progress be made. Citizens' initiatives are based on such self-determination and responsibility. Humanists should play an active role in these initiatives.

There exists a harmonious order in the world of living nature from which human beings are far from excluded. The functions and structures of our environment maintain the species and the system; that is the product of more than two billion years of evolution.

Evolution doesn't mean that there is no end for certain species. More species exist now than have lived on earth during the past two billion years. But if we consider an untouched tropical rainforest, we understand the meaning of order and organization in the living nature as well as in the lifeless nature—in the natural cycle.

Many hope that our instinct will enable us to develop abilities that have a positive chance to save even our species. Organisms don't destroy themselves; that would be against the most vigorous driving force in the history of evolution, the instinct of self-preservation.

To use our positive instincts we must liberate our thinking, make our minds free. Our enemies are not others—foreigners, Russians, Nicaraguans, immigrants.

Our enemy very often is our own mentality. It is not necessary that we be redeemed. We have to awaken, awaken to peace with our neighbor, our fellow-animal, our whole environment, the whole of nature. I appeal to a holistic rather than an anthropocentric approach in a new environmental ethic.

One can distinguish five levels of environmental-ecological ethics:

1. The *egocentric* level, with a mere utilitarian sense of using the natural resources without reflecting on the results.

2. The *anthropocentric* level, with the arrogance of speciesism, noted by David Ehrenfeld in 1978. Nature is more than the environment for the human species; the ideology of dominating nature has to end.

3. The *pathocentric* level we find in Jeremy Bentham's *Introduction to the Principles of Morals and Legislation.* In it the founder of utilitarianism wrote, "The question is not, Can they reason? nor Can they talk? but, Can they suffer?"

4. The *biocentric* level we find in quite a number of Asian religions; it includes the respect of all living nature.

5. The *holistic* level. As an example we can take the "land ethic" postulated by the American ecologist Aldo Leopold, one of the first human beings with an ecological ethic: "A land ethic . . . implies respect for [our] fellow-members, and also respect for the community as such." It includes the lifeless nature too.

Increasing numbers of human beings who feel obligated to such an environmental—I would rather call it ecological—ethic, and seek to live in harmony with nature. In the history of human development, important social changes took part despite existing structures of power. But a pioneering change can and will take place only when the drive behind it has become strong enough. Human beings give institutions their publicity, effect, and power. Without the mandate of committed human beings no institution can act. That implies the strength of alternative movements, and we should be conscious of that. During the 1986 IHEU World Congress at Oslo, the sociologist John Galtung said, "Without the great engagement of the worldwide peace movement, we wouldn't have reached the status we have now." I hope that our humanist and ethical optimism gives us the power and confidence to continue to support and strengthen alternative movements. We all set for ourselves priorities in our actions according to our own responsibility and self-determination.

I will end with a poem by one of our members of the Bund Freireligiöser Gemeinden Deutschlands (Union of Freereligious Societies and Communities of the Federal Republic of Germany). Kriemhild Klie-Riedel, of the Free Humanists of Lower-Saxony, published a book called *Zwischen Allmacht und Ohnmacht (Between Allmightiness and Powerlessness)* and called the poems "Käfiggedichte" ("Cage poems"):

| Zeigt es deb mächtigen | Show it to the Mighties |
|---|---|
| *Wo viele Bäche*<br>*ineinanderfließen*<br>*wird leicht ein Strom*<br>*draus über Nacht.*<br>*Wo viele Schwache*<br>*sich zusammenschließen*<br>*wird Ohnmacht*<br>*MACHT.* | Where numerous rivulets<br>flow together<br>there will be easily a stream<br>after all.<br>Where a lot of weak persons<br>combine,<br>powerlessness will become<br>POWER. |
| *So sammelt euch,*<br>*ihr scheinbar Schmächtigen*<br>*zeigt es*<br>*den Mächtigen!* | So unite all of you,<br>you apparently unmighties,<br>make your power clear<br>to the mighties! |

## References

Bentham, Jeremy, *An Introduction to the Principles of Morals and Legislation*. Ed. by J. H. Burns and H. L. A. Hart (London: University of London, The Athlone Press, 1970; first published 1780).

Birnbacher, Dieter, *Environmental Ethics: A Priority Rule for Environmental Ethics,* vol. 4 (New York: Doubleday, 1982).

Birnbacher, Dieter, *Ökologie, Ethik und neues Handeln,* 1987.

Ehrenfeld, David, *The Arrogance of Humanism* (New York: Oxford University Press, 1978).

Leopold, Aldo, *The Sand County and Sketches Here and There* (New York: Oxford University Press, 1949).

Meyer-Abich, Klaus M., "Wege zum Frieden mit der Natur," *Praktische Naturphilosophie für die Umweltpolitik* (München: Carl Hanser, 1984).

Partridge, Ernest (Ed.), *Responsibilities to Future Generations: Environmental Ethics* (Buffalo, N.Y.: Prometheus Books, 1980).

Rieser, Armin. "Frieden und Menschlichkeit," *Der Humanist,* 14. 1987. Jg., H. 2, 38–43, Ludwigshafen.

Rollin, Bernard E. *Animal Rights and Human Morality.* (Buffalo, N.Y.: Prometheus Books, 1981).

Teutsch, Gotthard M., *Lexikon der Umweltethik* (Vandenhoek & Ruprecht, Göttingen, Patmos Verland, Düsseldorf, 1985).

Watson, Richard A., *Environmental Ethics: Self-Consciousness and the Rights of Nonhuman Animals and Nature,* vol. 5 (1979).

Weizsäcker, Carl F. von, *Die Einheit der Natur* (München: Hanser, 1971).

Zaidi, Iqtidar H., *Environmental Ethics: On the Ethics of Man's Interaction with the Environment: An Islamic Approach,* vol. 3, 1981.

# Learning to Control Human Exuberance: The Key to Human Survival

Lester W. Milbrath

(United States)

The threatening problems faced by our species stem from our very success as a species. We are a "successful" species in that we have been able to defeat and bend to our will every other species. We are "successful" in that we have been able to appropriate for our own needs a great proportion of the planet's biological productivity—even dipping into the earth's crust to extract accrued productivity stored there long before we evolved as a species. We are "successful" in that we continue to reproduce at record rates while we reduce populations of other species, or eliminate them altogether. Human population is now more than five billion and promises to double to ten billion in only fifty years. But we must learn to control our exuberance, or our "success" will lead to our extinction.

Our ability to learn has enabled us to do better and better those things that we have always tried to do. We wanted our children to survive and live long and good lives, so we reduced infant mortality, conquered disease, and mended or replaced broken body parts. We wanted sufficient food, so we appropriated much of the earth's bioproductivity for our own use. Now we are faced with a veritable explosion in human population.

We wanted to live more comfortable lives, so we isolated ourselves from extremes of weather. We wanted excitement, so we learned to travel swiftly to the far corners of the globe and to bring into our homes a vast array of entertainment. Our science and technology delivered into our hands ever greater power to manipulate the planet's resources to our own enjoyment. With this kind of success, why are so many of us worried?

We have failed to take into account the long-term consequences of doing what we have always done, only better. Doubling the world's population in fifty years will more than double the burden we place on the environment, since most of those billions of people will strive to attain ever higher standards of living. We are using up the planet's resources at an unprecedented rate—particularly fossil fuels, and we surely will encounter severe shortages of many of them. All of those consumed resources will eventually turn to waste and be cast back into the environment. The biosphere is disrupted not only by the sheer volume of such wastes but also by the fact that many wastes are unnatural compounds that biospheric systems do not know how to absorb and recycle.

In effect, we have built a society and an economic system that cannot sustain its trajectory.

How serious is the disruption we are inflicting on planetary systems? The damage may be far greater than we currently believe. The drought in the midwestern United States during the summer of 1988 signals that it may already have begun. The build-up of greenhouse gases, due to the burning of fossil fuels and to other production and consumption activities, has already initiated a global warming that will change climate patterns, perhaps more swiftly and more drastically than we thought possible even a few years ago.

Think for a moment about the proportion of investment decisions that depend on the premise of continuity, especially climatic continuity: choosing a place to live, building a house, starting a business, buying stock in a business, accepting collateral for a loan, making contributions to a pension fund, and so on. A review suggests that about 90 percent of investment decisions are premised on continuity. If climate changes foreclose continuity over large proportions of the globe, and scientists are now reasonably confident that they will, the socioeconomic disruption will be horrendous. Savings will be wiped out, families will be forced to move, some communities will die out while others will be devastated by uncontrollable hordes of in-migrants. Some localities will be under water and others will turn to desert; former deserts may be able to support new plant and animal communities, but first must build them. It seems likely that many people will die because we depend for food on plant and animal communities that are ill-adapted to a changing climate and therefore will become extinct or lose productivity.

Devastation from climate change will be exacerbated by other global biospheric effects: loss of the ozone layer; acid rain; the poisonous red tides of algae; the toxic pollution of soils, water, and air; species extinction. Nature may have many additional unpleasant surprises in store for us. When these effects are combined with resource shortages, we may well wonder how we can continue to support even the five billion people already living, much less the additional billions that are destined to arrive, even if we strive vigorously to limit population growth. An additional population doubling, from ten to twenty billion, seems unthinkable.

Many people believe we can surmount these difficulties by developing more and better science and technology. The power of science and technology is the main reason our species is so successful, is it not? Perhaps it was in the past, but it holds little promise for the future. Not only does technological advance seem a puny weapon to forestall climate change and loss of the ozone layer, but it carries with it another great problem—the danger that we will lose our freedom. We sought the development of science and technology to give us control over our lives, but now the prospect looms that the forces we have unleashed will control us. Science and technology are likely to become runaway forces that no human institution can control. They carry the promise of so much power that acquiring them dominates the human enterprise and threatens to enslave those not winning control of them. A technology may even escalate out of human control and devastate all life on the planet. For example, three recently developed technologies have sufficient power to change nearly *everything* in our physical/social world.

We all know about and are fearful of nuclear power. We all realize that we must avoid a global nuclear war, since if the war itself did not destroy most life on earth, the ensuing nuclear winter almost certainly would. The power in nuclear energy—for peace or war—is generated in large physical installations that are visible and detectable, and thus, in principle, are controllable. There have been, and will be, mistakes made, but political institutions are developing some capability for the control of nuclear power.

Recombinant DNA technology, sometimes called bio-engineering, has the potential to be equally powerful and is, in principle, much more difficult to control. It gives to some humans the ability to "play God." It contains great potential to do good and equally great potential to do harm. Scientists and their supporters tell us only about the good and downplay the potential for evil. Scientists could develop and release new creatures with no natural enemies—such creatures could reproduce epidemically and wreak havoc with delicately balanced ecosystems. Governments and scientific organizations are trying to develop effective controls, but this technology is inherently difficult to control. A new creature could be developed in any laboratory in any country. The potential of this technology to confer great wealth and power on its developers will motivate individuals and corporations to avoid controls. In a global economy—but a politically fragmented world—multinational corporations will pursue recombinant DNA development in "out-of-the-way" corners of the world with few or no controls.

Nanotechnologies are exceedingly small but have the potential for more power than either nuclear power or recombinant DNA. Nanofabrication is analogous to nature's method of making things—molecule by molecule. It would revolutionize fabrication away from "bulk" methods toward the molecular level. Imagine a computer 100,000 times more powerful than existing ones, but as small as a bacteria. The potential for good is enormous; the potential for evil is equally great. Whoever controls nanotechnology will have the power to change everything in our world.[1] Such power is also the power to subjugate. How could technologies so small and easily hidden ever be controlled? For the sake of our own survival, we had better learn how.

These are only three recent scientific discoveries. What else will flow from the fertile brains of our scientists? Have we created a monster that will deprive us of our freedom or devastate our life-supporting ecosystems? Control of science and technology will likely become the dominant political concern of the twenty-first century. Meeting this challenge will require decisive change in the way we think and in the way we conduct politics. We will have to find ways to review the potential effects of a line of inquiry, or the deployment of a technology, before it has advanced so far that it is too late to curb its possible ill effects.

We already fail to recognize the social-structural impact of technology. We should perceive technology as a kind of legislation that structures our behavior. Consider the impact on social structure and politics of such technologies as television, computers, automobiles, and nuclear power. We carefully consider and debate the expected impact of a proposed law, but we never do this for a proposed technology. Yet the effects of an attractive and powerful technology are more pervasive and permanent than most laws. We can repeal a law, but we do not know how to repeal a technology.

In order to learn how to control technology we will have to learn how to have an effective discourse about values. We cannot choose the kind of society in which we would like to live without coming to some agreement on this topic. Reasoning together about values is the essence of politics and will be essential to the preservation of our civilization and of our species. Inquiry into values can be just as rational and objective as any other kind of inquiry—but we must learn how to do it. We need to be more forthright in our discussion of values. We must become aware of hidden assumptions, learn to question everything, learn to have rational discourse, learn to systematically inquire into values. We must seek out the hidden values in science, technology, power, competition, traditional practices, and more—and carry out a rational discourse about them. We must do much better in distinguishing means from ends. In the process we will learn how to use values to give meaning and clear direction to our politics.

In our politics we also must shift from a reactive to a pro-active mode. I call it a *learning mode,* in which we utilize a holistic framework and think in a long-term perspective. We should learn how to routinely anticipate the cumulative consequences of just doing what we do every day—and seem always to have done. Also, new technologies, new projects, new programs should be reviewed for their ultimate consequences. Governments will need to develop an improved capability for anticipating and assessing the consequences of proposed initiatives. To do this, I propose the development of a new branch of government, a "Council for Long-Range Societal Guidance."

At an even more fundamental level, politics must eventually abandon its central focus on power and domination. Our civilization is a dominator civilization; it is oriented to allowing some people to subjugate others. We no longer condone outright slavery but the many forces of domination have the effect of bending the will of weak creatures to serve the desires of the powerful. Power is so ingrained in our thinking that most humans believe they have a right, even an obligation, to dominate nature. Many men and women believe that it is right for men to dominate women. Nations believe that they should strive to dominate each other—eat or be eaten. Americans believe they must maintain world-power status.

This emphasis on domination is a central evil in our civilization. It leads us to injure each other. We are driven to acquire power in order to compete—we believe we cannot decide *not* to compete, not to be strong, not to control and dominate. It drives us to destroy our biosphere.

As we think about what we will do in the future we need to be much more aware of and sensitive to biospheric systems. These systems are essential to life, and without life there is no meaning for other goals. Therefore, we must give *top priority* to maintaining the good functioning of biospheric systems. No other end or goal can be urgent enough that we would be willing to disrupt biospheric systems in order to achieve it.

We must turn our whole society around. We must curb our exuberance—our thrust for growth, power, domination, and thrills. There is no magic formula for doing this; we can only learn. Learn how to think in the long term. Learn how to think holistically. Learn how nature works. Learn how to think about values. Learn the need to learn from one another. Make a learning society. Design a politics that emphasizes learning. Be an active participant in that politics and help our fellows to learn.

## Note

1. See K. Eric Drexler, *Engines of Creation* (Garden City, N.Y., Anchor Press/ Doubleday, 1986) for an imaginative, yet chilling, discussion of the potential of this new technology.

# IV.

# Global War, Global Peace

# On the Nature of War and Affirmations for Life

## Matthew Ies Spetter
### (United States)

In their abhorrence of the possibility of nuclear war, liberal-minded people have a tendency to concentrate upon the terrible aspects of such a conflagration. This tendency may be partially due to genuine anxiety for the fate of the world, and partially to a rising anger against the existing sociomilitary power structures. But whatever the motivation, adding to fear is no way of stimulating alternatives to war.

To resist the power of paralyzing ideas of doom, it is instead necessary to comprehend the nature of war and the preparation for it.

Because of my concern about this, I will start out with a few conclusions:

1. Humanists can work for the integration of nations (as is now happening in Europe) and a *functional* internationalism, rather than for ideological concepts.

2. Since the preparation for war has an enormous impact upon the economies involved, humanists need to develop concrete alternatives concerning productivity for peace, employment, business activity, and investment of capital.

3. Humanists can play a crucial role in the psychological reorientation required for an integrated world economy that will stress the concept of the Family of Humankind, the context of the global consequences of peace-making, and the celebration of life rather than isolation and collective hostility.

Wars do not "just happen." They are ingrained in the human saga. This aspect was perhaps best expressed by one of the Fascist generals of Franco's

Spain, who liked to end his addresses to the soldiers by crying out, "Long live death!"

Today, with the United States' and the Soviet Union's rapprochement, conflict has not miraculously disappeared, but we see at least some new beginnings. France and Germany, once considered "inevitable" enemies, now are integrating their economies and even their armed forces. And we have lived to see the day that at least some nuclear weapons are being destroyed, both in the Soviet Union and the United States. The pathology of merely military thinking (conceiving the world in terms of power and domination) may now slowly be replaced by a notion of "planethood," as coined by Benjamin Ferencz, assistant U.S. prosecutor at the Nuremberg International War Crimes Tribunal. The issue then becomes how to organize power in the world on a global scale, since nuclear determent cannot, in the long run, be seen as a reliable means for preventing nuclear war. Cold War habits can be overcome step by step as leaders and nations no longer feel obligated to express unrestrained hostility toward their perceived adversaries.

## War as Necessity?

The late sociologist C. Wright Mills wrote that in industrialized societies war has become the human condition, while peacetime has become but an interlude. Today, there are twenty-four wars going on around the world, according to the New York *Times*. Since the end of World War II an estimated forty to fifty million people have been killed in such armed conflicts. This is the central issue as we as humanists seek to assist in the transformation from global war to global peace.

Large and small nations have indeed come to accept war and the preparation for war as the legitimate business of governments. Thus violence has become institutionalized with the planet as its ultimate target. Preparation for global war is considered a "necessity" in the official definition of reality. The wars in Vietnam and Afghanistan are but the latest examples of the involvement of the superpowers in this fallacious world view.

The American anthropologist Margaret Mead offered this definition of war in our time: "War is that situation in which clearly defined societies engage in purposeful, organized, and socially sanctioned combat with the purpose of killing one another."

Since 1914 we have lived in a state of perpetual mobilization for war. The psychological climate "justifying" sacrificing human life requires that all social, economic, and psychological forces remain so organized. In the Iran-Iraq war we again saw two social structures aiming not just to dominate, but to simply destroy, for no purpose or advantage to their peoples. Poison gas, which we hoped we had seen the last of when the Nazis murdered twelve million people in the concentration camps, was again employed. Thus the fatal race continues between life and the preparation for mass death around the world. Even if the terms of the INF treaty between the United States and the Soviet Union are executed, only 3 percent of existing nuclear arms will have been destroyed; uncounted hellish machines of death will still stand ready to tear into human flesh. A malignant cloud still hovers over humankind and Western nations, Latin American nations, and Communist nations still compete feverishly in producing and selling arms to all comers.

What can we as humanists propose?

Simply this: that every living soul has the absolute human right to live out his or her life free from the hoarse threats of annihilation.

But a right is only as good as the ability to claim it. If we want to be peacemakers and peacekeepers, humanists have to become skilled and effective in this new global work. To be part of protest movements may be laudatory. But the real task is to become pioneers on the frontiers of planetwide thinking and acting.

## To Unlearn War

Preparations for war, as war itself, are not a natural given. They are culturally determined. Nature did not equip human beings with the teeth of a shark, nor with the talons of a vulture. We are by nature naked, rather defenseless creatures. The tools of war were developed because of that weakness. Human beings have the capacity to learn to kill. Animals competing with one of their own species for a mate or for food very rarely kill after domination is established. Human beings are missing that restraining gene, and so killing becomes a culturally determined social activity.

We venerate the killing hero. In war we feel the elation of shared hostility, pride, courage, discipline, service, physical fitness, self-sacrifice. People serving in armies feel like a homogeneous mass; social barriers between them become unimportant; drab lives and boredom are overcome by a new sense of solidarity.

The central humanist proposition is that, as killing can be learned, it can also be unlearned; that murderousness can be intercepted and replaced by different, life-affirming goals.

War and preparations for war require technology, productivity, education, research, information, and analysis. Modern warfare is applied human intelligence, par excellence; armies function almost like universities. Men, and, increasingly, women as well, are taught how to use space-satellites, radio, radar, laser beams, tanks, submarines, rockets, missiles, and complicated technologies for gathering intelligence and the detection and destruction of targets. Armies today need scientists, technicians, researchers, chemical engineers, and more, both in and out of uniform.

There are the sociologists and social psychologists who create propaganda aimed both at the opponent and at the home front. There are writers, filmmakers, entertainers, and preachers to keep those under arms appeased. There are merchants for food, clothing, medications, shoes, nerve gasses, and, of course, oil. There are hospitals, physicians, nurses, surgeons, psychiatrists, artificial-limb specialists, and today even obstetricians to administer to our soldiers.

War is a total social activity. In modern warfare combatants need not be passionate. It is an impersonally planned and executed machinery. To turn that total social activity around will take far more than an abhorrence of war. It will take a technology for peace. In the past, nations could trust that after mass bloodletting, their own social structure would go on. The human sacrifices could be portrayed as guarantees for survival. This will never be true again. There is no permissible dose of increased global radiation.

A new solidarity for life, a new solidarity for the resolution of conflict, a new solidarity for peacemaking and peacekeeping can be learned. In this, humanists the world over can make concrete commitments provided that we accept this changed social activity as humankind's essential commitment.

Those are the central issues for our time. Our task is specific. It is to counterbalance the very real human capacity for evil with the weight and the power of a new global ethics based upon the collective stewardship for life. Humanists can be instrumental in helping to usher in the next phase of human evolution, the next breakthrough toward an open world rather than one of paranoia; toward a world of trust, of knowledge of the human capacity for good, of greater equity between nations.

That means learning to use power in the real world because power does matter. And as there is the power to enslave, so is there a power of emotional and moral liberation for mutuality and solidarity.

## Beyond the Scenarios of Doom

Ever since the Middle Ages, Christian cultures have preached the delusion of "the end of the world." Predictions of doom have been ingrained with fear and insecurity as tools of control.

In our time we have learned to live with "an interior holocaust complex."[1] But it is not invisible powers that control human destiny. It is our choices that do.

One of our greatest psychological challenges is to outgrow the assumption that peace is not possible. The real question is whether the people of the world want collective security enough to reorder global priorities and to demand of their governments a transformation to caring for life rather than seeking death.

We are not helpless. The ancient repressive norms set by authority can be changed. We need an expressive rather than a repressive morality; a morality of clear-thinking and functional bonds between nations. We can teach ourselves limited rather than absolute sovereignty and yet maintain our own cultural identities and values. This will make possible as well an outgrowing of what the sociologist Seymour Lipset has called "psychic numbing," replacing drift with the hard-hitting willingness to comprehend the factors that have led to the militarization of our planet.

The world confrontations and conflicts—especially between the superpowers—have now come down to what value we place on human life, what creatures we really are. Are we fit only for polarized collective hostilities? Can we, at last, grasp what nature and our bodies tell us—namely that survival and a decent life are only possible through symbiosis, the coming together of the life-preserving forces?

We can do our part in building up confidence. Not cheap confidence, not "hoping for the best," but the knowledge of our shared humanity, our abilities to be contributing members of the world community. Human beings emerged from the caves and jungles and have made incredible progress in all directions. Notwithstanding our "crimes and follies," a sober hope is justified that we can learn to make life worth living and struggling for.

I will close with an event of our time that many of you may remember: A little American girl named Samantha Smith died a few years ago in a plane crash. She was a very special twelve-year-old. One morning she had awakened and asked herself, "Could this be the last day of the earth?" She was afraid of the arms race and decided to write a letter to the then Soviet leader, Yuri Andropov.

She wrote, "I have been worrying about Russia and the United States getting into nuclear war. Are you going to have war? If you are not, please write me how you are going to help avoid such war."

To everyone's surprise, a letter came back from Andropov. He invited her to come to the Soviet Union and see for herself. Samantha Smith went to Moscow and soon made many friends with Russian girls and boys her own age. This youngster, with her easy smile, broke through the barriers. She was not afraid to be called naive or too idealistic. For adults it is often hard to break through the fog of propaganda, but Samantha had no such trouble. She was not suspicious or cautious as adults would be. She was not there to make points for the American estabishment. She was just a child among children. And when she died in that plane crash the Soviet government wrote to her mother, "Samantha has captured our imagination and our hearts." Children can do such things. All the children of the world are our children. Maybe that young life, snuffed out so sadly, will yet help this poor world and its leaders to remember what humankind's destiny is really all about.

## Note

1. See Spencer Weart, *Nuclear Fear* (Cambridge, Mass.: Harvard University Press, 1988).

# The Moral Irrelevance of the Distinction Between Conventional and Nuclear War

## Robert L. Holmes
### (United States)

It is commonly held that nuclear war is the paramount threat facing humankind today, and that it represents the greatest evil the world has ever known. It is also commonly held that as rational beings with a concern for life and what is of value and importance in the world, we must spare no effort to avert such a confrontation.

I find this incontrovertible. But I do not find incontrovertible a conclusion often drawn from it—not explicitly, as a rule, but implicitly in the attitudes that accompany the preoccupation with nuclear war. This is that the problem of war in general can wait; that, as desirable as it would be to rid the world of war, to do that is a project for the future, after the nuclear threat has been defused and we can be confident there will be a future. Accordingly, the growing opposition to nuclear war has been accompanied by a growing acceptance of conventional war; indeed, to the point where many feel that nuclear disarmament, or even a significant reduction in nuclear weapons, must, in the interests of national security, be accompanied by a buildup of conventional forces. Conventional war is thus acquiring a kind of respectability. It represents an acceptable compromise between the magnitude of the violence of nuclear war on the one hand, and the abhorrent quality of the violence of terrorism on the other.

I accept the premise of this argument. In fact, it is less obvious than is often supposed. We have known for years that as the sun ages and gradually enlarges, it will incinerate the planets in orbit around it. Our solar system will come to an end, and with it—barring transfers to distant regions of the universe— life on earth will end as well. That this will happen we know with greater certainty

---

than that there will be a nuclear war, or if there is one that it will extinguish all life. Yet this fact occasions no comparable concern. Governments remain indifferent; ordinary citizens take no notice. That the one end would result from the natural evolution of stars and planetary systems, the other from human actions, makes a difference as to whether we can assign responsibility for them—but not as to their relative calamitousness.

My point is that nuclear war is the greatest threat to humankind only if we mean the greatest threat *today*. It is not a greater threat in the long run than are such things as ozone depletion, destruction of the environment, or overpopulation.

But I shall assume that it is the greatest threat. And, further, that defusing it should be our top priority. Why, then, am I concerned about the character of the growing preoccupation with it?

First, because I believe that what is wrong with nuclear war is wrong with conventional war as well, and that in this sense there is no moral difference between the two; and second, because from a practical standpoint, I believe there is no realistic hope of counteracting the one threat without dealing with the other as well. The acceptance of conventional war makes nuclear war virtually inevitable.

Assume for the moment the legitimacy of war. If a nation may justifiably go to war in some circumstances, what may it justifiably do in the course of waging war? Should it restrain itself, or is moderation in war—as the Prussian military strategist Karl von Clausewitz maintained—an absurdity?

The answer is yes or no, depending upon what we take the question to mean. Moderation is not an absurdity if we suppose it to require only that we refrain from inflicting gratuitous death and destruction beyond what is necessary for the attainment of the ends of war. The so-called principle of humanity sometimes cited among the laws of war demands no less. But the answer is arguably yes if one means that nations should exercise restraint in the sense of deliberately doing less than is minimally necessary to achieve their objectives. If one feels it necessary to resort to such bloody and destructive measures as war represents, it must be because, morally, the objectives are thought to warrant them. If, then, once these measures are undertaken, one deliberately does less than what is necessary to achieve them, it would indeed seem absurd; a violation of the tenet of rationality that to will an end is to will the indispensable means to its attainment. This tenet is but an adaptation of the principle of military necessity. And it is probably accepted by every nation that goes to war.

This means, I suggest, that given the rationale behind resorting to war in the first place, in any circumstances in which attainment of the objectives of war requires the use of nuclear weapons, they should be used; and when they are not possessed but the need for them is foreseeable, they should be acquired. The logic of war demands it. The fact that the weapons are nuclear *in and of itself* makes no difference. Moreover, in circumstances in which they are possessed and national survival is at stake, it is virtually certain that they will be used. How many world leaders would preside over the destruction of their country if they thought that by using nuclear weapons they could prevent it?

The evidence for the truth of these two claims is substantial. The only wartime use of atomic weapons occurred when the United States determined it could further its objectives by dropping them on Japan. And those weren't even basic objectives; the war was already won. They were the subsidiary objectives of minimizing the loss of American and perhaps Japanese lives. As for acquisition, the superpowers today frenetically multiply the numbers of nuclear weapons they possess, and the nonnuclear nations scramble to acquire them.

But might not the resort to nuclear war risk crossing a threshold beyond which one's objectives *could not* be achieved, because it would threaten a level of destruction that would jeopardize the attainment of *any* objectives at all? And wouldn't the logic of war, with or without a principle of military necessity, preclude such resort?

Nuclear war does indeed risk crossing such a threshold. But it does not necessarily involve crossing it. The atomic bombings of Hiroshima and Nagasaki did not cross that threshold, but *did* serve American objectives. Many scenarios for nuclear war do not involve crossing that threshold. In fact, many projected limited nuclear wars involve fewer casualties than have major convenional wars of the twentieth century. The more than fifty million killed in World War II would probably equal those killed in a fairly large nuclear war. Resort to war of any sort risks an outcome in which one's objectives become unattainable, if only because going to war risks losing; and inasmuch as no war has more than one winner, and some have none, history is replete with examples of conventional war taking one or the other or both sides over that threshold.

Still, it is true that conventional war rarely takes a nation over the threshold beyond which no objectives can be attained *ever again,* in the way in which all-out nuclear war would. But it has happened. The Romans annihilated the Carthaginians in the third Punic War as effectively as if they had dropped a nuclear bomb on them. And it could happen today. A third world war fought without nuclear weapons but with the large-scale use of chemical and biological weapons could rival a nuclear war in its effects. And if not the third, then the fourth or the fifth or the nth world war could do so. The sophistication, accuracy, and destructive power of conventional weapons is rapidly closing the gap between conventional and nuclear war. Nuclear weapons will always have greater destructive potential, and they are quicker. But insofar as the threshold in question is concerned, once war of either sort can destroy civilization, those differences become relatively unimportant.

Even if this were not so, the preceding consideration argues only against *crossing that threshold,* not against using nuclear weapons. True, using nuclear weapons at all increases the probability of crossing that threshold; and it is doubtful that nations could be expected to exercise sufficient restraint to avoid that outcome. But if it is unrealistic to expect nations to deploy nuclear weapons but restrain themselves from using them in times of conflict, is it not equally unrealistic to expect them to make full use of conventional weapons and yet to restrain themselves from *producing* nuclear weapons if they are able? Why suppose that the restraint necessary to refrain from using nuclear weapons in an otherwise conventional war, or to limit their use if they are resorted to, is greater than that necessary to refrain from producing them if rising tensions, or the exigencies of a long war argue for it? And is that not what is supposed when it is proposed to ban nuclear weapons but allow conventional armaments, or to allow nuclear weapons but limit their numbers and kinds? Except that they can more readily be used if they are possessed than if they are not possessed, it is hard to see a difference. If we want to minimize the prospects of annihilation, we won't go to war at all, conventional or nuclear.

Thus, while we can assuredly discern a moral difference between *all-out* nuclear war and most conventional wars, we can also see a moral difference between all-out conventional war and most nuclear wars. My point is that nuclear war is not *in itself* any worse morally than conventional war, even if (which I doubt) the worst possible nuclear war might be worse in destructive power than the worst possible conventional war. Death and destruction are central to both, as is the inevitability of killing innocent persons; and the magnitudes can vary on either side.

What I have said thus far, of course, is more or less theoretical, in the sense that the situation we actually confront in the world today is one in which both superpowers are heavily armed with nuclear weapons and prepared to use them if necessary. And there is little likelihood of that changing in the near future.

This situation underscores the difficulty, perhaps the near-impossibility, of both preserving conventional war and eliminating nuclear weapons, even if it should be conceded that there is a significant moral difference between the two. On the one hand, as I have said, the increasing destructiveness of conventional weapons and the refinement and sophistication of both conventional and nuclear weapons are blurring the distinction between the two. When a few B–52 bombers can in a matter of minutes drop explosives equivalent in power to the atomic bomb that leveled Hiroshima, and when nuclear weapons can be made so small that they can be fired from conventional "dual capacity" weapons and used on the battlefield, there is a merging of nuclear and conventional weapons into a single war-fighting capability. If military necessity calls for a job to be done that can be done more efficiently by tactical nuclear weapons than with conventional ones, we can have little confidence that the use of such weapons will long be foregone. Nor, if one accepts the premises underlying the resort to war, is it easy to see why it should be.

On the other hand, the use of nuclear weapons has been so integrated into policy planning as to make their elimination virtually impossible—at least short of dramatic changes in such planning. When I say the "use" of such weapons, I do so advisedly. As the economist Daniel Ellsberg has pointed out, nuclear weapons have been used and are being used today, and can be expected to be used in the future. Not that they are being detonated; that has not happened in wartime since Hiroshima and Nagasaki. But that is not a requirement of their being used. An armed robber uses a gun when he sticks it in your ribs and demands your money. He does not need to fire the gun. And so the United States uses nuclear weapons when it makes it known that it may use them (in the sense of firing them) unless an adversary backs down, as it did against the Soviets in the Cuban Missile Crisis; or when it gives reason to believe that it may use them unless certain conditions are met, as it reportedly did against China during the Korean War and against North Vietnam during the Vietnam war. And the very threat of retaliation that is at the heart of nuclear deterrence is a use of nuclear weapons, even if it is not the actual detonating of them.

Moreover, nuclear weapons are used when they are relied upon as an express or implied threat in escalation. And that threat is an integral part of current strategic thinking. The former Secretary of Defense Caspar W. Weinberger made this clear when he wrote that an adversary "must know that even if his aggression should succeed in achieving its immediate objectives, he faces the threat of escalation to hostilities that would exact a higher cost than he is willing to pay." He then added, "Thus the United States must maintain a credible threat *both of escalation and of retaliation* to secure deterrence across the spectrum of potential conflict."[1] (Italics added.)

When the United States refuses to renounce a first use of nuclear weapons in Europe, it is to convey to the Soviets that we might initiate a nuclear war in response to a conventional attack against NATO forces. Indeed, the positioning of U.S. troops so they will unavoidably become engaged with Warsaw Pact forces at the outset of hostilities constitutes a tripwire, involving us and providing a rationale for resorting to nuclear weapons if that should be deemed necessary. The recently formed Rapid Deployment Force, or Central Command, serves a similar function in the Middle East. It has in fact been called a "portable Dien Bien Phu," in reponse to the decisive battle of the French Indochina War, during which the United States was prepared to use nuclear bombs to break the Vietnamese siege. British unwillingness to support such a use dissuaded Eisenhower from proceeding with the plan. Moreover, the threat of escalation to nuclear war provides a protective covering for U.S. intervention in the Third World, as it did in Cuba and later in Grenada, and as it does today in Nicaragua. It is virtually inconceivable that the Soviets would commit troops to combat in those areas under a threat of U.S. escalation. This gives the United States a free interventionist hand to wield the conventional sword under a nuclear shield. This makes it highly improbable—assuming a continuation of the kind of thinking found in the Reagan administration—that the United States would ever agree to a plan like the Gorbachev proposal to eliminate all nuclear weapons. We are too dependent upon them.

For all of this, there is symbolic significance to the distinction between conventional and nuclear war: It represents a kind of "firebreak," if you will. Once that line is crossed, it will be easier to cross it again, or having crossed it, to escalate to all-out nuclear war. To the extent that keeping that line clearly in view lessens the likelihood of a nuclear holocaust, it is important to do so.

But there should be no illusions about the chances of success, so long as the assumptions and values underlying the readiness to wage war of any sort are left unchallenged. Any line *can* be crossed—whether in the use of weaponry or in its production when the capability is possessed. What makes the difference is the attitudes toward war itself. The risk of nuclear war is a function of more than the mere possession of nuclear weapons; it is a function of attitudes concerning ideology, national interest, self-defense, conflict resolution, and, perhaps most importantly, toward the use of violence and the taking of human life. Leave these unchanged, and there is virtually no chance of eliminating the risk of nuclear war. The war system has a momentum and logic of its own. When a country's economy is permanently war-oriented, when nearly half of its scientists and engineers work on military-related projects, and when force and the threat of force are accepted features of its foreign policy, one can hardly expect to reverse a movement that is a logical product of these forces. *We minimize the magnitude of the problem of nuclear omnicide if we suppose that anything short of a radical change in our thinking has the remotest prospect of success in dealing with it.*

John Dewey recognized the futility of trying to deal with the problem of war in piecemeal fashion. In thoughts that have relevance to our present concern, he said:

> The proposition . . . is not the moral proposition to abolish wars. It is the much more fundamental proposition to abolish the war system as an authorized and legally sanctioned institution. . . .
>
> How long have we been taking steps to do away with war, and why have they accomplished nothing? Because *the steps have all been taken under the war system.* It is not a step that we need, it is a right-about face; a facing in another direction. . . .
>
> If there be somewhere some grinning devil that watches the blundering activities of man, I can imagine nothing that gives him more malicious satisfaction than to see earnest and devoted men and women taking steps, by improving a legal and political system that is committed to war, to do away with war.[2]

This, regrettably, is what one sees so much of in the anti-nuclear movement. In leaving the war system essentially intact, and leaving the readiness to wage war unchanged, in effect we are saying that we want to continue playing the game but not have to accept the consequences to which it naturally leads. We want to keep the war system but eliminate the risk of nuclear war.

If the likeliest way a nuclear war will start is by escalation of a conventional war, then we must deal with the threat of conventional war. And if the readiness to wage conventional war is a function of the institutionalization of violence on a massive scale, we must find ways to de-institutionalize the commitment to violence. It is not nuclear violence alone that is the threat to humankind. It is the willingness to kill and destroy our fellow human beings—those who are innocent as well as those who are not—for political ends. Unless we are willing to redirect our time, energy, and resources away from perfecting the means of mass destruction of whatever sort, and into exploring nonviolent alternatives to war itself, our efforts to combat the threat of nuclear war are likely to be of no avail.

But isn't this asking too much? Whereas people might conceivably be prepared to dismantle nuclear weapons, isn't it too much to expect that they come to grips with the whole problem of the war system itself?

Perhaps. But that is only to say that we may be incapable of saving ourselves. A man overeats, smokes heavily, drinks too much, and gets no exercise. He learns he has high blood pressure and a weak heart. He decides to switch to filtered cigarettes, drink a little less, skip seconds on desserts, and walk a few blocks now and then. Is that not a step in the right direction? Certainly. But it probably won't save him. What he needs is a change in his whole way of life. We, too, can go on fueling the furnace of war and take our chances on being able to control the heat. It certainly is easier. But let us not deceive ourselves that this is likely to save us. The whole history of civilization shows that we never have been able to resist heaping more and more fuel onto the fire, or to avoid burning ourselves with increasing severity. Doing less of what we have been doing wrong isn't good enough. We must stop doing it.

What the people of today's world need first and foremost is ruthless honesty about themselves and about their condition—for it is more serious than they want to believe.

## Notes

1. Caspar W. Weinberger, "U.S. Defense Strategy," *Foreign Affairs,* Spring 1986, vol. 64, no. 4, pp. 678, 679.
2. Quoted in Joseph Ratner (ed.), *Intelligence in the Modern World: John Dewey's Philosophy* (New York: The Modern Library, 1939), pp. 515, 523.

# Is There a Need for Multilateralism?

## Johan Nordenfelt
### (Sweden)

The creation of the League of Nations at the end of World War I—which had seen some ten million people die—was an acknowledgement by the powers of the day that international conflict had become intolerable because of a vastly enlarged destructiveness in warfare capabilities. But unfortunately, the recognition was not strong enough to influence governments to place the common interests of the community of nations above individual national ambitions and concerns. They tended increasingly to rely on unilateral action, rather than common action within the league. And the United States never joined it, even though President Woodrow Wilson had been its chief proponent.

Amid the mass unemployment and despair of the depression years, caused in large measure by shortsighted trade policies, aggressive Fascist regimes rose to power, riding the waves of vehement nationalism and discontent in their countries. The league's inability to restrain them caused it a fatal loss of credibility. World War II soon followed. Its death toll was vastly larger than that of the first.

Could timely multilateral action and preventive diplomacy have kept the peace? The people who created the United Nations—American statesmen were again among the prime movers—would have said yes. It was that belief which led them to give the postwar system of international organization a wide-ranging and activist mandate.

Influenced by the experience of the wartime alliance, the founders of the United Nations expected the great powers to coordinate their policies and harmonize their actions in case of threats to or breaches of the peace, and in acts of aggression. But the East–West chasm opened immediately after the founding of the United Nations, and, as it meant the collapse of the great power consensus, it froze the basic assumption behind the scheme of collective security envisaged in its charter. The point, therefore, can be easily conceded that, set against the world of concord and harmony envisaged by the framers of the charter, the United Nations has indeed fallen short of expectations.

But, in the real world in which it has functioned—the world of tensions between the great powers, the arms race, collisions of national interests, resentments born of past violations or neglect, economic disparities, cultural differences, poverty, drought, and famine—the United Nations has done as well as it was permitted to do and, in many ways, better than what could have been anticipated. The world of today is not tidy, but few can doubt that it would have been more disorderly and much less manageable without the United Nations.

Let me now give some examples of how the United Nations has served as the catalyst and agent of peaceful change. The process of decolonization has led to the establishment, for the first time, of an international system representative of virtually all peoples of the world. In that sense the United Nations certainly represents the reality of today. Even before this process gathered momentum, the United Nations set standards for the observance and protection of human rights against which the behavior of governments may be judged. It made human rights a matter of legitimate international concern. Never before had this been the case. Violations are no doubt taking place, sometimes deplorably on a massive scale. But the occurrence of these violations is not an argument against the value of these standards, any more than the occurrence of crime negates the value of law.

In the highly complex world of sovereign states and conflicting interests, only a generally acceptable international legal order can provide the basis for international confidence and the necessary framework for multilateral cooperation. The United Nations has formulated and codified more international law than was done in all previous history.

In the field of arms limitation and disarmament, multilateral action has led, for instance, to treaties preventing the proliferation of nuclear weapons to more countries and to certain environments, such as the seabed and outer space, and to the prohibition of biological weapons.

It is paradoxical that, as the need for cooperation increases, the machinery through which it can be realized has in the past decade or so been increasingly bypassed, rebuffed, and disdained. There has been a tendency to disregard obligations to which states have committed themselves under the United Nations charter and to revert to methods known to have failed in the past.

I believe there is some confusion about what traditional diplomacy can and cannot do. Although many of the problems on the agenda of the United Nations have remained unsolved, they are there because states have not been able to solve them otherwise. The inability of the United Nations in such cases is caused not by defects in its machinery, but by lack of cooperation of the governments involved. The analysis should relate not only to the nature of the problems but also to the way the instrument of the United Nations has been used; governments cannot blunt it and then complain that it lacks a sharp edge.

Like it or not, we live in an interdependent world; this is reflected in so many ways that it cannot be ignored. In a world overshadowed by nuclear arsenals capable of obliterating human civilization as we know it several times over, it is understandable that one's vision tends to narrow down to the relations between the two superpowers. It is also understandable that intensive and complex negotiations between them have preoccupied policymakers and officials in Moscow and Washington at some cost to a thorough exploration of multilateral possibilities.

But it is also quite clear that member states, including the great powers, appreciate that the United Nations continues to offer a uniquely valuable instrument for containment and settlement of conflict, and that they are ready to use it, as has been demonstrated lately. The Soviet withdrawal from Afghanistan is now being monitored by United Nations personnel. A U.N. team recently came back from the Persian Gulf area after investigating instances of the use of chemical weapons, and the organization played a role in bringing to an end the war between Iran and Iraq, which lasted for more than eight years. Plans for the settlement of the Western Sahara conflict also rely on an active U.N. role.

It is quite obvious that some of our most serious problems know no national boundaries, and that countries, no matter how powerful, cannot hope to solve them alone or even bilaterally. Leaving armed conflict aside, the gradual destruction of the ozone layer, acid rain, airborne radioactive contaminants like those resulting from the Chernobyl disaster, drug trafficking, disease, and international terrorism are only a few examples of problems that have increased our awareness that multilateral solutions are needed.

The same goes for arms limitation and disarmament. It is true that only the nations that have nuclear weapons can achieve disarmament, and it is, indeed, encouraging that the superpowers have recognized this by concluding the first nuclear disarmament agreement. But it hardly serves any purpose to conclude bilateral agreements on limitations or the abolition of weapons and technologies to which many states have access. Such a prohibition must be global in scope; despite its complexities, it has to be negotiated multilaterally, and its compliance must be verified multilaterally.

Although space-weapons technology may at present be pursued by only a very small number of states, space technology as such is no longer a monopoly of two or three. A critical analysis of where new technological developments may take us, when replicated on many sides, points to the need for multilateral agreements. Witness the Non-Proliferation Treaty. Nuclear-weapons technology is by no means known only to the existing nuclear-weapon states. The relative success achieved thus far in perventing the proliferation of nuclear weapons is due to a concerted and ongoing multilateral process.

Verification of compliance with the obligations not to acquire nuclear weapons under the Non-Proliferation Treaty is carried out by the International Atomic Energy Agency. For a long time its safeguards system has been the only substantive multilateral verification mechanism in operation.

One of the many interesting features of the transformations taking place on the international scene is the shared appreciation of the important confidence-building role of verification. Although the major powers possess to varying degrees their own so-called national means of verification, usually by means of satellite monitoring, the INF Treaty demonstrates the United States' and the Soviet Union's recognition that verification may have to be more intrusive. Multilateral agreements in the future will require multilateral verification arrangements, since states are not likely to become parties to treaties that can be verified only by very few.

All this constituted the setting for Third Special Session of the General Assembly. In hindsight, it may be clear that it was somewhat premature to convene a third special session on disarmament in 1988. Perhaps the international community had not had sufficient time to digest the remarkable transformation taking place not only in the superpower relationship, but also in other relationships, and to grasp fully the factors that transcend national boundaries and compel cooperation. In any event, after four weeks of discussion and negotiation, the participants were unable to reach consensus on the text of a concluding document.

Although the outcome of the special session may seem disappointing, I believe it is no more than a temporary setback. For in fact member states were able to agree on the bulk of the informal draft for a concluding document. Many member states said that they could go along with the draft text in its entirety, though they were not completely satisfied with all parts of it. There was general acceptance of most of sixty-seven paragraphs of the draft with some amendments.

What is significant is the attempt to adopt a fresh approach to global disarmament issues, using the final document adopted at the first special session in 1978 as a foundation to which member states have varying degrees of attachment. Instead of using U.N.-ese, the language in the text is largely simple and direct. Taking into account encouraging recent developments in the Washington/Moscow negotiations, including the conclusion of the INF Treaty, the underlying approach in the paper is forward-looking without being euphoric. There is also a willingness to face the questions of national security in a broader context of global interdependence and the close interrelationship among social, humanitarian, economic, ecological, and technological factors.

Three sections of the draft—the introduction, "Assessment," and "Machinery"—were largely agreed upon, leaving two sections—namely "Directions for the Future" and a conclusion—subject to further consideration. Reading the agreed paragraphs, it seems evident that:

1. There is acceptance of the notion that national security must be looked at and looked after in the broader context of global issues and international concerns.

2. While arms limitation and disarmament constitute a crucial element in the pursuit of international peace and security, there is an interrelationship between the pursuit of disarmament and U.N. endeavors in other areas, such as peaceful settlement of disputes, peacekeeping, economic and social development, self-determination, and human rights.

3. Disarmament will be promoted when root causes of international tension are addressed and ancillary measures—such as confidence-building, greater openness and honesty, comparability in military expenditures—are achieved.

4. Disarmament is not the sole responsibility of the two major powers; all member states, large and small, must contribute their ideas, initiatives, and efforts both in their own regions as well as in global forums.

5. While nuclear disarmament continues to be a high priority, conventional disarmament has acquired a new importance and urgency.

6. It is vital to strengthen further the nuclear nonproliferation regime.

7. The earliest conclusion of a chemical-weapons convention is of great importance, and the forty-nation Conference on Disarmament in Geneva should devote maximum effort to achieving it.

8. The qualitative aspect of the arms race, or the manner in which science and technology are mobilized for armament and disarmament should not be ignored, but considered together with the quantitative aspect.

9. All states, particularly those with major space capabilities, should contribute actively to the objective of the peaceful use of outer space, and to the prevention of an arms race there.

10. Arms transfers should not be treated as taboo, but should receive greater attention from the international community.

11. The potentially important role of the United Nations in the verification of multilateral disarmament and arms-control agreements deserves in-depth study.

12. While the relationship between disarmament and development and welfare may not be direct or "organic," the way the finite resources of the earth are used for these competing objectives must be of interest to all.

On the whole, the session was characterized by a remarkable spirit of compromise. Those countries that were sharply critical of the United States' position on three issues—the nuclear test ban, the use of outer space, and naval disarmament—were in the end willing to delete any reference to naval disarmament and to accept formulas negotiated with the United States on the test ban and outer space. The Soviet Union's flexibility was noticeable throughout the negotiations.

It may therefore seem a matter of some surprise and certainly regret that a few remaining issues—such as nuclear weapon-free zones, zones of peace, the relationship between disarmament and development, the question of the nuclear capability of South Africa and Israel, and the role of the Secretary General in investigating the use of chemical weapons—proved to be stumbling blocks to a final agreement. In truth, however, these items simply happened to be the ones remaining when time ran out.

The divisions between various national positions and attitudes were really of a more fundamental nature. The last few hours of negotiations on the informal text showed that national and regional concerns continue to cast long shadows over questions concerning war and peace and disarmament. Yet there is a growing acceptance of the need to find a universal approach to many of these matters. At present, we undoubtedly stand at the confluence of these two opposing forces and crosscurrents.

While there will continue to be setbacks now and then, it seems to be imperative that we not lose sight of the direction in which the tide is running. That direction is positive. The relentless search is on for more rational and multilateral methods to attain security. Thanks partly to the third special session, the international agenda concerning disarmament efforts has broadened.

The third special session confirmed an emerging common outlook on disarmament. It also showed where the remaining obstacles are. New items on our informal agenda will no doubt be more pragmatic and balanced. This, it seems to me, augurs well for the future.

Is there a need for multilateralism? The answer is decidedly yes. The international dimension of the causes and consequences of a great number of problems imply the necessity of international cooperation in their analysis and solution. Multilateral cooperation is a functional response to the complex interdependence of the modern world. To treat it as optional is a deadly mistake. Despite the narrow vision of polemics or actions prompted by short-term interests, member states, including the great powers, have often shown that they recognize this fact. The United Nations is there. It provides a system and a structure. It has competence and experience. It is inexpensive. It has served the international community well under circumstances vastly more difficult than those foreseen by its founders. It is ready to continue to serve.

# Soviet/American Scenarios for the Next Fifty Years

Paul H. Beattie
(United States)

One of the mistakes that democracies are prone to make is to view foreign policy in terms of short-term results. This short-term world view leads to disappointments as well as terrible mistakes. Perhaps the most obvious example in our century was the way in which the English and French foreign-policy establishments watched the largest military build-up in all of history occur in Germany until it was almost too late. If Hitler had not attacked Russia and declared war on the United States, Western Europe and England might have witnessed the onset of a dark age of horrendous ferocity and oppression. My goal in this brief paper is to consider the Soviet/American relationship in terms of a fifty-year scenario; in my opinion, while it may be possible to project an ever-better relationship between the two countries, achieving a stable peace between them will take at least that long.

While numerous scenarios can be imagined regarding the possible relationship between the two greatest world powers, the initial distinction to be drawn in constructing these scenarios must be between those that envision a war of some sort and those that do not.

## Scenario One

Although unlikely, some sort of nuclear exchange could occur between the Soviet Union and the United States. It could be an exchange involving a massive attack by each on the other over a confrontation of some sort (even the possibility of a sudden and unexpected first-strike effort cannot be entirely discounted); it could be a relatively small exchange involving just a few missiles. In this second case, a limited nuclear exchange could be caused by each nation going to the brink over some issue and then backing down, or it could be caused by a mistake that is brought to an end before total war occurs.

Another possibility for war involves the accidental or planned launch of a missile or missiles by some third party. As nuclear proliferation has developed, involving such countries as England, France, China, India, and possibly Pakistan, Israel, Libya, and more, the possibility of such attack, planned or accidental, looms ever larger. While some detection systems can pinpoint the source of such a missile, they are not foolproof, and with many different interacting parties the possibilities for miscalculations and accidents, as well as for a planned launch, are almost infinite.

As a result of the possibilities mentioned above, I think that all countries should build Strategic Defense Initiative (SDI) systems (not necessarily dependent on laser technology) that are designed to stop as many incoming missiles as possible. Work is going on both in the Soviet Union and in the United States to achieve such a system. While the Americans may have a slight technical lead, the Soviets have an operational missile-defense system around Moscow and may well have the beginnings of a much larger system that may become operational in the not too distant future. In a smaller nuclear exchange between superpowers, strategic-defense systems might reduce the damage incurred and lead to a quicker termination of the hostilities. In the case of the launching of missiles by a third party, especially if the launch were an accident, the missile might be intercepted by such a defense system. What is more, some form of SDI will also ensure that any nuclear deterrent will remain a deterrent because it will be less vulnerable to a first strike by either side.

Obviously, if a nuclear exchange is large enough, all life on this planet might be threatened with extinction. In a small exchange that catastrophic consequence would not necessarily be the case; then, survivability would depend on the size of the exchange and the civil defense measures in place in each country. While we hope that a nuclear exchange will never occur, prudence dictates that all countries ought to have an active civil-defense program. The Soviet Union has a very active program of building nuclear shelters and other civil-defense measures, while the United States has almost no program at all to shield or help the populace should a nuclear exchange of any sort occur. Not only would a shelter program help survivors in a limited exchange, but its very existence also strengthens the confidence of the populace.

Democracies have a hard time thinking about foreign policy over the long run, but they have an even harder time maintaining defense establishments (offensive and defensive) against the pull of domestic needs and pacifist sentiment. An example of such failure can be seen in England's inability to face Adolf Hitler's relentless military build-up prior to World War II. In many countries the right to conscientious objection is illegal and the defense budget is not publicly scrutinized by the population or voted on by elected representatives; for that reason it is my belief that to have a peaceful world with freedom will require the United States to do something that no democracy has ever done (and I include all democracies from Athens to the present). No democracy has ever been able to "hang tough" for many years running in the face of an authoritarian or totalitarian government that has opposed it.

Before continuing with this analysis comment must be made about the extraordinary events taking place in the Soviet Union under the guidance of Mikhail Gorbachev. We may be witnessing the beginning of a long process of change that will lead to the development within the Soviet Union of one of the key essentials of true democracy, the right to protected dissent. In a democracy like the United States, if a treaty is violated (for example, supposed that the United States agreed not to make chemical weapons and then surreptitiously began making them), there would be a number of whistle-blowers within the industry or government; the matter would be exposed in the press and the public alerted. In democratic societies treaties designed to achieve peace are monitored internally. Until recently, the Soviet Union has been a closed society with a controlled press, but under Gorbachev this appears to be changing. If these changes keep occurring and become ingrained in Soviet society, then the Soviet Union too will develop an internal monitoring system. This is to be devoutly wished; however, achieving that degree of societal change will take many years to occur and become secure, and I think that some American foreign policy effort ought to be directed toward encouraging such a change.

Another consideration concerning the Gorbachev-inspired changes is that they may not succeed and, indeed, may be reversed. Consequently, U.S. foreign policy must proceed cautiously so that the defense posture of the United States is always appropriate, no matter what happens in the Soviet Union; so long as disarmament treaties are adequately monitored and truly symmetrical, neither country has anything to fear from the other.

A very perceptive recent article by Constantine Menges pointed out that Gorbachev's reforms actually mark the fifth time since World War II that the Soviet Union has appeared to be moving toward accommodation with the West.

> Nowadays, the term detente is usually reserved for the prolonged period of "eased tension" inaugurated by Richard Nixon and continued during the Ford and Carter Administrations. But a careful look at the history of Soviet–American relations since World War II shows that detente is not an isolated phenomenon, but a recurring temptation: in at least three other periods, Washington attempted friendly relations with the Kremlin. Each period was marked by Summit meetings, arms-control accords, and high expectations of a new era of cooperation. Each was ended by an act of Soviet aggression. And, when the dust settled, each period of detente left the West in a relatively worse position.[1]

Menges finds that the first period of detente ended with the Berlin blockade, the second with the invasion of Hungary by Soviet troops to crush the freedom movement there, the third with the erection of the Berlin Wall, and the fourth with the Soviet invasion of Afghanistan. His point is that, despite our hope for the continuation of the Gorbachev policy of mutual, peaceful accommodation and coexistence, U.S. foreign policy must be geared to the possibility of a Soviet reversion to an aggressive stance. A democracy must be wary of becoming so sanguine in its hope for change that it becomes defenseless through obsolescence, bad strategic planning, or a single-minded paring away of the defense budget.

America must remain aware that Gorbachev presides over the military empire that has had the largest military build-up (strategic and conventional) of any nation in all of history. The Soviet Navy has greatly increased its size so that it often equals (and in some ways excels) that of the United States; the Soviet Union has vastly superior conventional forces, more intercontinental ballistic missiles, and a modern bomber aircraft in large-scale production, whereas the United States does not. The pace of this vast military program, occurring in every area of weapons development and placement, apparently has not slowed under Gorbachev, and the size of this military build-up exceeds anything that has occurred in the United States under President Reagan's administration either in real terms or in terms of the percentage of each nation's budget.

Another cause for concern among the Western democracies is the Soviet Union's gigantic propaganda and disinformation apparatus, which is still in place. The Soviet Union also has the largest spying establishment in the world, specializing not only in military intelligence and information for foreign-policy purposes, but also dedicated to industrial espionage and theft. No other nation on earth has such a large percentage of its diplomatic corps involved in spying; estimates are that about a third of all Soviet diplomatic personnel, whether at the United Nations or as Soviet representatives to other nations, are primarily engaged in espionage. This shocking fact is not calculated to inspire Western confidence in Soviet motives. On June 14, 1988, the Los Angeles *Times* carried the story of the arrest in Ottawa of a Newfoundland man accused of being a spy for the Soviet Union. Similar reports about the representatives of the Soviet Union are all too common. The Soviets often counter the expulsion of their diplomats by expelling innocent diplomats from other countries. While all countries engage to some extent in propaganda, disinformation, and spying, the Soviet Union is perhaps most at fault in this regard; and, ultimately, this situation will have to change if real progress is going to be made in peaceful coexistence without fear and distrust.

There is no doubt that the Soviet Union has had a kind of paranoia about invasion by the North Atlantic Treaty Organization (NATO) or the United States, but under the present Western governments such a development is highly unlikely. The Soviet Union need fear nothing from the Western democracies; and the more treaties of agreement that are symmetrical and verifiable, the better for all concerned.

In the past one of the fears that seems to have driven the Soviet Union has been that of open windows of freedom to the West. If, under Gorbachev, that fear can be eroded through the development of protected personal freedom within the Soviet Union, then great possibilities for developing a trust worthy peace exist. The Soviet Union has never wanted to conquer the world, but there is a tendency to want to destabilize the world and to silence any window of freedom that is unsettling to the Soviet system. We may be seeing the end of this kind of negative motivation; let us hope so. We will not be certain for many years.

As noted earlier, there are, broadly speaking, two types of scenarios that could develop between the Soviet Union and the United States during the next fifty years, one set leading to war and a second set in which war does not occur. Let me now outline the second set of possible scenarios; those that avoid war. First, I will first present the best possible scenario for the future, the one in which the Gorbachev program remains in place and prospers; then I will present those scenarios that assume a Soviet reversion to a more aggressive policy.

## Scenario Two

If the Gorbachev program of glasnost and perestroika continues to florish and takes deep hold in the Soviet Union, then we can reasonably hope that the next fifty years will see increased trade and other exchanges with the Soviet Union and its satellites. As the modern world progresses, the logic of the scientific method, the reality principle of technocracy, and democratization can lead to the reform of the Soviet system. We can hope that, similarly, in the West, democracy will increasingly come to be *knowledge-oriented* rather than ideological or oriented toward the enhancement of power for leaders. Information will gradually come to be shared on a worldwide basis, and protected dissent will be recognized and accepted in the Western world and in Russia. Such conditions could result in the international control of all armaments by some sort of world federation, a federation both stronger and less politicized than the United Nations of the 1980s. This glorious prospect will occur only if positive evolution continues in both countries: if the Soviet Union increasingly learns to trust the West and openness, and if the United States maintains an adequate military deterrent for long enough while, at the same time, committing itself to increasingly total, symmetrical, verifiable treaties that gradually reduce armaments first between the superpowers and later throughout the entire world.

The great dangers in this scenario are that the democracies will not maintain their will and strength long enough, thus tempting Russian adventurism, and that the Soviet Union will find it impossible to remain deeply committed to glasnost and perestroika in the best sense of those words. The possibility of achieving, in Kant's phrase, "perpetual peace" can be glimpsed as a real possibility during the next fifty years, and if this happens, no one will be due more honor than Mikhail Gorbachev. But the way will be long and arduous, and fraught with temptations and dangers.

Now we must look at the less happy scenarios, scenarios in which the Soviet Union reverts to its prior, more aggressive role. Should that happen I see two possible lines of development during the next fifty years; one or the other might occur depending on the whether or not the Western democracies and especially the United States maintain their will to maintain their freedom.

## Scenario Three

If the Soviet Union, in reaction to the Gorbachev program, reverts to a more aggressive approach toward the rest of the world, and the United States loses its will to resist, then, during the next fifty years the free world would grow increasingly fatigued by living with the balance of terror. Then, through a "failure of nerve," or what Alexander Solzhenitsyn called the "Munich mentality," the free world could succumb to a worldwide dystopia in which people are fed and clothed but at the price of the loss of the civil liberties so cherished in the West. The dystopia of a Finlandized world, a world controlled by conformity to Russian aims, would come closer each day due to the fear of nuclear Armageddon. Almost total Soviet domination would eventually be welcomed with relief; candidates for public office in the Western world would begin to vie with each other to see who could most self-righteously and indirectly proclaim principles whose realization would result in accommodation to the goals of Soviet leadership. Eventually the democracies would be led by politicians and bureaucrats whose promise to their constituencies would be to get the most for the least effort; elected by the democratic process, they would follow the policies dictated by Soviet pronouncements. Then, through informal agreements (for example, between the CIA and the KGB), the Soviet Union would increasingly control the free world to a degree somewhere between its current firm control of Poland and its indirect control of Finland.

The democratic forms would remain in place, though paralyzed. Such control might be accepted in the West for supposedly idealistic and altruistic reasonings, for it would represent an end to the arms race and to the threat of nuclear war. There would also be the promise that all people would be fed, even on the basis of worldwide scarcity. We would live in an impoverished version of Aldous Huxley's *Brave New World,* offering "community, identity, stability"; but, as in Huxley's dystopia, there would be no individualism and no liberty. Such a program would likely be presented as a move in the direction of a more egalitarian society, domestically and internationally, and for this reason many "intellectuals" would be drawn to its standard. Resources of the wealthy nations would be shared with the less fortunate nations, in the same way that Czechoslovakia and other satellite nations have "contributed" to Soviet imperialist schemes in many parts of the world. Environmentalists would be assured that the new order would ensure that the most effective measures for the protection of the environment would be undertaken; just as the integrity of the environment is guaranteed today in the Soviet Union.

Finally, let me outline the scenario that might occur should the Soviet Union revert to an aggressive stance and the United States find more of a will than it now has to maintain its independent existence with freedom.

## Scenario Four

With no signs of modification of the Soviet system and glasnost and perestroika dead in all but name, and with the United States in a state of military readiness, anxious to maintain its liberty and independence, the world could face a power struggle between these two nations and their allies that would drag on for fifty years or longer. The sword of Damocles—the threat of the extermination by means of nuclear war—would continually hang over the world with no hope of relief and with precious resources constantly being wasted in the endless struggle.

I end on this somber note because, while "perpetual peace" is possible, it will only be achieved by means of a long, difficult, and courageous struggle. Prometheus was condemned by Zeus because he wanted to save the human race from extinction. In agony, torn apart each day and tormented with thirst, he hoped in his heart—indeed, he believed with all his might—that ultimately his torment would end, he would achieve peaceful reconciliation with Zeus, and humankind would survive. Yet he refused to bow his head to the god who tormented him. Such a struggle must be waged by human beings if they would achieve perpetual peace; to assume it can be accomplished by nothing less than a desperate struggle and a long-range commitment is absurd.

## Note

1. Constantine C. Menges, "The Four 'Detents,' " *National Review,* June 24, 1988, pp. 37-40.

# V.

# Human Rights

# Church-State Separation and Freedom of Conscience

## Edd Doerr
### (United States)

Church and state, or government and organized religion, have always been two of the most important institutions in society. Historically they have in nearly every society been very closely related. In some societies religion has dominated government and used it as an engine for its purposes, while in others the situation has been the reverse. At still other times and in other places religion and government have engaged in a symbiotic relationship, each helping the other. In all of these arrangements dissenters, minorities, and women have been met with a range of unpleasantries: denial of equal rights, discrimination, persecution, exile, prison, even death. Wars over religion have killed literally millions of people and laid waste to nations.

The situation is somewhat the same in most of the world today, though the penalities for minorities, dissenters, or nonbelievers are generally much less harsh than they were in the past. Many Muslim states barely tolerate religious minorities and do not allow a great deal of true freedom of religion or freedom of conscience. In some it is even a capital crime to convert from Islam to another religion. Even in democratic, progressive, modern Western Europe, church-state relations models from the past continue in force. Established churches in the Scandinavian countries still cause discrimination against dissenters and unbelievers. Citizens are compelled through taxation to contribute to established churches in West Germany, Norway, and elsewhere. In the Netherlands, Belgium, France, the United Kingdom, Ireland, and other countries taxpayers are compelled to support religious indoctrination and religious segregation in private schools. In West Germany, citizens can still be persecuted for "blasphemy." Switzerland, Israel, Canada, Australia, and New Zealand have an assortment of church-state entanglements that reduce full religious liberty—by which I mean, of course, complete freedom of conscience and choice with regard to religious belief and disbelief.

The countries of the Eastern bloc are not models to follow either. They discriminate as often against humanism as they do against traditional religions.

Among the church-state issues that directly affect he lives of citizens are equal treatment of all under law, laws and regulations bearing on marriage and divorce, laws and regulations regarding birth control and abortion, women's rights, religious indoctrination and discrimination in tax-supported public education, compulsory tax support for religious institutions, and special relations between national governments and the Holy See, which have the effect of discriminating against non-Catholics and even against those Catholics who do not see eye to eye with the Vatican leadership.

While there is much that we Americans can learn from other countries, I think it is fair to say that the United States has developed an approach to church-state relations that may provide a useful guide. When the first Englishmen came to North America in 1607 they brought with them the religious and political institutions with which they were familiar in Europe. This meant that they were rather intolerant toward people of other religious beliefs. Indeed, 1988 marked the 350th anniversary of the expulsion of Anne Hutchinson from the British colony of Massachusetts for the crime of holding unauthorized religious meetings in her own home. She was also expelled for the crime of being the wrong gender to lead religious discussions. Since the time of Anne Hutchinson and the hanging of Quakers in Massachusetts, the development of religious pluralism throughout what was to become the United States has led to sharp dissatisfaction with the European model of state establishment of religion. At the same time that the British colonies in North America were conducting an armed revolt for their independence, they went through the process of separating religion from government, an arrangement found today in our federal Constitution and in all fifty of our state constitutions.

The separation arrangement was included in the first article of the Bill of Rights of our Constitution, which provides that, "Congress shall make no law respecting an establishment of religion or prohibiting the free exercise thereof." President Thomas Jefferson, in 1802, referred to this section of the Constitution as erecting "a wall of separation between church and state." The courts and the people of the United States have generally adhered to and advanced the separation principle throughout most of our history. Unfortunately, the Reagan era saw the beginning of a regression. The issues of concern in the United States today are the role of religion in public education, the question of tax support for sectarian private schools and sectarian child-care centers, attempts to restrict the right of women to decide for themselves whether or not to continue problem pregnancies, and the Reagan Administration's formal diplomatic recognition of the Vatican state, thereby discriminating against all other religions and life-stances in the United States.

It is interesting to note that Italy and Spain, each of which has a rather bad historical record with regard to religious liberty and separation of church and state, have made enormous progress toward separation during the past decade. It is ironic that their progress has occurred at the same time that we have noted the beginning of a regression in the United States.

There seems to be a consensus among humanists the world over that there should be a separation of church and state—as strict a separation as can possibly be arranged. Each country, of course, has its own history, legal traditions and procedures, religious demography, and circumstances. Consequently, achieving chruch-state separation requires different strategies in different countries. It is my belief that each of our countries can learn from the others. Each must solve its own problems, but this may be made easier by cooperation not only among humanists around the world but between humanists and people of other religious persuasions or life stances.

Though the United States has advanced legal machinery for the defense and progression of church-state separation, this is not the case elsewhere. The American occupation of Japan after World War II led to that country's adoption of an American-style separation. Australia imitated the American separation model at the turn of the century, but, unfortunately, the Australian High Court has chosen to use British definitions of religious establishment rather than American definitions, contrary to the intentions of the framers of the Australian constitution.

European humanists may find it fruitful to experiment with the relevant United Nations declarations regarding human rights in their quest for the furtherance of separation. Humanists the world over have arrived at the point where we can and must work together and with persons of other persuasions and life stances to advance church-state separation and the complete freedom of belief (or nonbelief) and conscience.

# Human Rights: The Right to Work

## Renate Bauer
### (West Germany)

As a member of the Free Religious movement in Germany and a leader of one of its communities, I am deeply concerned with the question of the right to work. From its inception in the middle of the nineteenth century, the Free Religious movement has evolved parallel to and in close association with the German labor movement. From the start it has advocated the right to work, to earn a just wage and a decent living. We have consistently held that conditions of employment constitute the crucial difference between freedom and oppression, self-determination and dependency, morality and immorality.

Although the situation of the Third World is certainly deplorable and many problems there relate to the right to work, industrialized nations are facing serious problems in this regard as well. These nations are running out of paid work. Technological advances are dictating progressive automation and increasing productivity while reducing the number of workers engaged in the productive process. The result has been a progressive rise in unemployment.

Unemployment not only strikes society's marginal groups; even highly qualified workers can become at least temporarily unemployed. Industrial development encourages this process, which is leading to a widening gulf between those with secure employment and those whose employment will become more and more erratic. A cynical new form of social darwinism based on the ideological concepts of free competition and achievement became popular under Reaganomics and Thatcherism. These are mechanistic solutions to social problems. The inhumanity underlying these concepts does not stand up to close scrutiny.

In addition to increasing insecurity in the workplace, changing conditions of employment tend increasingly to isolate the individual. Demands for mobility, flexibility, and constant professional self-development are turning working people into solitary fighters, struggling to maintain their positions in hostile environments. Interpersonal relationships between individuals and solidarity within the group are increasingly becoming luxuries that few working people can afford to enjoy. More obviously than ever before, economic developments are determining the whole shape of society. The changes surrounding marriage and family life illustrate the larger changes in society. There has been a steady decline in the marriage index for men and women from 1965 to 1984—in Germany, Sweden, the United States, and even in predominantly Catholic countries like Ireland and Italy. The percentage of couples who live together without a legal consent is rising. In Sweden the percentage of unmarried women twenty-five to twenty-nine years old living with their partners grew from 17 percent in 1975 to 31 percent in 1980. Fifteen years before, about 90 percent of this age group had been married. In the countries mentioned the ratio of "complete" families has dropped drastically, especially in big cities with a rising number of singles in all age groups. In all of these countries fewer children are being born, and on the average the number of divorces has more than doubled from 1965 to 1984. Economy profits from these developments, since a single person needs about the same number of appliances and many other household products as does a whole family.

What are the societal consequences of these developments? Confronted with the increasingly existential insecurity of their lifestyles, people have been losing their faith in the validity of social norms and mores. Traditional forms of marriage are losing their primacy over looser pair-bonds, sex-roles are breaking down, religions are taking on new forms of expression. The tendency is toward transient relationships, and consequently toward isolation and loneliness. Isolation not only raises the demand for psychological and other forms of help, because social nets diminish and grow weak, but it affects mores and self-control as well. Lonely people become demoralized. They neglect themselves and their surroundings; they lose their manners, which I consider to be a symbol of losing contacts with and awareness of other people; they grow helpless in the art of meeting people and of maintaining relationships; they cannot get their daily lives into shape. These processes that we can observe from the outside—and quite often abhor—are signs of an underlying inner disintegration.

Many groups are hit by the fear of becoming unemployed, but at the moment they are still able to earn a living. Middle-class groups—teachers, social workers, managers, and others who are fairly well-educated—struggle with the knowledge that they can lose their jobs easily and have a hard time to finding comparable ones; they also find it difficult to break into the "real world" after they have finished their training. They often react by becoming less rational. They have learned to be progressive and to seek out new directions. Often, however, they seek direction from sources that are difficult for some of us to understand, given the level of education of these people. Occultism, astrology, spiritualism, faith-healing, and shamanistic wisdom seem to many to offer better solutions than do the constantly changing insights of rational science. Irrational predictions seem to correspond more closely to perceived reality than do logic or reason, for rational thought demands the ability to stand aloof from a problem—an exercise that can be strenuous and, at times, painful as well. Many people live today under constant emotional stress. Why should they take on even more?

The situation young people experience has its own touch of inhumanity. Twenty years ago they could assume a direct correlation between their educational and professional backgrounds and their chances of employment. Today only the cream of the crop even qualifies for consideration, and still there are no guarantees. Today's really critical qualifications are not formal criteria, but influential contacts, good looks, and the ability to sell oneself effectively. These factors are irrelevant to ability in most fields. It is certainly rational for employers to use such criteria when there are more than enough qualified people, but those who have to present themselves often receive inhuman treatment in being selected like cattle. Since these criteria are hard to quantify it is also hard to control them, so what does one do? One takes a talisman with oneself.

With such insecurity, work and a life based on the ideology of work seem meaningless. To fill the gap some people resort to political extremism; others are driven to drug-abuse, crime, or mental illness. This affects us all; quite literally, each of us pays the price. Also, as life becomes more insecure and solidarity withers, each of us becomes less charitable to others and less willing to accept help when we need it ourselves. These are all symptoms of economic and industrial developments—their structural changes affect the whole of society in a complex way. The problems mentioned cannot be dealt with by appeals to the individual or by alms-giving, even on a political basis. The bottom line is that industrial and institutional changes have to be made.

But what can we do?

The labor movement, embodied in the unions, seems to be the one institution that thus far has been able to protect people from unconditional surrender to the dictates of economic and industrial development. In principle these federations of working people have for the most part been able to protect at least their own members. In some countries they have been able to secure better working—and therefore better social—conditions for the entire working population. Though in practice unions can become corrupted by a corrupting system, this is not an argument against the principle behind the unions. The same holds true on the other side. One charitable employer does not change the inhumanity of others or of the system of the working process.

Today the unions have to struggle with a bundle of changes. They are in danger, particularly where classical factory structures have been supplanted by computer-based technologies. These technologies break down the old patterns of mass production, the environment in which the unions grew strong. The speed of change has overtaken the unions, making them seem prehistoric and irrelevant to the new class of technical workers. But the unions must be strengthened; they advocate commonly recognized values and foster group solidarity. They are indispensible in keeping the weak from being driven from the workplace and banished to the margins of society. The simultaneous growth of multinational corporations and the rebirth of cottage industries demand new forms of organization in the labor movement, leading to more participation in managerial decisions that affect employees. As more and more corporations diversify into the international market, the need for international labor organizations becomes more pressing. Unions have the capability of monitoring and influencing developments of economic, social, and technological importance. The important role of labor organizations as a control organ for scientific and technological research can hardly be overemphasized. Scientists and engineers are too often ill-prepared to weigh the potential effect of their work in the larger sphere. Critical scientists can easily be silenced by bribes (also called incentives) and threats of unemployment. By the time criticism or warnings reach the concerned public, decisions have already been made, money invested, possible alternatives discarded. Once this stage has been reached, there is little chance of retrieving the situation. A major concern of humanists and labor organizations alike must be to analyze new developments and to weigh their effect on nature and humanity alike, before such vested interests evolve.

Humanists eschew the concept of a deity, rely upon science, and believe therefore in the freedom of scientific inquiry. The difference between "good" and "bad" science is for us a question of public and private morality: The term "bad" as applied to science can only mean science that refuses to examine itself critically, to inquire into all of the ramifications implicit in its discoveries. So defined, much of the research conducted by industry must unfortunately be termed "bad," since it serves only economic aims and must be turned to profit. Other important aspects of research are all too often neglected out of greed or ignorance. Science underlies every form of industrial and technological progress. It is therefore the concern of every one of us, because it affects all of our lives. Society—and as a part of society, the working person—has the right to ask critical questions of the scientific community, to call for moratoria on forms of research whose implications are not fully understood, and to resist the introduction of objectionable scientific discoveries in the form of products of dubious social and ecological worth.

We humanists hold that freedom is inseparably bound to responsibility. This means that all people have the duty to examine their own actions, to judge the consequences and possible effects of those actions, to weigh their benefits for mankind and act accordingly. We all must pay the price of poor decisions or missed opportunities; it is therefore only fitting that we should have a share in fixing the price. We humanists must be aware of the synergy between economic developments and ideological formulae and the way in which they predicate and reinforce each other—we must be particularly aware of this when examining our own ideas. Only then will we be able to approach our goal of rational enlightenment.

It is also our duty to take up our share of the burden of solidarity. Freedom and responsibility lead us to ask what we can do to strengthen the bonds between people, to help others grow so that they may be able to live fuller lives. Humanism means more than just defending freedom and human rights. It calls us to act upon our principles, to give hope, to enable growth not only for ourselves but for others too, without forcing our way of life upon them.

Our duty extends to the individual threatened by recurring or prolonged unemployment. This threat hangs over each of us and is one of the foundations of our solidarity, for each of us will have to learn to cope with it, directly or indirectly. Not every individual can learn to cope on his or her own; nor can all find meaning in their lives without outside help. Humanists recognize the self-perpetuating nature of poverty. In societies like ours, which are built around work, the unemployed quickly cease to be productive members of society. Thrust to the margins of society, they lose the ability to educate and socialize their children, who are then unable to take their place at the workplace. Like the four horse-men of the Apocalypse, the plagues of poverty, lack of education, alcohol and drug abuse, and early parenthood descend upon the children of the unemployed, perpetuating themselves through generations. A vicious circle evolves, which under the current circumstances is widening to enclose more people every day.

This brings us back to our original proposition, that the industrialized world is running out of work. We need to reexamine the work ethic in light of the increasing numbers of unemployed. Is employment the only activity that gives meaning to life? What about love, empathy, caring, and spiritual and intellectual growth? But all these possibilities are rooted in the right to earn a decent living in a humane way, and to have a proper share in work and wages. Industrial society represents a fairly new stage in human history, and probably is transitory, as were all the stages before it.

The ideals of humanism are based upon the ideals of the Renaissance and of antiquity, when those who espoused these ideals were not "employed" as we define the word today, but instead sought to develop other goals and talents such as wisdom and art—including the art of relating. Our task now is to redefine goals such as these, that will lead to a better life for humankind and for nature as well. Though in the past people depended on the productivity of slaves and serfs to allow them to pursue other goals, we must live our ideals of freedom, responsibility, and solidarity so that everyone may take part in the work process and fill his or her life with other meanings as well.

# Human Rights: The Indian Experiment

## R. A. Jahagirdar
### (India)

Though India emerged as a nation independent from colonial rule in 1947, the thirty-year struggle leading to that independence bore the seeds of what later came to be recognized as fundamental rights. In 1931, at the Karachi Congress, a resolution on fundamental rights was adopted that is now generally accepted to be the handiwork of M. N. Roy, who at the time went by the name of Dr. Mahmood. At that time Roy was a Marxist—perhaps a better term would be Communist. Even then he realized the importance of fundamental rights as a part of the program for independence. Subsequently, as is well known, Roy became a humanist. He formulated what is now known in India as the New Humanism or Radical Humanism. India finally became free after a blood-bath of communal violence that resulted in the death of hundreds of thousands. Large masses of people migrated from what are now Pakistan and Bangladesh into India and vice versa in what has been characterized as one of the largest exoduses in the history of mankind.

Fortunately the shadow of the tragic events of 1947 did not have a depressing effect upon the framers of India's Constitution. If they had been gripped by the fear of continuous unsettled conditions, the authors of the Constitution probably would have endowed the state with draconian powers. The great debates that took place in the Constituent Assembly disclosed an intense awareness on the part of the Constitution's framers of the need for translating the philosophy of the pre-independent era into the realities of an independent India. The Constitution freely draws upon the libertarian philosophy of France, England, and the United States, though prior to colonial rule, fundamental rights were not known in India. During the struggle for independence, the authors of the Constitution and the population at large recognized that some provision was necessary regarding fundamental rights.

This was not merely fancy; it became a legal provision to be found in Part 3 of the Constitution. In innumerable judgments since, the courts have held that any law that contravenes Part 3 of the Constitution is invalid. This is in sharp constrast to the experiences of other countries that became independent after World War II. Of all the countries in Asia and Africa that were freed from the yoke of foreign domination after the war, India is the only one that has sustained its democratic institutions for more than four decades. India has held every general election as scheduled—be it for the Central Parliament or the State Legislature—as envisaged in the Constitution and the Representation of the People Act. It could be suggested with some justification that the elections have not always been model in all respects, but in a sea of authoritarian and totalitarian regimes in the countries surrounding India, she stands as an island of democracy and freedom.

In a recent article in the *London Economist,* the philosopher Karl Popper suggested that the true test for judging a society to be democratic is whether the possibility exists that an alternative government could effectively displace the government in power. The application of this test leaves little doubt that India can be regarded as a democracy. There are of course several shortcomings in the prevailing system, and those who have been entrusted with power are far from perfect. Despite these imperfections and failings, one cannot but appreciate the manner in which India has carried on its democratic experiment despite four wars and several periods of almost anarchical conditions.

The Universal Declaration of Human Rights was adopted by the United Nations General Assembly on December 10, 1948. The International Covenant on Civil and Political Rights and the International Covenant on Economical, Social, and Cultural Organizations were drafted in 1954 and adopted by the United Nations in 1966, but were not enforced until 1976. Even while these efforts were being made, the framers of the Indian Constitution had quietly but surely started working on their chapter on fundamental rights.

The two different but inseparable aspects of human rights—that is, civil and political rights on the one hand and economic, social, and cultural rights on the other—are to some extent reflected in the Constitution of India. The realization of civil and political rights was considered a goal within immediate reach, which economic, social, and cultural rights were regarded as ideals toward which the country should constantly strive. There is in the Indian Constitution a recognizable but not airtight distinction between the two classes of rights. Civil and political rights mainly deal with freedom from the power of the leviathan state of today; therefore they are often expressed in negative terms. Economic and social rights are regarded more as promotional. This distinction, however, should not be overemphasized, since ultimately the sum total of human rights is a complex amalgam. India is multiracial, multilingual, and multireligious. Nearly 80 percent of its population is Hindu; nothing would have been easier than to declare India a Hindu state, and the framers of the Constitution might have got away with it given the political conditions of 1950. In the long run, however, history would not have forgiven this. Fortunately the idealism that inspired the framers of the Indian Constitution prevented them from falling prey to the narrow considerations of the community.

Part 3 of the Constitution provides for fundamental rights that may not be contravened by the legislature or by the executive. Part 4 contains what are clalled the Directive Principles of State Policy, which are not enforceable but nevertheless are fundamental in the governance of the country. It is the duty of the federal and regional governments to apply these priciples in making laws.

Article 14 provides that the state shall not deny to any person equality before the law or the equal protection of the laws within the territory of India; this applies to noncitizens as well as to Indian citizens. Recent legal developments recognized that it is not merely the denial of equality that invites the wrath of Article 14; if a provision is not discriminatory but is unreasonable or arbitrary, it could be held to be in contravention of this section of the Constitution. By so holding in a series of judgments, the Supreme Court of India has assimilated into the Consititution the principle of substantive "due process of law," a feature heretofore peculiar to the Constitution of the United States. The Supreme Court of India has said:

> Equality must become a living reality for the large masses of the people. Those who are unequal, in fact, cannot be treated by identical standards; that may be equality in law but it would certainly not be real equality. Existence of equality of opportunity depends not merely on the absence of disabilities but on presence of abilities. It is not simply a matter of legal equality. *De jure* equality must ultimately find its *raison d'etre* in *de facto* equality.

In Article 16, the principle of equality is extended to mean equality of opportunity in matters of public employment. However, in view of the peculiar conditions prevalent in India in the form of the existence of several backward communities, Article 16 permits a state to make provision for the reservation of appointments in favor of citizens who, in the opinion of the state, are not adequately represented. This is consistent with the principle of nondiscrimination as mentioned in the International Law of Human Rights, which says: ". . . the law must treat all members of the protected class with complete equality, regardless of their particular circumstances, features, or characteristics."

Article 19 of the Constitution originally contained what have been described as seven lamps of freedom: freedom of speech and expression; freedom to assemble peaceably without arms; freedom to move freely throughout the territory of India; freedom to reside and settle in any part of the territory of India; freedom to acquire, hold, and dispose of property; and freedom to practice any profession, or to carry on any occupation, trade, or business. In 1979 an amendment removed the right to acquire, hold, and dispose of property; instead, in Article 300-A it is now provided that no person shall be deprived of his or her property save by authority of law. Thus this right has slipped from its lofty position in Part 3 of the Constitution to a subordinate place.

It must be added, however, that fundamental rights are not absolute; the state has been given power to impose reasonable restrictions on their exercise. This is somewhat akin to the due process of law noted in the American Constitution, but provides for the possibility of imposing restrictions that are reasonable and uphold the Constitution.

There is a provision in the Indian Constitution that a person may be convicted only for the violation of a law in force at the time that the act was committed; furthermore, no person may be subjected to a penalty greater than that which might have been inflicted under the law in force at the time of the commisssion of the offense. Provision has also been made that no person shall be prosecuted and punished for the same offense more than once, and that those accused of an offense shall not be compelled to witness against themselves.

The next and probably the most celebrated section in the Indian Constitution, insofar as it relates to civil and political liberty, is Article 21, which provides that "no person shall be deprived of his life or personal liberty except according to procedure established by law." In 1975 a state of emergency was declared in India, which continued until Febrary 1977; provisions in the Indian Constitution permitted the president to suspend fundamental rights during this time.

Subsequently, however, in the case of *Maneka Gandhi* v. *Union of India,* the Supreme Court held that the right to travel abroad was considered to be a liberty as mentioned in Article 21, and that a person could not be denied a passport under a law that did not afford an opportunity to answer the objection of the issuing authority. The case thus held that a "law," as it is used in Article 21, must be "right, just, and fair," and not arbitrary, fanciful, or oppressive, since an unreasonable, unfair, or arbitrary provision is no procedure at all, and the requirement of Article 21 could not be said to be satisfied under such conditions. The fresh look at Article 21 that the Supreme Court took in Maneka Gandhi's case and in subsequent cases has helped the growth of India's tree of liberty. New dimensions have been given to the expression of life and liberty.

The state of prisoners all over the world is always pitiable; before and after conviction they are the most unprotected citizen of every country. They are held behind stone walls—not merely behind barbed wire, where they could be seen. Behind those stone walls things happen that would shock a civilized society but are not always known to the outside world. In a series of decisions the Supreme Court of India has pointed out that those who have been convicted may lose their freedom of movement, but conviction may not deprive them of their life or personal liberty, except, of course, according to the procedure established by law. In 1978, Charles Shobraj challenged the Superintendent of Jails, who had put him in bar-fetters for an unusually long period; he also challenged the provisions that permitted the authorities to use this method for holding a prisoner. The Court held that such punishment should be given only in those cases where absolute necessity demanded it, and ordered the removal of the bar-fetters.

In the case of Sunil Batra the undesirable practice of putting a prisoner in solitary confinement was subjected to a searching inquiry. In this decision the Supreme Court invoked the Declaration for the Protection of all Persons from Torture and Other Inhumane and Degrading Punishment adopted by the U.N. General Assembly in 1975. The judges also set out guidelines for the protection of prisoners, directing that these guidelines be strictly followed. These two judgments are know as "Operation Prison Justice." The guidelines included the requirement that a prisoner's handbook be prepared in the local language and that each prisoner receive a copy. The Supreme Court also mentioned that the state would take steps to follow the Standard Minimum Rules for Treatment of Prisoners recommended by the United Nations. An overhauling of the Prisons Act and the Prison Manual was recommended to bring it into consonance with constitutional values, therapeutic approaches, and tension-free management.

In another series of decisions, the case of prisoners awaiting arraignment was highlighted and remedial measures were suggested. The shocking state of affairs of such prisoners in India and in particular in Hazaribagh Jail was brought to the notice of the country by the dedicated work of human rights activists. An alert court contributed to the exposure, and ordered the release of all persons who had been held for an inordinately long time pending arraignment. The Supreme Court stated:

> We are talking passionately and eloquently about the maintenance and preservation of basic freedoms. But, are we not denying human rights to these nameless persons who are languishing in jails for years for offenses which perhaps they might ultimately be found not to have committed? Are we not withholding basic freedoms from these neglected and helpless human beings who have been condemned to a life of imprisonment and degradation for years on end? Are expeditious trial and freedom from detention not part of human rights and basic freedoms? Many of these unfortunate men and women must not even . . . remember when they entered the jail and for what offense. They have over the years ceased to be human beings; they are mere ticket-numbers. It is high time that the public conscience is awakened and the Government as well as the judiciary begin to realize that in the dark cells of our prisons there are large numbers of men and women who are waiting patiently, impatiently perhaps, but in vain, for justice—a commodity which is tragically beyond their reach and grasp. Law has become for them an instrument of injustice and they are helpless and despairing victims of the callousness of the legal and judicial systems. The time has come when the legal and judicial systems have to be revamped and restructured so that such injustices do not occur and disfigure the fair and otherwise luminous face of our nascent democracy.

For me and for other human rights activists, the continued presence of the death penalty on the statute book of India has been a great source of anxiety and embarrassment. Attempts to find it in contravention of Article 21 have so far failed. Though the Supreme Court has upheld the constitutional validity of the death penalty, its actual use has become increasingly rare. It is only one of the two sentences that can be awarded to a person convicted of murder. The alternative sentence is life imprisonment. The Supreme Court has stated on more than one occasion that the life sentence is the rule and the death sentence is the exception, to be handed down in the rarest of rare cases. The principles that the burden of proof rests with the prosecution and that a person is innocent until proven guilty are an integral part of the criminal justice system in India, and hence are not mentioned in the Constitution.

Thus there is a constitutional background of human rights, and the judiciary in India has upheld and even enlarged those rights. Unfortunately, in the legislative field there has not been the same degree of awakening. This must be said with certain qualifications as we cannot forget, for instance, the recent enactment of law providing for free legal aid to the poor and needy, and the passing of the Equal Rights and Civil Rights Acts.

One of the unsatisfactory features of the Indian Constitution has been the provision relating to preventive detention. Article 22 provides that no person who is arrested shall be detained in custody without being informed of the grounds for arrest, and shall not be denied the right to consult and be defended by a legal practitioner of the defendant's choice. This article, however, does not apply to those who have been detained under any law providing for preventive detention; this has led to several abuses. An overwhelming majority of detentions are set aside by the courts on the ground that they are in breach of the constitutional safeguards. However, the fact that so many wrong arrests are made should be a matter of great concern to lovers of freedom, particularly in a country that does not provide for compensation for wrongful arrest and detention. If such a provision were made, in all probability it would bankrupt the government since quite a sizable number of those tried are acquitted.

India is a land of many religions, many languages, and many races. Since the country has refused to accept Hindu as the state religion, provisions had to be made for freedom of religion. Article 25 of the Constitution has bestowed upon all persons in India freedom of conscience and free profession, practice, and propagation of religion. This, however, does not prevent the state from regulating secular areas that may be affected by religious practice. Thus the state protects religious minorities and their right to establish and administer educational institutions. The extent of this right under Article 30 of the Constitution has been the subject of several decisions; the last word is yet to be heard.

In India the imparting of religious instruction in an educational institution wholly maintained out of state funds is prohibited. An overwhelming number of educational institutions in India receive large grants from the government; only a small measure of the funding is provided by individuals or agencies, who unfortunately are not covered by Article 28. India is not secular in the sense that the United States is, because there is no clearly defined separation between church and state.

Part 4 of the Constitution deals with economic, social, and cultural rights and prescribes several norms, principles, and policies to be followed by the state. Most of the articles in this section of the Constitution pay homage to the doctrine of human rights. As has been pointed out in a judgment of the Supreme Court:

> The Fundamental Rights and the Directive Principles constitute the "conscience" of our Constitution. The purpose of the Fundamental Rights is to create an egalitarian society, to free all citizens from coercion or restriction by society and to

make liberty available for all. The purpose of the Directive Principles is to fix certain social and economic goals for immediate attainment by bringing about a nonviolent social revolution.

In what has come to be known as the Asiad workers' case, poor working conditions in Delhi were exposed—thanks to the alertness of organizations engaged in the cause of human rights—and the Supreme Court handed down a series of directives to employers. After the Bhopal tragedy, pollution has also attracted the attention of social action groups and the courts.

Also, the Equal Rights Act states that men and women shall receive equal pay for equal work. It contains a provision requiring the state to direct its policy toward securing, for both male and female citizens, the right to an adequate means of livelihood; however, since India is not very affluent, this had proved difficult. Primary education in India is free and compulsory, but higher education still is not within the reach of all sections of the community.

Article 50 of the Constitution commands that the state shall take steps to separate the judiciary branch from the executive; this separation is an aspect of the principal of the rule of law, and fortunately, it has been practically complete.

All of this has been possible due to an alert judiciary and to socially active groups. Public interest litigation has come to stay in India. But surprisingly, no political party there is taking an active interest in ensuring human rights. They pay lip service to the cause of human rights, but the nature of their activities completely eclipses their concern for human rights in whatever little measure it might exist. Laws have been passed. The judiciary is doing its duty. But there is no satisfactory machinery to implement the laws. Nor is there any agency to monitor the progress toward achieving the goal of human rights.

In 1976 a new section, "Fundamental Duties," was inserted into the Constitution. These include the duty "to develop the scientific temper, humanism, and the spirit of inquiry and reform." But these duties have not been translated into statutory obligations, and, in the absence of law, they will remain ineffective.

Surely India is not a paradise of human rights. But it is an experiment being sustained by groups interested in human rights and a judiciary that is sufficiently responsive to the need of upholding such rights. It may serve as an example to those Western nations that make the doubletalk distinction between a totalitarian state and a friendly authoritarian state. As far as human rights are concerned there is no distinction between totalitarian and authoritarian states. It may be a requirement of the *real politik* to be friendly with "authoritarian" regimes. But let it not be said that such foreign policies are dictated by the concern for human rights.

Forty-eight years ago, Franklin Delano Roosevelt propounded four freedoms as necessary for peace abroad and contentment at home: Freedom of speech and expression, freedom of religion, freedom from fear, and freedom from want. In India, the first two are prevalent in sufficient measure. Freedom from fear, too, has more or less been attained in India, though the laws of preventive detention are often abused and, to our lasting shame, many deaths result from encounters with police.

Freedom from want, however, is a distant dream, despite the *Garibi Hatao* ("Banish Poverty") slogans. No sustained programs for the elimination of poverty have been successfully launched, and the size of the population in India remains a great impediment.

One must admire India for not succumbing to the temptation of becoming a religious state despite the overwhelming number of Hindus. A religious state is by its very nature is antihumanist. Many countries make the distinction between a theological state that is useful to further their foreign interests and a theological state that has taken a hostile attitude toward the Western world. Iran and Pakistan have recieved many inconsistent assessments at the hands of Western political and social analysts. Attempts are now being made to establish an Islamic state in Bangladesh, which, until recently, was a good experiment in secularism. I cannot do better than to quote M. H. Beg, a former Chief Justice of India, from a recent article in the *Times of India:*

> Human rights imply justice, equality, and freedom from arbitrary and discriminatory treatment. These cannot be subordinated to the interests of the rulers in the name of Islam. No one can be subjected to coercion for holding particular religious beliefs. The doctrine of national sovereignty cannot justify violations of human rights.

Nineteen-hundred and eighty-eight was the third centennial of the Bill of Rights that followed the Bloodless Revolution in England. It is apt, therefore, that we rededicate ourselves to the maintenance of human rights. Indeed, at that time there was no such concept as human rights. We now realize that human rights are an aspect of humanism. Humanism is not possible without the maintenance of human rights.

Human rights are not acquired, nor can they be transferred, disposed of, or extinguished by any act or event, because they are universally inherent in all human beings. The primary duties in connection with human rights fall upon the states and their public authorities. Because of these two distinctions, says the writer and human-rights activist Paul Sieghart, three consequences follow. The first is nondiscrimination between individuals belonging to different groups; the second is the rule of law whereby people are governed by law and not by other people; and the third is that there are remedies available for the violation of human rights. According to these three criteria, India has come a long way toward the realization of human rights. But we still have a long way to go before we have done all that is possible.

# The Separation of Church and State in Western European Countries

## Oldrich Andrysek
### (Netherlands)

The position of nonbelievers varies greatly from country to country. One of the goals set by the Council of Europe when it was established some thirty years ago was the building of Europe by means of "equality of opportunity, justice, the realization of human rights and social progress combined with maximum personal liberty."

Each of the council's twenty-two member states has highly developed industry, a correspondingly high standard of living, and deeply rooted pluralistic democratic traditions committed to the rule of law.[1] Each also boasts a highly developed human-rights protection system set up under the European Convention on Human Rights (also known as the 1950 Treaty of Rome).

The conventions that entered into force in 1953 instituted an unprecedented international guarantee for basic rights and freedoms, and covered most of the civil and political rights enshrined in the United Nations Universal Declaration of Human Rights of 1948.

While very similiar, no two Western European countries are identical in their treatment of religious issues and church-state relations. In many cases the situation differs widely even within a country, with different laws applying to the various regions under the state's jurisdiction.

Even a brief inspection of the situation shows that wide approaches to the question exist. Next to the established (state) churches of England, Scotland, and most Scandinavian countries, we may observe the implementation of Concordats with the Holy See (as in Italy and the Federal Republic of Germany) or countries that have separate church-state issues by law (the Netherlands and France). The states that adhere to the separation principle are in the minority, and alarmingly, the principle has recently come under constant attack and is being openly and covertly eroded (as we see in France, for instance).

Naturally, international law reflects national legal systems and permits such arrangements and subsequent diversity. Unfortunately the conclusions that we can draw from the situation in Western Europe are far from comforting.

In the struggle for true recognition of their rights, humanists must take the only way open to them and claim what is rightfully theirs by invoking laws that to a greater or lesser degree protect their freedom of—or from—religion. Naturally this can be confusing, as a humanist is a rational being who does not believe in or worship a god. The Latin word *religio,* which means "fear of and reverence for the gods," says it all. I believe that matters of such importance should be clarified, and that one of the decisive traits of humanists is that they are not religious.

Existing national and international legislation protects active forms of freedom of religion; that is, the right to worship, observe, practice, manifest, profess, or change one's religion. Needless to say, such wording offers great doubts as to the effectiveness of protection afforded to individuals who do not adhere to any given religion.

In their legislative and administrative practices, many states clearly or tacitly presuppose that everyone within their jurisdiction is religious. This is proved by the wording of the relevant legal and administrative provisions and by numerous examples in everyday practice. For example, the case of a man who was convicted of drunk driving in the state of Maryland parallels many situations in Western Europe. His sentence of twenty days in jail was suspended under the condition that he be placed on eighteen months' probation and attend Alcoholics Anonymous meetings during that time. The person involved just happens to be a professed atheist, and AA meetings are loaded with references to God, a "Higher Power," or "A power greater than ourselves."

What are a person's rights in such a case? What about those who do not believe? Are their rights protected by the same provisions of law as those that protect the freedom of religion? Jurisprudence tends to maintain that they are. If an individual has the right to worship, by argument á contrario the same individual has the corresponding right not to worship. Further, the interpretation of various terms—such as thought and conscience—provide us with some leeway in handling the rights of nonbelievers.

I believe, however, that the rights of nonbelievers should be protected in explicit terms and quite unequivocally, as are the rights of believers. I consider that to be the only way that the existing potential for discrimination—not only for nonbelievers, but also for religious people—finally can be done away with.

Further, there exists in Western Europe a high level of complacency with regard to the level of protection of human rights. This is true in political, legal, and administrative spheres, as well as among scholars and jurists. The prevailing opinion is that infringements on nonbeliever rights are so marginal, insignificant, or even nonexistent that there is no need for alarm, let alone changes in law.

In defense of compulsory religious education one often hears the argument that the history, values, morals, and ethics of the state are so closely linked to the Christian way of life that the curriculum must integrate or at least reflect religious teachings in order to raise the youth to have a love for their country.

But in this day and age, with mass movements of people across borders, rapid telecommunications, and weapons of mass destruction, this argument and others like it are so shallow that they just cannot stand up to critical scrutiny.

While the numbers of nonbelievers swell (again linked to the overall progress humankind is experiencing), subtle or open aversion to atheism is growing. In some cases, nonbelievers and humanists are even portrayed by religious groups as presenting a threat to the very moral fiber of the societies in which we live (for instance, regarding the abortion issue, humanists are called antilife or even murderers). Such forces have organizational structures and finances that humanists unfortunately cannot match.

Examples abound of efforts to smuggle religion into our lives, often through ingenious methods. Since the 1950s, every U.S. paper bill bears the words "In God we trust." Do we? In Great Britain, the Royal Post Service added the text "Jesus saves" to every letter that was to be stamped (for a price, of course). Classrooms in Italy are equipped with crosses.

Our societies are being polarized. Tolerance is suffering and civil strife is a real threat (take the appalling situation in Northern Ireland, for instance). Though the number of churchgoers is declining and the number of atheists growing, there are some very disturbing signs as well. For instance, fundamentalism and religion-based movements and sects are on the rise. This is most disturbing and calls for urgent action.

Considering these facts and that nonbelievers face a variety of real problems in areas ranging from intolerance to discrimination, from religious tax laws to blasphemy proceedings, and from family laws to education, action is more than timely.

In a recent case in Sweden, a woman did not want her six-year-old daughter to attend compulsory religious lessons sponsored by the Swedish state church. According to Swedish law such lessons are compulsory and an exemption may be granted only if (1) the parents (in this case the woman involved was a single mother) wish so and (2) "provided that the pupil belongs to a religious community which has obtained the permission of the government to arrange for religious education as a substitute for the school." In other words, the situation is truly pathetic; atheists hardly ever belong to a recognized church that is considered capable of providing religious education.

The case was litigated without success right up to the Ministry of Education, and was finally brought to the attention of the European Commission on Human Rights. In desperation, the mother even refused to send her daughter to school; police threats were used against her, and certain teachers turned against her, saying that she was "ridiculous and disorderly" to deny her daughter Christian instruction. It is noteworthy to remember that all of this and more happened in the presence of a minor entitled to some protection.

The woman's complaint was dismissed by the European Commission on a legal technicality. Sweden has since made a reservation to the part of the convention that guarantees that "education and teaching is in conformity with [the parent's] religious and philosophical convictions." A second child in the family has reached school age since then.

Certain avenues could be followed in order to ensure that rights of nonbelievers would be truly guaranteed. First, human(ist) rights must receive more than the lip service they seem to be getting now.

Assuming that humanists by their very nature are not indifferent to life around them, we must mobilize our own interests in the issue and subsequently make a concerted effort to awaken the public to the dangers lurking in religious meddling into state affairs. Each humanist and each humanist organization have a role to play in this regard according to the situation in the country concerned. Only then can the International Humanist and Ethical Union (IHEU) step in and coordinate such actions. Working in isolation within the narrow constraints of one's country would be very ineffective. Here we should be prepared to take lessons from bodies like the World Council of Churches or even the Vatican.

Humanists need some serious scientific analysis in this field. The IHEU is perfectly suited to coordinate such efforts. I strongly recommend that we embark on a project that would on a systematic, country-by-country basis report on the situation between state and church in all the relevant fields.

## Note

1. The member states of the Council of Europe include Austria, Belgium, Cyprus, Denmark, France, the Federal Republic of Germany, Greece, Iceland, Ireland, Italy, Liechtenstein, Luxembourg, Malta, the Netherlands, Norway, Portugal, San Marino, Spain, Sweden, Switzerland, Turkey, and the United Kingdom.

# Humanism and Artistic Freedom in Mexico

## Mario Mendez-Acosta
### (Mexico)

In January 1988, something happened in Mexico City and in the neighboring town of Puebla that reminded us that the humanist struggle for the maintenance of freedom of artistic expression is far from over in that country.

Mexico is one of the few Catholic countries in which church-state separation has been attained. Since the 1850s there have been laws that establish civil marriage and registration, divorce, the secularization of burial grounds, and the prohibition of real-estate ownership for the churches (before this, the Catholic Church had been the largest landowner in Mexico). The 1917 Constitution extended separation to public education and severely limited the participation of the clergy in politics.

Needless to say, there was much opposition to this from the Catholic church; in 1925, when President Plutarco Elias Calles tried to strictly enforce the new Constitution, the church renewed its battle with secularism. This wrought a long and bitter rural struggle. Peasant Catholic armies—the *cisteros*—fought peasant government armies with great cruelty and hatred. In 1929, the church's hierarchy asked for a truce with the new regime. The state loosened somewhat the anti-Catholic restrictions set up in the constitution, while the church agreed not to stir up any more trouble. Because of this, many of the regulations regarding the separation of church and state have not been strictly enforced for more than sixty years.

So many years of a peaceful status quo have caused Mexican authorities to become complacent. Consequently, great confusion ensued when, unexpectedly, fringe groups of the religious right-wing physically attacked several artistic exhibitions in a number of museums and galleries, demanding the immediate removal and destruction of many pieces that were considered irreverent by the demonstrators.

The protest was far from peaceful; on the contrary, it was very threatening and fearsome, and was organized by one of the most dangerous right-wing groups in Mexico, which also has demonstrated violently against birth control and legal abortion. Its leaders have repeatedly made public death threats against liberals and leftists.

In this case, the aggression against the artists was so vicious and menacing, and the intimidated authorities responded so blandly, that the intellectual class in Mexico organized for the explicit purpose of taking definite actions in defense of the freedom of artistic expression.

The main target of the *Pro-Vida* (Pro-Life) group was an exhibition by the Guatemalan artist Rolando de la Rosa at the Mexico City Museum of Modern Art, the most important gallery of its type in the country.

De la Rosa belongs to a contemporary art school that specializes in a kind of expressionist pop-art. With its plastic work, this group satirizes bitterly the manipulation of the Mexican people by so-called popular idols. Wrestlers, soccer players, pop-singers, and B-grade actors are pictured in sordid atmospheres and are grotesquely caricatured through paintings and sculptures with great visual impact.

De la Rosa's crime was to involve some of the most "sacred" religious images in this parody, mixing them with nonreligious icons that represent many of the most popular show-business and contemporary sports figures of Mexico. For example, in one piece, de la Rosa substituted the apostles' faces in Da Vinci's *Last Supper* with those of famous Mexican movie actors. Jesus had the face of Pedro Infante, a greatly revered Mexican movie star who was killed in a plane crash in 1957. A picture of Our Lady of Guadalupe bore the smiling face of Marilyn Monroe, and an image of the child Jesus was shown wearing little boxer's gloves, shorts, a flashy sequin embroidered silken robe, and a little towel thrown over his back.

Other exhibitions threatened by Pro-Vida included Gustavo Monroy's showy plastic creations that bluntly expressed the repressed sexuality in classic and baroque religious art, and Jesusa Rodriguez's play *Council of Love,* which satirized some proceedings and mannerisms prevalent within the Catholic church.

In the case of de la Rosa's exhibition, faced with the threat of physical violence, museum authorities yielded and agreed to close the hall and dismantle the pieces. However, the federal-education and fine-arts authorities, instead of lending their support to the museum and offering police protection, *fired* the director of the museum.

Naturally this foolish conciliatory measure was as far as they could go, for the Pro-Vida group also demanded the resignation of the Director of Fine Arts and the Secretary of Education.

Faced with this blatant and unpunished attack on the freedom of artistic expression, a large group of intellectuals, writers, journalists, artists, playwrights, and art critics established a National Committee for the Defense of the Freedom of Expression. Its immediate goal was to demand of authorities the strict application of the law for the protection of Mexican artists and thinkers and for the free exhibition of their work. Everyone in Mexico was surprised by the effectiveness of this movement and the enthusiastic response it received from the public. A magnificent artistic festival was organized in a public square in downtown Mexico City, opposite the ancient Palace of the Holy Inquisition. A great number of artists, musicians, actors, comedians, and intellectuals proclaimed with outrageous deeds our right to be irreverent even against the most "sacred" concepts, which throughout the centuries invariably have been used to exploit the poor and ignorant people of Mexico. The media effectively aroused public awareness of what was really jeopardized in this scandal: the freedom of any person to express his or her feelings, particularily through the arts.

A few months later, the Pro-Vida group launched a new campaign; this time its target was the government-sponsored campaign for the prevention of AIDS. The fanatics objected to the use of the word "condom" in nationwide publicity directed toward education about the deadly disease. Of course, they suggested that the only way to eliminate AIDS was to isolate homosexuals and to recommend sexual abstinence for everyone. This action caused a great deal of awe and indignation among the educated sector of the public who weren't quite so sure when Pro-Vida's victim had been a scandalous foreign avant-garde artist. Naturally, health authorities reacted with firm rejection of the group's fanatical demands and the airing of much more information about AIDS.

Mexican society has learned a great deal from this brief awakening of medieval intolerance and barbarism. The Pro-Vida group has been widely ridiculed and the more prudent members of the Catholic church have somewhat dissociated themselves from this right-wing fringe. Special protection of law has been granted to artistic activities, and the authorities have warned against any further acts of violence that may affect the artistic work of any group or individual.

It requires eternal vigilance to keep hard-won freedoms: their enemies are merely dormant, not extinct.

# The Struggle for Abortion Rights in Canada

## Henry Morgentaler
### (Canada)

On January 18, 1988, the Supreme Court of Canada struck down this country's abortion law as being in violation of Section 7 of the Charter of Rights in the Canadian Constitution of 1982, which guarantees "life, liberty, and security of the person." This momentous decision in the case of the *Queen* v. *Morgantaler, Scott, and Smolling* affirmed the dignity and equality of women in this country, breathed new life into the Charter of Rights, and added a new dimension to democracy and liberty in Canada.

To quote Chief Justice Dickson: "Forcing a woman, by threat of criminal sanction, to carry a fetus to term unless she meets certain criteria unrelated to her own priorities and aspirations, is a profound interference with a woman's body and thus an infringement of security of the person."

Madam Justice Bertha Wilson said: "The right to reproduce or not to reproduce is properly perceived as an integral part of modern woman's struggle to assert her dignity and worth as a human being." In her concurrent opinion for the majority, Madam Wilson also stressed the right to freedom of religion and conscience and, in ringing terms, the autonomy and dignity of the individual in a democratic society.

For me, this Supreme Court decision was the culmination of a twenty-year struggle that resulted from my commitment to humanism and my involvement with the humanist movement.

I joined the Humanist Fellowship of Montreal in 1963 and became its president the following year. Humanist philosophy appealed to me not only because it was devoid of dogma, arbitrariness, and supernatural claims, but also because it had a framework of values that seemed relevant to the concerns of contemporary society. The ideals of fulfillment, human dignity, responsibility for ourselves and the community, the seeking of joy and happiness in this life, the brotherhood and sisterhood of people of various origins, and the striving for democracy in relationships and institutions: These and other humanist ideas form the basis of my philosophy of life.

When I became president of the Humanist Fellowship of Montreal I tried to make the organization more active, not only in publicizing humanist philosophy through the media, but also in seeking for issues where we could translate our principles into meaningful action. The first such issue was in the area of education. In Québec, the school system is confessional; that is, only Protestant and Catholic schools are paid for out of general taxation. No public secular schools exist. This system is inefficient, outmoded, and discriminatory against those of other religions and those without religious affiliation. In 1964 I organized the Committee for Neutral Schools, whose objective was to replace the confessional school system with a public secular one, working hand in hand with the francophone Mouvement Laique de Langue Française in Québec, which shared the same objective. We have had limited success in raising the consciousness of the people regarding freedom of religion and conscience, and in slowly transforming the Protestant system into a secular one. So far we have been unable to achieve our objective because of a combination of factors, including the entrenchment of Catholic and Protestant education through the British North America Act of 1867, formerly the Canadian Constitution; the anxieties of the English minority in Québec, which fears for its linguistic rights and views the guarantee of Protestant rights as a safeguard; and the vested interests of the Catholic and Protestant establishments. Within the Charter of the Canadian Constitution we have guarantees for freedom of religion and conscience, which presumably means equality of all persons regardless of their religious affiliation. Under this charter the legal basis for the confessional school system in Ontario was rejected by the Supreme Court. Sadly, Canada does not have separation of church and state spelled out as well or as clearly as does the neighboring United States.

The second big issue we tackled as a humanist group was that of abortion law reform, which has been in the forefront of public opinion for the past twenty years, hotly debated and, to this day, one of the most controversial of public issues, pitting fundamentalists against humanists and religious liberals. It was natural for a humanist group to adopt this issue for many reasons: the defense of women's rights and the empowerment of women to be equal and autonomous members of the community; the elimination of the scourge of illegal clandestine abortion with its toll of death, injury, and suffering; and the realization that "wanted" children given love and affection in their formative years would be more likely to grow up into emotionally healthy individuals and responsible members of the community. The fundamentalists—mainly the official Catholic church and some Protestant churches with arbitrary dogmatic notions—had no concern for the fate or welfare of women or for the healthy development of children.

In 1967 Great Britain passed a liberal abortion law. The medical establishment in Canada wanted that country's law changed to reflect more liberal attitudes and the government responded by establishing a committee of the House of Commons to examine changes to the abortion legislation. At that point, abortion was considered to be a major crime punishable by life imprisonment, and was justified only if the pregnancy endangered the woman's life. The Humanist Fellowship of Montreal prepared a brief to the Health Committee of the House of Commons on the subject. Since I was a physician and interested in this area, I did all of the research on the subject and wrote the brief. Thus, when I presented the brief of the Humanist Fellowship of Montreal, endorsed by the humanist groups of Toronto and Victoria, to the House of Commons Health Committee on October 19, 1967, the humanist movement in Canada was the first public body to advocate *abortion on request*. At that time it was a novel and revolutionary concept in Canada, and it attracted a great deal of media attention. One of the byproducts of this was that the various humanist groups in the country found themselves bound by a common ideology and decided to form a national organization, the Humanist Association of Canada, with groups in Montreal, Toronto, Vancouver, Windsor, and Ottawa. I was its first president.

The attention that our humanist beliefs had received in the media and the continuing debate on the question had a great effect on me that I had not anticipated. Women started coming to my medical office seeking abortions. They could not wait until the law changed; they needed help immediately. Initially I refused these requests, conscious of the many unpleasant consequences that might result from an act of civil disobedience to the law. My moral dilemma became acute. In refusing these women the help I had publicly stated they deserved, I was condemning them to unsafe back-alley procedures and possibly infertility, injury, or death. If, on the other hand, I decided to help them, I was risking my medical license, the security of my family, and possibly a long jail term and financial ruin.

Eventually, after a great deal of soul searching, I decided that it was my duty as a doctor and a humanist to practice what I preached and to help women in need of abortions in order to protect their lives, health, and dignity. I knew I was taking an enormous risk and that criminal prosecution was likely to follow, but I was confident that if I was given a chance to explain my action to a jury of my peers they would understand and acquit me. I started to provide abortions in my medical office in 1968, and was probably the first doctor in North America to use the vacuum suction technique, which is now widely used and recognized as the safest and best method available.

I had established for myself two principles to guide my abortion practice. First, that it should be as safe as possible, which meant the use of modern, safe techniques, and second, that no woman should ever be refused an abortion because of inability to pay. My abortion practice grew at a very fast pace, reflecting the desperate need of women across Canada and the United States. I was receiving referrals from a group of counselors who called themselves Clergymen Counseling on Abortion. They were mostly liberal religious leaders, Baptists, Methodists, Unitarians, and Jews, who tried to alleviate the suffering of women by referring them to reputable doctors for safe abortions. Bob McCoy, a former president of the American Humanist Association, had established a counseling agency in Minnesota together with some Protestant ministers, and was referring cases to me. Others were coming from similar groups in New York and Boston. Faced with the enormous demand, I trained four other doctors to perform abortions with the safe method I had pioneered, and Montreal became, for a while, the safe-abortion mecca for the eastern United States, as far away as Minnesota, as well as for the whole of Canada.

In August 1969 the new Canadian abortion law came into effect. It followed the recommendations of the Canadian Medical Association, which made abortion legal if approved by a committee of three doctors on the grounds that the continuation of the pregnancy was likely to endanger the life or health of the woman. It had to be done in the hospital, not in a doctor's office or clinic. The new law, although a vast improvement, remained seriously deficient. It did not force all hospitals to provide this service, and sixty percent of them did not establish it for reasons of religious affiliation. Thus, it limited access to metropolitan areas that had hospitals with liberal abortion policies, while discriminating against women in rural areas or areas where only Catholic hospitals existed, and it applied varying criteria to the notion of need and to the interpretation of the health clause. The worst aspect of it was that not only were many women denied access to medical abortion, but where they were able to receive it the delays involved rendered the procedure more dangerous. It is now accepted medical knowledge that the sooner an abortion is performed, the better. Every week of delay increases the danger of complications by twenty percent. Canada unfortunately has the distinction of having the second highest incidence of second-trimester abortions in the world (India ranks highest) and a corresponding rate of complications.

At any rate, when the new law was enacted only a few non-Catholic hospitals in the province of Québec started performing abortions; the majority, which were Catholic, did not. Thus my abortion practice was still needed, not only by Canadian but also by American women. My clinic was raided on June 1, 1970, and charges of illegal abortion were laid against me. While preliminary legal skirmishes lasted until October 1973, I was able to continue providing abortion services in my Montreal clinic. In the meantime, New York had liberalized its abortion law in July 1970. In January 1973 the United States Supreme Court, in its famous and historic *Roe* v. *Wade* decision, invalidated all state laws against abortion and ushered in the era of abortion on request during the first six months of pregnancy. Suddenly U.S. abortion laws became much more liberal than those of Canada. Inspired by the Supreme Court decision and confident that the tide was running in our favor, I spoke to a packed hall in Toronto on April 18, 1973, declaring that I had performed five-thousand abortions with an excellent safety record and pointing out the flaws in the Canadian abortion law. I followed up by performing an abortion in my clinic, which was televised by the second-largest national network (CTV), in order to show the Canadian public that clinical abortions are safe, that the stipulation that they must be performed in hospitals is ludicrous, and that Canadian women were suffering needlessly from a restrictive law.

My first trial took place in Montreal before a French Canadian Catholic jury. It lasted four weeks, and I was acquitted, just as I had expected. It was a great victory. I had hoped that it would establish the right of any doctor to provide medical care to any woman seeking an abortion, as the Bourne case had done in 1939 in England. In that celebrated case a British doctor, Dr. Eric Bourne, had performed an abortion on a fourteen-year-old girl who had been raped by soldiers. He was acquitted and his case could henceforth be used by British doctors to point out the distress of women seeking abortions. In fact, almost no doctors were prosecuted for illegal abortion in England even before the law changed in 1967.

However, the Canadian story unfolded quite differently. The government of Québec, which was prosecuting me under its mandate to enforce the federal Canadian Criminal Code, appealed the jury acquittal to the Québec Court of Appeal. The right to appeal a jury verdict of innocence does not exist in the United States or in Britain but it does in Canada. What is worse, the Court of Appeal had the right to cancel the verdict of the jury and to substitute its own. This right had been enacted in 1930 but had never been used before; for the first time in Canadian history, a Court of Appeal overruled a jury by declaring that I was guilty. I was sentenced to eighteen months in prison. The case was appealed to the Supreme Court of Canada, which, on March 26, 1975, approved the verdict by the Québec Court of Appeal by a majority vote of six to three, with the Chief Justice Bora Laskin dissenting. On March 27, 1975, I started to serve my sentence in Montreal Bordeaux jail. The Québec government, trying to break my morale and possibly achieve a jury conviction, proceeded with another trial against me while I was in prison, on similar charges of performing an illegal abortion on another woman. After another three-week trial I was once again acquitted by a French Canadian Catholic jury.

Thus I had been granted two jury acquittals but I was still in prison. This created an uproar among civil libertarians concerned with human rights in Canada and with the unfairness of the judicial system. The former prime minister, John Diefenbaker, introduced a bill that would no longer allow a Court of Appeal to overturn a jury verdict, thus depriving Canadians of the right to be judged by their peers, a right going back to 1215 with Britain's Magna Carta. There was widespread support for this bill, and the government eventually enacted it as the Morgentaler Amendment. No longer can a higher court substitute its own verdict for a jury verdict of "not guilty." All it can do is order a new trial if it finds errors in law. I am therefore the only Canadian in history to have ever been convicted by a higher court and sent to prison despite a jury acquittal. All subsequent Canadian administrations have refused to grant me any compensation for this injustice.

The Québec government arrested most of the doctors I had trained in Montreal and charged them with performing illegal abortions. While their cases awaited the final disposition of my case, Québec women were forced to travel to New York State, as far as Manhattan, to obtain safe, legal abortions.

In January 1976, after I had served ten months of my prison term, the Minister of Justice of Canada annulled the verdict of the Court of Appeal of Québec and ordered a new trial—retrial on the first charge. Not double, but triple jeopardy! On September 18, after a two-week trial, a French Canadian Catholic jury acquitted me for a third time. The Québec government promptly announced that another trial would be held in December of that year. It was that kind in insensitivity to public opinion, represented by three juries, together with corruption and contempt for the people of the province, that brought about the downfall of the Bourassa government in November 1976. The new government of René Leveque promptly announced that the projected trial would not be held and no further prosecutions would be made against doctors providing safe medical abortions. The new attorney general of the province declared that the law was deficient and unenforceable and invited the federal government to change it, an invitation that successive federal administrations have ignored to this day.

Québec opted not to enforce the federal abortion law. As a result, my colleagues and I reopened our clinics. The Community Health Centers, or Centres Locaux de Services Communautaires (CLSC), which provide storefront medicine while emphasizing prevention and public health education, approached me some time later with the request that I train their doctors so that they could provide abortion services in their institutions. Eventually others learned the technique and today, in the province of Québec, access to abortion has become better than in any other province in Canada, available not only in hospitals but in clinics, doctors' offices, CLSCs, and women's health centers. This is a great victory; rights to safe medical abortion are entrenched in the province, with beneficial results for the population.

Why is abortion more readily available in Québec, the most Catholic province of Canada? Québec is no longer a reactionary, backward province dominated by the Catholic hierarchy. While the majority of the people are still nominally Catholic, they do not follow Catholic doctrine on matters of personal sexual morality, and the Catholic church has lost much of its power and prestige. Québec society has become secular, democratic, and more open. The loss of power by the Catholic church has brought about a flowering of creativity in the arts and a broadening of horizons. It is fair to say that nowadays Québec is one of the most progressive of all Canadian provinces.

While the situation in Québec was steadily improving, however, it was deteriorating in the rest of the country. The anti-choice movement, consisting almost entirely of conservative Catholics and fundamentalist Protestants, the same mix as in the United States, concentrated on the weakness of the Canadian legislation by organizing campaigns to take over hospital boards with the purpose of eliminating abortion services. They were surprisingly successful in some provinces. Access to abortion became increasingly difficult as hospital after hospital gave in to pressure tactics. In some cases, like in Saskatchewan and Prince Edward Island, provincial governments worked hand in hand with the anti-choicers to deny abortion services to women. In view of that situation, I decided in 1982 to launch the second phase of my campaign, which was to bring safe medical abortion services to the women of all the other provinces. I had accomplished it for the women of Québec, had had a few years rest from my first campaign, and had finally been able to pay off the legal debts that had remained from my previous battles.

After a long period of preparation I opened an abortion clinic in Winnipeg, Manitoba, on May 1, 1983, and another in Toronto on June 16, 1983. In both cases the clinics were raided and charges of conspiracy to perform abortions were laid against me, my colleagues, and the staff. The Toronto clinic was raided three weeks after its establishment. At the trial, two colleagues and I challenged the validity of the law under which we were being tried. The judge rejected this challenge and the trial proceeded. On November 8, 1984, another jury acquitted us. On December 10, I reopened the Toronto clinic and it is still in operation today.

The government of Ontario again appealed the jury verdict and the Court of Appeal again cancelled the jury decision—but, due to the Morgentaler Amendment, they could no longer send us to jail. They ordered a new trial. We appealed this decision to the Supreme Court of Canada, which heard the case in October 1986. Sixteen months later the historic decision came down invalidating the abortion law.

## The Morality of Abortion

The issue of the morality of abortion provides the best illustration of the profound difference between humanist ethics and traditional religious attitudes. The former are based on concern for individual and collective well-being and are able to incorporate all available modern data and knowledge, whereas the latter are bound by dogma and tradition to sexist, irrational prohibitions against abortion and women's rights, and are completely and callously indifferent to the enormous, avoidable suffering they themselves are inflicting on individuals and on the community.

Most of the debate that has been raging about abortion around the world has surrounded the question of morality. Is it ever moral or responsible for a woman to request and receive an abortion, or is abortion always immoral, sinful, or criminal?

When you listen to the rhetoric of the anti-abortion faction, or read its imprecise terms about the unborn, you get the impression that every abortion kills a child; consequently it cannot be condoned under any circumstances, with the sole exception of where the life of the pregnant woman is endangered by the pregnancy, a condition that is now extremely rare. This position—that abortion is always wrong and that there is a human being in the womb from the moment of conception—is a religious idea mostly propagated by the doctrine of the Roman Catholic church and espoused by many fundamentalist Protestant groups, though not by the majority of Catholics and Protestants.

Let us briefly examine this idea. At the moment of conception the sperm and the ovum unite, creating one cell. To proclaim that this one cell is already a full human being and should be treated as such, is so patently absurd that it is almost difficult to refute. It is as if someone claimed that one brick is already a house and should be treated with the same respect a full house deserves. Even if you have a hundred bricks, or two hundred bricks, it is not yet a house. For it to be a house it needs an internal organization, it needs walls, it needs plumbing, it needs electricity, it needs a functional organization. The same is true for a developing embryo. In order for it to be a human being it needs an internal organization, it needs organs, it especially needs a human brain to be considered fully human. This entity is the result of sexual intercourse, where procreation is often not the goal, and whether it is called a zygote, blastocyst, embryo, or fetus, it does not have all the attributes of a human being and thus cannot properly be considered one.

It may be called a *potential* human being. But remember that every woman has the potential to create twenty-five children in her lifetime. The idea that any woman who gets pregnant as a result of nonprocreative sexual intercourse must continue with her pregnancy does not take into consideration the fact that there is a tremendous discrepancy between the enormous potential of human fertility and the real-life ability of women and couples to provide all that is necessary to bring up children properly. The morality of any act cannot be divorced from the foreseeable consequences of that act. Should a girl of twelve or a woman of forty-five, or any woman for that matter, be forced to continue a pregnancy and be saddled with bringing up a child for eighteen years without any regard for the consequences, without any regard for the expressed will or desire of that woman, or of the couple? The anti-abortion people say yes. Again, this proposition is so absurd that it is almost difficult to refute. Haven't we learned anything by observing events in countries where abortion is illegal, where women are forced to perform home abortions, where they are forced into the hands of quacks, where many die and more are injured for life or lose their fertility? What about the children often abandoned to institutions where they have no father or mother, where they suffer so much emotional deprivation and trauma that many become psychotic, neurotic, or so full of hate and violence that they become juvenile delinquents and criminals who kill, rape, and maim? When a person is treated badly in childhood, that inner violence manifests itself when he or she is grown up.

The pro-choice philosophy maintains that the availability of good medical abortions protects the health and fertility of women and allows children to be born into homes where they will receive love, care, affection, and respect for their uniqueness, so that these children grow up to be joyful, loving, caring, responsible members of the community, able to enter into meaningful relationships with others.

Thus, reproductive freedom—access to legal abortions, to contraception, and, by extension, to sexual education—protects women and couples and is probably the most potent preventive medicine and psychiatry, as well as the most promising preventive of crime, in our society.

## Consequences of Liberalizing Abortion Legislation

Wherever abortion legislation has been liberalized, particularly in countries where abortion is available upon request, the effects on public health and on the well-being of the community have been very positive. The drastic reduction of illegal, incompetent abortions with their disastrous consequences has almost eliminated one of the major hazards to the lives and health of fertile women. There has been a steady decline in complications and mortality due to childbirth, a drop in newborn and infant mortality, an overall decline in premature births, and a drop in the number of births and of unwanted children. It is of utmost interest to examine the consequences and effects of the liberalization of the abortion laws.

Where abortion has become legalized and available and where there is sufficient medical manpower to provide quality medical services in this area, the consequences have all been beneficial not only to individuals but to society in general. In countries where there is a high level of education and where abortions by qualified medical doctors are available without delay, self-induced or illegal abortions by incompetent people who do not have medical knowledge eventually disappear with tremendous benefit to the health of women. Also, the mortality connected with medical, legal abortions decreases to an amazing degree. In Czechoslovakia in 1978, for instance, the mortality rate was 2 per 100,000 cases; in the United States it was .5, or one death per 200,000 abortions, which is extremely low and compares favorably with the mortality rate for most surgical procedures.

Another medical benefit is that the mortality of women in childbirth also decreases in countries where abortion is legal and the medical manpower exists to provide quality service. This is because the high-risk patients like adolescents, older women, and women with diseases often choose not to continue a high-risk pregnancy; consequently, the women who go through childbirth are healthier, better able to withstand its stresses, and more resistant to inflection. Generally, the children born to such women are also healthier, more resistant to infection, and better able to withstand the stresses of childbirth; thus, infant mortality and neonatal mortality rates have decreased consistently in all countries where abortion has become available.

But probably the biggest benefit of legalized abortion and the one with the greatest social impact is that the number of unwanted children is decreasing. Children who are abused, brutalized, or neglected are more likely to become neurotics, psychotics, or criminals. As adults they often do not care about themselves or others, are prone to violence, and are filled with hatred for society and for other people. If the number of such individuals decreases, the welfare of society increases proportionately.

Medical abortions on request and good quality care in this area are a tremendous advance not only toward individual health and the dignity of women, but also toward a more loving, caring, and responsible society, a society where cooperation rather than blind submission to authority will prevail. Indeed, it may be our only hope to survive as a human species and to preserve intelligent life on this planet in view of the enormous destructive power that mankind has accumulated.

The right to legal abortion is a relatively new achievement, only about twenty-five years old in most countries. It is part of the growing movement of women toward emancipation, toward achieving equal status with men, toward being recognized as full, responsible, equal members of society. We are living in an era when women, especially in the western world, are being recognized as equal, where the enormous human potential of womankind is finally being acknowledged and accepted as a valuable reservoir of talent. However, women cannot achieve their full potential unless they have freedom to control their bodies, to control their reprodutive capacity. Unless they have access to safe abortions to correct the vagaries of biological accidents, they cannot pursue careers, they cannot be equal to men, they cannot avail themselves of the various opportunities theoretically open to all members of our species. The emancipation of women is not possible without reproductive freedom.

The full acceptance of women might have enormous consequences of humanizing our species, possibly eliminating war and conflict, and adding a new dimension to the adventure of humankind. Civilization has had many periods of advance and regression, but overall it has seen an almost steady progression toward the recognition of minorities as being human and their acceptance into the overall community. It has happened with peoples of different nationalities and races. It has happened with prisoners of war, who would be treated mercilessly. It has happened quite recently, actually, with children, who were in many societies considered the property of parents and could be treated with brutality and senseless neglect. It was only a few generations ago that we recognized how important it is for society to treat children with respect, care, love, and affection, so that they become caring, loving, affectionate, responsible adults.

Finally, most countries now recognize the rights of women to belong fully to the human species, and have given them freedom from reproductive bondage and allowed them to control their fertility and their own bodies. This is a revolutionary advance of great potential significance to the human species. We are in the middle of this revolution and it is not surprising that many elements of our society are recalcitrant; are obstructing this progress; are acting out of blind obedience to dogma, tradition, and past conditions; and are hankering for the times when women were oppressed and considered useful only for procreation, housework, and the care of children.

The real problems in the world—starvation, misery, poverty, and the potential for global violence and destruction—call for concerted action on the part of governments, institutions, and society at large to effectively control overpopulation. It is imperative to control human fertility and to only have children who can be well taken care of, receiving not only food, shelter, and education, but also the emotional sustenance that comes from a loving home and parents who can provide love, affection, and care.

In order to achieve this, women across the world have to be granted the rights and dignity they deserve as full members of the human community. This would naturally include the right to safe medical abortions on request in an atmosphere of acceptance of specifically female needs and in a spirit of the full equality of women and men in a more human and humane society.

It is often said that it is impossible to stop the success of an idea whose time has come. But good ideas come and go and occasionally they are submerged for many years due to ignorance, tradition, resistance to change, and the vested interests of those frightened by change. Occasionally, good new ideas will gain slow and grudging acceptance. More often, they will be accepted only after a period of struggle and sacrifice by those who are convinced of the justice of their cause. The struggle for reproductive freedom, including the right to safe, medical abortion, could be classified as one of those great ideas whose time has come.

# VI.

# Ethics of the Future

# The Ethics of Humanism

## Paul Kurtz
### (United States)

Humanists have been under sustained attack worldwide by religious conservatives who maintain that we are in a serious state of moral decline. They attribute this to the growth of humanism, which they believe has corrupted the young and undermined the very fabric of society. The underlying cause of our moral degradation, they insist, is that we have departed from religious morality: Only by returning to "traditional values" can we be saved from sin and immorality. They blame humanists for the violence, crime, drugs, pornography, and sexual freedom that they claim are signs of the decline. Humanists surely don't condone crime, violence, or the irresponsible trafficking of drugs or pornography; yet this, the fundamentalists maintain, is humanism.

There is something tragicomic about such indictments, for it should be abundantly clear by now that professed belief in the Bible or Koran is no guarantee of moral virtue. The double standard is all too apparent. Some preach a gospel of love while condemning enemies—foreign and domestic—and insisting upon our being armed to the teeth. Others arouse fear of an impending Armageddon that will destroy the world and pave the way for the rapture of true believers. Unscrupulous faith-healers work unsuspecting crowds, promising miraculous healings.

There has been a revival of neo-fundamentalist religious orthodoxy worldwide. Committed believers are all too willing to slaughter one another in the name of God: Muslims and Christians in Lebanon, Shiites and Sunni in Iraq and Iran, Jews and Muslims in Israel, Catholics and Protestants in Northern Ireland, and Sikhs and Hindus in India. Paradoxically, religious sects often attribute contradictory moral commandments to the will of God. For example, orthodox Jews and Christians extol monogamy; Muslims, quoting the Koran, find polygamy morally exemplary.

Many conservative theists hold that morality requires religious foundations and that one cannot be a responsible person unless one accepts theistic religion as a guide to life. The question that is often raised is this: Can one be a good citizen, raise loving children, contribute to society, find life meaningful, and be aware of one's moral duties, yet not believe in a deity or follow conventional religious observances?

## The Trees of Knowledge and Life

There are at least two approaches to morality in our society. The first, religious morality, attempts to deduce moral rules from God's commandments as found in the Bible, the Book of Mormon, the Koran, or the sayings of Mary Baker Eddy or the Reverend Moon. Here the chief duty is obedience to commandments that are usually taken as absolutes. Religious piety precedes moral conscience.

In the Old Testament, Jehovah forbids Adam and Eve to eat the fruit of the Tree of Knowledge of Good and Evil. They disobey him and are expelled from the Garden of Eden. Jehovah expresses his displeasure and his fear that they might next be tempted to eat the forbidden fruit of another tree in the garden, the Tree of Life.

There is a second historic tradition, however, whose primary imperative is to base ethical choices precisely on eating the forbidden fruit of the Tree of Knowledge of Good and Evil and the Tree of Life. This tradition begins with the philosophers of Greece and Rome—Socrates, Aristotle, Hypatia, Epicurus, and Epictetus—and the Chinese sage Confucius. It was expressed during the Renaissance by Erasmus, Spinoza, and others, and many philosophers, such as Immanuel Kant and John Stuart Mill, seek to develop ethics based on rational foundations. Even the founders of the American republic—James Madison, Thomas Jefferson, Tom Paine—were deists and humanists, showing confidence in the power of reason to ameliorate the human condition. Robert Ingersoll, John Dewey, Bertrand Russell, A. H. Maslow, Margaret Sanger, Carl Sagan, Sidney Hook, Isaac Asimov, and others express humanist values.

This deep cultural stream of civilization runs side by side with Judaic-Christian-Muslim tradition. It cannot be dismissed or labeled "immoral," though its critics would like for it to be. The ethics of humanism is an authentic approach to moral principles and ethical values, and, far from corrupting men and women, it has contributed immeasurably to human culture. It is a great disservice to our democratic society that secular humanism has been unfairly attacked as lacking ethics. On the contrary, if it is anything, humanism is the expression of an authentic ethical philosophy—one that is especially relevant to the present world.

## The Common Moral Decencies

The question is constantly asked: How can one be moral and not believe in God? What are the foundations on which the ethics of humanism rest? Let me outline some of the main features of the ethics of humanism.

First, there is a set of what I call the "common moral decencies," which are shared by both theists and nontheists alike and are the bedrock of moral conduct. Indeed, they are transcultural in their range and have their roots in common human needs. They grow out of the evolutionary struggle for survival and may even have some sociobiological basis, though they may be lacking in some individuals or societies since their emergence depends upon certain preconditions of moral and social development.

Nevertheless, the common moral decencies are so basic to the survival of any human community that meaningful coexistence cannot occur if they are consistently flouted. They are handed down through the generations and are recognized throughout the world by friends and lovers, colleagues and coworkers, strangers and aliens alike as basic rules of social intercourse. They are the foundation of moral education and should be taught in the schools. They express the elementary virtues of courtesy, politeness, and empathy so essential for living together; indeed, they are the very basis of civilized life itself.

First are the decencies that involve personal *integrity: telling the truth,* not lying or being deceitful; being *sincere,* candid, frank, and free of hypocrisy; *keeping one's promises,* honoring pledges, living up to agreements; being *honest,* avoiding fraud or skulduggery.

Second is *trustworthiness.* We should be *loyal* to our lovers, friends, relatives, and coworkers, and we should be *dependable,* reliable, and responsible.

Third are the decencies of *benevolence,* which involve manifesting *good will* and noble intentions toward other human beings and having a positive concern for them. It means the *lack of malice* (nonmalfeasance), avoiding doing harm to other persons or their property: We should not kill or rob, inflict physical violence or injury, or be cruel, abusive, or vengeful. In the sexual domain it means that we should not force our sexual passions on others and should seek *mutual consent* between adults. It means that we have an obligation to be *beneficent;* that is, kind, sympathetic, compassionate. We should lend a helping hand to those in distress and try to decrease their pain and suffering and contribute positively to their welfare. Jesus perhaps best exemplifies the principles of benevolence.

Fourth is the principle of *fairness.* We should show *gratitude* and appreciation for those who are deserving of it. A civilized community will hold people *accountable* for their deeds, insisting that those who wrong others do not go completely unpunished and perhaps must make reparations to the aggrieved; thus, this also involves the principle of *justice* and equality in society. *Tolerance* is also a basic moral decency: We should allow other individuals the right to their beliefs, values, and styles of life, even though they may differ from our own. We may not agree with them, but all individuals are entitled to their convictions as long as they do not harm others or prevent them from exercising their rights. We should try to *cooperate* with others, seeking to negotiate differences peacefully without resorting to hatred or violence.

These common moral decencies express prima facie general principles and rules. Though individuals or nations may deviate from practicing them, they nonetheless provide general parameters by which to guide our conduct. They are not absolute and may conflict; we may have to establish priorities between them. They need not be divinely ordained to have moral force, but are tested by their consequences in practice. Morally developed human beings accept these principles and attempt to live by them because they understand that some personal moral sacrifices may be necessary to avoid conflict in living and working together. Practical moral wisdom thus recognizes the obligatory nature of responsible conduct.

In the Old Testament Abraham's faith is tested when God commands him to sacrifice his only son, Isaac, whom he dearly loves. Abraham is fully prepared to obey, but at the last moment God stays his hand. Is it wrong for a father to kill his son? A developed moral conscience understands that it is. But is it wrong simply because Jehovah declares it to be wrong? No. I submit that there is an autonomous moral conscience that develops in human experience, grows out of our nature as social beings, and comprehends that murder is wrong, whether or not God declares it to be wrong. We should be highly suspicious of the moral development of one who believes that murder is wrong *only* because God says so. Indeed, I believe that we attributed this moral decree to God simply because we apprehended it to be wrong.

Today a great debate rages over whether moral education should be taught in the schools; many are violently opposed to it. But we do have a treasure of moral wisdom that we should seek to impart to the young, and all too often this is not actively taught in the home. We need to cultivate moral intelligence, a capacity for rational thinking about our values. This is where the debate intensifies because some of the critics of humanism are opposed to any reflective questioning of values.

## Ethical Excellences

The common moral decencies refer to how we relate to others. But there are a number of values that we should strive toward in our personal lives, and I submit that we also need to impart to the young an appreciation for what I call the *ethical excellences*. I believe that there are standards of ethical development, exquisite qualities of high merit and achievement. Indeed, in some individuals nobility shines through; there are, according to the Greek philosopher Aristotle, certain virtues or excellences that morally developed people exemplify. These states of character are based upon the golden mean and provide some balance in life. I think that these classical excellences or virtues need to be updated for the present age. What are they?

First, the excellence of *autonomy,* or what Ralph Waldo Emerson called self-reliance. By that I mean our ability to take control of our own lives; to accept responsibility for our own feelings, our interpersonal relationships and our careers, how we live and learn, the values and goods we cherish. Such people are self-directed and self-governing. Their autonomy is an affirmation of their freedom. Unfortunately, some people find freedom a burden and thus are willing to forfeit their right to self-determination to others—to parents, spouses, or even totalitarian despots or authoritarian gurus. A free person recognizes that he or she has only one life to live and that how it will be lived is ultimately his or her choice. This does not deny that we live with others and share values and ideals, but basic to the ethics of democracy is an appreciation for the autonomy of individual choice.

Second, *intelligence* and reason are high on the scale of values. To achieve the good life we need to develop our cognitive skills; not merely technical expertise or skilled virtuosity, but good judgment about how to make wiser choices. Unfortunately, many critics of humanism demean human intelligence and believe that we cannot solve our problems. They are willing to abdicate their rational autonomy to others. Reason may not succeed in solving all problems—sometimes we must choose the lesser of many evils—but it is the most reliable method we have for making moral choices.

Third is the need for *self-discipline* in regard to one's passions and desires. We must satisfy our desires, passions, and needs in moderation, under the guidance of rational choice, recognizing the harmful consequences that imprudent choices can have upon ourselves and others.

Fourth, some *self-respect* is vital to psychological balance. Self-hatred can destroy the personality. We need to develop some appreciation for who we are as individuals and a realistic sense of our own identities, for a lack of self-esteem can make one feel truly worthless, which is neither healthy for the individual nor helpful to society at large.

Fifth, and high on the scale of values, is *creativity.* This is closely related to autonomy and self-respect, for independent persons have some confidence in their own powers and are willing to express their unique talents. The uncreative person is usually a conformist, unwilling to break new ground, timid and fearful of new departures. A creative person is willing to be innovative and has a zest for life that involves adventure and discovery.

Sixth, we need to develop *high motivation,* a willingness to enter into life and undertake new plans and projects. A motivated person finds life interesting and exciting. One problem for many people is that they find life and their jobs boring. Unfortunately, they are merely masking their lack of intensity and of commitment to high aspirations and values.

Seventh, we should adopt an *affirmative* and positive attitude toward life. We need some measure of optimism that what we do will matter. Although we may suffer failures and defeats, we must believe that we shall overcome and succeed despite adversity.

Eighth, an affirmative person is capable of some *joi de vivre,* or joyful living, an appreciation for the full range of human pleasures—from the so-called bodily pleasures such as food and sex to the most ennobling and creative of aesthetic, spiritual, intellectual, and moral pleasures.

Ninth, if we wish to live well then of course we should be rationally concerned about our *health* as a precondition of everything else. To maintain good health we should avoid smoking and drugs, drink only in moderation, seek to reduce stress in our lives, and strive to get proper nutrition, adequate exercise, and sufficient rest.

All of these excellences clearly point to a *summa bonum*. The intrinsic value humanists seek to achieve is *eudaemonia:* happiness or well-being. I prefer the word *exuberance* or *excelsior* to describe such a state of living, because I believe it is an active, not a passive, process. I believe that the end or goal of life is to live fully and creatively, sharing with others the many opportunities for joyful experience. The meaning of life is not to be discovered only after death in some hidden, mysterious realm; on the contrary, it can be found by eating the succulent fruit of the Tree of Life and by living in the here and now as fully and creatively as we can.

Yet the humanist is condemned for focusing on happiness as a goal. For some salvational theologies this life has no meaning—it is only a preparation for the next. But this is an escapist theory for those who are unable to find significance in their personal lives and seek to be released in the next. Even if immortality exists, that is no reason to denigrate life in the here and now. The important point that is often forgotten is that whether we find life meaningful depends in large part on what we give to it. Life presents us with opportunities and possibilities, and whether or not we tap these depends on our capacity for autonomy and creative affirmation.

There are those who maintain that the ethics of humanism, since it focuses on joyful, creative living, is corrupting and demeaning and may lead to libertarian licentiousness and hedonism in which "anything goes." For them, morality is repression, the body is despised, sexual expression for reasons other than procreation is sinful, and the world is a tragic vale of tears. They believe that they are incapable of solving their own problems or obtaining happiness on earth by their own efforts, and create the myth of solace to help them escape from the trials and tribulations of mortal injustice. They are laden with guilt and a sense of sin and try to assuage this by preferring comfort to truth.

This point of view is extremely pessimistic (and, I might add, contrary to the spirit of American optimism), for it demeans and denigrates our intelligence and our capacity for high achievement. In its excessive form it is profoundly anti-human, even pathological. It masks a deep fear of one's own capacities to live autonomously, and it expresses a lack of self-respect and even shows self-hatred.

## The Need for Creative Ethical Thinking

Thus far I have focused on two areas of ethics: (1) the common moral decencies, and (2) the ethics of personal excellence. The ethics of humanism is anything but self-centered or egoistic; it involves a deep appreciation for the needs of other human beings, as well as a recognition that no person is an island and that among our highest joys are those we share with others. Indeed, the common moral decencies point to the need to develop the excellences of integrity, truthfulness, beneficence, and fairness—and these excellences directly concern our relationships with others. The ethics of humanism prizes strength of character. I believe that most members of our society can accept the principles and values I have enumerated and that we do share more common ground than is usually appreciated. But we live in a period of rapid technological and social change in which we are constantly confronted by new ambiguities and new problems. The quest for absolute certainty is impossible to satisfy. We cannot simply draw upon the moral wisdom of past generations; we must be prepared for some revision of our traditional moral outlook. We need to adapt to the new challenges that confront us and develop new principles and values appropriate to the twenty-first century and beyond. The age-old morality contains many tested principles, but much of it—particularly our religious morality—was developed by early nomadic agricultural societies. It is difficult to apply these ancient moral codes to the highly technical post-industrial society in which we now live. How, for example, shall we deal with the problems of medical ethics engendered by new technologies that can keep people alive far beyond the time when there is some significant quality of life? How shall we deal with organ transplants, given the widespread need and limited supply? How will society be able to support the growing number of nonworking elderly? These issues pose new moral dilemmas with which a classical biblical religion, for example, is unable to cope. These situations simply did not exist for previous generations; this is the age of space travel, the computer-information revolution, biogenetic engineering. Dramatic new scientific and technological breakthroughs provide enormous opportunities for human betterment, but they also raise moral dilemmas concerning possible dangers and abuses.

We cannot cope by retreating to the absolutes of the past; fresh thinking in the future is essential. Critical intelligence is the most reliable tool we have— it is not perfect, but nothing is when dealing with moral dilemmas.

This position is often attacked by those who do not understand the nature of moral deliberation. They condemn it as "situation ethics"—but the point of situational reasoning is that we often encounter new contexts in human experience unlike anything that has been faced in the past, and we need to bring to bear creative inquiry to deal with them. If there is any excellence that society should develop it is the need for pooled ethical wisdom and social intelligence. Instead of resorting to shrill denunciations, we should be willing to engage in cooperative rational dialogue and develop, where needed, new values and principles appropriate to the emerging world. This is also the primary quality of mind we should seek to impart to our children: to think not only about facts, but about moral principles and values as well.

There are many moral philosophers today who are engaged in creative ethical thinking, and they have come up with new moral guidelines. In the field of medical ethics, for instance, the principle of informed consent is a basic general moral principle that is applicable to health care; that is, patients have rights and their consent is required concerning the nature and extent of their treatment.

## Privacy

This brings me to another point, which is particularly relevant to those who cherish an open pluralistic and democratic society. It regards the importance of the principle of privacy in ethics. That is, a free society should grant adult individuals some autonomy and responsibility for their own lives, especially in regard to those areas that concern intimate beliefs and values. Society should not unduly interfere with the free exercise of these rights.

I will not here develop the full implications of the privacy principle—euthanasia, the right to confidentiality, abortion, responsible sexual freedom, and so on. These issues are at the center of intensive national debates in our society, as revealed during the mudslinging 1988 presidential campaign; in the battle over Judge Robert Bork's nomination to the Supreme Court; in the mushrooming of the anti-abortion movement called Operation Rescue; in skirmishes regarding censorship, creation vs. evolution, and school prayer; and in other hot political issues of the past and coming decades. I believe we should defend the right to privacy as a fundamental human and civil right.

## Responsibilities to the World Community

There is also an urgent need today to expand the horizons of our ethical concerns from our parochial national societies to the world community. Each of us as an individual has obligations and responsibilities to ourselves, to our immediate family and friends, to our coworkers and colleagues, to the community in which we live, and to our nation as a whole—but I would also add that we have a responsibility to the broader community of humankind. Heretofore, the moral systems of the past have been rather chauvinistic, focused on preserving our own race, ethnic group, religion, or nation over others. We need to break out of that narrow focus, for it is abundantly clear that we are now living in an *interdependent* world, and that what happens in one part often reverberates in every other part.

National governments can no longer cope with economic problems in haughty isolation—unemployment, fluctuations in currency rates, and equitable trade and commerce are problems of the worldwide economic system. Multinational corporations have discovered that the entire world is their market. The depletion of natural resources and the despoilation of the environment are problems that need to be addressed on a global scale: The hunting of whales or the damage to the ozone layer is a problem that transcends the self-interest of any particular nation and is a concern to the entire world community. What this means is that we need to develop a new *global ethics* in which each of us fully recognizes our responsibility to every other member of the human species. The classical religions, in the best sense, have recognized the brotherhood of human beings. Our ethical concern today and in the future must be truly planetary. Civilization is international in scope and philosophy and the arts and sciences cannot be limited by narrow political or ideological barriers. We need to develop a new ethical awareness that transcends the divisiveness and intolerance of the arbitrary barriers of the past. Intercommunication, travel, the free exchange of ideas, and the intermingling of peoples will no doubt accelerate in the future. We want a democratic world in which individual human freedoms and rights are everywhere respected. But given intense nationalistic opposition, it will be no easy task to extend the ethics of humanism to a planetary scale. The ethical imperatives implicit in this task should, however, be apparent to all who are concerned with preserving and enhancing the human species on this planet, not only for our time but for future generations.

# Humanism as a Life-Stance

## Harry Stopes-Roe
### (Great Britain)

The ethics of the future should be something we can all share, with well-founded confidence. But there are problems: What will give our ethics a good foundation? How can we be confident? How can we *share* the ethics, the foundations, and the confidence? In short, then: How can we have a global ethics?

What are the responsibilities of Humanists toward the ethics of the future? Basic to Humanism is the recognition that one of the essential features of humankind is ethical sense; that is, the recognition that there is a curious sort of pressure to do some things and not others, and the recognition that this pressure is important, in some objective sense as well as personally. But what does this mean? Philosophers have been asking this question for two millennia; but its significance has been resisted until the past hundred years or so. Now, however, the public at large realizes that it has no effective answers. There are many contradictory claims, and no security. As a result, the world is a society in moral confusion; and so are the societies to which we each belong—I think this is true of most of us.

This moral confusion is extremely damaging, because the quality of life in a society depends on the values that prevail in it. The society will be worth living in only if the values that prevail are such that individuals develop all that is best in their potential, and actually find worthwhile fulfillment. If human beings are to develop their potential, then their environment and particularly their upbringing must be such that their human spirit is encouraged to grow. As uncertainty eats into the moral values of a society, the processes that support growth, development, and enjoyment decay, and the quality of life suffers. Humanists recognize this, and hence join in the widespread aspiration for a new global ethics—"new" at least in its recognition as the global ethics. (The ethics itself can hardly be truly new.)

Our forebears in the Humanist tradition were powerfully concerned with these problems. Of these, the ethical movement is the most important, for it has been particularly concerned with developing and maintaining the moral quality of individuals and of society. Holyoake's secularism was quickly overlaid by Bradlaugh's ideas; and these, along with freethought, rationalism, atheism, and agnosticism, have been more concerned with freeing us from improper constraints—an essential precondition, but no more—rather than the foundations and the building of a new ethics. Unfortunately, however, the ethical movement was founded on inadequate philosophy and over-hopeful psychology. We must now move forward, and build on better foundations.

It is of the nature of ethics that any understanding of it must be founded on a set of claims about reality—claims both about how things are and about what is important. One cannot get ethics a priori: a substantial ethics must refer to something. And one cannot simply say "Ethics has been devised by human beings," for there are genuine constraints.

Further, it is of the nature of human psychology that no amount of evidence will lead everyone to accept any one set of assumptions on these matters. Human beings are not so motivated by reason. Thus if we are to be realistic, our ideal must be an open society, and we must allow that there will be a powerful God-religious presence well into the twenty-first century and beyond. But this is not the end of all ideas of a global ethics.

Let us take up the philosophical issues first. Ethics is not just casual good will; good will requires direction. How is this determined? When an agent must consider which action to perform among various alternatives, the rightness or wrongness of each depends on the prevailing facts of the case, which determine what would actually happen following each alternative. But all of that is only background: which of these alternative outcomes *ought* to happen? This is a matter of value, not of fact, and must be assessed by moral criteria.

For example, suppose that you are a doctor whose terminally ill patient is suffering grossly, and the actual circumstances are such that many Humanists would say that voluntary euthanasia is morally right. What are the values that should be considered? We should consider the patient's suffering as well as the benefits and drawbacks to those who care for the patient. Further, we should consider the social and the individual benefits and drawbacks involved in the alternative social rules that might prevail. These would either allow doctors to act so that death is hastened in appropriate cases, or require doctors to act so that the patient continues to suffer. (These are, logically, the only options.) All of these benefits and sufferings are clear, and each is known to the individual who benefits or suffers. A Humanist would say that these are the *only* values involved. But other people might say that there are other values: that the life of the patient has a value that transcends all the values that inhere in the natural world. Some people say, "God loves all his creatures"; "Suffering in this life gives value in the afterlife"; "Life is sacred." If these are true, then euthanasia, however "voluntary," might be a moral wrong, because moral value might lie in these other, transcendent evaluations, which might cancel the drawbacks of continued suffering.

What is in dispute here is the identity and nature of what is ultimately important in the universe, or at least in our part of it. Is it the natural suffering of the patient, or the superpurposive love of God? What is ultimately important?

This brings me to my first major point: *Any understanding of ethics must make substantial and controversial assumptions.*

I chose my example to introduce this point. More particularly, the example introduces a particular assumption that is critical in any fundamental discussion of ethics, and more broadly, of life-stances: namely, that the universe is naturalistic, or superpurposive, as the case may be. People make different assumptions on this matter.

I use the word "superpurposive" rather than the more common "supernatural" because the latter has unfortunate associations. *The universe is SUPERPURPOSIVE if there is purpose or design that does not belong to a material body, or value that is not an evaluation belonging to a material body. The universe is NATURALISTIC if there is nothing like that.*

God is the most interesting example of something superpurposive, if he is real. So one of the things that one is saying when one says that the universe is naturalistic is that there is no God, nor any power or purpose like him. The Judeo-Christian idea of God is superpurposive because, first, he is supposed to have had a purpose in creating the universe, and in particular he has a purpose for human beings; and, second, he is not limited by anything material, even the universe—quite the other way round!

The fundamental difference between Humanism and Christianity lies in what each finds to be ultimately important: Humanism looks to the joys and sorrows of sentient beings, and the moral sensibility in human nature; Christianty finds God in Christ, and his love, to be ultimately important. These two life-stances make these contradictory value claims, and from these follow their respective ethics. But note that Humanism cannot be founded merely on the claim that "Happiness is ultimately important": Mill recognized this in his attempt to develop ultilitarianism. The point is that Humanism looks to human nature, not "God," to find the constraints on "happiness"; human nature (we say) is the key to understanding the heart of life.

Thus any understanding of ethics has implicit within it fundamental assumptions on matters both of fact and of value. These implicit assumptions also constitute the principles of the life-stance that underlies the ethics.

People's assumptions, of course, are not always explicit; they are implicit in the way one makes moral judgments. And though the moral rightness of an action depends on the nature of what is ultimately important, it does not necessarily follow that every decision in life that is of moral significance is determined exactly. But the example of voluntary euthanasia shows that one cannot arrive at a sufficient understanding of morality without reaching an implicit decision on the reality of superpurposive powers.

The decision whether or not there are "superpurposes" goes beyond what can properly be called science, and so do certain of the other decisions basic to ethics and life-stances. Though these assumptions are subject to evidence and argument, they are and will remain resistant to definitive answers. They may reasonably be called metaphysical, while importing nothing derogatory by this.

Humanism uses many scientific conclusions, but this neither gives science the status of Humanism, nor Humanism the status of science. This is the answer to Judge Hinds and the fundamentalist attack on evolution in U.S. schools. It has nothing to do with whether Humanism is or is not called a religion. A life-stance is not the same as a science, or a philosophy; it is more than both.[1]

My second major point, or rather pair of points, sums all of this up: *A LIFE-STANCE is the expression of an individual's or a community's relationship with that which is of ultimate importance; the concept includes the presuppositions and commitments of this, and the consequences for life that flow from it. Those aspects of a life-stance that are particularly concerned with the guidance of behavior are called ethics.*

*Humanism is a life-stance.* We are perverse if we claim some sort of neutrality for Humanism, as against other naturalistic or god-religious life-stances. Certainly, Humanism has its distinctive beliefs, which give it direction and motivation.

I now turn to the psychological naivety of the ethical movement: It overrated the power of reason in human beings. Even if the balance of evidence on the above matters were to shift very heavily one way or the other, very many people would continue in their respective traditions well into the foreseeable future. More particularly, it seems that many people have an emotional need for the support of superpurposive powers.

What, then, is the role of Humanism? We have seen that it cannot be to demonstrate the independence or "autonomy" of ethics, in any significant sense. The ethical movement was right, certainly, to say that ethics does not require god-religious foundations; but it does require foundations in a life-stance. These give it direction, and it does matter what this direction is.

*The role of Humanism is to be that life-stance, which is the foundation to ethics.* We claim no *authority* for our position: we simply present reasons why Humanism is close to the heart of life. Further, our aspiration is only that Humanism is *close* to the heart of life; it is the best life-stance available. And we act on these commitments.

At various times in the past people have supposed that the true foundation of ethics was one god-religion or another. Now we make a similar claim, in a very different way: we claim nothing beyond the reasonings we offer, and we by no means claim that we have everything just right. We are sensitive to evidence and good argument, and adjust our beliefs accordingly; we bear sharply in mind that it is logically possible that we might have to abandon Humanism.

We now come to the practical difficulties: we must cope with two conflicting points, and one overarching fact. First, no one knows which life-stance is closest to life, and no life-stance can aspire to universal acceptance; second, perhaps Humanism actually is the best available! The overarching fact is that all this matters to human happiness and welfare.

Again, there are problems with pluralism: in particular, it can easily induce an acceptance of relativism and a sense of anomie, creating an environment in which the lowest values win. It has been well said that for evil to flourish it is necessary only that good people do nothing. But "good will" is not enough: what does the good woman or man do?

The absence of agreement does not mean that good people are impotent. One basic thing people of good will can do is to work for the open society. This is a reasonable basic aspiration. The open society is one in which there is a prevailing concern for ethical values, even though there is disagreement on what, exactly, they are; the state is neutral with respect to all life-stances (or rather, all that are worthy of respect); and finally (but most important), there is consensus on basic facts and values.

In particular, in the open society all public affairs should accept that one can be a good citizen without any assigned beliefs on the ultimate questions of life. The public provision of education should accord with this. More delicate is the principle that law should be based only on naturalistic value. If this were so, the rules that limit medical practice would permit voluntary euthanasia as well as abortion. Overall, no Western country is very close to the ideal of open society.

The open society is a sound foundation for a good society, and it brings me to my fourth and final claim. *Humanists have a particular responsibility toward the open society: To come together, and to work for the advancement of Humanism.*

There are a number of points here. First, Humanists have a particular responsibility for the open society. There are problems about the open society, for it is a threat to the revelation inherent in all life-stances that are based on superpurposive assumptions, and it is rejected (for contrary reasons) by ideological Marxism and by Buddhism. More particularly, it rejects the Evangelical claim that rebirth in Christ is essential to being a good person. Only Humanism finds it truly congenial, and only Humanism can give it a full-blooded fundamental justification. But on the other hand, the open society is implicit in the Western liberal tradition. (One might say it is pretty much the American ideal.) Thus, though in a fundamental sense the idea is Humanist and we are responsible for it, we are not sectarian when we assume it or seek to advance it.

Beyond that, Humanists have particular responsibilities in the open society. First, though there is no hope of a single, total global ethics, there is much agreement among people of different life-stances, and therefore there is the possibility for shared purpose in many important, ethical values. A more limited global ethics is possible, but this requires effort. Christians have in the past established a reservoir of concern and confidence in these basic values; now the superpurposive life-stances are in decline—because, with their belief in superpurposes, they are not in harmony with what really is ultimately important. The responsibility, therefore, passes to Humanists to maintain the validity and importance of those principles of value that are agreed upon by all mature life-stances. Humanists have in the past been too much inclined to live on the capital Christians have generated, doing little to maintain it. With the decline of

Christianity, we must take over the maintainance of moral sensibility in individuals and in society. But it would be quite improper for us to do as the Christians do: they say this shared morality is "really Christianity"; we must not say it is "really Humanism."

Finally, in an open society it is Humanists who have the responsibility of maintaining the social influence of Humanist values, and the personal availability of the Humanist life-stance. The advancement of Humanism is important because Christianity, ideological Marxism, and even atheistic Buddhism are wrong on many very important moral issues. Voluntary euthanasia is a clear and simple example of a moral issue where the god-religions have a particular tendency to err, though I could have taken contraception (still rejected by Rome) or many other issues.

The world will be a better place if Humanists come together to fulfill their responsibilities: To keep pressing for the open society; to maintain those parts of ethics that can be global; and to secure the influence of Humanism where there is dispute. Thus far a global ethics *is* possible, if Humanists undertake their responsibilities: The open society could give the world both a spirit of unity and a living core of practical unity. And, after all, if Humanism *is* the best life-stance available, it *may* become the focus for the one comprehensive global ethics.

## Note

1. Randall D. Eliason discusses the attack on evolution in *Free Inquiry* 8 (2), Spring 1988, pp. 59–62. I discuss the concept of life-stance in *Free Inquiry* 8 (1), Winter 1987/88, pp. 7–9, 56.

# Ethics and Human Nature

## Tad Clements
### (United States)

## The Nature of Ethics

If ethics is ever to become a respectable scientific discipline, it must be grounded in the realities of human nature, human experience, and the objective external realities that condition human existence. Many biologists, psychologists, and medical people find such a statement quite reasonable, since many of their professional activities implicitly or explicitly assume some such position as this. The vast majority of moral philosophers, however, condemn such a view, insisting that it is fundamentally mistaken. Most insist that it commits various fallacies, among them the so-called naturalistic fallacy of trying to derive *ought* from *is*, of trying to deduce normative, prescriptive statements from descriptive, factual statements. They also accuse anyone who attempts to ground ethical concepts in scientific theories of committing scientism, of worshiping science and mistakenly thinking that it is the only paradigm of reliable knowledge and should be applied even to areas not amenable to scientific treatment. They have even subdivided scientism into categories depending on which science is primarily used to mistakenly attempt the derivation of ethics. Thus, according to these philosophers, one may be guilty of biologizing (à la E. O. Wilson) or psychologizing (à la Abraham Maslow) ethics.

What would these moral philosophers have us do instead? What is their conception of ethics? And how do they seek to establish ethical principles and define ethical conceptions? They insist that ethics must be an autonomous discipline independent of the empirical sciences, which they call irrelevant; we should instead consult either conscience, practical reason, God's will, or the pronouncements of some other absolute authority on the one hand, or certain absolute ideal ends derived from such sources as intuition and common sense on the other. In either case, the resulting ethical system must be deductively internally consistent; that is, it must be a formal, rational system containing truths that are universalizable, more like mathematics than a probabilistic, open-ended, inductive, factual science.

Moral philosophers have carried on their discourses about ethics and meta-ethics with this conception in mind for so long that it seems to most of them almost self-evident that there cannot be any other legitimate way of doing moral philosophy. There is, however, another tradition that has its roots at least as far back as Aristotle, one that is not only possible today but much more justifiable than the approaches they have almost universally accepted. It offers an alternative to the common prejudice among the majority of moral philosophers that is more promising than their a priori assumptiveness and that seeks to create an empirical ethics derived inductively and involving only probable generalizations.

## Human Nature

Nearly everyone would probably concede that in the nonhuman sphere the way to understand the nature of any kind of organism nonassumptively is to examine reliable samples of populations of such organisms to reveal common characteristics and the range of variations within these characteristics. If we wish to proceed nonassumptively, two kinds of investigative modalities are employed—reductive studies that analyze organisms into various kinds of constituent structures, and contextual studies. There seem to be, in principle, no good logical or scientific reasons that such considerations should not be applicable to understanding human nature nonassumptively. Indeed, reductive studies of human beings have already resulted in a large body of reliable knowledge. The sciences involved already have revealed a great deal about the structural and physiological features of human beings, including much about ranges of variability.

Most of the problems associated with understanding human nature contextually—if we ignore for now the obfuscations created by unscientific theologies and philosophies—have resulted from contextual myopia. That is, investigations of human nature have often placed an undue emphasis on certain levels or other features of the contexts conditioning human life. Thus, for instance, some have placed almost all of the emphasis on human social realities. Others have emphasized human life almost totally in terms of geographic and climatic complexes. And still others have treated human nature almost entirely in terms of inherited evolutionary processes. All of these, and other, contexts are important, but if we are to avoid simplistic fallacies we must try not to be like the blind men and the elephant of legend.

Having said this, I'm not sure I can avoid all the pitfalls myself. To avoid promising more than I can deliver, let me say that what I shall suggest is simply that—a *suggested* way by which clues may be discovered as to the kind of beings we are.

If we look at human beings transculturally and transhistorically, an interesting fact emerges. No matter how diverse the individuals and groups examined, certain kinds of activities seem to be nearly universal. Adults almost universally engage in at least rudimentary forms of play, work, sexuality, parenting, art, religion (in some sense of that term), science, morality, philosophy, and politics.

The small minority of individuals who do not engage in one or more of these activities are usually considered unusual or even eccentric, and societies make it possible for all of their members in good standing to engage in such activities to some extent or other. Why should this be the case?

I suggest, as a hypothesis, that if we ask *why* people play, work, become parents, accept and promote moral codes, and so forth, certain plausible satisfactions come to mind that may operate as underlying reasons or causes. It is important in proceeding in this way not to take superficial answers as fundamental ones. To illustrate, let us take the varied activities that may be called "political." If one were to ask why people engage in political activity, one might be tempted to accept the superficial answer "Because they desire power." The reason this is superficial is because it makes perfect sense for someone to then ask, "Why do people desire power?" As long as the "why" question can be asked and reasonably answered, we haven't arrived at the ultimate springs of the behavior. However, when the ultimate satisfactions are revealed we simultaneously have a picture of the underlying needs and desires that may reasonably be taken as characterizing human nature. The underlying fundamental human needs and desires characteristic of human nature appear to fall into three categories: (1) physiological needs, such as food, water, and shelter; (2) psycho-social needs, such as sexual expression, the need to give and receive intimate affection, a sense of belonging, the need to have a sense of self-identity, and the need to feel moral; and (3) aesthetic and intellectual needs, such as science, religion, philosophy, and enjoyment of other forms of beauty.

## The Ethical Theory

From the point of view of any individual organism, human or otherwise, whatever pattern of existence harmoniously satisfies all of the constituent underlying needs and desires characteristic of its nature over the longest period of time possible constitutes what is good for that organism and is therefore what it should ideally try to achieve. For individual humans, this means being healthy and happy; happiness and health are two ultimate ethical goals for individuals.

However, individuals do not exist in a vacuum: they exist and function, either well or poorly, within various contexts. Each of us must constantly respond adaptively to other components of the global ecosystem, which encompasses a number of important subsystems, if we are to optimally attain and maintain our individual good. The global ecosystem includes the human population, but it also includes all of the nonhuman aspects of the natural environment of the earth—its physical, chemical, and biological life-support systems. If any individual is to attain and maintain long-term health functioning and happiness, his or her interactions with human and nonhuman environments must be realistically adaptive. This means that for each individual, environmental integrity is another ultimate value. Environmental ethics thus becomes another central foundation of a realistic and intelligently pursued human ethics. Environmental integrity, however, implies a reasonable stand on population size. So another strand of this naturalistic ethics entails commitment to limitation of the human population. Long-range quality of life must commit all of us to attempt to limit human population growth and thus maintain the integrity of the global environment.

For most ethicists what I have said so far has barely touched on the true domain of ethics—the domain of human interpersonal relationships. What does an ethical system grounded in individual human nature and environmental integrity have to say about this? There is ample evidence that the human species is not social in the sense that ants, bees, and termites are. We form social associations, but often our interests conflict. However, there are features of human nature that may be developed in order to increase the tendencies to cooperate in the interest of what is good for all of us, individually and as a species. First of all, most of us are born with some capacity for empathy, for identification with others, to project our long-term goals into an indefinite future, and to think in terms of enlightened self-interest. These capacities can be developed in ourselves and others, and since what is good for all of us (happiness, health, and adaptation) and for the integrity of the global ecosystem depends on their adequate development, we have a moral duty to develop them.

However, much of moral reasoning involves real or imaginary scenarios in which dilemmas of choice are involved. How should these cases be decided? I think that it is a mistake to seek, as moral philosophers generally do, a priori universalizable moral principles supposedly applicable to all similar cases. We should try to be scientific in ethics. The principles to be applied should be scientific, inductively developed generalizations derived from our commitment to human good and ecosystemic integrity, with careful consideration of each case for both similar and dissimilar features. In general what is needed in resolving any particular moral dilemma is an approach that is situational (as suggested by Joseph Fletcher) and pragmatic (as developed by John Dewey) applied within a naturalistic bioethics and environmental ethics (as suggested by V. R. Potter and E. O. Wilson). Probably the person who has developed the most successful synthesis of those tendencies so far is Colleen Clements, a medical ethicist associated with the University of Rochester and Strong Memorial Hospital. The question to be asked in each specific problematic case is: What, in these specific circumstances, is most likely to promote the maximum happiness, health, and adaptation for these particular individuals in the long-run? Neither communal good nor individual good would automatically take precedence. Both are mutually interdependent in an ideal systems approach; only a careful situational analysis can determine the best resolution in conflict situations.

Let me discuss for a moment an example from real life to illustrate the sort of considerations that might enter into the possible resolution of such an issue. In the rice-growing areas of Thailand, the peasants are dependent upon rice for their subsistence. In these rice fields there were many cobras which, as far as the peasants could see, served no useful purpose and were a danger. Then an apparent bonanza happened. The peasants discovered that there is a lucrative market in China for cobra venom, which is mixed with cobra blood and other ingredients to make a "health" drink. Soon the peasants were doing a lively trade in cobras. They have improved their lives considerably and would like to continue the capture and sale of cobras indefinitely. However, the exhaustive hunting has now made the cobras very scarce. And now the chief food of the cobras—various rodents—are enjoying a population explosion. The rodents eat rice, so the rice crops are seriously threatened. The peasant farmers' solution is to hunt more cobras in order to survive. We can see in this situation how all of the values are systematically interrelated. Individual good (happiness, health, and adaptation), communal good (the well-being of the social group), and the integrity of the environment (the rice-farming subsistence environment) are all intertwined. What is good for any one is good for all of the system. And this is what the people involved must be encouraged to realize through adequate education and other measures.

The situation in North Africa is similar. The ever-increasing desertification and the resultant famines are in large part due to unwise population pressure and the destruction of the environment from overgrazing and other such activities. And on a much vaster scale—one bound to affect all of us adversely—the destruction of the tropical rainforests at an almost unbelievable rate (they will probably be gone by early in the twenty-first century) poses a similar problem with similar possible solutions.

To summarize, my purpose here had been to build on some of the ethical insights of various naturalistic humanists and environmentalists who have, in a variety of ways, sought rational, naturalistic, scientific foundations of ethics. I have suggested that much of recent ethics has led us down blind alleys in pursuit of absolute, universal nonscientific principles, whereas what is needed in ethics is a scientific approach—one that is empirical, inductive, tentative, and situation-relative. To develop such an ethical perspective and methodology we must start with an adequate, though provisional, understanding of human nature and the contexts within which human existence and experience occur.

The central thesis is that certain fundamental, functionally interdependent values—human happiness and well-being and environmental integrity—emerge as natural ultimate goals when studies are conducted of human nature and its contexts. And these central ethical goals should guide our selection of ethical proposals meant to resolve ethically problematic situations.

Sometimes limited systems-analysis and proposals are sufficient in resolving ethically problematic situations, but we should realize that seemingly limited and insulated situations are also functional aspects of wider systems and, ultimately, of the global ecosystem. It follows that global ecosystemic considerations should also have weight in seeking to resolve any ethically problematic situation to attain the central ethical goals.

The ultimate goals imply a moral duty to cultivate certain features frequently found, to some extent, in human beings—the capacity for empathy, the capacity to project long-range goals, the capacity to think in terms of enlightened self-interest, and so forth—since these features increase the likelihood that the central values can be attained.

# The Inseparability of Logic and Ethics

## John Corcoran
### (United States)

Logic and ethics are too often regarded as separate, if not somehow in opposition
to each other. But many great logicians, including Aristotle, Ockham, Bolzano,
De Morgan, and Russell, were capable of incisive contributions to ethics and
of heroic actions grounded in ethical insight. Likewise many exemplary moralists,
including Socrates, Plato, Kant, Mill, Gandhi, and Martin Luther King, showed
by their teachings and actions a deep commitment to objectivity, the ethical
value that motivates logic and is served by logic. This essay explores the role
of logic in ethics and the role of ethics in logic.

It is important to investigate the hypothesis that the ethics of the future
must accord logic a more central and explicit role. Connections between ethics
and irrational subjectivities must be severed; human dignity and mutual respect
can be based to a greater extent on the universal desire for objective knowledge.

Likewise it is important to investigate the hypothesis that the *logic* of the
future must accord *ethics* a more central and explicit role. Logical principles
are important because they serve ethical goals. Logic is peculiarly and essentially
a human pursuit; the alleged disconnections between logic and human involvement must be refuted.

The caricature of logic as a meaningless game of symbol manipulation and
the caricature of ethics as a rationalization of blind emotion must both be exposed.
Logic and ethics are in fact inseparable and each is served by explicit recognition
of its involvement with the other.

## Objectivity

Aristotle observed that all humans by nature desire to know. Our attention
is thereby drawn to objectivity, to the intention to make up one's mind in accord
with the facts, whatever they may be, whether they fulfill or frustate hopes,

whether they intensify or allay fears, whether they are compatible or incompatible with previously accepted beliefs. Objectivity involves what has been called love of truth, devotion to truth, loyalty to truth. It is recognized as a characteristically human trait that serves to unify the human race. It is at the same time an ethical virtue that requires cultivation. The primary goal of logic is the cultivation of objectivity. Logic aims at concepts, principles, and methods that are useful in making up one's mind in accord with the facts.

If humans were omniscient or infallible there would be no logic because there would be no need for it. If they were indifferent to truth or lacked concern for it, again there would be no logic because there would be no desire for it and no motivation to develop it. The human condition is replete with unfulfilled and perhaps unfulfillable aspirations. Here we juxtapose human ignorance and fallibility with the aspiration to knowledge.

Logic might be said to begin with observations about this gap between accomplishment and aspiration. Belief is not necessarily knowledge. The feeling of certainty is not a criterion of truth. Persuasion is not necessarily proof. Indeed, one of the perennial problems in logic is the perfection of critieria of proof, the development of objective tests to determine of a given persuasive argumentation whether it is a genuine proof, whether it establishes the truth of its conclusion. But alongside the negative observation that humans are neither omniscient nor infallible are the positive observations that the desire to know the truth can be fulfilled to a greater extent than it has been thus far, that it is possible to approach the ideal ever closer, and that objectivity can be cultivated.

The three facts that begin logic—that humans are neither omniscient nor infallible, that humans seek knowledge, and that improvement is possible—are three facts that serve to bring humans together. It is possible to cooperate in the goal, at once noble and practical, to overcome ignorance and fallibility as much as possible. Objectivity automatically involves cooperation and avoidance of deception, whether deception of others or by others, or even deception of oneself. It is said that the most destructive lies are those we tell to ourselves.

Objectivity, which, as already noted, involves the intention and the capacity to make up one's mind in accord with the facts, is an important virtue. But taken alone it might appear to be cold, alienating, and to some extent even dehumanizing—it might even appear to conflict with and exclude other virtues. But these appearances are based on several errors.

It is obvious of course that being objective requires being dispassionate. But being dispassionate does not exclude being passionate. Some of the most moving stories of the triumph of objectivity involve people who were passionate in their dedication to truth and who were moved to heroic personal sacrifices in order to develop and test their ideas. Being disinterested is not the same as being uninterested. Being an impartial observer is not the same as being an indifferent observer. Being dispassionate and impartial requires care, concentration, and energy; passionate dedication to truth can supply that energy.

Moreover, being dispassionate does not exclude being compassionate. Indeed, in order for compassion to be effectual and beneficial it must be accompanied by objectivity. For example, the practice of medicine is often motivated by compassion for human suffering, but without objectivity, attempts to alleviate suffering can be expected to be self-defeating. In many cases, compassion and objectivity enhance each other.

Compassion not only does not exclude, but actually *requires* objectivity, and this is not an isolated case. All virtues are compatible with objectivity, and most, if not all, virtues require it in order to be effectual and beneficial. Without objectivity the other virtues are either impossible or self-defeating or at least severely restricted in effectiveness. In fact, in many cases lapses in objectivity tend to turn the other virtues into parodies, mockeries, or perversions of themselves. Attempts at kindness without objectivity often end up as insulting paternalism. "Justice" without objectivity is arbitrariness. "Courage" without objectivity is rashness. "Integrity" and "moral steadfastness" without objectivity tend to become willful stubbornness and even fanaticism. Worthy causes have been embarrassed by lapses in objectivity by their ardent supporters. A worthy cause can have as much damage done to it by an overzealous supporter as by a detractor. With unobjective friends, a cause does not need enemies.

Objectivity is a rather distinctive virtue. We tend to value people for their objectivity and to be disappointed and even annoyed with people when they suffer avoidable lapses in objectivity. When there are important decisions to be made or a job to be done, we try to surround ourselves with people noted for their objectivity—regardless of whether we enjoy their company for other reasons. But what is even more distinctive is that objectivity gives rise to both pride and humility. Objectivity gives a person a sense of self-worth and dignity. People take just pride in their objectivity. At the same time, objectivity makes people especially alert to their own fallibility and thereby inspires them with a sense of humility, caution, and modesty.

To get a measure of how objectivity tends to unify humans and to transcend accidental differences such as age, sex, race, nationality, religion, and class, just consider international cooperation in mathematics, science, technology, and, perhaps most importantly, the human-rights movement. When people focus on making up their minds in accord with the facts in order to accomplish a common objective, accidental differences recede into the background. What matters is not who a person is or even what he or she believes, but rather how those beliefs were arrived at and what attitude he or she has toward them—in particular, whether he or she is ready to have those beliefs objectively examined.

## Cultivating Objectivity

Although the desire for objectivity seems to be universal and natural, the process of becoming objective requires skills and attitudes that many people at first do not find natural or easy to acquire. Perhaps the first such skill is that of making a hypothesis, of setting forth a proposition for investigation. There is little difficulty when the proposition is not already believed to be true and not already believed to be false. In such a case, there is rarely any resistance to the project of submitting the proposition to examination and testing.

Logicians use the word *hypothesis* to refer to a proposition that is neither known to be true nor known to be false by the relevant community of investigators. They also extend this usage so that the word refers to a proposition that is taken, for purposes of reasoning, *as if* it were neither known to be true nor known to be false. The point of making a hypothesis is to test it objectively, to review the evidence pro and con, to critically evaluate the relevant argumentations, to determine whether errors have been made, to see how it will stand up to objective investigation. The initial process of hypothesis-making has been referred to as *bracketing,* as *suspension of belief and disbelief,* and as *methodological doubt.*

When people have been deceiving themselves about the cogency of their evidentiary processes they are naturally afraid to have their own beliefs submitted to investigation. But even sincere people who have not had experience in this process tend to regard it as dangerous. When bracketing a proposition or setting forth a hypothesis, one sets aside all preconceptions about it, however well-established these preconceptions may have appeared.

In an open community every attempt to prove or disprove a proposition is at the same time a bracketing of the proposition. Every attempt to settle a hypothesis is automatically an invitation that it be critically examined. In fact, in order to follow a proof it is necessary to doubt the conclusion and to see that the proof removes the doubt. This is part of what is meant when we say that knowledge comes from doubt.

The disinclination to have a belief considered as a hypothesis is often a sign of dogmatism, closed-mindedness, and self-deception. But sometimes it is simply a reflection of ignorance of logical methodology. If a proposition is true, its adherents have nothing to lose by having it critically investigated. On the contrary, they have much to gain. On the other hand, if a proposition is false, the sooner it is recognized as such the better. Shielding a proposition from critical examination serves no useful purpose.

Sometimes we are afraid to go to the doctor when we suspect that we have incipient symptoms of illness. Sometimes it takes courage to face up to the truth. But the clearer a person becomes about the ultimate desirability of knowing the truth in a given case, the less courage is needed to put the issue to the test.

To a community of objective thinkers, any attempt to shield a proposition from the testing process reflects badly on those who believe it to be true. Shielding a proposition from testing is seen as shoddy, undignified, and ultimately absurd. A proposition not worth testing is not worth being taken seriously.

Another thing that facilitates willingness to submit beliefs to the test is knowledge of logical principles. For example, a person who cannot recall evidence for a given belief may become gripped with fear when that belief is raised as a hypothesis. It is a feeling similar to that encountered when one cannot locate money to pay for a meal already consumed. But it is clear that the analogy does not carry over once a person is aware of the principles of evidence. The *fundamental principle of evidence* can be stated roughly as follows:

> The absence of positive evidence by itself is never conclusive negative evidence and the absence of negative evidence by itself is never conclusive positive evidence.

At first it may seem that this principle conflicts with the *principle of excluded middle:*

> Every proposition is either true or false.

But it becomes clear that there is no conflict as soon as it is realized that there are distinctions both between *true* and *proved to be true* and between *false* and *proved to be false.* The *principles of nonomniscience,* which embody these distinctions, are in part as follows:

> Not every proposition is either proved to be true or proved to be false. Not every true proposition is proved to be true. Not every false proposition is proved to be false.

Ignorance of the fundamental principle of evidence has been exploited by unscrupulous persons and groups. An unscrupulous person may make a baseless charge and, when challenged to present evidence, try to turn the situation around by asking for evidence to the contrary in order to give the impression that the absence of evidence to the contrary is actually evidence in favor of the charge. In recent years purveyors of unsafe consumer products have delayed having their products rejected by using tactics that exploit the ignorance of the consumers regarding the fundamental principle of evidence. The tobacco industry has tried to get people to believe that cigarettes are safe by reiterating that scientists have been unable to prove conclusively that smoking causes various illnesses.

The dispassionate search for truth tends to bring out the best in people. The study of logic, not as a system of external rules, but as an intensely personal attempt to be objective about objectivity, contributes to this search. On the other hand, attempts to defend preconceived beliefs by whatever means necessary, even deception and coercion, tend to bring out the worst in people.

## The Hypothetico-Deductive Method

In logic the word "proof" and its cognates are used in the strict sense. A proof that a proposition is true actually establishes that it is true; such a proof produces objective knowledge of the truth of its conclusion. The same thing holds, with the obvious changes, for proof that a proposition is false.

The hypothetico-deductive method is often preliminary to proof and sometimes it actually results in proof. The simplest form of this method of investigation consists in setting forth a hypothesis and seeing which propositions can be deduced from it and also which propositions it can be deduced from. The object, of course, is to determine what else would be true if the hypothesis were true and what else, being true, would explain the truth of the hypothesis—in other words, to find out what would be explained by the hypothesis being true and what would serve to explain the hypothesis being true. In short, two questions are asked:

What are the logical consequences of the hypothesis?
What is the hypothesis a logical consequence of?

People who are not accustomed to using this method are often amazed at the clarity it produces and at how many things come to light once it is used.

Quite apart from the fact that the hypothetico-deductive method sometimes leads to proof, it is useful in cultivating objectivity because it leads to a better understanding of the hypothesis in that it produces knowledge of what to expect were the hypothesis true and of what would result in the hypothesis. If the statement of the hypothesis is ambiguous, this process often brings the ambiguity to light and provides suggestions for revisions. If the hypothesis is vague, this process can locate the vagueness and provide suggestions for sharpening it.

How can this method lead to proof or disproof? There are several possibilities, only two of which will be considered here.

First, let us imagine that from the hypothesis we have deduced a proposition that was already known to be false or that was subsequently determined to be false, say by experiment. In this case we have a disproof of the hypothesis, a proof that the hypothesis is false. This is so in view of the following principle:

Every proposition that implies a false proposition is itself false.

This is the familiar *principle of false consequence,* which is the basis for much productive thinking. It is the principle most often used in exonerating innocent defendants and, more generally, in rejecting false hypotheses.

There are of course many other ways in which knowledge of this principle leads to cultivation of objectivity. For example, by focusing on the principle of false consequence we are reminded of the fact that a proposition is false if even one of its consequences is false, and that a person making an assertion is as responsible for each of the consequences of the assertion as for the assertion itself. This should move an objective person to be a bit more cautious and to do some deductions before making an assertion.

Second, let us imagine that we have deduced the hypothesis from a proposition that was already known to be true or that was subsequently determined to be true. In this case we have a proof of the hypothesis in view of the following principle:

Every proposition implied by a true proposition is itself true.

This is the familiar *principle of true implicant,* also known as the *principle of truth and consequence.* This principle is also the basis for much productive thinking. It forms the basis for the reasoning employed in the axiomatic development of the various branches of mathematics, and it is involved in understanding mathematical proof, which is a kind of ideal standard against which to measure argumentations that fall short of mathematical proof.

## Proof

In order to discuss the concept of proof, it is useful to have a typical example in mind. Consider the Euclidean proof of the Pythagorean Theorem. Its premise-set consists of axioms and definitions for plane geometry, which presumably are known to be true by the audience. Its conclusion is the Pythagorean Theorem. Its chain of reasoning extends over several pages and includes over forty intermediate theorems, and its final passages involve a clever recipe for dividing the square on the hypotenuse into two pieces, each adjacent to a leg of the triangle and each equal to the square on the adjacent leg.

In order for this proof to be conclusive for a given audience it is necessary for the premises to be known to be true by that audience. There is no way to base knowledge on premises not known to be true. When the audience does not have knowledge of the premises, the argumentation is said to *beg the question* or to *commit the fallacy of unwarranted assumption.* But the conclusiveness of the proof also requires that the chain of reasoning make clear that the evidence is sufficient, that the premise-set actually implies the conclusion. When this is lacking, the argumentation is said to be a *non sequitur* or to *commit the fallacy of inadequate reasoning.*

The main idea here is the familiar fact that every proof has three parts: a conclusion, a premise-set, and a chain of reasoning. Normally the chain of reasoning is by far the longest part. In a proof the chain of reasoning shows that the conclusion is implied by the premise-set. The chain of reasoning by itself does not show that the conclusion is true but only that it is implied by the premise-set. In order for the conclusion to be recognized as true by means of the chain of reasoning, the person doing the recognizing must have already verified that the premises in fact are true.

Analogous considerations apply in argumentation that falls short of mathematical proof. It is necessary to establish the premises—in other words, to make sure that what is alleged to be evidence is accurate as it stands without regard for what it is supposed to be evidence for. In addition, and this is an entirely different issue, it is necessary to establish that what is alleged to be evidence for the conclusion is sufficient to imply the conclusion. If this is not so then the conclusion is not proved even were the alleged evidence correct. To summarize, there are two things to check: whether the alleged evidence is accurate, and whether the chain of reasoning makes it clear that the alleged evidence, if true, would warrant acceptance of the conclusion.

Fallacious reasoning from warranted premises is no better than cogent reasoning based on unwarranted premises. In many cases of shoddy argumentation people waste their energy squabbling over the premises when a cursory examination of the reasoning would bring down the argumentation like a house of cards.

There are two arts involved in proof. There is the art of producing or discovering proof (a *heuristic* art), and the art of recognizing proofs (a *critical* art). This critical art brings us back to the problem of perfecting criteria for proof. In order for an argumentation to be a proof of a given conclusion for a given audience, it is necessary that the argumentation persuade the audience of the truth of the conclusion. But persuasion is not sufficient, and criteria are needed to prevent deception and error.

Whether a person is creating a proof or critically evaluating an argumentation offered as a proof, the underlying guiding principle is the *golden rule of proof:*

Argue unto others as you would have them argue unto you.

When you have produced an argumentation and you are wondering whether it is a proof, ask yourself whether you would find it acceptable were a respected adversary to offer it to you. Likewise when an argumentation is offered to you as a proof and you are wondering whether you should accept it, ask yourself whether you would offer it to a respected adversary and whether you could stand behind it.

## Conclusion

In the above discussion we have reviewed only a few facets of the interrelatedness and interdependence of logic and ethics. We have seen that ethical practice involves logic insofar as the other virtues require objectivity in order to be effectual and beneficial, and in some cases even for their very existence or realization. There was, unfortunately, no room in such a short discussion to explore the role of logic in ethical theory. The importance of consistency and of criteria of consistency in ethical theory was not mentioned, nor was the role of logic in the analysis of ethical concepts and propositions.

One of the most important points is one that is often overlooked and that may have not been treated before to the extent that it has been treated here. I have in mind the fact that logic can be seen as an ongoing, imperfect, incomplete, and essentially incompletable attempt to cultivate objectivity, to discover principles and methods that contribute to the understanding and practice of objectivity, which is an ethical virtue standing alongside kindness, justice, honesty, compassion, and the rest, and which is characteristically human in the sense that an omniscient or infallible entity would have no use for objectivity and no use for logic. Logic is a humane and humanistic science; it is one of the humanities in the renaissance sense.

## Postscript and Acknowledgments

Late one afternoon about a year before his death, I had been discussing with the logician Alfred Tarski the influence that his various works had had on the modern development of logic. I asked him whether there was any aspect of his contributions that had not received the attention that it deserved. Naturally, I was wondering whether there might be among his discoveries one whose ramifications had somehow been overlooked by the logical community and that might be, so to speak, a rich vein as yet unmined. To my surprise, he replied that his deepest regret in this connection was that the ethical dimension of his work had gone largely unrecognized and unappreciated. The memory of this conversation was before me when I decided to write this article. It is my hope that attention will be drawn to the ethical dimension of Tarski's work and more generally to the interrelations of logic and ethics.

The many persons with whom I discussed these issues before and during the writing of this article share in whatever merit it may have. I want to mention especially Ray Lucas, Newton Garver, Joseph Morton, Michael Scanlan, Stewart Shapiro, Timothy Madigan, Ralph Argen, Susan Woods, James Gasser, Arthur Efron, and Susan Williams.

# Beyond The Ten Commandments

## Lester Mondale
### (United States)

It is all but self-evident that if any group is to be a community and remain as such, it must abide by rules of conduct that prescribe how members are to behave with respect to one another's persons and property. Otherwise, with the breakdown of rules—that is, the breakdown of the administration of law and order—theft and destruction of property, murder and rape, are likely to be the order of the day. Hence we have the Code of Hammurabi, the Ten (plus) Commandments, and comparable proscriptions the world over.

The Judaic code has to do primarily with the sancrosanctness or inviolability of property, including one's servants, livestock and wife—and of one's person and that of others. It was a code that, despite interwoven priestly ordinances, was directed primarily to the holding and disposition of things physical.

However, immediately beyond this realm of the physical and its safeguarding Decalogue looms the realm of intermingling self-to-self, ego-to-ego relations. Among these relations, Sinai's safeguarding commandments that forbid killing, stealing, and the removal of landmarks, are of little pertinence. Here a physical possession—one's automobile for instance—has value less for transportation than for what it affirms about its owner in a society of intermingling egos. One's residence similarly affirms the place one has made for oneself in one's own estimation as well as that of others. It is shelter more for ego than for flesh and bones.

In this society of interacting psyches there is, of course, never enough place for everybody. Therefore, in the making of a place for oneself, one must contend with others whose hearts and minds are set on similar, if not identical, objectives. In this rivalry, education, personality, drive, brainpower, shrewdness, and charm are the essence of success. Accordingly, introduction to a stranger customarily evokes an instant and covert appraisal: What is the stranger's state of culture? The posture of shoulders? Expression of lips? Inclination of nose? Tenor of voice? Fit and choice of clothes? Does it all add up to one who is a formidable scion of a city's Main Line, the product of generations of affluence and consequence? Or is he or she obviously of a rural background? Of the wrong side of a city street? In this supraphysical, psychological society, position or status spells assurance, security, well-being, even ego survival.

In this social nexus, persons supposedly no longer shoot or knife one another in personal encounters, and no longer piratically commandeer the house, the bread, the spouse of another. But behind its conventional façade of law-abiding politeness and seeming consideration lurks a Hobbesian jungle, a state of nature wherein the ego that survives as a self-regarding and other-regarded individual must be a competent adversary. It is a society in which one's ego is relatively insecure in challenging-to-threatening surroundings. Even in circles of polite sophistication, a university environment, say, there is always the threat of the knowledge-is-power Goliath who, with his or her learned specialty, delights in making others into spectacles of misinformation or ignorance. And who among us is not tempted at times to play the knowledgeable Goliath . . . or the David?

This psychological—and to a large extent lawless—state of nature raises the question, "What about a possible code that might do for this jungle of intermingling, often jangling, selves what codes of Mosaic style have done for the realm of the more physical?"

Conventional wisdom and piety would have us supplement the Mosaic Decalogue with the Christian code of the Golden Rule and the Sermon on the Mount. We will consider this Christian response presently; and with that, a humanist response I would advocate. Meanwhile, I invite you to consider an intermediate code that has taken over and all but religiously prescribes the values and dominates the interego conduct of the Western world and the United States in particular.

This intermediate code, far from condemning ego-assertion and the besting of others in the innumerable contests and conflicts of the daily intermingling of persons, lauds conflict. Conflict, as this code has it, strengthens and ennobles the contestants themselves. It selects those who are to be the most honored and esteemed. They are the winners of the contests.

The code to which I refer is that of the sports world. There, winning—Vince Lombardi to the contrary—is *almost* everything. The good and best are the sportsmanlike: resolute and able to take rough and tumble, as well as to dish it out with skill and power. Superiority of performance, teamwork, superhuman effort: such is the goodness of the code. The athlete is our revered and acclaimed secular saint. He or she scoffs, martyr-like, at personal injury, however serious or painful. Saintly again, he or she smiles with spiritual detachment after an encounter lost but well fought, with, "Yes, you win some, you lose some—but the *game's* the thing." Life is nothing for the sports world if it is not an all-inclusive game of winning and losing, playing without cheating, without weakness, without ineptitude or stupidity—and always to win.

The extent to which this code has taken over on the American scene was nicely attested in a recent article in the sports supplement of the *Wall Street*

*Journal:* "In the big cities, sport is part of a larger culture. In the big corporations, its jargon and images are now common, part of that culture too. But in countless small towns across the country, sport is much more than that. It practically *is* the culture, the social cement that holds these towns together."

Adds the coach of a Texas high-school football team, "Football is part of our curriculum. It teaches life."

And a corporation president: "Turning the workplace into a playing field can turn our subordinates into athletes, dedicated to performing to the limits of their abilities." Sports celebrities, the supplement continues, are, as a consequence, "showing up at corporate functions in record numbers . . . to motivate and pass out advice: how to become leaders, how to be competitive, how to win."

In athletic purview, the world of intermingling psyches is a universal playing field of the innumerable contests of everyday living. And there is no divergence from the norm, no difference of any order—from jogging speeds to bait-casting skills—that isn't a potential contest in which to experience "the thrill of victory or the agony of defeat." Here, in a word, is a code that evokes in humankind the morale that can make the ugliest of contests of everyday living into games to be taken in the "joyful spirit of competition."

For all of the respect that is the just due of the valiant and accomplished athlete, the sober fact remains that the culture that is being athletized is also, in essence, an invidious culture, made no less so by the athletes and their contests. Therein, every office desk's position, every college examination, every party gown, every summer residence, and every dinner check is a poignant reminder to the beholder of where one stands—that is, how far from the economic, social, or political top. That reminder, ever before us, is the all-but-holy mission of the billions of advertising dollars annually devoted to creating dissatisfaction and inferiority—and a specious superiority.

Since the beginnings of recorded time, the occasional Buddha, Tolstoy, Gandhi, or Schweitzer has reacted with revulsion to egos forever contesting and denigrating egos, to the predominance of the invidious. Profoundly injured, they have protested the idea that the jungle is the natural order of intermingling psyches. We humans were created, they have said, for a more healthful, secure, sustaining, joyously abundant mingling. We are better suited by head and heart and gut for a more finely feeling order of coexistence.

Such has been the protest of persons of marked sensitivity—like my own father, a Methodist minister and farmer. As a young man, he was horrified by the hurtful insensitivity of young male studs boasting of their sexual conquests in a brutal and inhumane manner, and likewise by the false respect commanded, by and large, by the number of acres of one's farm or the number of head of livestock of one's herd.

My father's was a spirit that knew that there just had to be a more satisfying, supporting, healthful, considerate, dignified mingling of psyches. But on whose authority? The rebelling assertion of his own feelings? He, like other rebels of his day and locale, had only one authority to see as ultimate: the word of God as revealed in the New Testament precepts of the Golden Rule and the Sermon on the Mount. Those precepts condemned the culture, the low spirituality of the invidiously adversarial. Moreover, in the Sermon on the Mount and the Golden Rule there was also, supposedly, the word of God specifically laying out, it was commonly believed, a more peaceful, happier, more healthful mingling of psyches.

At this juncture one runs into a strange and profoundly fundamental contradiction between what my Christian father accepted as the commanding word of God, and what was even more authoritative and commanding: the word of his own heartfelt feelings and humanistic good sense. The word of God commanded, in no uncertain terms, "Sell all thou hast. Give to the poor." However, for all of my father's commitment to the code of the crucified savior, he didn't sell all he had, which then was substantial. Further, despite his supposedly Christian commitment, my father had plenty of thought for tomorrow though scripture told him not to. He didn't love or forgive the local saloon keepers he had righteously decided to put out of business. He did give way to anger when his eldest son's behavior demanded reproof that would not likely be forgotten. And lust in the heart? How account, otherwise, for his remarriage and for the issue of his second family?

In fact, the bulk of what my father seemingly got from the Christian code was what he read into and selected out of it. What was Christian for him was the acceptance of others as human like himself, with tender feelings and a sensitivity like his own. Accordingly, his was a helping warmheartedness that embraced child and adult, neighbor and stranger alike. It was a spirituality, a finely sensitive regard that he gave to others; it was the respect that any wholly human being must have for another if one is to evoke the fully human. All of this was selected from and read into the precepts of Christian revelation and the stories of the life of Christ. To anyone of humanist persuasion it is obvious that the gospel he preached and lived by and his dislike of the invidious were not revelation, but his own heart and mind in interaction with the hearts and minds of others. The result was an empathy, a spirituality that had the external vestments of Christian theology, but that also had all the interior substance of the humanistic.

So we ask now: Why not espouse an avowedly humanistic spirituality standing on its own as the antithesis of the invidious? Certainly the invidious that dominates our culture can be as contortingly injurious and as hurtful for humanist as it was for Gandhi, Tolstoy, Schweitzer, and Mother Teresa, and for my father as a young man. The basic inhumanity of the invidious can, and probably should bring the humanist, as it did my father and countless others, to the inescapable conclusion that there must be a more satisfying, supportive, considerate, dignified, healthful mingling of psyches.

What about an avowedly self-confessed humanist spirituality? Is there any reason why anyone under the humanist aegis shouldn't be an exemplar of empathy as much any avowed Christian or Buddhist? This order of spirituality bespeaks the protesting authority of the mind and heart of any invidiously beleaguered man or woman—an authority that I strongly believe it is our duty as humanists to reclaim and assert. It belongs to us to research, to advocate, to experience as it does not belong to born-again fundamentalists, mystics, or revivalists who preach love so hatefully. I envision humanism as the expression of a down-to-earth code—not something for saints vainly proclaimed as the harbinger of a miraculous and utopian world peace—a code to be aspired to, to be incorporated into the everyday lives of individuals to the fullest possible extent.

I cannot conceive of any more valid profession of or identification with the cause of empathy than a humanist profession and identification. What group is better qualified—indeed, more obligated—to take over from the revelationists and become *the* advocate of the empathetic?

I want to think of humanism not only as incorporating the ideal of the Renaissance man and woman and not only as the very incarnation of power and courage in any battle for personal and civil liberty, but also as the embodiment of an ideal personhood, a personalized rather than merely ethical standard by which I can and should measure my own daily performance.

Called upon to be the helping hand and heart, I will—to paraphrase my minister father and his doing *the Christian thing*—do the humanist thing. In measuring my performance I will face up to some such question as, "Is mine the discernment that sees beyond someone's show of hostility or overbearing superiority to the early hurts and repressions that may well have driven this person to express himself or herself in such a self-defeating, alienating manner?" For the shattered ego of one whose sense of self-worth has been based on stocks that have crashed, on salary bonuses that are now nonexistent, on a top job from which he or she has been summarily dismissed—how insightfully reassuring and nonpatronizing is the solace or counsel I try to offer? And for those who are homeless in spirit or in actuality, the alienated of an invidious environment, to what extent am I being the sheltering friend? In sum, as a humanist, how consecrated am I to an ever more supportive, considerate, dignified, healthful, empathetic, joyous mingling of selves?

Empathy, let us not overlook, includes *tenderness:* the tenderness of the mother for the infant at her breast, the tenderness extended to include the self-regard and the hopes and dreams of young and old, feelings that come as near to the sacred as anything one of humanist persuasion can conceive.

Asked, "Are you a Christian?" my father's typical response was, "I'm trying to be." Similarly with humanism: Am I a humanist? I must answer, "That's what I'm *trying,* doing my damnedest, to be!"

# VII.

# Sex and Gender in the Twenty-First Century

# Expanding and Contracting Constructions

## Elizabeth Rice Allgeier

### (United States)

Early this summer, my husband Rick and I bought a cottage on a lake in Michigan, and the former owners left a number of old novels. There's one published in 1959 called *Dr. Jane Comes Home,* and its cover carries the blurb, "Woman or doctor?"[1] We are told that "A lovely young doctor tries to bury her woman's need for love in a brilliant medical career." Another, published in 1966, is titled *Once A Nurse . . . But Always A Woman.*[2] When I saw this I thought, Goodness, how silly it would seem if it were titled *Once A Doctor [or Nurse], But Always A Man.* But these titles and jacket blurbs simply reflect attitudes common twenty-five years ago about gender, sexuality, love, and their interactions.

During the 1960s, I became very involved in protests against the Vietnam war. I did not get the least bit involved with the movement toward gender equality, however, as I didn't see the humanist connection—the right to self-determination—between the two movements. I must confess that I failed to understand the objection to the generic use of "he" for both males and females. At that time, I also missed the point being made by those who objected to the title "Mrs." I loved being female, I loved babies, and my big goal in life was to obtain that "Mrs." title and start having those babies. I don't know what your motives were for entering college, but the only reason that I enrolled in 1959 was that my mother told me that if I didn't go, she would not allow me to date!

There was one other popular book that I read at that time that focused directly on the differences in the "healthy" sexuality of men and women. I am not a supporter of book burning, but should my attitudes toward censorship ever change, Marie Robinson's book, *The Power of Sexual Surrender,* would be one of the first that I would throw into the fire.[3] Robinson's general point was that a healthy woman was receptive to her mate whenever *he* (it was never a female mate, of course) desired sexual stimulation and release. The woman should surrender to her mate's desires, and her arousal and response should occur as a direct result of sexual stimulation by him. However, she should not preempt his prerogative to initiate sex. These beliefs were reinforced by the man I was married to at that time, who was, after all, socialized during the same period and by the same culture that had shaped me. Although I independently experienced feelings that I might now describe as horniness (though at the time I understood horniness to be an exclusively male phenomenon), I was embarrassed by those feelings and was convinced that there was something animalistic and wrong with me. It didn't occur to me to question the dominant constructions of female sexuality that existed in the early 1960s.

Thus, had I been asked to give this address twenty-five years ago, my perspective would have been very different than it is today. The sociologist Alice Rossi made a marvelous statement that captures nicely, if more eloquently, what my viewpoint would have been. She said, "Modern society is a mere second in our evolutionary history, and it is naive to assume that our audacious little experiments in communal living, birth control, sexual liberation and sex-role equality can overturn in a century, let alone a decade, millennia of custom and adaptation."[4]

Incredible shifts have occurred in the past quarter of a century among some segments of industrialized societies in assumptions about what it means to be male or female. Parallel shifts have also occurred regarding the meanings attached to sexual expression over the past few decades. In short, during the past twenty-five years, our "audacious little experiments" involving contraception, sexual liberation, and gender-role equality have had a monumental impact on the ways in which at least some people construe the meanings of sexuality and gender.

Several extensive movements relevant to sexuality and gender have been going on during the past few decades: One of them is sociopolitical with social and legal ramifications, another is scientific with social and technological ramifications. In the sociopolitical realm, the free-speech movement in the United States during the 1960s questioned the taboos associated with sexual language, and the experiments with utopian marriage and group-living arrangements challenged some of our assumptions and taboos associated with sexuality. The women's movement, led by the National Organization for Women, challenged the age-old belief in the appropriateness of assigning roles on the basis of gender, and in particular, the traditional restriction of opportunity for women beyond the borders of their domiciles.

Within the sciences, initial attempts to understand the meaning of sexuality and of being male or female focused on obtaining *facts.* The Kinsey group sought to obtain information about sexual behavior: Who did what to whom under what circumstances? Masters and Johnson also focused on "facts"—the physiological responses of the body during sexual arousal, orgasm, and resolution. Neither research group was particularly concerned with how the people they studied construed their experiences. Various research groups also sought to understand ways in which gender programmed people to behave in particular ways, such as why women were relatively more verbally skilled and men more quantitatively adept. Was it due to biological differences or sociological and socialization factors?

Politics entered the scientific arena, with some social scientists emphasizing what Rachel Hare-Mustin and Jeanne Maracek have described as an alpha bias.[5] Bias as they define it means perspective, not necessarily error. An alpha bias is an emphasis of the differences between people as a function of their gender. Other social scientists were guided by beta bias—an emphasis on similarities and equalities between males and females—and sought to demonstrate the relative uselessness of gender as a predictive variable. Even when scientists operating with a beta bias reported a difference between the average male and the average female in some attribute—for example, aggressiveness—they also pointed out that the mean, or average, of a group doesn't capture the whole story. With the exception of a few characteristics tied to reproductive capacities—ovulation, insemination, gestation, and lactation—most behaviors and attributes of men and women are arrayed on distributions that overlap. The practical implications of this are that although the average female may have more highly developed verbal skills than the average male, for instance, some men have greater verbal skills than the average woman.

Scientists focusing on the attempt to understand and explain sexuality and gender have been involved in a quest for facts and the interpretation of these facts, and have produced a plethora of correlational findings with researchers bowing to the problems of sorting out the influences of biological, sociological, and socialization factors. Into this fray has stepped the social constructionist movement. To some extent, social constructionists have just begun to do, scientifically, what the contemporary sociopolitical movements concerned with sexual liberation and egalitarianism began doing in the 1960s. These political movements challenged the ways in which society construed sexuality and gender, and questioned constructions of sex as solely or primarily for the purpose of reproduction. More recently some scientists have begun to study the meanings and constructions of *sexuality,* as Leonore Tiefer has pointed out.[6] The political movements challenged the construction that women and men should appropriately operate in quite distinct spheres, with the men earning and the women baking the bread. Within scientific circles, the social constructionist movement has also begun to study the meanings and constructions societies attach to *gender.*

Let me give a very personal example of what the terms "construe" and "social construction" mean. In 1959, shortly after I entered college to be allowed to date, I fell in love, quit going to classes, was put on academic probation at the end of my first year, and happily withdrew to do what I really wanted to do—marry and have babies. By 1967, I had had three of my four children. I was also experiencing considerable boredom and depression because I wanted to return to college, but I construed that as an extreme violation of my responsibilities as a mother to remain at home until my children had entered school. Although at that time I hadn't read the constructions of healthy femininity by Freud or any of the other psychoanalytic writers, I had certainly absorbed the idea that if I were a healthy woman, I would find my role completely satisfying, and the man to whom I was married at that time ardently agreed. The fact that I was distressed led me to seek therapy so as to become better adjusted. I thank the gods that in my random search for a therapist, I didn't land in the office of a psychologist who construed my difficulties as stemming from penis envy. Instead, I happened to find a therapist team who construed my problem as one of isolation and understimulation. Their "prescription" was to reenter college. They gave me their authoritative permission to "be all that you can be," and told me that they saw no need for further therapy. Although many women have experienced the same sense of boredom and depression, most of us here construed our responses as the result of our own individual defects rather than as the normal responses of healthy adults to a structure in which they are isolated and understimulated. I think that this common situation illustrates the wide-flung ramifications of society's construction system for people's lives.

With increasing pressure from humanists and political groups to examine those societal constructions that limit the development of individual potential, and with increased interest by scientific groups in the ways in which humans create social constructions—a movement from a Lockian to a Kantian perspective—I think that our understanding and tolerance for human diversity will be increased during the twenty-first century.

If we continue in this vein, the construction of the meanings and purposes of sexuality will expand in the twenty-first century. We are familiar with some of the ways in which sexuality is currently construed, at least among a few relatively educated people: not just for reproduction, but also as an expression of intimacy, self-knowledge, relaxation, recreation and fun, and so forth. Open discussion of sexuality may also reduce some of the less desirable subsidiary uses of sex such as its employment as a vehicle through which men and women subjugate other men and women. By the way, some have claimed that as sexuality loses some of its taboo status some of the passion associated with it will be lost. To the extent that feelings of anxiety and guilt may contribute to a sense of arousal, feelings of arousal *without* anxiety and guilt may indeed be subjectively experienced as a decrease in passion. But insofar as anxiety and guilt can also reduce our ability to experience passion and intimacy and just plain old sensation, I frankly prefer my passion straight without the unwanted emotional calories of those negative feelings.

In contrast to a general expansion of common acceptance of the diversity of the meanings of sexual expression, I believe that constructions about the meaning of being male versus female will experience constriction. Instead of gender conferring a set of roles throughout one's lifespan (goat herder vs. baby-sitter, initiator vs. recipient, work outside the home vs. work inside the home, bread-earner vs. bread-baker, dominator vs. submitter, and so forth.), gender will have a few relatively limited meanings. At the most personal level, gender is important when you are seeking a person with whom to share your genes in conceiving a third person. At a very broad level, the continued study of gender-related issues is important for understanding humans in general in all our diversity. As we continue to pursue research with an alpha bias—that is, a focus on gender differences—we may learn more about human functioning and potentialities. But the beta perspective—the focus on how we are similar— may increase the ability of societies to accept the dreams and gifts of males and females as individuals.

## Notes

1. A. McElfresh, *Dr. Jane Comes Home* (New York: Bantam Books, 1959).

2. W. D. Roberts, *Once A Nurse . . . But Always A Woman* (New York: Ace Books, 1966).

3. Marie Robinson, *The Power of Sexual Surrender* (Garden City, N.Y.: Doubleday, 1959).

4. Alice Rossi, "The Biosocial Side of Parenthood," *Human Nature,* vol. 1, pp. 72–79.

5. Rachel Hare-Mustin and Jeanne Maracek, "The Meaning of Difference: Gender Theory, Postmodernism, and Psychology," *The American Psychologist,* vol. 43, pp. 455–464.

6. Leonore Tiefer, "Social Construction and the Study of Human Sexuality," in P. Shaver and C. Hendrick (eds.), *Sex and Gender* (Beverly Hills: Sage, 1987), pp. 70–94.

# Sex Repression in Contemporary China

## Fang Fu Ruan
### (China)
## and Vern L. Bullough
### (United States)

Since the time of Charles Darwin the urge to reproduce has been recognized as a biological imperative. The sex drive is part and parcel of being human, and whether it is repressed, sublimated, redirected, or handled in any one of a number of other ways, it remains a powerful force. Still, at various times in human history, organized groups—usually religious but sometimes political—have felt the need to control sexual practices. One of the more repressive traditions has been that of the Catholic church. Until the time of St. Augustine in the fourth century, the ideal life was conceptualized as an asexual one, even though this would have led to the elimination of the human species. Augustine, however, recognized that not all people had the dedication to remain completely chaste, and permitted sex within marriage provided it was engaged in for the purpose of procreation and in the proper position, that is, the so-called missionary position.

As history demonstrates, the Christian church has only rarely been able to enforce its beliefs about sexuality, and in fact many modern Christians find such teachings an embarrassment. Still, it is the Augustinian position on sex that allows the pope to stand firm against any form of contraception and provides the theological justification for celibacy. For centuries the Augustinian position dominated the American and English legal systems, making almost all forms of sexual expression against the law. It is only in the past three decades that a major legal challenge has been mounted to these assumptions.

Despite its great efforts, however, Christian society as a whole has not been as effective in enforcing its will on sexual practices as has China under Communist rule. The one thing that usually saved even the most sexually active individuals in the past was the Christian willingness—indeed, obligation—to forgive the sinner. There was a widespread assumption that though the spirit was willing the flesh was weak. Moreover, the church was rarely in a position to enforce its sexual code until after the sin had been committed. This has not been the case with the Chinese Communists.

Ancient Chinese society was very open about sexuality. There are numerous ancient manuals giving advice and instruction about sexual activity, and a vast tradition of Chinese erotica dating from ancient times up to the end of the nineteenth century. Though Chinese attitudes changed somewhat during the Sung dynasty (960–1279), the result was to discourage public discussion about sexuality rather than to change sexual practices. Many of the Chinese sex classics either were destroyed or went underground; many of the sex manuals, in fact, survived only through Japanese versions. Despite this official prudery, Chinese attitudes about sexuality were far more liberal in the nineteenth and early twentieth centuries than were official Western attitudes, except regarding such matters as public nudity.

All of this changed after the Communist Revolution. Officially, after 1949, the only legal and moral kind of sexual behavior permitted was between married heterosexual couples. Polygamy, long practiced among the rich and powerful in China, was banned, as was prostitution, premarital sex, extramarital sex, nonmarital cohabitation, pornography, nudity, homosexuality, and all forms of variant sexual behavior. All social activity that seemed to have the least connotations of sexuality, including social dancing, was banned as well.

Though both were hostile to sex, the difference between the Chinese Communists and the Christian church was that the Communists had the kind of political control required to enforce their edicts, as well as the additional desire to assert the authority of the government over individuals. Harsh punishments were given to those who were caught violating the officially established norms. The power of the party and the government were everywhere. In order to get married, individuals had to get permission from their leader in the local community or in their workplace. This permission had no correlation to the marriage license required in the West, since the primary concern was serving the state and not the individual. To get pregnant, married women also needed permission from the same official. Sometimes wives were officially inspected by other women to make sure they adhered to the standards expected of them, and did not attempt to become pregnant without permission. (Though the Chinese law code provided for equality of the sexes, a kind of double standard continued to exist). Chinese officials discouraged intimacy among married couples by assigning husbands and wives to different parts of the country and allowing them to meet only for brief vacation periods during the year. In the cities, holding hands and kissing in public were forbidden, making it difficult to demonstrate affection since privacy, even in the home, was very limited. Obviously control was more effective in the city than in the rural countryside, and among the rank and file Party members than among the rest of the Chinese, but still, those who were caught violating the norms could be summarily punished. The major exception was high-ranking party officials, who bent the rules to suit their own needs. Several, for example, had mistresses, and the first transsexual operation in China was performed during the 1980s on the son of a powerful military figure.

With the emergence of the People's Republic the government clamped down on the dissemination of information about sex. Pre-1949 sex manuals were banned and replaced by a prudish translations from an unsophisticated Russian manual designed for married couples. Eventually even that disappeared from the bookstores, and was replaced by unsophisticated and moralistic Chinese originals. The result, particularly in the cities, was the rise of all kinds of misconceptions about sex. During a good part of the 1960s and early 1970s even information about contraceptives was banned. By officially deemphasizing sex, the government could more easily justify its control.

Still, sex continued to be a troublesome problem for the government. In fact, one of the stated purposes of the Cultural Revolution proclaimed in May 1966 was to eliminate all remaining evidence of bourgeois culture, particularly any that showed lustful or decadent patterns of sexual behavior. Enforcement was entrusted to the Red Guards, who traveled around the country reprimanding those who adhered to "bourgeois practices." Of course, this was like charging the fox to guard the henhouse, since these cadres of young men and women at the height of their sexuality moved from city to city and commune to commune far removed from any adult authority. Accommodations and sleeping arrangements were haphazard and the guards often ended up sleeping together, regardless of sex, in a variety of places, including open fields, crowded barracks, and railroad stations. Though the Party control over the sexual discipline of the Red Guards often broke down, they still denounced the decadent sexuality of others, and adopted as their slogan one that appeared on Beijing walls in 1974, at the height of the Cultural Revolution: "Making love is a mental disease that wastes time and energy." Those who were found to have strayed from the Party doctrine were harassed, forced to confess their errors, and punished.

As the excesses of the Cultural Revolution were brought under control, the Chinese officials realized that a whole generation had grown up without any information about sex. Particularly uninformed were the women, who, surveys indicated, often believed they could become pregnant by kissing. By 1980, the government again permitted some pamphlets on sex education to be published, but in highly censored form. Michael Weisskopf, a correspondent for the Washington *Post,* in 1980 described one of the first of these books. He stated that the only sex manual he ever saw in China was a pamphlet entitled *Sexual Knowledge.* It took a strict view "of the need to limit the frequency of intercourse . . . with a [recommended] normal routine of 'once every week or two' [for newly married couples]. But the guidebook . . . was sold out within hours after it went on sale in the New China Bookstore near the Peking Hotel." Gradually, more sophisticated manuals went on sale, and in 1985 the Chinese government allowed the publication of Fang Fu Ruan's *Handbook of Sex Knowledge.* Also in 1985, there was a national conference of educators to plan a program of sex education in China, which was implemented in 1988. Official opposition to the dissemination of information about contraceptives was withdrawn; indeed, a new program was initiated specifically to teach about birth control.

These programs, however, should not be taken as evidence for any radical change. The purpose of the sex education program was to give some basic information about sex and contraception and to discourage any sexual activity except between married heterosexual couples. With the Chinese emphasis on the one-child family, adequate information about contraceptives is deemed essential. However, about the same time that the government seemed to be starting to come to terms with sexuality through its sex-education program, it reasserted its power by moving against those who experimented with different forms of sexuality. During the past two years, in fact, there have been a series of arrests of foreigners who engaged in sex with Chinese prostitutes, of Chinese who were cohabiting together without official permission to do so, of prostitutes, of homosexuals, and of those who disseminated "pornography," a term rather broadly defined since even the widely recognized classic of the seventeenth century, *The Golden Lotus,* has been classed as pornographic. Large quantities of published material, videotapes and audiotapes, and the machines on which they were played, have been seized and destroyed. Fines are steep and punishment is drastic. In 1988, the police urged all Chinese who either possessed or read pornography to turn in their materials to the police and confess. One young man who failed to do so was discovered with nine pornographic tapes that he allegedly played at sex parties. He was given the death penalty. To further combat illegal cohabitation in university dormatories, female students have been given strict curfews, and nightly bedchccks are performed.

The major effect of the government policy has been to make it difficult for Chinese who do not have spouses to have lawful outlet for their sexual drives, which, of course, remain strong. Eighty percent of the women recently surveyed in Shantung Province admitted to having had sex before they were married. Also, incidents of rape and other sex crimes have increased. Between 1979 and 1983 rape cases rose by 377 percent in Shanghai and by 340 percent in China as a whole. There has been a corresponding rise in crimes such as voyeurism, the physical harassment of women, and prostitution, both homosexual and heterosexual.

In sum, the attempts to control sexual expression have been slightly more successful in modern China than elsewhere in the world or in history, and have emphasized just how much control the official government has. When individuals need permission to attempt to conceive, we have reached the ultimate police state. It is noteworthy that the greatest repression of sex we know of in history has not occurred through the efforts of any unenlightened religious group, but through a modern secular government that claims to know what is best for its people. It has been more effective than past attempts at control because modern techniques allow it to be so. China began to modify its position in 1985, but after 1989's student uprising, it reverted to some of the sex repression of the past. China has a long way to go before it reaches the ideal of toleration advocated by the International Humanist and Ethical Union.

# Roadmap to the Humanist/Feminist Future

## Gina Allen
### (United States)

A funny thing could happen to us on our way to the twenty-first century. We could get lost and end up in Kalamazoo. We most certainly will get lost if we don't know where we're going.

That's why we need to create a roadmap to the future. It will be a humanist future if we humanists can make it so at this late date. It is already a feminist future. Feminists worldwide have been working on that for generations.

The feminists of today in this country are the great-grandchildren of the feminists, both women and men, who gathered in Seneca Falls, New York, in July 1848, for the first Feminist Convention. Other countries too have their historic feminist awakenings, but I shall focus on the progress of women in the United States, because that is what I know.

When it comes to women's rights the United States is not the most progressive country in the world. It ranks far behind the Scandinavian countries—Norway, Sweden, and Finland, for instance—and in recent years the United States has been losing ground.

It is, in fact, rather like Iran, where I lived for several years before the reign of the Ayatollah. The years I spent in Iran were a very exciting time for women there, when they were discarding the veil, learning to read and write, and even being admitted to Iran's colleges and universities. But then the country got religion and descended into hell.

That's a problem with religion—once you get it you don't know where you're going. Only God knows, and who can read his capricious mind? Of course, as a woman I was always as leery of going to heaven as to hell. Oh, I knew, as a religious child, that hell was hot and heaven was made of gold, but I also knew that the God who had made earth had also made heaven and no doubt divided up labor the same way there as here. So I figured it was the male angels who sat on fluffy clouds playing their golden harps, or maybe playing golf, while female angels spent eternity washing golden dishes at golden sinks. Who needs it?

I became an atheist so that I wouldn't have to worry about where I was going; later I became a feminist and a humanist. Now I am again worrying about where I'm going—where we're all going—not in the hereafter but in less than a dozen years.

I worry that when the humanists get to the twenty-first century they'll see that it is a feminist century and drive on past, looking for a future that is more familiar. The present humanist and ethical revival was achieved by men half a century ago and for many years these men simply neglected to invite women to the feast—or to the boards or to the platforms of humanist and ethical organizations. A few women wandered in to stay and were tolerated and sometimes even elevated to offices. But there was little or no outreach to women.

It was as if when humanists spoke of working for the best possible life on earth for all mankind they truly meant men only. It wasn't that they didn't like women. They had wives and sweethearts and mothers and daughters, but these women didn't exist independently—not even in the files of humanist organizations. I found out when I investigated that married women members were listed only as "and Mrs." under their husband's names. And I walked into a humanist board meeting one day to hear a man recommending a new book on humanism as follows: "This book is written in such simple terms that even your wife will understand it."

That took me right back to the Old Testament, where women are admonished that they shouldn't speak up in church but should save their questions for their husbands, who will explain it all to them. And I feared then that American humanists, at least, weren't as far removed from their Judeo-Christian roots as they thought; that, indeed, against all scientific evidence, and with the fundamentalists and the authors of the Bible, they believed that the seat of the mind is in the testicles.

And I guess this wasn't strictly an American phenomenon. For years, when the IHEU World Congress program came out, Bette Chambers and I wrote protesting that there were no women participants. I guess the IHEU finally got tired of hearing from us, for token women began appearing on conference programs. And now! Look at this program! We've come a long way, baby. So I can stop worrying, I think. Humanists are ready for a feminist twenty-first century.

Why do I keep calling the next century a feminist one? Because while humanist men were talking to one another about what men consider important, feminists were not only waging a feminist revolution on behalf of women's equality but they were also bringing up the next generation, the adults of tomorrow who will shape the next century.

Just as feminists have raised one another's consciousness around the globe, so have they raised the consciousness of their children. And they have done a remarkable job. As Sonia Johnson, excommunicated from the Mormon church for her feminist activities, has observed, "Consciousness raising is the genius of the women's movement."

Certainly it has had a profound effect on college students. In an attempt to find out what causes have most influenced college students in the past two decades, two sociologists, Alexander Astin and Kenneth Green of UCLA's Higher Education Research Institute, compiled and analyzed studies conducted over that time on more than a thousand college and university campuses. These studies surveyed the attitudes and aspirations of six million college students.

Analysis of these studies revealed that in recent years the women's movement—of all causes—has had the most significant and enduring effect on college students. "The women's movement has penetrated every aspect of college life," say the researchers. "And its impact is not diminishing. The changes seem irreversible. Women will surely never go back to where they were two decades ago."

Nor will men go back. They don't want to, according to a survey of 2,800 business executives made by the American Management Association. Eighty-three percent of these highly successful businessmen reported that success in the business world did not equal happiness.

They wanted more. Not more money or more recognition, but more time with their families. More opportunity for creative self-expression. More possibilities to savor life and love, maybe to carry out the dreams of their youth. Some of them wanted the same choices their wives had to pursue careers or stay at home and enjoy the children and pursue interests that might be economically costly but were personally and often socially productive.

The young women and men that feminists have been bringing up during the past quarter of a century are going to take these choices for granted. If he wants to stay home and take care of the children and write or compose or paint, she'll be the breadwinner and he won't feel less the man because she's earning the living. Or she can stay home. Or both will pursue careers. Not because two careers are forced on them through economic necessity, as is often the case today, but because they have choices and aren't so bound by traditional sex roles that they can't accept these choices.

So now we know our destination—not only a new century but a new world in relationships between women and men. And where do we start mapping our journey? I would suggest the campuses. The road ahead looks wide and smooth and easy—but beware, there are hidden potholes all around us.

In a recent study reported in the *Journal of Academe,* researchers found that women who teach at universities are paid less, on the average, than their male colleagues. Elizabeth Scott, professor of statistics at the University of California at Berkeley, says that at major universities throughout the United States, "the average annual increase in salary for men is about twice that for women. Women start lower and move up more slowly. Salary dfferences get worse with time."

The research proves this. A female assistant professor makes only $2,000 less annually than a man who was hired at the same time; but when both become full professors, the woman earns on the average $10,000 less a year than the man. This can't be excused on the basis that women take time out to have children, since women without children experience the same salary differentials.

Humanists meet on college and university campuses all the time, and many of those at the forefront of the humanist and ethical movement teach in colleges and universities. Why, then, does this injustice go unchallenged?

The eighth item in the Declaration of Principles of the International Humanist and Ethical Union states that "Human justice is the progressive realization of equality." Equality on university campuses, as elsewhere, should be a humanist and ethical concern. When we drag our feet on such issues we aren't moving ahead toward the next century. We're letting others get there before us to shape the world of tomorrow.

So let's get a move on. We start out, mapping our way to the future, on a beautiuful highway, despite the hidden potholes. This fine road, though eroded here and there, is paved with hard-fought victories from the past: the Civil Rights Act, the Equal Pay Act (which works better at McDonald's than it does on college campuses), the Higher Education Act, Affirmative Action, and women's right to control their own bodies and make their own reproductive decisions, without which all other rights are meaningless.

Humanists were pioneers in the long struggle in this country for reproductive freedom. Margaret Sanger, who fought for birth control, was honored in 1957 by the American Humanist Association (AHA) as the first woman Humanist of the Year, though it would be twenty-one years before we had another woman Humanist of the Year; indeed, of the thirty-five Humanist of the Year awards, only eight have been presented to women.

But if the AHA neglected women when it was handing out awards, it didn't forget women's important right to reproductive freedom. Long before the Supreme Court decision on *Roe* v. *Wade* gave women in this country the right to safe, legal abortions, the AHA became the first organization to work actively for a woman's right to terminate an unwanted pregnancy, and actually helped pregnant women to find competent abortion providers.

This was accomplished through the Society for Humane Abortion, founded by the humanist Pat Maginnis with support and assistance from the AHA. In those dark years before *Roe* v. *Wade,* practically everything this group did was illegal and its leaders spent years defending themselves before the Supreme Court put the stamp of approval on their courageous, pioneering work. AHA's part in this effort on behalf of women stands as one of humanism's finest hours in this country.

What was so gallantly won then must not be lost now for lack of vigilance. Abortion is constantly under attack in this country and is denied in Third World countries in large part because of the United States' arbitrary restrictions on funding, which also endanger all methods of birth control where they are most desperately needed.

Think of it—in the Third World and in poverty-stricken areas of the United States, five million women are killed every decade by motherhood. In the Third World perpetual pregnancy is the leading killer of women of childbearing age. These deaths are almost entirely preventable when safe, legal abortions and low cost, effective birth control are available. Hundreds of thousands of lives have been saved by legal abortion in most industrialized nations since the 1970s.

And abortion is about to become safer and easier than ever before—but not in this advanced country. In other developed countries where abortion is legal, a new abortion pill has been released that terminates pregnancy within the first trimester without an operation and without major side effects. It won't be available here because the so-called pro-lifers threaten to boycott the drug companies that market it. The farm workers get heavily fined when they try to boycott, but others keep their religious tax exemption while politically imposing their religious beliefs on the rest of us.

Obviously, though the highway to the future that we have been charting looks smooth enough, it requires constant vigilance, like the freeways in southern California where drivers take potshots at one another just for the sport of it. And—look out ahead! There's a barrier on our map that is labeled "The U.S. Constitution." The map doesn't call it a barrier. It says it stands there to protect the rights of those who travel this road. It's been standing over the highway for two hundred years, heavily guarded, but the guards let some people through and turn others back.

It is rather like St. Peter's gates that stand at the entrance to heaven. There the guards ask men who approach to spell "God" and if they can do so they are admitted. The guards ask the women to spell "Albuquerque."

But even women who can spell Albuquerque aren't offered the protection of the U.S. Constitution. It's for men only. And all the gains of the past that pave the highway on which we travel to the future are in danger of obliteration until the rights of both halves of the population of the United States are protected by the Constitution. That they aren't should shame us all.

To proceed on our way you who are men can pass through the barrier. My sisters and I will scramble around as best we can. On the other side of the barrier the going gets rough. We join other women struggling toward the future—Third World women, many of whom are veiled, considered property, sold into marriage or concubinage, used as beasts of burden, raped and killed during wars, starving where there is famine, carrying babies dying of hunger.

There are women from East, Central, and Southern Africa who have been sexually mutilated at puberty, which makes sexual intercourse and childbirth excruciatingly painful and leaves them particularly susceptible to the AIDS virus, of which they are the main carriers in that part of the world and which they pass on to their babies at birth. Officials of the World Health Organization say that AIDS in these areas of Africa threatens more human lives than famine, drought, or refugee problems.

Has this glimpse of the Third World depressed you? We can hurry on to the developed world, but we can't escape AIDS. It's everywhere. In the United States it is complicated for many of its victims by homophobia. Other victims are young drug users who share needles and practice unsafe sex.

Many girls who are drug users become mothers while they are still children themselves, their pregnancies complicated by their youth and lack of prenatal care, their babies born addicted, or with AIDS, or both, and often with other problems as well. The deaths of their newborns swell our disgracefully high infant-mortality rate, which, in poverty pockets such as Detroit, is as high as it is in Third World countries such as Zimbabwe.

In this country where female college graduates earn, on the average, the same as male high-school dropouts, these young single mothers have little hope. With their children they will join the ranks of the homeless and impoverished, a growing army in this affluent land.

Indeed, children under fifteen years of age, most of them from single-parent families headed by women, make up the largest, fastest growing poverty population in the United States. Many of these children were born into the middle-class and were plunged into poverty by divorce. The average American man's standard of living rises by 42 percent in the first year after his divorce. The standard of living of the mother with custody of her children, on the other hand, drops by 73 percent.

Less than 60 percent of mothers are awarded child support by the court and fewer than half these actually get any child support. Even those who do receive support get only half what it costs them for day-care while they work. Most ex-husbands' monthly car payments are higher than their child-support payments.

Around the world children—our hope for the future—are our most wasted resource. In this country alone, ten thousand children die of poverty each year. Only 5 percent of the American military budget would keep every child in America out of poverty. A day's worth of military spending worldwide would end starvation everywhere.

But most children who die in this country and around the world don't die from starvation. Imagine, if you can, as we map our route to the future, two hundred jumbo jets packed with children crashing every day on our roadways. Half of these children are killed and half are crippled for life. That's thirty thousand children who die every day and thirty thousand who are irreparably damaged.

If they actually crashed in jumbo jets we would pay attention. But they don't. Nor do they die of anything as dramatic as starvation, war, or AIDS, though many children worldwide do. No. These children die of diarrhea and of diseases that could be prevented easily with inexpensive immunization and proper care, says the Executive Director of UNICEF, James Grant, writing in the UN Children's Fund annual report, 1987. These children die from our neglect.

We must take the burden of these neglected children with us into the twenty-first century, along with the other burdens we have collected along our way. It's a heavy load. Fortunately, we don't have to carry it far, for there, just ahead on our map, is our destination.

The feminists who got there before us are gathered to greet us and to help us with the cargo of problems we've brought with us for solutions in this future that we both now share. They don't chide us that we're tardy. They don't say what I said—that the twenty-first century is a feminist century. They say what Feminist leaders—Betty Friedan, Aileen Hernandez, Gloria Steinem, and others—have been saying for a quarter of a century: "What we are all about is humanism." Feminism is, after all, just another face of humanism.

And that's fortunate. For building a world community in the new century, a community dedicated to equality, to peace, to the cherishing of children, is too large a task for humanists or feminists to accomplish alone. We'll do it best if we do it together.

# Building a New Ethics:
# Contingencies and Predictions in Sexology

## John Money
### (United States)

When the ethics of any new century undergoes change, its divergence from the ethics of the past is neither totally arbitrary nor totally engineered. Prophecies and predictions, whether of moral doom and destruction or of moral redemption and utopia, may be as inconsequential as fairy dust. Or they may be contingent on changes in either technology or demographics, the two great sources of change in the ethics and ideology of how the members of a society conduct themselves in relation to one another.

Technological innovation may be the product of a homegrown invention, or it may be borrowed directly or by progressive diffusion from its place of origin. Demographic alteration of a population may be a product of changes in its overall density, its sex ratio, or its age ratio, all three of which are, in turn, products of differential changes in mortality, longevity, and incoming or outgoing migration.

In conformity with the principle of inertia, a society's ethics of sexuality and eroticism remain constant until disturbed by technological or demographic change. Such a change took place among cultures of the West during the 1960s and 1970s. It was of sufficient magnitude to earn the title "sexual revolution." Since it lacked the characteristics of an armed uprising, it is more accurately named a sexual reformation, even more accurately because it was a continuation of a reform movement dating back to the middle of the nineteenth century. The agenda of the movement was the destereotyping of rigidly stereotyped male/female roles and relationships, and an equal-opportunity ethics for both men and women, sexually and otherwise.

The first stage of the sexual reformation extended into the first quarter of the twentieth century. It culminated when women gained the franchise and had equality with men at the ballot box. The second stage peaked between mid-century and the present. It culminated with increased equality of educational and vocational opportunity, but with the Equal Rights Amendment put on hold in the United States.

The third stage, quietly gaining momentum, will continue into the twenty-first century. It has on its agenda equality of economic opportunity in the marketplace for women, and equality of domestic opportunity and child care for men.

Equal economic and domestic opportunity constitutes social androgyny, which correlates with erotosexual androgyny to a variable degree. Bisexuality is one manifestation of erotosexual androgyny. The statistics of AIDS have unmasked the statistics of bisexuality and shown its prevalence to be of sufficient magnitude that the ethics of homosexual as well as heterosexual orientation is assured a place on the agenda of the third stage of the sexual reformation in the forthcoming century.

## Technology and Sexual Reformation: Past History, Future Lessons

Within the household and family during the present century, the reformation of male/female roles into equal-opportunity roles with respect to child care has been dependent on technological innovation in infant nutrition. Even though formula milk and prepared baby food are compatible with infant health, their preferred use in early infancy is as supplements, not substitutes, for breast milk. Whether before weaning or after, however, the existence of alternatives to breast milk allows the father to participate in infant care, or even to be solely responsible.

Other changes in domestic technology, insofar as they reduce the amount of time spent on household chores, enable both men and women to find time for two careers, one domestic, and one extradomestic.

Until the beginning of the industrial age, barely two centuries ago, the bimodal division of labor between males and females was dictated in part by the contingencies of their different reproductive roles, and in part by differences contingent upon their reproductive hormones. Women were tied by pregnancy, breast-feeding, and the effect of their reproductive hormones on sexually dimorphic physique to a less mobile lifestyle than were men; whereas men were tied by the sexually dimorphic effect of their reproductive hormones on skeletal and muscular size to a lifestyle of more labor-intensive lifting, pushing, and pulling.

With the invention of labor-saving heavy machinery and, subsequently, its automation and computer-operated control, the ethics of bimodal stereotyping of male and female roles on the criterion of brute strength became subject to revision and reformation. Industrial technology changed the erstwhile hard-labor occupations of males into equal-opportunity occupations that could be performed by both sexes.

Following the discovery, in the mid-nineteenth century, of the vulcanization process to produce rubber, the manufacture and distribution of rubber diaphrams and condoms was criminalized. The invention of the latex rubber process in the 1920s, and the mass-production of rubber condoms distributed in vending machines, then a novelty, marked the true onset of the birth-control era. Contraceptive technology, advancing rapidly to include hormonal contraception, by the 1950s produced the Pill. With the Pill, women gained more than just another self-applied pregnancy regulator. It was put respectably into the mouth, not into the vagina; and the act of taking it was separated by time from the act of copulation.

The Pill, together with the revival of the IUD, the diaphragm, and the condom, allowed the scheduling of pregnancies to be an equal-opportunity endeavor that separated procreational sex from recreational sex. Contraceptive technology relieved people from being locked into an ethics of unequal opportunity that coerced both sexes into breeding too often, and locked woman into the role of brood mare and housewife and man into the role of breeding stud and breadwinner. The equal opportunity provided by contraceptive technology was essential to the reformation of sexual ethics that, put into practice, became known in media parlance as the sexual revolution.

Whereas contraceptive technology gave both sexes equality of opportunity to make a distinction between procreational and recreational sex, and to schedule their genital activities accordingly, antibiotic technology promised equality of opportunity to be protected against sexually transmitted disease. Penicillin, the first antibiotic to be discovered, was initially mass-marketed in the late 1940s. It proved to be effective against the two most dreaded of sexually transmitted infections, syphilis and gonorrhea. It protected all who were exposed to infection, including the unborn, and it protected those who were exposed homosexually as well as heterosexually.

The combined effect of contraceptive and antibiotic technology was to provide both sexes with equality of opportunity to revise the patriarchal stereotype of male/female sexual interaction in monogamous marriage, and to substitute one of what became known as the alternative lifestyles. These alternatives, rather than being newly discovered, were culturally borrowed or historically revived. Among the alternatives were the polygynous or polyandrous household, or both combined in communal or group-sex sharing. Open marriage abolished the traditional possessiveness of monogamy, and the vituperation associated with adultery. Betrothal and living together in pre-Roman Europe was a universal custom that provided proof of fertility prior to marriage. It had survived only in Arctic Scandinavia, whence it was borrowed back into the mainstream of new-age youth culture. Some lived alone and had more or less casual affairs as singles. Some lived as the head of a single-parent household. In the United States, this custom had an antecedent in African-American slavery, within which marriage, as a legal right, did not exist.

Antibiotic technology's great deficiency was that it did not protect against sexually transmitted viral disease. A vaccine was developed to protect against viral hepatitis, but there is no vaccine to protect against the virus for genital herpes. Both of these viral diseases pale into insignificance in comparison with AIDS, the newly recognized lethal disease for which the human immunodeficiency virus (HIV) is responsible. AIDS changed the lifestyle focus from equal opportunity to equal responsibility for safe sex.

More than a hundred years prior to 1960, the age of puberty in Europe and America began decreasing by approximately four months every ten years, from age seventeen or eighteen to twelve or thirteen—more or less. Two centuries ago, courtship, marriage, and a sex life followed on the heels of puberty—and necessarily so, for the average life expectancy was only thirty-five years. The younger the age of puberty, however, the greater the pressure to revise the age-related sexual ethics of youth. To some extent, young people have been establishing a revised ethical consensus for themselves, in advance of formal ratification of the revision. Thus the age for beginning a sex life is scheduled earlier than the age of marriage. Dependent on local traditions, the age of first parenthood also antedates marriage, and the three-generational, extended kinship household takes precedence over the two-generational, nuclear-family household.

## Demographics and Sexual Reformation: Past History and Future Lessons

At the end of the eighteenth century in Maryland, the infant mortality rate between birth and one year of age averaged 50 percent. For the survivors, the average life expectancy, as aforesaid, was thirty-five years. By the end of the nineteenth century, the average life expectancy was forty-five years. Now, even before the end of the twentieth century, the average life expectancy for is women eighty to eighty-five years, and for men seventy to seventy-five years. Expansion of the life span expands also the number of years in which men and women are emancipated from the obligations and duties of breeding. Some of those years of emancipation are years of equal sexuoerotic opportunity, and some are years when the briefer life expectancy of the male changes the sex ratio and there is a surplus of older women. Thus, a revised, nonprocreative sexual ethics for the proverbial life after forty is needed. Formal ratification of a revision, as in the case of youth, has been dilatory.

It would appear to be an all-species principle that population density is not self-limiting until the size of a population and the size of the ecological resources for its sustentation reach a critical ratio. There are many signs that for the human species this critical ratio has been reached, and that the human population has already begun the destruction of its ecological resources to the point of exhausting and exterminating them. With insufficient resources, the human species would be in danger, if not of its own extinction, then of its decimation. This is not an era when the human population needs to breed prolifically to maintain itself. Rather, it will maintain itself by breeding less prolifically. Men and women may, therefore, reduce their breeding and add to their expanded life expectancy even more years of a revised, equal-opportunity, nonprocreational sexual ethics.

## Demographics and Sexual Reformation: Projections and Prophesies

If, in the twenty-first century, the age-related sex ratio should become radically imbalanced, then in populations in which one sex greatly outnumbers the other, a revision of sexual ethics would be logically expected. Without human intervention, a radical change in the sex ratio is improbable. One possible human intervention would derive from advances in the biotechnology of fertilization. A brave-new-world sexual ethics favoring a contrived imbalance of the sex ratio is science-fictionally possible. Over the long term, however, a balanced sex ratio is the more likely realization.

As compared with a change in the sex ratio, a change in the age ratio of a population is not science-fictional. Such a change has already been observed in several populations in which there has been a change in the ratio of births to deaths. In the United States, the bulge in population growth after World War II, known as the baby boom, is an example. Like a wave, the bulge rolls forward and will create a geriatric bulge and a funeral bulge. Large-scale shifts in the age ratio necessitate revision of social policy with respect to the rate of population growth, which, in turn, involves revision of sexual ethics.

In this effect on the revision of sexual ethics, shifts of the sex ratio or age ratio within a population are minor in comparison with shifts in population density. The Malthusian dread of catastrophic overpopulation has dominated contemporary projections of population density in the upcoming century. A corresponding dread of catastrophic depopulation, despite the history of populations decimated or annihilated by war, famine, and plague, has seldom entered into the calculations of future statistics. Nonetheless, depopulation as a sequel to ecological pollution, for example, or the ozone hole, or the greenhouse effect, is a possibility. In addition, no one knows how to predict the extent of depopulation from the viral plague of AIDS.

Because AIDS is, to a significant degree, a sexually transmitted disease, its effect on the revision of sexual ethics has already been made apparent. It is not only the threat of depopulation, however, but also of overpopulation that will necessitate a rebuilding of next century's sexual ethics.

## Technology and Sexual Reformation: Projections and Prophesies

In the history of science, so many future-changing discoveries have been made serendipitously that they could not, ahead of time, have been accounted for in any estimate of the effects of technological change on ethical change. At best, one takes account of those technological changes that are already on the horizon of possible realization. Among them are advances in the control of fertility and infertility, which will include male contraception and nonrandom determination of the sex of offspring before conception.

It is already known that a human pregnancy can be carried to term in the abdominal cavity without a uterus. Thus one may expect, by inference from animal evidence, that the same will happen, by way of an in vitro fertilization of a donor egg, in the abdominal cavity of a human male. One may expect also the development of a technology that will allow an in-vitro fertilized zygote to be transferred into the uterus of a surrogate of another species or, going one step further, to be grown to term in an extrauterine incubator.

Eventually, the fertilization of two cells, egg and sperm, in vitro will itself become optional, for the technology of cloning will allow a single cell to grow into a replica of its donor—a technology that is already well established for plants. Even without technology, there are some species of whiptail lizards that reproduce by cloning. These lizards have no males and no females, but are parthenogenic. In other words, each lizard grows from one parent cell alone. It becomes an exact replica of the parent.

The technology of DNA sequencing is already sufficiently developed to have put the prospect of mapping the entire human genome on the drawing board. Provided the enormous cost of financing the project can be met, and competitive rivalries can be resolved, it will be accomplished. Everything in human development that is genetically coded will ultimately be traceable, once the genome map has been completed. The range of technological applications is of an enormity too great to be encompassed in present-day thinking. There will certainly be a technology of genetic engineering—in media language, the utilization of designer genes—that will be applicable before conception, in utero, and postnatally.

Genetic engineering will open up the possibility of evolutionary engineering, applicable to all species, including Homo sapiens. One can envisage the designing of human subtypes and varieties—and, perhaps, an annual best-of-show championship contest for each! With designer genes, cross-species hybridization is also a technological possibility.

Needless to say, all of the foregoing potential innovations in technology will provoke intense ethical dispute in which the forces of reformation line up against the forces of counterreformation. Whatever the outcome, it will not be the fossilization of today's sexual ethics but an updating of them to meet the as-yet-unforeseen contingencies of a changed technology.

## Counterreformation Tyranny

Worldwide, there are multiple ideologies of pair-bonding, procreation, and marriage, each one ethically viable within its own larger sociological context. If the forces of counterreformation prevail, they would, as during the Inquisition, tolerate only one ideology—their own. Should the counterreformation consolidate its power under a charismatic demagogue, Hitler-style, then be prepared in the twenty-first century for a sexual tyranny enforcing the antisexual ideology of a self-defined moral elite. Be prepared for a tyranny that criminalizes sex and uses secret-police tactics of entrapment to prove criminality. Be prepared for the first strategy, the criminalization of pornography. The sexual tyrant knows that he can co-opt even those who will admit in private that pornography as an erotic form of entertainment has had no corrupting influence on them. In public, these same people will self-righteously declare that they are against pornography.

Be prepared, next, for the disenfranchisement of liberation and feminist politics, and for the criminalization of abortion, contraception, homosexuality, and bisexuality, all of which controvert the dogma that sex should be exclusively for reproduction. Nonreproductive forms of sexual expression, including manual and oral sex, will be prosecuted as perversions and crimes against nature. Only penovaginal sex will be permitted, with the man on top, and woman below, in her patriarchally subordinate position of obedience.

The forms of sexual expression already listed in the criminal code as perversions punishable by imprisonment or death will be expanded to include all the forms, harmless or otherwise, of kinky sex, properly known as paraphilias.

Mystified by the bizarre manifestations of some of the paraphilias, and afraid of them, the public buys into the long-outmoded, prescientific dogma that they are caught by social contagion. The contagion, according to this false dogma, is spread not only by those who already are carriers of a syndrome of paraphilia, but also by representations of them in narratives, pictures, photos, movies, or videos, legally defined as pornography. An even more ominous error in this dogma is that the contagion can be caught from "pornography" that depicts normal, healthy sex. The explanation given is another dogma, namely that normal pornography incites to lust, which causes loss of precious vital fluids, especially semen. As the semen drains away, degeneracy sets in, ending in progressive sexual depravity, disease, and death. Degeneracy dogma belongs with semen-conservation dogma. Both have their origins in prehistory.

The tragedy of the public that buys into the error of semen-conservation dogma is the tragedy that befalls their children. To ensure that they will conserve semen and be saved from degeneracy, children are subjected to an ideology of sexual prohibition and the criminalization of sex. A sex-is-punishment, sex-is-crime environment backfires, however. It increases the risk of growing up to be sexually abnormal. Sexual abnormality is passed on like an epidemic of a slow-growing virus. It is an epidemic that expands, exponentially, from one generation to the next. The paradox of antisexualism and the criminalization of sex is that, instead of eradicating or reducing the sexual abnormality that it prohibits and criminalizes, it actually increases it.

The sexual tyrant self-righteously fails to comprehend this paradox. Do not be surprised, therefore, to encounter a counterreformationist proposal to set up utopian, patriarchal breeding colonies, inhabited exclusively by a quarantined, antifeminist breeding elite. In the twenty-first century, such colonies may well be extraterrestrial, their inhabitants hand-picked according to ideologically dictated criteria. One of the criteria might be a preliminary segregation to ensure that they are AIDS-free and HIV negative.

Whatever the criteria on which a utopian breeding colony might be founded, its founding ideology would be unrecognizably transformed in the outcome.

Likewise its ethics. That is always the fate of utopias. Too many unforeseen and adventitious factors intervene and alter the predicted outcome.


## Reformation Democracy

If the ideology of the sexual reformation survives the tyranny of counterreformation, then the ideological prospectus for sexual ethics in the coming century is one in which sexual democracy will no longer be considered a subversive threat to political democracy. The ratification of sexual democracy would grant equality of opportunity to men and women in the bedroom as well as in the boardroom and allow the activities of both locations to be uncensored topics in the public domain. Both could be discussed explicitly and without fear of self-incrimination as safely in the media as in private.

It is self-incriminating to admit to having experienced, even only in fantasy, any expression of sexuality that is, according to the criteria endorsed by society, morally or criminally abhorrent. The penalties of self-incrimination are so great that in Washington, D.C., one among many jurisdictions where oral sex, even between spouses, is a crime, no politician or public personage would dare to admit to ever having engaged in it. The dangers of self-incrimination apply at all ages, with potentially devastating consequences on the young who, quite literally, dare not speak the unspeakable, lest they incriminate themselves. Among minors, the range of the unspeakable is broad. It includes juvenile sexual rehearsal play, masturbation, pubertal and adolescent copulation, contraceptive protection, safe-sex to avoid AIDS, and precocious parenthood.

The unspeakable and self-incriminating sexual topics include also the anomalies of sexuoerotic function that, for those who have them, are experienced as shameful, blameworthy, guilt provoking, or criminal. To speak of them is to betray oneself to public humiliation, scorn, or reprisal. To not speak of them is to betray oneself to private suffering, self-denigration, and risk of being unmasked. This is a classic example of being entrapped in a Catch-22 dilemma of being damned if you do and damned if you don't. The terrible price to pay may be personal—as, for example, when the trauma of sexual abuse is so unspeakable that it induces a response of elective mutism and disabling phobic pathology and somatic impairment.

The terrible price may also be paid by society, as is the case of the sex-offending paraphilias, the syndromes of sexual behavioral disorder known legally as perversions. Erotophonophilia, the syndrome of serial lust murder, is an extreme example. The boy whose erotic dreams and masturbation fantasies reveal to him that he is potentially a lust murderer does not incriminate himself by talking about his paraphilic imagery. He is deprived of the benefit of early therapeutic intervention, and damned by his silence to develop the full-blown syndrome. He may kill alone, or with an accomplice. Females with the syndrome are, according to data available, more likely to have an accomplice. Either sex may kill homosexually or heterosexually. They may kill dozens or hundreds of times before being apprehended. That is the terrible price that society pays.

There is a Catch-22 paradox that applies here, namely, that the very behavior that is outlawed and prohibited as immoral or criminal is not thereby eradicated, but only concealed. In concealment it flourishes, and escapes the scrutiny of science. It will be the research of science, not the paraphernalia of punishment, that eventually discovers the cause, the treatment, and the prevention of all the sexual disorders. That will be a task for the twenty-first century. For the realization of this task, it will be imperative to have a new sexual ethics—one in which the pathological manifestations of the sexual syndromes, instead of being criminalized, will be biomedicalized. Biomedical ethics are not irresponsible. They are the ethics of etiology, diagnosis, treatment, quarantine, and prevention. If psychosis and epilepsy had not been biomedicalized, then criminalization would still be the fate of psychotics and epileptics.

The decriminalization of sex will permit the development in the next century of a genuine science of pediatric sexology. It will expose the errors of the now widespread twin doctrines of sexual behavior in the juvenile years, namely that sexuality in childhood is a developmental nullity, and that manifest evidence of juvenile sexual behavior is, de facto, evidence of criminal molestation and abuse.

The decriminalization of sex will release minors of all ages from the Catch-22 of being damned if they do disclose their sexual activities and damed if they don't. With no Catch-22, there will be no self-imposed retribution, and no penalties or reprisals imposed by others as the price of either silence or speaking out. Instead of being forced by the system into being either self-incriminating, self-reproachful, or adversarially destructive, the person who speaks out will be entitled to mutually fair and constructive intervention that will be maximally beneficial to all parties. In addition, those who investigate and those who render biomedical services will not become conscripts of the social-science and medical arm of the police.

The decriminalization of sex will have a positive ancillary effect on issues of sex that, though not criminalized, are subject to opprobrious stigmatization. In the sexual ethics of the twenty-first century, one such issue will pertain to the open availability of explicitly accurate information, pro and con, concerning abortion, contraception, the curriculum of love and sex education, and the relationship between the ideological economics of a culture and the age of first parenthood. In twenty-first-century ephebiatrics, the twentieth-century statistical obsession with teenaged pregnancy as a disease, even up to the age of nineteen, will be seen as the ideology of those in power imposed on cultural minorities whose cultural history regarding age of first parenthood stems from a different, although not necessarily inferior, ideology. With adequate economic support, an early beginning and early ending of breeding may well be seen as a viable alternative to a late beginning and late ending—especially when viewed in the context of equal-opportunity for careers, other than parenthood, for both the father and the mother.

Another ancillary effect of the decriminalization of sex is that, in the twenty-first century, it will be possible to use pornography positively and constructively as an illustration of paraphilia and impairment of sexual health on the one hand, and of normophilia and enhancement of sexual health on the other. Even before the twenty-first century, there is a positive urgency in establishing a constructive relationship between pornography, masturbation, and AIDS.

Masturbation in Latin means, literally, "hand rape." "Hand practice," the term used in India, sounds better. Hand practice, today, is just about the only sure-fire guarantee against catching the virus that causes AIDS. I strongly recommend hand practice, especially to those entering adolescence, but also to people of any age who want, at all costs, not to expose themselves inadvertently to the infected body fluids of someone who is already, even though invisibly, carrying the virus.

Masturbation accompanied by a masturbation fantasy is a rehearsal for a sexual relationship with a partner. Masturbation fantasies have been around for as long as the human race has been on earth. Only in the twentieth century, however, have filmmakers converted the mental tapes of their own and other people's fantasies into erotically explicit movies and videos, and produced them commercially so that others may share them. Sharing is possible, however, only when a person's own erotic fantasy matches the fantasy on the movie or video-tape. People with healthy or normophilic erotic fantasies do not get turned on sexually by books, films, or videos made for people with unhealthy or paraphilic (kinky) erotic fantasies—and, as aforesaid, they do not catch a paraphilia by reading or watching an example of paraphilic kinkiness.

My recommendation to young people is to select technologically superior and erotically healthy videos, and to use them to become champions of virtuoso hand practice. To begin with, you can watch them alone. Then you can watch them with your lover, engaging in mutual hand practice, but still avoiding contact with one another's body fluids. In that way you will buy time to discover how well-matched you are for a long-term, pairbonded love affair, and maybe marriage. Eventually the day will arrive when you can make a solemn contract of pairbonded fidelity, which means that, as long as you stay together, neither one will risk infecting the other by breaking the contract and bringing back someone else's AIDS virus.

My additional recommendation is that all young people educate all people of the older generation to be rationally open-minded, and to accept my advice. Otherwise the older people will be condemning their children and grandchildren to becoming, in the prime of life, very ugly corpses, loved to death by a virus.

# Humanism and the F-Word

## Betty Friedan
### (United States)

Around the time when I signed the Humanist Manifesto II, the women's movement was emerging as one of the greatest movements of social change of its time. I wanted to emphasize the importance of feminism within the humanist movement.

Until the women's movement, women, in their passivity and dependence, were perhaps the largest group of people in our society to be easily manipulated by dictator and demagogue, by priest and profiteer. Then fully half the human race, which had been oppressed throughout history, suddenly began to move toward social equality and to define themselves as a people, empowering one another and gaining control over their lives. Of course, the fundamentalists, the authoritarians—virtually all groups, economic and political, whose power rests on keeping people passive—were threatened by this, and the political climate of this country began to change, largely because of their reaction.

Today, secular humanism has become a dirty word; feminism has become a dirty word; liberalism has become a dirty word. Now, after eight years of the Reagan Administration and the growth of right-wing fundamentalist reaction to human progress and to the changes that happened so fast in our society, the conventional wisdom calls it "special interest" when the government pays attention to the needs of the people—of working people, women, minorities, old people, poor people. Today the only thing that government can do is protect the profits of the powerful.

But these are *not* special interests. I watch in a kind of horror when my colleagues go along with this, and say that they are not feminists. Feminism has become the new F-word.

Young women today say, "I'm not a feminist, but I'm going to be an astronaut"; "I'm not a feminist, but I'm going to be a lawyer and sit on the Supreme Court—if I don't become the president instead"; "I'm not a feminist, but I don't mind if my husband isn't all that successful"; "I'm not a feminist, but maybe some day, when I get around to it, I'll have children."

I want these young women to say, "I am a feminist."

The women's movement is not finished yet. Unless young women today *do* something about changing this nation, they won't be able to become astronauts or Supreme Court justices or presidents.

The United States is the only industrial nation in the world other than South Africa that does not have a national policy of child care and parental leave. During the Reagan era we saw the erosion of laws on sex discrimination in employment, on racial discrimination, on affirmative action—another dirty word. We cannot fight this by saying, "Oh, no, I'm not a liberal"; "Oh, no, I'm not a feminist"; "Oh, no, I'm not a humanist."

Well what am I?

I think we have to say, "I am a humanist." But what is a humanist? A humanist is someone who values existential responsibility for carrying on our part in the evolution of human society, someone who believes we have a responsibility for the evolution of morals as well as of science and technology. We have to bring awe and wonder into humanism; it is reason and emotion together.

And just as humanism must evolve, so must feminism. It is no longer either/or, woman against man, feminism or family. We have entered the second stage of feminism that shall go beyond the male model of equality and affirm the values of life and of the family in a gestalt in which the equality and personhood of woman is a vital element.

Traditionally, woman kept to the private sphere, where she was specialized for nurture, while man roamed free in the public sphere to dominate amd make war. We must bring into the public sphere the values of life, a sensitivity and flexibility toward life. We can no longer afford to specialize women to nurture, and leave the men free to make wars that no one can win and that will eventually destroy the planet.

Feminism must evolve; humanism must evolve. We must stop answering the rhetoric of reaction with the rhetoric of reaction. Feminism, liberalism, and humanism are *not* dirty words! We can't fight the phonies unless we say what we're really for. Labor is not a dirty word, union is not a dirty word; poverty and homelessness should be dirty words. We cannot continue to step over the homeless on the streets of New York or the beaches of Santa Monica. We cannot step over them and say, "Now is not the time to take on the problem of the homeless," because now is the time to take on this problem and many more, before they become completely beyond our control.

I come from a generation that had the GI Bill and affordable mortgages; nearly everyone was able to obtain housing. This was because of government innovation and because of a great president—his name was Roosevelt—who proved that we *can* do something about our problems. We as a nation can do something when we see the government as the vehicle of the people. That is what we have to restore.

And we can't do it by speaking the language of dirty words. That is why I'm saying, "Yes, I am a feminist. Yes, I am a humanist. Yes, I am a kind of liberal." It is our responsibility to keep alive the torch of truth, of human values, and of our own commitment to the evolution to our society. We must pass that torch along, and not allow ourselves to conform to the notion that all of the values for which we stand have become dirty words.

# VIII.

# Religions of the Future

Sponsored by the Committee for the
Scientific Examination of Religion

# The Bible in the Twenty-First Century

## Gerald A. Larue
### (United States)

At the inception of the twentieth century, biblical studies enjoyed a rich heritage of critical scholarship. The Pentateuch had been analyzed and different sources were recognized. It was clear that, despite what Jesus may have thought, Moses could not have authored the Torah. Different literary types had been identified. The discovery of poetic parallelism and the recognition of Hebrew meter made possible the identification of Hebrew poetry outside of the Psalms, which led to the discovery that fully one-third of the Old Testament is in poetic form.

The magnificent Oxford edition of the Apocrypha and Pseudepigrapha, edited by R. H. Charles, enriched research into apocalytpic thought and intertestamental literature. Frazier's *Golden Bough* provided basic materials that encouraged comparative studies. Hastings's *Dictionary of Christ and the Gospel* and *Dictionary of the Bible,* together with the *Encyclopedia of Religion and Ethics,* brought the research of experts into public libraries. Ancient Egyptian hieroglyphs had been deciphered, enriching appreciation of the cultural and material impact of the Nile civilization on Palestine. Cuneiform tablets from Mesopotamian excavations provided sources from which, it was clear, some biblical writers had borrowed motifs. For those who studied the available material, it was becoming obvious that the Bible was not the unique, original book that many Jews and Christians thought it to be.

During the twentieth century, continuing exploration, analysis, and research has broadened our understanding of the interrelationship between ancient Israel and its neighbors. Scores of ancient texts have been found, including the Canaanite library from Ras es Shamra, the Dead Sea Scrolls from Qumran, the Nuzi texts, the texts from Elba and Nag Hammadi, and so on. Under the auspices of local governments, and with participation from universities throughout the world, hundreds of tombs and sites in the Near East have been probed and excavated, providing mute testimony concerning homes, villages, and life-settings. Linguistic studies have clarified difficult passages in the Bible and have provided new understanding of biblical language. The scope of modern biblical research is broader and greater in depth than ever before.

At this point, as we prepare to enter the twenty-first century, the natural question to be raised is, What have we learned?

Once the Bible is studied in the broad context of developing human history and without isolation from the rest of the ancient world, it can be recognized for what it really is: a collection of selected Hebrew, Jewish, and Christian religious literature composed, edited, and preserved by individuals and groups associated with cultic centers, who lived in the ancient Near East and the Mediterranean world some two to three thousand years ago. Like written material from other ancient political and religious centers, the Bible contains a variety of literary types, including myths, legends, folktales, sanctuary tales, hymns, wisdom sayings, novellas, some solid historical data, tracts, personal letters, and collections of teaching ascribed to one person or another. The quality and character of the biblical writings are no better or no worse than comparable writings found in the surrounding cultures. The theological angles of vision may differ, the god-names may vary, but the human concerns, including the search for meaning and the quest for reasonable understanding of natural forces, were the same.

We know something of the selection processes and of the debates and arguments that determined which writings came to be included in the different biblical canons. We possess Jewish and Christian writings that were excluded from our present canons, including the Pseudepigrapha and such items as "The Shepherd of Hermas," "The Didache," and so on.

We can recognize the work of editors and compilers. Many writings can be related to established historical events. In some instances, the human situations out of which particular writings came can be identified. For example, the words of Isaiah of Jerusalem can be best understood in the context of the explosion of Assyrian power in the eighth century B.C.E. The proclamations of Jeremiah, recorded by his secretary Baruch, can be directly related to the threatening power of Babylon in the seventh century B.C.E. The words of the unknown prophet in Babylon, whose writings came to be attached to those of Isaiah of Jerusalem, can be linked to the sixth century B.C.E. growth in power of Cyrus of Persia, whose name is mentioned in Isaiah 45:1. The letters of Paul are, for the most part, directed toward problems associated with the evolving Christian sect.

The literary forms of prophetic pronouncements have been analyzed. The Pauline epistles have been compared favorably in terms of style, format, and language to letters from the same period written by travelers to their families at home. The nonbiblical communications contain many of the same phrases and features found in Paul's letters. The two letters to the Christians in Corinth have been demonstrated to be an intermingling of several separate Pauline documents.

Some biblical literary units can be identified as temple fiction. For example, ancient priests justified the presence of the Canaanite serpent symbol in the Hebrew temple by creating a sanctuary legend that linked the sacred icon to the tales of the Hebrew desert wanderings (Num. 21:6–9; 2 Kings 18:4).

The setting of the invisible presence of the Hebrew god Yahweh enthroned between cherubim on the sacred ark of the covenant in the dark back room of the temple reflects the monarchical seat of rulers as depicted on the sarcophagus of the Phoenician King Ahiram, who was also enthroned between cherubim. Near Eastern archaeologists have uncovered Canaanite shrines that demonstrate that the temple of Solomon, built by Phoenicians (I Kings 5), was modeled on the architectural pattern of Canaanite shrines.

Consequently, we can say that when studied in context, the biblical accounts reflect not only some particular features of the Hebrew people and the early Christian church, but also the commonality of biblical beliefs and ordinances, the ordinariness of the heroes of the faith, and the blandness of much biblical thought. When placed in its historical context in the ancient Near East, that which was once cherished as unique is rather common. The cosmological view was the same whether expressed in Hebrew or Eygptian or Mesopotamian myths. Hebrew psalms and prayers were addressed to Yahweh, Mesopotamian psalms and prayers were addressed to local gods. Hebrew wisdom literature stressed morals and ethics associated with Yahweh; Egyptian wisdom literature reflected many of the same attitudes, but in terms of Egyptian theology. The divine laws, presumably revealed by Yahweh on Mount Sinai, are like laws found in Mesopotamian codes and attributed to the particular god of a given locality. The precepts given by Jesus on the Mount of Beatitudes are similar to teachings given by Jewish sages of the same period. Thus, the Bible is unique in its Hebrew/Jewish/Christian orientations, in its presentations of Yahweh as the sole deity, in the attribution of events and happenings to Yahweh, and in its provincial or peculiar interpretations of history. It is common in its ethical and moral stances, in its world view and in its general theology, in that the acts of Yahweh are like the actions attributed to other gods in surrounding cultures.

The developmental pattern of ancient Judaism and Christianity echoes what has occurred in the growth patterns of other religions. Both Judaism and Christianity became enmeshed with politics, just as other religious belief systems have done throughout human history. Through the combined power and authority of church and state, the selected faith literature acquired the aura of revealed or divinely inspired writings, separate from all other such writings; the temple and church became dominant institutions with control over the lives of individuals. Consequently, for Jews and Christians, the Bible is not just a book, it is *the* book, a Holy Book, an authoritative book, even though many of its teachings and concepts no longer fit into modern life and thought.

If we have learned anything during the past century, it is that the faith approaches of church and synagogue cannot be the methodology employed by the scholar. For the open-minded, critical researcher, the Bible must be perceived not as divine or revealed, but as a human product involving nothing mysterious or supernatural despite its supernaturalistic outlook. The only authority possessed by Jewish and Christian scriptures or by the faiths to which they are related is the authority given by humans. Any other approach automatically suggests that the documents that each and every religion claim are divinely given must be examined only from the faith position of the particular religion.

A devout Muslim might accept the notion that the angelic voice of Gabriel provided Mohammed with the sacred words of the Koran, and that consequently the Koran should be recognized a holy, divinely revealed book. The critical non-Muslim scholar can recognize this notion as a faith statement rather than as an historical reality. For the scholar, the Koran is to be approached as literature that came out of a definite time and place setting, subject to the best analytical and critical approaches available. At the same time, the scholarly researcher can be aware of and can appreciate the fact that for millions of Muslims, the Koran is a sacred book. Most Christian and Jewish scholars have no problem with this approach to the Koran.

However, when the believing Jewish or Christian scholar approaches the Bible, the attitude can be completely different. There is, first of all, the religious conditioning to which many of us have been exposed during our growing years. Some acquired their basic training in biblical studies in seminary settings, where the focus was on the role and responsibilities of the clergy. Some were ordained into one denomination or another. Some may still be affiliated with a particular faith group. Within the college and university setting, there are pressures from student believers, sometimes from their parents, and quite often from colleagues, that encourage the instructor to avoid critical approaches that might induce questioning of the faith. Perhaps, after tenure, some instructors can become more reckless; many continue to follow the modes established prior to tenure. The language of the university classroom in biblical studies often echoes the language of the seminary and, in some cases, of the pulpit. The Bible is the "Holy Bible," God "speaks" through his prophets, and so on.

There seems to be little point in emphasizing the obvious: If Christian scholars can analyze objectively the Koran or the Vedas or any other literature deemed sacred by one or another segment of the human family, then the Bible cannot be exempted from the same analysis. On the other hand, if divine revelation is to be accepted for the Bible, then the angelic voice heard by Mohammed and the revelations that came through Joseph Smith and Mary Baker Eddy might also be accepted as genuine. Should that happen, then, it seems to me, Jewish and Christian groups will be obligated to accept the Koran and all other so-called revealed literature as a continuing and varying disclosure of the divine.

It becomes clear that for the scholar, despite the claims of the synagogue and the church, the Bible must be recognized as a human creation. It is time that the adjective "holy" be dropped from its title. The Bible is no more "holy" or "inspired" than any other ancient or modern work.

The Bible is a literary product of two faith systems that originated in Palestine. It not only reflects ideas that were common to other ancient religions, but it contains material borrowed from surrounding cultures. If the Genesis 1 creation myth is "divinely inspired," then the Babylonian creation myth *enuma elish,* from which its format is derived, is also divinely inspired. If the flood myth is divinely inspired, then the Babylonian Gilgamesh epic, which relates a similar flood story, is divinely inspired. If Proverbs 22:17 to 24:22 are divinely inspired, the Egyptian "Instruction of Amen-em-ope," which served as the model for the biblical material, can be accepted as inspired. If Psalm 104 is inspired, then the magnificent Hymn to Aton found in the tomb of Ay at el-Amarna may also be recognized as holy or inspired, inasmuch as the biblical psalmist apparently drew directly from the Egyptian hymn.

Of course there are Christian scholars who would deny such interpretations. For example, when Donald Redford discussed the relationship between Psalm 104 and the Akhenaton hymn in *Biblical Archaeology Review*, he treated the similarities as "thematic," and stated "there is no literary influence here." He explained the parallels as resulting from "similarities in cultural milieu."[1] Some of us prefer to go along with J. H. Breasted, who proposed a direct relationship between the two poems.[2]

Biblical scholars identify the Bible as a product of its own time. Nevertheless, through continuing reinterpretation by synagogue and church, during the past two thousand years it has made an impact on much, if not most, of the world, as if its contents were eternally modern, up-to-date, and relevant.

As one might expect, problems associated with some biblical teachings have arisen from time to time. Clergy have been compelled to keep its so-called "eternal message" in constant flux as they sought to force it to conform to societal changes. When slavery was in fashion, the preaching of the churches supported the status quo; when slavery was outlawed, biblical preachers found texts to support the social change. The emergence of the women's movement has been an embarrassment to synagogue and church. The Bible in its entirety is a patriarchal document. In it women are clearly second-class persons and under male control as property. Now, slowly, despite what the Bible teaches, women have taken giant strides toward freedom and equality. Within church and synagogue, the ordination of women has finally become acceptable in some of the male-dominated denominations. There are now ordained female rabbis and ministers but, as yet, no female priests. The election of the first female bishop, the Reverend Barbara Harris, by the Episcopal Diocese of Massachusetts in September 1988 troubled some of the Anglican community. It was pointed out that the apostles chosen by Jesus were all males, that sacramental acts, such as ordaining priests, would be invalidated if performed by a woman, and that the attempted rapproachment between Anglican and Roman Catholic hierarchies would be negatively affected if the Reverend Harris was accepted as a bishop by the church as whole. It should be pointed out that since 1976 the Episcopal Church in the United States has ordained nearly one thousand female priests and four hundred female deacons.[3] It is reported that only five other groups within the Anglican Communion have approved of female priests (the Episcopal Church of Brazil, the Anglican Church of Canada, the Church of the Province of New Zealand, the Diocese of Hong Kong, and some dioceses in Kenya). Perhaps the election of a woman bishop will be accepted as a new revelation of divine will, in much the same way that the Mormon church accepted blacks into the priesthood after a divine revelation.

Almost simultaneously, on September 30, 1988, Pope John Paul II issued an apostolic letter "On the Dignity and Vocation of Women" (*Mulieris Digni-tatem*), in which he reaffirmed his strong opposition to the ordination of women to the priesthood, using the same arguments as those put forth by the anti-feminists in the Anglican community. An amazing contradiction in papal think-ing is obvious. On the one hand, the pope may affirm the dignity, freedom, and equality of women, and on the other, he may deny them the freedom to be priests equal in status to males. The argument that Jesus is "the same yes-terday, today, and forever" (Heb. 13:8) gives notice that the patriarchal, male-dominated notions of first century C.E. Christianity will continue to control Ro-man Catholic policy so long as the present pope and his ultra-conservative colleagues are in control. In both Anglican and Roman Catholic communities, the ancient past continues to influence the present.

The maleness of the biblical deity troubles some Christians and Jews. One need only look at the tortured efforts to produce a unisex god through retranslat-ing biblical passages and rewording hymns, prayers, and articles of faith to be-come aware of the extent of the problem. Consider this effort of the National Council of Churches to desex the patriarchal God of the Bible in the familiar John 3:16 passage:

> For God so loved the world that God gave God's only Child, that whoever believes in that Child should not perish but have eternal life.

In this passage even Jesus is desexed, he is not a "son" but simply a "child." Honesty would compel religious leaders to admit that the Bible is a dated, if not an outdated, sexist, male-oriented literary collection. To force translations to conform to modern ideas of universal equality, freedom, and justice is to violate the nature of the biblical material, whose orientation is particularistic, not universal, and to deny the Bible its rightful place in the historical process and in the history of human ideas.

In an attempt to view the Bible for what it really is, one can only conclude that it is a human document providing no more insight into whatever might be the nature of the divine than any other ancient or modern collection. Its very cosmology has been destroyed by modern science. There is no heaven above to which Elijah or Jesus could have ascended and where God and the angels dwell, nor is there an underworld or hell below from which the shade of Sam-uel may have come at the bidding of the necromancer of Endor, or to which Jesus could have descended as part of his death experience. Nor is hell a place where the devil and his cohorts abide, as some modern preachers would have us believe. These ideas are silly, out-of-place, and irrelevant in our modern con-text. They reflect obsolete, ancient world views.

Much of the Bible's basic ethic and teaching have been abandoned as out-of-touch by our modern society. Men and women marry and divorce without regard to what Jesus may have taught (Mark 10:10–12; Matt. 19:3–12). Church women are no longer submissive to their husbands (Eph. 5:22; Col. 3:18), nor are they plainer in dress with fewer adornments than women outside of the church (despite the teachings of I Peter 3). The Bible is irrelevant so far as these issues are concerned. But the church and synagogue have refused to admit this. Leaders in modern denominations continue to use church formulas, reading the Bible as "the sacred word" from lecterns and pulpits as though its concepts were binding, and then "spiritualizing" or finding "spiritual insights" in the archaic passages so that they may be applied to modern situations. The process is as comical as Rabbi Akiba's allegorization of the Song of Songs. Modern scholarship recognizes these ancient stanzas as love poems, perhaps associated with wedding festivals, or more likely derived from sacral sexual poems associated with ancient fertility cults. Rabbi Akiba argued that the verses reflected Yahweh's love for Israel. Later, the Christian church claimed that the poems reflected Christ's love for his church. As one reads the frank sexual allusions in the poems with these "spiritualized" interpretations in mind, the result can only be amusement. But the process continues in the modern religious settings. It is time for the pattern to be exposed for what it really is: a lifting out of context of biblical verses and subjecting them to a present-day allegorizing process disguised under the cloak of "finding the spiritual meaning."

We have become aware of the changing image of the deity throughout the scriptures. When the Hebrew tribes entered Canaan, Yahweh was portrayed as a tribal war god, represented by the sacred box or ark that the Hebrew warriors carried into battle (Num. 10:35–6; Joshua 3:3–11). When the Hebrews controlled the land and settled as agriculturists, their deity became like the Canaanite fertility god Ba'al, an agricultural deity. The Genesis 2 creation myth depicts Yahweh as one who planted a garden, just as the settled Hebrews were doing. He had been transformed from a tribal to a territorial god. His kingdom embraced Israel. Other gods controlled the surrounding nations and territories. This was a time of monolatry in theological thinking: Each nation worshipped its own controlling or dominant deity and the existence of other gods controlling other nations was not denied. The Hebrew appreciation of that concept is reflected in the commandment "Have no other god beside me" and other passages (Exod. 20:3, 34:14; Deut. 5:7, 6:14, 13:6–7).

When the Jews went into exile and wondered how they could worship their territorial deity, Yahweh, in a foreign land where the god Marduk held sway (Psalm 137), the unknown prophet of the exile argued that Yahweh was the sole god of the world and could be worshiped anywhere (Isaiah 40–45). Thus the monotheism that was to affect the Western world was born. During the exile, the Jews became acquainted with *enuma elish,* the Babylonian creation myth that extolled the creative cosmic organization accomplished by Marduk of Babylon. Consequently, by imitation, Yahweh too became a creative cosmic organizer—a notion reflected in the Genesis 1 creation myth.

As a cosmic deity, Yahweh became more remote. Indeed, by New Testament times, humans appear to have lost the ability to communicate directly with Yahweh. In the book of the Revelation the prayers of the believers were delivered in the form of incense in golden bowls by twenty-four angelic beings ("elders") and four zoomorphic monsters ("living beings") to the enthroned deity

(5:8). The New Testament portrays the judgment of humans by a demanding father-god who condemns to everlasting punishment those of his human children who fail to live according to Christian standards (Rev. 20:15). John 3:16 refers to a God who so loved his human creatures that he preplanned to have his own son killed to effect reconciliation between the human and the divine. Such an image of fatherly love is anything but comforting. Once again, the scholar and the thoughtful reader are confronted by archaic notions of sacrifice and reconciliation that only serve to keep alive savage notions that many of us wish to outgrow.

What is most disturbing is to find that in our universities, which are supposed to be centers of learning and research, the curricula of Departments of Religious Studies are often modeled after the seminary, and the classrooms are often staffed solely by seminary-trained personnel.

I must admit that my training in biblical scholarship was in seminaries. St. Stephen's College, where I commenced my religious studies, was a college within the University of Alberta in Canada. I was fortunate in that some of my seminary instructors were products of schools emphasizing critical thought. They believed that the best findings of biblical research ought to be part of the honing of the clerical mind. In my case, the results of the historical/literary/analytical approach reinforced my skepticism.

Many present-day college instructors in biblical studies use textbooks written with a Christian bias. I can recall the insecurity among some of my colleagues in the School of Religion at the University of Southern California when I changed textbooks to introduce more critical analysis. Because we were in a courtship relationship with Hebrew Union College, I could argue honestly and on the basis of experience that the texts that had been used previously were offensive to my Jewish students. The books I selected avoided Christian biases.

Today, one of the most popular Old Testament textbooks used in college classes makes numerous references to Christian interpretations. Footnotes and commentaries in the Old Testament section of the *Oxford Annotated Bible of the Revised Standard Version,* almost all which were written by Christian seminarians, contain frequent references to New Testament themes that have nothing to do with the understanding of the passages in question, but that direct the reader to early Christian (New Testament) uses of the passages. Such information is unimportant for the study of the Old Testament per se, and can be offensive to non-Christians. I am not attempting to argue that seminarians cannot be good scholars, but rather that because of their professional responsibilities to train men and women to be leaders of religious faith groups they tend to think and respond along traditional church and synagogue lines. When seminarians move into university teaching positions, they may tend to choose textbooks with which they became familiar in the seminary but which slant teaching into traditional church–synagogue patterns.

In Biblical scholarship, as in any other university discipline, the evidence must lead the researcher rather than the researcher leading the evidence. If I begin my study convinced that I am dealing with the sacred word of God, with the church's book whose influence and authority is to be protected and preserved, then teaching, my research track, and my conclusions easily tend to accord with my prejudgments. If, on the other hand, I begin my study as a historian and literary analyst and treat the Bible as I would any other ancient document, then my discipline, not my belief system, becomes my guide and my conclusions will not be the result of theological prejudgments.

For many educators raised in the faith, the critical approach can become difficult. Their research may lead them to the kind of conclusions I have been discussing, namely that the Bible is simply a collection of Jewish–Christian writings primarily created in a Palestinian context between two and three thousand years ago, and that their "Lord and Savior Jesus Christ" is no more than one of many Jewish teachers whose thinking was locked into the ethos of his own era. Some, when confronted with such conclusions, make a leap of faith, which means that their thinking process is bifurcated. One mode of thinking is directed toward analytical scholarship; in the other mode one remains a believer despite the presence of evidence that may challenge beliefs. Such researchers develop a kind of mental numbness, which renders the religious concepts safe and secure from conclusions that call into question traditional faith assumptions. A wall of separation is raised between faith and scholarship, and whenever research tends to affect faith concepts, the wall comes into being. In the classroom the professor attempts to divorce inmost beliefs and commitments from teaching; in other words he or she seeks to be "objective" in the educational mode. At the same time, while in this professional role, the educator tends to avoid controversial issues and when confronted by them faces inner turmoil. On one occasion, due to a conflict in schedule, I asked a colleague to replace me as a guest lecturer in a class on human sexuality and to talk on "Sex and the Bible." Due to his faith-stance, and perhaps also due to his personal homophobia, he panicked and was unable to deal with questions that challenged the biblical view of homosexuality.

University professors are expected to publish. One way of handling the faith-research problem is to direct inquiry into safe peripheral areas. A New Testament teacher may focus on various kinds of work or labor current in the first century C.E. For example, one will study the role of the carpenter to understand Jesus' home life, the role of the tentmaker to appreciate Paul, the task of fishermen to gain a grasp of the work done by Peter and Andrew, and so on. Another will focus on schools of thought current in New Testament times, such as the Stoics or perhaps the Gnostics. The Dead Sea Scrolls provided a virtually safe treasure trove for such scholars. The beliefs of the Qumran Jews could be approached critically without fear of offending true believers. Where the Qumran group entertained ideas similar to those found in the New Testament, this fact could be admitted, but it could be pointed out that there was a lack of the spiritual insights of Jesus and Paul.[4] In such cases, one may safely ignore the conclusion that Jesus and Paul probably borrowed some of their ideas from the Qumran group.

Others turn to linguistics and their research relates to philological problems that keep faith issues at a distance. All such studies relate to and make some contribution to our understanding of the biblical text and world, but they concentrate on noncontroversial areas. These teachers publish in acceptable journals and receive promotions and salary increases as validation of their scholarship. Their students are robbed of the vitality that comes from instructors who, without regard to the impact on faith positions, examine and reexamine critically the literary, historical, archaeological, and cultural contributions made by those who are on the cutting edge of progressive education and who share what they find with their students. To personally engage in critical studies and not hesitate to evaluate the Bible in terms of the findings, and to share the exciting new information with students, is to fulfill the high academic calling of educator.

We have witnessed the treatment of exciting research by scholars like Bultmann, who not only demythologized the New Testament but through his faith proclamations engaged in a theologizing or remythologizing designed to preserve the faith. If one follows the implications of demythologizing and does not feel the need to make defensive theological compromises, the Bible loses its sacral status and becomes a source book for study of the ancient Near Eastern world.

What can we say of the future?

It is clear that biblical scholarship will continue to be centralized in the seminaries and in universities, where the majority of researchers are committed to faith positions concerning the Bible. There can be no hesitation in saying that excellent critical analyses will result from many of these studies.

At the same time, we recognize a growing body of nonfaith researchers in some university settings and among Israeli archaeologists who are primarily historians and who use the Bible as they would any other ancient document that might cast light on their research. There are literary analysts through whom literary terms, including myth, legend, fiction, and temple tales, intrude increasingly on biblical studies. Genesis 1 can no longer be disguised for students as "poetic language"; it is mythic language. As the literary analysts influence those who write for the general public as novelists and columnists, critical language will penetrate the public domain.

I do not expect any great change in the understanding of the Bible to come through the pulpits. I can recall when some of my Canadian seminary classmates, inspired by scholarly instructors and by preachers like Harry Emerson Fosdick, sought to introduce the language and findings of critical scholarship to their congregations. After fragmenting the harmony of several churches, they either began to follow safer paths in their preaching and teaching, or left preaching and sought employment in some other calling.

Many church leaders and church members are threatened by biblical criticism and analytical thought. To see this threat in action, one need only follow the adventures of the popular but conservative *Biblical Archaeology Review*. Whenever the editor, Herschel Shanks, dares to publish the comments of scholars whose research does not support conservative or fundamentalist biblical thought, he is taken to task and subscriptions are cancelled.

We have seen challenges to the teaching of evolutionary thinking in public schools by those who choose to deny evolution and profess belief in the biblical creation accounts. The opposition to these challenges has come, in large part, from secular organizations. Why were the voices of the liberal synagogue and church not raised in protest? Why were the rabbis and pastors of the liberal organizations and their denominations silent? These educated men and women know the difference between science and myth. The biblical creation story is not fact, it is fiction and the educated clergy know this. If the patterns we have witnessed during the past decades give any clues to the future, we will find that the silence of the clergy will continue to be the policy when issues like creation versus evolution arise. I find this to be most discouraging. It gives promise of continuing naivete and ignorance in the congregations.

It seems to me that the responsibility for placing the results of good biblical scholarship in the hands of the public will rest with groups like the Committee for the Scientific Examination of Religion, which is sponsored by the Council for Democratic and Secular Humanism and was developed to examine the claims of well-established and newer sects of Eastern and Western religions in the light of scientific inquiry. It is time that the interpretation and study of the Bible and other religious works like the Koran not be left in the hands of true believers and the clergy.

Biblical analysis will continue, enriched by findings from archaeological research, the study of concepts originating in neighboring cultures that have had an impact on biblical thought, and the open nontheological approach to biblical literature. Consequently, for those who pay heed to such studies, the Bible will emerge more and more as a most human book. As such it belongs to our humanist heritage, as does all writing. It is the product of one segment of our human family as that segment sought to come to grips with existence in this very complex world. It reflects one dimension of our ancestral heritage that helps us to understand how these ancient peoples responded to their neighbors, to their environment, and to one another.

Where noble insights are present, they can be accepted and, together with similar profound and important observances from other times and cultures, studied to affect the future. Where mean, destructive, and demeaning attitudes are found, we can record them together with all similar expressions as outmoded notions that should remain in the past or that we may still struggle to overcome.

Because the Bible is a human book, it has importance for the humanist. It is important because of the positive and negative influence it has had throughout history and will continue to have in the twenty-first century. Humanists must claim the Bible as their own, as a human—and in places humanistic—document. It is human in that it was forged by human hands and minds; it is humanistic when its writers rise above narrow parochialism and nationalism and focus on human rights, human justice, and human decency. This I hope and project for the future.

## Notes

1.  D. Redford, "Similarity Between Egyptian and Biblical Tests—Indirect Influence?" Biblical Archaeological Review, XIII: 3, 1987.

2. J. H. Breasted, *The Dawn of Conscience* (New York: Scribner, 1933), pp. 366–370.

3. Russell Chandler, "Woman Bishop Puts Anglican Unity to the Test," *Los Angeles Times,* Sept. 27, 1988.

4. See G. Graystone, *The Dead Sea Scrolls and the Originality of Christ* (New York: Sheed & Ward, 1956).

# The Study of the Gospels as Literary Fiction

## Randel Helms
### (United States)

In 1979, Frank Kermode published a study of the narratives in Mark, *The Genesis of Secrecy*. In 1981, Robert Alter published a landmark work, *The Art of Biblical Narrative*. In 1982, Northrop Frye published *The Great Code: The Bible and Literature*. In 1986, Frank McConnell edited *The Bible and the Narrative Tradition*, and in 1987, Alter and Kermode published another major work, *The Literary Guide to the Bible*, in which they declare that "Literary criticism, long thought to be peripheral or even irrelevant to biblical study, has emerged since the mid-1970s as a new major focus of academic biblical scholarship."[1] All of these writers are professors of literature—Frye at Toronto, McConnell and Alter in California, and Kermode at Cambridge.

Much of the future of biblical studies lies in the secular world, particularly the secular universities; such a future is the consequence of the recognition that the Bible is a human book—or collection of books—produced by imaginative human writers, a literary text that can be read with the same skills we bring to any other text. Serious reading of the Bible is becoming a humanistic activity.

Of course, unscholarly readers will continue to study the Bible for devotional purposes, and professional theologians for scholarly insight. But there is a major split among theologians that involves two radically separate traditions of theological study of the Bible. The first is rational, humanistic, and the child of the Enlightenment, the other is at war with the Enlightenment; I call these two traditions "serious" and "fundamentalist." The serious tradition is the one that has been fruitful, opening the way for such critics as Frye, Kermode, and Alter, the forerunners of the next century of biblical study. The fundamentalist tradition will continue, but will become increasingly peripheral, fighting a rearguard battle.

The split between the serious and fundamentalist scholars can be illustrated with regard to the question of miracles in the New Testament. The "serious" position has been well put by Ernst Käsemann:

> Over few subjects has there been such a bitter battle among the New Testament scholars of the last two centuries as over the miracle stories of the Gospels. . . . We may say that today the battle is over, not perhaps as yet in the arena of church life, but certainly in the field of theological science. It has ended in the defeat of the concept of miracle which has been traditional in the church. . . . The great majority of the Gospel miracle stories must be regarded as legends.[2]

On the other side we may put a book that pretends to seriousness but is in fact fundamentalist: *Gospel Perspectives: The Miracles of Jesus,* edited by David Wenham and Craig Blomberg and published under the auspices of the Department of Biblical Studies at the University of Sheffield in England. The pretense of the book's intellectual seriousness begins to become clear in its preface, which asserts that "serious historical and literary scholarship allows us to approach the gospels with the belief that they present an essentially historical account of the words and deeds of Jesus."[3] But this is, of course, precisely what serious historical and literary scholarship of the New Testament does *not* do; the preface is intellectually dishonest. Indeed, as James Barr puts it in his book *Fundamentalism,* fundamentalist biblical study is in the literal sense of the word, "unprincipled," its real goal, dogmatic argument, being disguised as objective investigation.[4]

The scholarly line of descent in which Käsemann stands, "serious" biblical study, goes back, in the twentieth century, to such scholars as Martin Dibelius and Rudolf Bultmann, whose schools of thought have come to be called Form Criticism and Redaction Criticism. The powerful insights and general acceptance of such approaches have made possible what will be the next century's approach: literary criticism. Bultmann taught at the University of Marburg in Germany until his retirement in 1951. His 1921 book *Geschichte der synoptischen Tradition (History of the Synoptic Tradition)* has remained authoritative:

> There was need of a cult-legend for the Kyrios [Lord] of the Christian cult. Since the pattern of the Christ-myth had to be illustrated, it needed to be combined with traditions about the history of Jesus. . . . Thus the Gospels are cult-legends. Mark has created this type. The myth of Christ gives his book . . . a unity which is not biographical, but simply based on the myth.[5]

That the outline of the gospel story is mythological and the content of the Gospel stories legendary, at least to some extent, is now the majority view among serious biblical scholars. Since myth and legend are *literary* categories, the Gospels are works of literature, available to the approaches of literary critics: such will be the legacy of scholars like Bultmann in the next century. Let me hasten to point out that for Bultmann to call the Gospel stories mythological is not to reject their spiritual or theological value but rather to establish the terms within which their real value can be grasped. And what must be stressed is that the theological parameters within which Bultmann finds the New Testament supremely valuable are humanistic at their core. As Bultmann wrote, "The real purpose of myth is not to present an objective picture of the world as it is, but to express man's understanding of himself in the world in which he lives. Myth should be interpreted not cosmologically, but anthropologically, or better still, existentially."[6] Bultmann's enemies in the fundamentalist camp have been quick to note his humanistic sympathies and to attack him for this aspect of his thinking. To quote from a bitter critic of Bultmann, Simon J. Kistemaker, professor of New Testament at Reformed Theological Seminary and author of *The Gospels in Current Study:*

> Bultmann puts man at the center of Scripture; he rejects the teaching that the center of Scripture is God, who reveals himself as Christ. He does not want to accept that God supernaturally enters history, that his Son was born supernaturally, that he died and was raised from the dead, that he ascended to heaven forty days after his resurrection, and that on the last day he shall return as Judge of the living and the dead.[7]

Though Kistemaker's tone is dismissive, his perception is accurate; Bultmann did not accept the first-century mythological constructions Kistemaker lists, and Kistemaker's unease stems from his recognition that Bultmann's views have triumphed among serious theologians. But let me point out what Kistemaker does not make explicit: that the list of propositions he says Bultmann does not accept constitutes a virtual paraphrase of the Apostles' Creed. For Kistemaker, biblical study is not a matter of disinterested scholarly investigation, but must instead be the servant of dogma; unless a scholar shores up the creed, he is suspect. Kistemaker's unprincipled fundamentalism is a subtext of his entire book.

The other major figure in twentieth-century New Testament study is Martin Dibelius, who applied Form Critical insights to the Gospels and Acts and showed them to be the largely fictional products of political concerns in the early church. His term for political concern was *Sitz im Leben,* the "life-setting" in the early church that called forth fictional stories about Jesus and the Apostles. Dibelius's major book, *From Traditonal to Gospel,* and his definitive essay, "The Speeches in Acts and Ancient Historiography," establish, for example, that Luke was much more like a Hellenistic novelist than naive readers have realized.[8] And other critics have followed in Debelius's path. Ernst Hänchen argues that in Acts, Luke was a literary craftsman, composing speeches and narratives, rather than a "historian" in the modern sense of the word.[9] The present consensus among serious scholars of Acts is that literary criticism is the appropriate approach to this book.[10]

Form Criticism established the idea that Gospel stories about Jesus are creations of the early church—that individual pericopes about Jesus could be works of what a literary critic would call imaginative fiction. Form Criticism set for itself the task of identifying and analyzing preliterate oral forms (units of folklore) that had been incorporated into Gospel written literature. Redaction Criticism followed after the Second World War, when the Evangelists began to be appreciated as authors in their own right; Redaction critics examined how each Evangelist creatively dealt with the kind of traditional materials uncovered by Form Criticism, and assumed that Gospel writers were fiction writers. These two forms of biblical scholarship, triumphing and coming to fruition in the first three-quarters of our century, have now freed the New Testament narratives into the world of secular humanistic studies. Now that the role of the Gospel critic has ceased having to be that of protector and enforcer of the creed, now that the Gospels can be recognized for what they are—fictional narratives about Jesus—they may be seen as the legitimate objects of the interest of secular and humanistic students of literature. As Frank McConnell puts it in the introduction to his book, *The Bible and the Narrative Tradition,* "Literary criticism and scriptural exegesis . . . are not so much to be wedded as to be reunited after a—surely rather long—trial separation."[11]

McConnell's book, published in 1986, is a fine indicator of much of the coming generation of work on the New Testament. He points out that the study of the New Testament narratives as fictions does not mean loss of interest in their theological content; rather it will mean a more sophisticated way to understand Martin Buber's insight about the Bible's own narratology: "Scripture does not state its doctrine as doctrine, but by telling a story, and without exceeding the limits set by the nature of a story."[12] McConnell's book contains essays by Harold Bloom, Frank Kermode, Herbert Schneidau, and James M. Robinson, among others, all of which deal in one way or another with what is coming to be called, in the current jargon of literary criticism, narratology, the theory of literary narrative. This way of reading sees any narrative as a kind of fiction, be it historical narrative, autobiography, biography, novel, or Gospel. Each narrative sets up or assumes its own realm, world, or system, seemingly analogous to the "real" world, but containing its own modes of coherence, and actions and outcomes meaningful in *that* world. For example, "The Gospels as Narrative," James M. Robinson's essay in this book, brilliantly combines Redaction Criticism with Derrida's conception of *différance;* having accepted Bultmann's demythologizing of the Gospels, Robinson begins the process, following Derrida, of deconstructing them. Robinson speculates on how the fictional narratives in the Synoptic Gospels were written. Arguing that the stories about Jesus saying and doing things are both anti-Gnostic propaganda and the effort of second- and third-generation Greek-speaking Christians to deconstruct the teachings of an outdated Palestinian Christianity, Robinson gives us an early example of narratological literary criticism of the New Testament.

New Testament study will continue, in the next century, to deepen its understanding of the truth of Buber's insight about the nature of biblical narrative as fictive, "literary." As Alter and Kermode put it, Scripture "now bids fair to become part of the literary canon. . . . Indeed, it seems we have reached a turning-point in the history of criticism, for the Bible, under a new aspect, has reoccupied the literary culture."[13] Their point is that now that what used to be called Higher Criticism has triumphed and entered the Western world's educated consciousness, now that such schools of thought or approaches to the Bible as Form Criticism and Redaction Criticism have done their work, "the interpretation of the texts as they actually exist has been revalidated."[14] As Alter wrote earlier, "prose fiction is the best general rubric for describing biblical narrative. Or, to be more precise, and borrow a key term from Herbert Schneidau's ... study, *Sacred Discontent,* we can speak of the Bible as *historicized* prose fiction."[15] The older methods of biblical criticism saw the texts as "more or less distorted historical records" and attempted to get "behind" the texts to the now-lost history that produced them—to the mental activities and life-settings of early Christian communities (Form Criticism) and the Evangelists themselves (Redaction Criticism). This work having been done, we are now free to look at the texts as *texts;* we can do literary criticism. And as Alter and Kermode point out, the most fruitful methods of literary criticism in the twentieth century—formalism, structuralism and post-structuralism—all have in common "a skeptical attitude to the referential qualities of texts and an intense concern for their internal relationships"; or, as one might say of the Gospels, they are not so much about Jesus as about their own attitudes concerning Jesus.[16]

To speak this way of the Gospels is to use the language of two interrelating methods or interests of literary criticism, narratology and intertextuality. These are already becoming central to the study of the New Testament narratives; both assume the fictionality or fictiveness of those narratives. I have described the first. The second, intertextuality, proceeds upon the insight, in Robert Scholes's words, that "texts are reworkings of other texts."[17] Northrop Frye has recently published a powerful work using this insight. The New Testament's intertextual relationship with the Old Testament prompts Frye to ask, "How do we know that the Gospel story is true? Because it confirms the prophecies of the Old Testament. But how do we know that the Old Testament prophecies are true? Because they are confirmed by the Gospel story. Evidence, so called, is bounced back and forth between the testaments like a tennis ball; no other evidence is given to us. The two testaments form a double mirror, each reflecting the other but neither the world outside."[18] Frye uses an intertextual insight to confirm narratological theory of the sort Alter and Schneidau have proposed: the Gospels set up their own world of fictive meanings.

I shall conclude with an example of intertextual fictionality in Gospel narrative—Luke's story of the resurrecting of the son of the widow of Nain. As Luke narrates (7:11-16):

> And it came to pass afterwards that Jesus went to a town called Nain, accompanied by his disciples and a large crowd. As he approached the gate of the town he met a funeral. The dead man was the only son of his widowed mother; and many of the townspeople were there with her. When the Lord saw her his heart went out to her, and he said, "Weep no more." With that he stepped forward and laid his hand upon the bier; and the bearers halted. Then he spoke: "Young man, rise up!" The dead man sat up and began to speak; and Jesus gave him back to his mother. Deep awe fell upon them all, and they praised God. "A great prophet has arisen among us," they said.[19]

This beautiful story is a prime example of the principle enunciated by Frye, that early Christians turned the Old Testament into a book about Jesus, finding in it stories they read as "prophecies" about him. As it happens, the miracle stories about Elijah in First Kings provided the basis for a number of miracle stories about Jesus. Elijah performs several striking miracles, among them the creation of much food from little and the resurrection of a dead son. If these sound familiar to readers of the Gospels, they should not be surprised. Luke, or a Greek-speaking Christian behind Luke, composed the story of the son of the widow of Nain on the basis of the Greek Septuagint version of First Kings, and its story of the resurrecting of the son of the widow of Sarepta's son:

> And it came to pass that the word of the Lord came to Eliu, saying Arise, and go to Sarepta of the Sidonian land: behold, I have there commanded a widow-woman to maintain thee. And he arose and went to Sarepta, and came to the gate of the city. . . .
> And it came to pass afterward, that the son of the woman the mistress of the house was sick; and his sickness was very severe, until there was no breath left in him. . . .
> And Eliu said to the woman, Give me thy son, and he took him out of her bosom. . . .
> And he breathed on the child thrice, and called on the Lord, and said, O Lord my God, let, I pray thee, the soul of this child return unto him. And it was so, and the child cried out, and he brought him down from the upper chamber into the house, and gave him to his mother.[20]

Both stories begin with a favorite Septuagintal formula, "And it came to pass" *(Kai egeneto)*. Both concern the dead son of a widow *(chēra)*. In both the prophet "went" *(eporeuthē)* to the town, where he met the woman at "the gate of the city" *(ton pylōna tēs poleōs,* LXX; *tē pylē tēs poleōs,* Luke), even though archaeological study has shown that the village of Nain in Galilee never had a wall or a gate; Nain's fictional gate is there for literary reasons—it is Sarepta's gate transferred. In both stories the prophets speak and touch the dead sons, who then rise and speak. In both stories it is declared that the miracle certifies the prophet ("Behold, I know that thou art a man of God," LXX; "A great prophet has arisen," Luke). And both stories conclude with precisely the same words: "and he gave him to his mother" *(kai edōken auton tē mētri autou)*.

Not all readers of the New Testament will feel free to see this sort of intertextuality between the Gospels and their literary sources in the Old Testament as part of a view of the literary and fictive character of the New Testament narratives, but those who do will be the most interesting readers and writers about the Gospels in the next century.

## Notes

1. Robert Alter and Frank Kermode, eds., *The Literary Guide to the Bible* (Cambridge, Mass.: Harvard University Press, 1987), p. 6.
2. Ernst Käsemann, *Essays on New Testament Themes,* trans. W. J. Montague (London: SCM Press, 1964), p. 48.
3. David Wenham and Craig Blomberg, eds., *Gospel Perspectives: The Miracles*

*of Jesus* (Sheffield, Eng.: JSOT Press, 1986), p. 7.

4. James Barr, *Fundamentalism* (Philadelphia: Westminster, 1978), p. 64.

5. Quoted in Bo Reicke, *The Roots of the Synoptic Gospels* (Philadelphia: Fortress, 1986), p. 15.

6. Rudolf Bultmann, "New Testament and Mythology," in *Kerygma and Myth,* H. W. Barsch, ed. (London: SPCK, 1972), p. 10.

7. Simon J. Kistemaker, *The Gospels in Current Study,* (Grand Rapids, Mich.: Baker House, 1980), p. 71.

8. Martin Dibelius, *From Tradition to Gospel* (London: Nicholson and Watson, 1934); and "The Speeches in Acts and Ancient Historiography," in *Studies in the Acts of Apostles,* Heinrich Greeven, ed., Mary Ling, trans. (London: SCM, 1956).

9. Ernst Hänchen, *The Acts of the Apostles: A Commentary* (Philadelphia: Westminster, 1971).

10. Alter and Kermode, ibid., p. 469.

11. Frank J. McConnell, ed., *The Bible and the Narrative Tradition* (New York: Oxford University Press, 1987), p. 17.

12. Quoted in McConnell, ibid., p. 14.

13. Alter and Kermode, ibid., p. 3.

14. Ibid., p. 4.

15. Robert Alter, *The Art of Biblical Narrative* (New York: Basic Books, 1981), p. 24.

16. Alter and Kermode, ibid., p. 5.

17. Robert Scholes, *Text Book: Introduction to Literary Language* (New York: St. Martin's Press, 1987), p. 129.

18. Northrop Frye, *The Great Code: The Bible and Literature* (New York: Harcourt, 1982), p. 78.

19. Luke 7:11-16.

20. III [I] Kings 17:8-10, 17, 19-23 LXX.

# The Future of Old Testament Research

## John F. Priest
### (United States)

The term "Old Testament" is unfortunate in that it reflects a distinctively Christian bias.[1] I use it simply because it has become a commonplace in our culture. Perhaps more important is clarifying the scope of what I consider to be "Old Testament" research. I am not referring only to the books considered scripture by Jews and Christians but to the communities that produced and preserved those writings and others not included in the canonical collections of either the Jewish or Christian religious establishments. The focus is on the community as well as the collection.

It is probable that advances will be made in the methodologies that have become the common property of biblical scholars over the past hundred-and-fifty years.[2] Work in textual, source, form, and redaction criticism will continue. The second limitation warrants a somewhat more extensive comment.

Four areas seem most promising for future Old Testament research: (a) new methods and methodology in archaeology; (b) new literary methods of interpretation; (c) examination of new literary remains from the Near East that have come to light, particularly in the past four decades; and (d) intensified use of the social scientific disciplines. I shall focus primarily on the last two, but a skeletal statement with respect to the first two is in order.

Archaeology, the study of the material remains of ancient civilizations, has for some two centuries made substantial contributions to understanding the biblical texts and, above all, to recreating the broader historical, cultural, and religious milieux within which the biblical communities emerged and flourished. Archaeologists of the present and future, making use of more refined scientific methods and technologies and interpreting old and new data in the context of broader cross-cultural conceptual models, will unquestionably enrich many dimensions of Old Testament research.[3]

New literary methods fall into two distinct categories. The first may broadly be called structuralism, though there are enormous differences among those scholars considered to be structuralists. Drawing upon the cultural anthropologist Claude Levi Strauss and the linguist Ferdinand de Saussure, structuralists assume that there are "deep structures" in human consciousness that are reflected in customs, traditions, oral tales, and even literary texts. These should not be understood in a straightforward way of surface progression (diachronic), but in a synthetic complex of sign/symbol meanings (synchronic). It is not only important to discover what language says, but also to discover the potentially empowering capacity of language itself.

I confess that the somewhat arcane language used by structuralists and their complicated charts, graphs, and diagrams leave me puzzled. Further, the results gleaned thus far by structuralist criticism and exegesis seem to elucidate what other methodologies have already established. But, since some of my best friends are structuralists, I retain an open mind as to the import of their future contributions.[4]

The second aspect ot the new literary methods draws upon the so-called new literary criticism, which addresses a text as a literary artifact in and of itself. The historical, social, and cultural conditions, and even the intention of the author, are not germane for interpretation. A piece of literature has no primary level of relationship with reality but creates a fictive world of its own.[5]

It is probable that diffidence about the new literary methods, both with respect to structuralism and the new literary criticism, is a legacy of my own training as a philologist and historian. Both structuralism and the new literary criticism are essentially ahistorical. This is, of course, an exaggeration, since many biblical scholars make considerable use of one or both methodologies without abandoning sensitivity to historical constraints. I have grave difficulty in approaching a text devoid of context, of interpreting a text solely in terms of the function of language in the "deep structures" of universal human consciousness (structuralism), or in terms of aesthetic evaluation of the fictive world created by an isolated literary product (new criticism). Nevertheless, I strongly suspect that some new and exciting insights will emerge from refined application of both of these new literary methods.

As important as continuing developments of the traditional critical methodologies, new contributions from archaeology, and the new literary methods may be, we now turn to the two areas that, in my judgment, are the most significant for the future of Old Testament research. Recovery of substantial collections of Near Eastern literary remains in the nineteenth century revolutionized biblical studies. The Asshurbanipal library, the finds at Nippur, Mari, Nuzu, the Amarna letters, and the Elephantine papyri, to mention only a few, brought to light unknown languages and little-known civilizations. Most of these impinged, indirectly at least, on biblical studies. The texts from Ugarit (Ras Shamra) discovered in 1928 laid bare details of the culture of Canaan within which the people of ancient Israel hammered out their own culture. Many of these earlier finds are still only partially published and those that are well known require new evaluation in the light of more recent discoveries. I shall not rehearse the earlier discoveries but shall focus on the three most significant ones that have appeared since 1945.[6] (Many other recent discoveries of lesser magnitude, in size at least, are also potentially of considerable consequence.) The three are the Ebla Archives, the Dead Sea Scrolls, and the Nag Hammadi Library.

## Ebla

Ancient Ebla, modern Tell Mardikh, a city of some 260,000 at its height, was the capital of a kingdom now recognized to have been of major importance from about 2600 to 2200 B.C.E.[7] The city, located about forty miles southwest of modern Aleppo in Syria, was the scene of excavations by an Italian archaeological team beginning in the early 1960s. In 1968 they found a modest number of clay tablets, and in 1974 and 1975 an amazingly large number of tablets were uncovered. Early reports of some 15,000 tablets were misleading, since there are some duplications and some tablets contain only two or three decipherable words. The most reliable reports suggest that some 1,800 significant texts can be identified.

The majority of the texts, according to the most recent reports, are economic, but historical, juridical, literary, and religious genres are also represented. When the first few scattered texts were made available, biblical scholars (as has usually been the case in the history of archaeological discoveries) immediately pounced on alleged parallels between Ebla and the Bible.

For instance, in a list of Eblaite kings, mention is made of Ebrum, considered to be the philological equivalent of Eber, the eponymous ancestor of the Hebrews (Gen. 10:21). Even more significant was the alleged parallel from Ebla of the list of the five cities of the plain, including ab-ra-mu (Abraham) were adduced. Another tantalizing item was mention of a site called Ur of Haran. Genesis 11:28 designates Ur of the Chaldeans, a city at the head of the Persian Gulf, as the birthplace of Abraham, but there is also a tradition that locates him in the land of Haran, which is immediately adjacent to Ebla. Is it possible that a later tradent who no longer knew of an Ur of Haran confused it with the still known Ur of the Chaldeans? Was there a close connection between the Abraham of the biblical tradition and Ebla? If so, the date for Abraham would have to be pushed back much earlier than any proposal made by the most conservative biblical scholars.

Further, there were reports of an Eblaite flood narrative and a creation story that reflected similarities with their biblical counterparts. A final example, and this by no means exhausts the list: It was suggested that there was a possible identification of an Eblaite god Ya(u) with the personal name of the Hebrew God, usually transcribed Yahweh.

From the beginning, many scholars questioned or categorically dismissed any direct bearing of the Ebla texts on biblical study. Most scholars today stand somewhere between naive credulity and historical nihilism. Decades of research will be necessary before any sound judgment can be passed on the contributions of Ebla for biblical studies.

In the meantime, the Ebla archives are already making two significant, albeit indirect, contributions to biblical studies. The first is lexical, the second historical and cultural. The Ebla texts are written in the Sumerian cuneiform system. Some are in the Sumerian language, but others use the system to transcribe a hitherto unknown language that, for convenience, has been designated Eblaite. There are also some bilingual texts that, like the Rosetta Stone for deciphering the Egyptian hieroglyphs, are of enormous value in unlocking the secrets of the new language. Eblaite is clearly Semitic, a precursor of biblical Hebrew (Canaanite), and may, like the earlier Ugaritic materials, clarify obscurities in many biblical passages. It is to be remembered that of the some 8,000 words appearing in the Hebrew Bible 1,700 are hapax legomena (words that appear only once). Lexical studies are so far in a nascent stage, but it is to be expected that they will be pursued with vigor.

Ebla was a flourishing kingdom vying for power and prestige with neighboring states, including Akkad, in the last half of the third millenium B.C.E. Its role in the politics and culture of that period will be of value in broadening our understanding of that era. Since the biblical community is in direct continuity, both geographically and chronologically, all information from Ebla will contribute to a richer understanding of ancient Israel.

I emphasize the focus of scholars on the general cultural significance of Ebla. Subsequent to the first flurry of somewhat sensational accounts that centered on "Ebla and the Bible," most researchers have turned to a consideration of Ebla as Ebla. As one scholar has wisely remarked, "Those who work on the tablets of Ebla are now doing their best to put all this hullabloo behind them and to look upon Ebla as a Syrian city producing material relevant to the culture and history of Bronze Age Syria . . . . The importance of the material at Ebla is not to be seen in its (direct) bearing upon the Bible, but for what it reveals about Bronze Age Syria."[8]

## The Dead Sea Scrolls

The Dead Sea Scrolls consist of a treasury of documents found in caves on the northwest coast of the Dead Sea between 1947 and 1956.[9] Closely adjacent to the caves are the remains of the ancient site of Qumran. Thus, "Dead Sea Scrolls" and "Qumran Scrolls" are used interchangeably. The present consensus is that Qumran was the home of a religious community that flourished from about 150 B.C.E. to 68/70 C.E. and is to be identified with some branch of the Essenes, a group already known from ancient literature, both Jewish and pagan. These Qumran Essenes were an ascetic group that had withdrawn from society to oppose what they considered to be the apostate leadership of the religious establishment. They understood themselves to be the True Israel and looked forward to an imminent eschatological denouement of the present age, the triumph of God over his (and their) enemies. They believed that their interpretation of the Law was the only valid one, and that the prophets of old had spoken explicitly (perhaps exclusively) of them.

The Qumran texts—and perhaps 20 to 40 percent of them have not yet been published—are quite diverse in nature. The following classification is intended to be representative but not exhaustive. First, there are manuscripts of every book of the Hebrew canon except of Esther. Many of these, to be sure, are quite fragmentary, but they do provide evidence for a Hebrew text a thousand years earlier than had been previously known.

Second, there are commentaries on biblical books or portions thereof. These commentaries are highly idiosyncratic in nature, relating the biblical books to the life of the sectarian community rather than providing historical data relevant for a historical understanding of the biblical book itself; but their citation of specific biblical passages attests to the text they had before them. Both the biblical manuscripts and the biblical citations in the commentaries are of inestimable value for scholars engaged in reconstructing the earliest stages of the formation of the text of the Hebrew Bible. The initial contributions of the scrolls, therefore, lies in the area of textual criticism.

Third, fragmentary copies of books included in the Greek canon of the Old Testament (Septuagint) but excluded from the Hebrew Bible have been found in their Hebrew or Aramaic originals.

Fourth, there are documents, substantial and fragmentary, that are included in neither the Hebrew nor the Greek canons but that are well known from other sources in antiquity. These are usually called the Pseudepigrapha, and their importance for reconstructing the worlds of early Judaism and Christianity is being increasingly recognized.

Fifth, a few Targums—that is, Aramaic translations of portions of the Old Testament—have been found. Hebrew had ceased to be a living language for most Jews some centuries before the beginning of the Common Era. The Bible was translated—paraphrased is more accurate—into the common language, Aramaic. Scholars have been sharply divided on the question of when written Targums emerged in the Jewish community. The Qumran evidence makes clear that they were in use, in some circles at least, before the beginning of the Common Era. The Qumran Targums also have importance for textual purposes and, since they are not strict translations but paraphrases, for enlarging our understanding of Jewish religious thought of the period.

Sixth, and finally, there are texts that seem to have been composed by the Qumran community itself. Only bare mention can be made of the documents that fall into this category. Texts that outline the organization of the community, set forth its peculiar religious beliefs, hymns, visions of the future, cultic regulations, and laws are representative. These otherwise unknown writings have made and will continue to make, when studied in an ever wider context, invaluable contributions to our understanding of the religious and cultural setting of Judaism and Christianity in the critical period from 200 B.C.E. to 200 C.E.

The relationship between Qumran and early Christianity remains moot.

Again, some early reactions were fraught with sensationalism. Claims that the birthplace of Christianity was not Bethlehem but Qumran; that early Christian theology, cult, and organization had been borrowed wholesale from Qumran; that the portrait of Jesus had been modeled on that of the Qumran leader the Teacher of Righteousness; and even that Jesus was the Teacher of Righteousness abounded not only in the popular press but, alas, in scholarly journals as well. Such fantasies have, for the most part, subsided, and scholars now focus on using the Qumran materials, early Christian texts, and a host of other documents written during the period to attempt to reconstruct the religious and social dynamics of this time so crucial for the emergence of early Judaism and early Christianity.

Many biblical scholars, spurred in part by discoveries such as those of Qumran and Nag Hammadi, have in recent years turned to fresh and intensive study of Jewish and Christian writings that were finally excluded by the respective religious establishments. Such study inevitably reopens the meaning and significance of canon. I shall cite two examples from Qumran, though a host of others could be adduced, and the principle may well be extended to the Qumran corpus as a whole. The examples are the Psalms Scroll and the Temple Scroll, both found in Cave 11.[10]

The extant Psalms Scroll contains about thirty of the biblical psalms, and the text conforms generally to the Massoretic version. The sequence of the psalms, however, varies considerably. Further, the scroll contains noncanonical psalms interspersed with the canonical, some psalms known also in the Syriac version, and a prose account of David's poetic activity; it concludes with a psalm not found in the Hebrew Bible but already an integral part of the Greek (Septuagint) version. This suggests, and other evidence seems to confirm, that at Qumran the canon was open-ended. Not only was there no officially established text of the canon, there were no formally established limits of the canon. The notion of a single, divinely inspired text is shaken to its roots. As Geza Vermes, one of the world's foremost authorities on the Scrolls, has remarked, "I am most curious to see how the conservative theologian, let alone the fundamentalist, will puzzle out this conundrum!"[11]

The Temple Scroll also exacerbates the issue of canonicity. This well-preserved document is the longest of the texts thus far published. It is some twenty-eight feet long, compared with the twenty-four-foot length of the complete Isaiah Scroll, and scholars have only begun to assess its significance for the Judaism of the time of its composition. One preliminary conclusion, however, seems clear: For the Qumran sectarians this scroll was as inspired and authoritative as the Torah itself. Indeed, the consistent shift from third-person statements (Moses) to first-person statements (God himself) may indicate that the laws in this scroll were considered not only equal to the biblical Torah, but in a sense a supersession of it. At the very least the Qumran materials require a careful reexamination of the nature and extent of canon for Jewish and Christian communities.

## Nag Hammadi

Two Egyptian farmers, probably in December 1945, discovered twelve codices (books) and portions of a thirteenth.[12] When scholars were able to examine them (how they came into scholarly possession is a fascinating tale), they were able to determine that there were fifty-two separate tractates, forty of which had not been previously known. The books were in Coptic, the Egyptian language written in Greek characters, with a few additional signs to represent sounds not found in Greek; but they were clearly originally written in Greek. Nag Hammadi is near ancient Chenoboskion (Chenoboskeia), site of a well-known ancient Christian monastery. It is possible that the Nag Hammadi Library has some connection with the monastery, or with one of the other monasteries that dotted the area in antiquity, though this cannot be established with certainty. When the books were written and when they were translated remain matters of debate, but it is evident that they were buried around 400 C.E.

The texts are conveniently available to the English reader in a preliminary translation edited by James M. Robinson, and critical editions of individual tractates are rapidly appearing. They are extremely varied in nature. Some are Jewish, some pagan—there is even a scrap of a poorly translated section from Plato's *Republic*—but most are Christian in origin or are adaptations of non-Christian works both Jewish and pagan. Most scholarly interest thus far has centered on two items: the nature of the community that wrote and/or preserved the texts, and the relationships between the contents of the Nag Hammadi Library and the canonical New Testament.

There is a general consensus on the former: The community reflects some form of Christian gnosticism.[13] We cannot here pursue this issue. The whole question of what Gnosticism is, whether it is only a Christian heresy or is Jewish in origin, whether there was a general Gnostic religion apart from either Christianity or Judaism, and so forth remains extremely complex and unresolved. The Nag Hammadi Library will undoubtedly make a significant contribution to clarifying these questions. There is also general agreement that the Nag Hammadi texts are later than the New Testament writings and in large measure dependent upon them. A significant exception is the Gospel of Thomas, a collection of 114 sayings attributed to Jesus. Many scholars feel that Thomas is independent of the Synoptic tradition and in some instances may be closer to the original Jesus tradition than the Synoptics. Both a fresh examination of Gnosticism and of the literary relationships between the Nag Hammadi Library and the New Testament will no doubt be a preoccupation of many New Testament scholars in the ensuing decades.

The concern with the Nag Hammadi texts in this paper pertains to the issues of canon and orthodoxy/heresy. Gnostics certainly considered themselves to be Christians, indeed, the true representatives of true Christianity. Their canon was *the* canon. Further, decisions about what constitutes orthodoxy and what constitutes heresy are always made in retrospect. The group that prevails are the orthodox, the losers the heretics. The Nag Hammadi Library provides invaluable information about the complexity of the situation when orthodoxy and heresy had not yet been determined.[14]

One might well inquire why the Nag Hammadi Library is included as source material for Old Testament research. It is increasingly clear that the Judaisms, the Christianities, and the pagan philosophies and religions of the first centuries of the Common Era cannot be studied in isolation. Indeed, when one reads certain texts from the period, it is by no means clear whether the author was Jewish, Christian, or pagan. A synthetic and comprehensive study is mandatory. Nag Hammadi contributes to that synthesis.

My final topic is sociological study of the Bible, the use of social scientific methods in Old Testament research.[15] Sociology, for convenience, will be used here as a cover term for the whole body of the social sciences. Sociological studies of the Bible may be divided into three broad categories, which at times overlap or become intertwined. They are social description, social history, and social theory. Social description is essentially the explanation and elucidation of the institutions and customs of the biblical community. The primary source is the Bible itself, though judicious use is made of relevant archaeological evidence, and occasionally limited use is made of information derived from ancient (only rarely modern) societies deemed comparable to the biblical community. Social history charts the changes that occurred in the biblical community, but normally does not attempt to explain the causes of those changes. Some social historians also pay more attention to factors omitted or minimized in traditional histories that emphasize politics, rulers, aristocrats, wars, and so on. They include family structures, the means of economic production, and the daily life of the mass of the population; their work, however, continues to be descriptive and not explanatory.

Social theorists seek a broader base. A primary feature of their program is the use of macro-social theory. Macro-theory concentrates on the total life of a society, uses cross-cultural models to illuminate data from that society and/or to fill in lacunae in the data, relies upon the generalizing conclusions of one or more recognized social theorist, and attempts to explain the factors lying behind social change. While the older understandings of social description and social history still claim some adherents, our concern will be with social theorists, as they show the most promise for new insights in Old Testament research.

Genuine sociological study of the Bible began in the mid-nineteenth century with the emergence of the disciplines of archaeology, cultural anthropology, and sociological theory. We cannot sketch even in outline form the early history of sociological studies of the Bible.[16] It is important to note, however, that when cultural anthropologists abandoned the sweeping approach of their fathers— for example Edward B. Tylor, who had the most influence on biblical scholars— biblical scholarship also largely withdrew from the anthropological arena. The influence of Max Weber, the most significant sociological theorist (for biblical studies at least), also waned. With a few important exceptions, sociological study of the Bible was ignored or pursued in a generally unsystematic manner.

The "new" sociological study of the Bible, not altogether new to be sure, began only about three decades ago.[17] Two features may be deemed distinctive of contemporary sociological study: (1) a more systematic use of macro-theory, and (2) more attention to the techno-economic factors in the study of society. Archaeology—particularly as it has shifted from emphasis on description to explanation—physical anthropology, geography, climatology, demography, economic analysis, and a host of other disciplines not usually reckoned among the social sciences are increasingly employed.

The new study, both in its use of macro-theory (especially in emphasizing cross-cultural contributions) and in its attention to techno-economic factors, has addressed a number of significant issues in biblical study. I shall limit myself to three examples: the study of Israel's origins, the phenomenon of prophecy, and a fresh look at apocalyptic.

It has long been a commonplace of biblical studies that Israel's origins are to be found in a nomadic or seminomadic society. This was true both for those who adopted a conquest model and for those who adopted a settlement model for the emergence of Israel in Canaan. Using cross-cultural models and techno-economic data, George Mendenhall and Norman Gottwald have spearheaded a radically different explanation: Israel emerged as a result of a peasant revolt against the Canaanite feudal lords. (Mendenhall and Gottwald differ significantly as to the role religion played in the revolt, but they agree that the nomadic ideal must be laid to rest.) Proponents of the new theory argue that both techno-economic data in the biblical texts and in cogent cross-cultural models support their thesis.

Social theory, social psychology, and cross-cultural anthropological studies have been used to reexamine Israelite prophecy. Special attention has been given to the social location of prophecy and the prophets, the social setting of prophetic oracles, the social function of prophecy (social maintenance or social change), prophetic authority, and prophetic behavior. The verdict is not yet in on the utility of these studies, but the prospects are exciting.[18]

A number of studies have examined the sociological factors that contributed to the ebbing—cessation is too strong a word—of prophecy and the emergence of apocalyptic. On the theoretical level it is proposed that the seedbed of apocalyptic lies in an experience of group alienation and/or a sense of felt deprivation. Anthropological studies of current or recent messianic/millenarian movements have been used to explicate the social setting of biblical apocalyptic. Conclusions based on sociological studies have been proposed about the date of the rise of apocalyptic and the nature of the sources that underlie it.[19] Again, the verdict is not in, but the prospects are exciting.

Much more could and should be said about the four areas I have selected, as well as about others that were totally omitted, but I hope that I have conveyed my profound impression that the future of biblical studies is full of promise. I believe that such studies will loose themselves more and more from notions of uniqueness, authority, and artificially imposed limits of canonical inclusion and exclusion.

I close with an observation that has grown in depth in the past months while I have been reviewing and reflecting in preparation for this paper. In a sense the four areas I have treated—archaeology, new literary methods, new literary data, and sociological approaches—do pertain to biblical studies, present and future. Yet there is a genuine sense in which their interest is not in the Bible itself, or at least in the Bible as traditionally conceived. The new archaeology is concerned with human culture. The new literary methods are concerned with human structure and human literary production. The new literary data are concerned with human interactions within specific social, cultural, and ideological contexts. The new sociological studies are concerned with the total scope of human societies.

I am not yet prepared to assent to John Miles's proposal that our era will witness "The debut of the Bible as a pagan classic,"[20] but I am in full agreement with that prescient pioneer of sociological studies of the Bible, Louis Wallis, that "the Bible is human,"[21] Future biblical studies will proceed most fruitfully within the context of that recognition.

## Notes

1. The relationship between the "two" testaments and Jewish and Christian interpretation of them is a matter of great significance for Jewish–Christian dialogue. It should be dealt with, however, in a specific theological context, which does not fall within the purview of this paper.

2. A valuable compendium of the history of biblical scholarship up to 1950 may be found in H. F. Hahn's *The Old Testament in Modern Research* (Philadelphia: Fortress, 1954), rev. ed. 1966. The survey is brought up to about 1985 in D. A. Knight and G. M. Tucker, eds., *The Hebrew Bible and Its Modern Interpreters* (Philadelphia: Fortress, 1985). This volume is abbreviated HBMI in subsequent notes.

3. See H. Darrell Lance, *The Old Testament and the Archaeologist* (Philadelphia: Fortress, 1981); W. A. Dever, HBMI, pp. 31–74; *Interpreter's Dictionary of the Bible, Supplement* (Nashville: Abingdon Press, 1976), pp. 44–52. This work is abbreviated IDBS in subsequent notes.

4. See Daniel Patte, *What is Structural Exegesis* (Philadelphia: Fortress, 1976); Robert C. Culley, HBMI, pp. 167–184.

5. See David Robertson, *The Old Testament and the Literary Critic* (Philadelphia: Fortress, 1977); IDBS, 547–551; Robert Alter and Frank Kermode, eds., *The Literary Guide to the Bible* (Cambridge, Mass.: Harvard University Press, 1987).

6. An invaluable introduction for the general reader is Raymond Brown's *Recent Discoveries and the Biblical World* (Wilmington, Del.: M. Glazier, 1983). It is highly recommended. See also J. J. M. Roberts, HBMI, pp. 75–121.

7. Most of the works on Ebla thus far have been directed toward specialists or are fraught with sensationalism. A balanced semi-popular work is Chaim Bermant and Michael Weitzman, *Ebla: A Revelation in Archaeology* (New York: Times Books, 1979). A popular but reasonably reliable introduction is in *National Geographic,* December 1978, pp. 730–759.

8. James D. Muhly, *Biblical Archaeologist* 47 (1984), p. 29.

9. The literature dealing with the Scrolls, both technical and popular, is enormous. Perhaps the best introduction for the general reader is still Geza Vermes's *The Dead Sea Scrolls: Qumran in Perspective* (Philadelphia: Fortress, 1978), and his translation of the major documents, *The Dead Sea Scrolls in English* (Baltimore: Harmondsworth, 1962, rev. ed. 1975). A brief treatment is in IDBS, pp. 210–219.

10. Perhaps the most convenient introductions are, for the Psalms Scroll, J. A. Sanders, *The Dead Sea Psalms Scroll* (Ithaca, N.Y.: Cornell University Press, 1967), and for the Temple Scroll, Johann Maier, tr. Richard White, *The Temple Scroll* (Sheffield, Eng.: Eisenbrauns, 1985).

11. Geza Vermes, *Journal for the Study of the Old Testament,* 39 (1987), p. 127.

12. The best place to begin for an overview is James M. Robinson's introduction to *The Nag Hammadi Library* (New York: Harper and Row, 1977, pp. 1–25). See also George MacRae, IDBS, pp. 613–619. For a lively but responsible journalistic treatment see John Dart, *The Laughing Savior* (New York: Harper and Row, 1976).

13. There is no scholarly consensus regarding the phenomenon of Gnosticism. The general reader may well begin with the articles on Gnosticism in the *Interpreter's Bible* (Nashville: Abingdon Press, 1962) by Robert Grant, pp. 404–406, and in IDBS by Elaine Pagels, pp. 364–368. John Dart, in the book cited in the previous note, gives a useful general introduciton.

14. Elaine Pagels, *The Gnostic Gospels* (New York: Random House, 1979) perceptively addresses this issue in nontechnical form. The book is a very good introduction to the broad range of Nag Hammadi studies.

15. A useful introduction is R. R. Wilson, *Sociological Approaches to the Old Testament* (Philadelphia: Fortress, 1984). Special attention may be called to Norman K. Gottwald's *The Hebrew Bible: a Socio-Literary Introduction* (Minneapolis, Minn.: Fortress, 1985). Gottwald utilizes the theoretical postulates of the theory in addressing the entire Old Testament.

16. See Hahn, pp. 44–82; pp. 157–184; Wilson, pp. 10–29.

17. See Culley, HBMI, pp. 184–200; Gottwald's bibliography is also very useful.

18. See Wilson, pp. 67–80; Gene M. Tucker, HBMI, pp. 325–368, esp. pp. 348–356.

19. See Paul Hanson, HBMI, pp. 465–488; IDBS, pp. 28–34.

20. John Miles, *Bulletin of the Council on the Study of Religion,* June 1976, pp. 1–6.

21. Louis Wallis, *The Bible is Human* (New York: AMS Press, 1942).

# The Future Of Religion

## Frank T. Miosi

### (Canada)

In the twenty-sixth year of the reign of Pharoah Ramses, while the king was in Thebes celebrating a religious festival, a messenger came from the prince of Bactria to say that Bentresh, the prince's daughter and the sister of Pharaoh's Syrian wife, was quite ill. "O King, my Lord, may your majesty order that a god be sent against this illness." Ramses sent the statue of the god, Khonsu, to Bactria. Upon the god's arrival, the prince and the chief officials of Bactria worshiped him and shortly thereafter, Khonsu cured princess Bentresh.

I tell this story, which was engraved on an ancient Egyptian stela, because it represents a religious spirit that is no longer present in the Western world. The Syrian prince believed in divine power. He did not believe that his own gods were the sole possessors of that power. He was willing to ask for and worship another god in the hope, if not the confident faith, that divine power could be found in many forms and that the beliefs relating to his own gods need not inhibit him from accepting other belief systems. This type of flexibility in religious beliefs, in humanity's ability to be creatively religious, changed dramatically with the onset of monotheism. This is not a necessary corollary of monotheism—there is a different way—but the fact remains that monotheism has been fraught with political and social intolerance, religious inflexibility, and the stifling of human initiative and creativity.

I do not blame religion for this. My view is that religion has become far too associated with belief structures and systems and too little understood for the faith that is at its core. My view is that the humanist, secular or otherwise, has or should have no essential quarrel with religion—only with rigid, stifling beliefs.

It is a very banal comparison, but just as one can quarrel with Keynesian or supply-side economics but not with economics itself, with existentialism or logical positivism but not with philosophy, with behaviorism or Jungianism but not with psychology, so also one can quarrel with Judaism or Islam or Christianity, but not with religion.

The historian knows full well that the actions of the prince of Bactria were not unique. When Alexander conquered Egypt, one of his first formal actions was to pay homage to the god Amon-Ra. Roman adoption of most of the Greek pantheon is well known. Post-Exodus worship of Baal by the Hebrews was a constant cause of prophetic concern. The examples are myriad: People had a fundamental faith and were willing to alter, adapt, and adopt belief systems that allowed them to better express and realize their faith. It is not surprising that in such a world the scholar is hard pressed to cite a single religious war. Of course, the gods were always invoked when a battle raged, but no one really claimed that "my faith is better than yours" or "we must conquer to convert the pagan."

There was an abrupt change, however, with the advent of monotheism. Behind the seeming pacifist nature of Pharaoh Akhenaton with regard to his Syro-Palestinian empire, one finds, for the first time, the desecration of Egyptian holy places and divine names for the honor of his sole god, Aten. This is the first monotheism of which we have any knowledge, and with it we see intolerance and violence. Not long afterward, in another Near Eastern monotheistic culture, we have what may be our first historical example of genocide. Suffice it to say that this pattern has continued, whether under the banner of Yahweh, Christ, or Allah. One can understand how such circumstances arise in conjunction with monotheism. A single god, almost always personified; attributed with human passions, logic, and motivations; all-powerful, all-knowing, omnipresent; able and willing to communicate directly with the created world, setting down codes of conduct—codes, by the way, that rarely address the inner thoughts and conscience of human beings, but instead heavily emphasize actions, duties, and attitudes that relate to the human being as a social animal—and all of this customarily being revealed in a sacred, inspired, inerrant book.

I contend that all of this is entirely of human origin and that it is and has been a sure recipe for disaster. I also firmly believe that this form of religious belief is fast losing its hold, its believability, as a result of the constantly developing analytical tools of modern scholarship. The grand, manufactured systems of traditional monotheistic beliefs have been attacked and have been found to be sorely lacking—indeed, they have lost. The job now is to inform and convince the common believer that this is actually the case.

Let us take a few moments to look at where we are today. We could make a very basic, two-part division in the attempts to challenge traditional monotheistic systems. The first encompasses technical scholarship and has been aimed at analyzing the sacred books of the various monotheistic systems. When it is contended that God intervenes in history, that God not only shapes and uses history for divine purposes but also becomes a player in or a maker of history, then the events so deemed are naturally subject to historical investigation. We need not dwell on this in depth, but once the inerrant, revealed word of God came under the critical scrutiny of the historian, archaeologist, linguist, anthropologist, chemist, biologist, botanist, paleontologist, and many more, the very occurrence of these religiously claimed *historical* events has come under serious question to say the least. From simplistic creation stories (so humanly authored that God even needs rest), or a historical Adam and Eve, or a historical flood that covered the world, or a Jericho that was abandoned and desolate when its walls were supposed to have come tumbling down; from Egyptian magicians whose canes became snakes, or a Jesus born during a census for which there is no record, a baptism that did and did not occur depending upon which Gospel one reads, a resurrection with no eyewitnesses, and ascension in one day and in forty days—the books claim historical fact, and insofar as they do, these facts are no different from George Washington's cutting down the cherry tree; they are subject to the normal process of verification, and they have consistently and critically been found to be unverifiable.

This process will only continue. Deeper analysis and more precise and sophisticated tools will uncover more of the facts and make obsolete more of the story as we have known it.

There is a second approach, much less technical, but possibly more sophisticated. Some of us have begun to look very closely at what our main religious traditions have given us as a description of God, and we are not at all comfortable with what we see. As examples of this approach, I would like to talk about miracles, free will, and evil.

Whereas the scientist or historian examines the physical evidence for miracles, for divine intervention into the processes and actions of nature and man—the theologian examines the very likelihood and the logical repercussions of the possibility of intervention. When looking at miracles, the theologian does not debate the historical facts of the event, but focuses instead on the nature of the god that is being described, if that god is either actually or even possibly a maker of miracles. If this is an option open to a god of creation, freedom, and love, then the theologian finds a dilemma. We would have a god who would work miracles for a very select number of people, but who is not prepared to do the same thing in order to prevent a Treblinka, a Hiroshima, or a Dresden, stop a famine or end a genocidal war in Ethiopia. The theologian will look upon this type of god as an idol, a truly false and dangerous characterization of the loving and forgiving god. If such a god were to actually exist, a god who prefers a few who do him obeisance over all the world's sufferers, then he would be the very devil and is not worthy of human faith. This, by the way, is just what the Christian Gnostics of the third century concluded about the god of the Old Testament.

There is only one way around this conclusion and that is to immunize God by claiming that the ways of God are mysterious, that human beings should not, indeed cannot, understand why he chooses to do what he does.

This naturally leads us to the next theological area of speculation: the believer's traditional portrayal of the god of monotheism as one who is omniscient and omnipotent. There was a time when people tried to play with these terms by creating spurious riddles. We are all familiar with these: Can God create a tree high enough that he could not cut it down? Can God create a thought so profound that he could not understand it?

Such questions no longer interest us. Again, we look at the portrayal, take it to its logical conclusion, and see what is left. When we examine the meaning of omniscience—a classic characteristic of a monotheistic god—we are left with someone or something that is totally powerless. Omniscience, as traditionally understood, means that God is outside of time. He knows all things, past, present, and future to us, but since he is eternal, timeless, all things are known by him at the same moment, including their temporal relationship. But this means that God cannot "decide" to act or to change things. Decision is a process, it represents movement from a state of inaction to action. But God cannot decide; his omniscience means that he knows what his actions are in advance, what his thoughts are before he thinks them. Omniscience, far from being a grand quality, is instead very limiting in human terms. For instance, the omniscient god can have no free will, for free will means choice, freedom to act; but the omniscient god is totally bound by his own omniscience. He always knows what is to happen, what he will do; everything is fixed and inflexible. The common portrayal of God results, then, in a sterile or powerless being, utterly incapable of "choosing" to do anything, of freely "acting" in any way. If you believe in the God of the Book who acts, decides, tires, has remorse, shows forgiveness, becomes enraged—if this is your god, then you must revise, indeed reject, your portrayal of that god as being omniscient and omnipotent. In one way or another, that god must be redefined.

This leads us directly to the third item for consideration: evil. This has been a fundamental religious question for millennia. The polytheistic religious systems had an easy out—the attributing of evil to one or more of the malicious or trickster gods within their pantheon. Monotheism has no such option—God is all-good, all-loving, all-forgiving, all-knowing, all-powerful, and, by definition, there are no other gods. We see strange creations, such as Satan and demon spirits and Islamic soul-snatchers, beings whose power and influence God is somehow unable or unwilling to eradicate immediately.

Both Christianity and Islam have constructed an eschatological system where God eventually conquers these evil beings, but it has not been generally realized that in either system, once there is a return to the pre-fall state, absolutely nothing prevents the entire process from being repeated—or another angelic revolution, another human transgression from happening. It happened once; it can happen again. It seems as if the Kingdom of God is not as final as has been believed.

Speculation on the relation between evil and a classically defined god is quite broad and profound. I do not intend to dwell on the various justifications and explanations that have been developed over the centuries. I would like, as before, to focus on the portrayal of God that the presence and continued existence of worldly evil gives us. We have in all monotheistic religions a god who has no hesitation in laying down moral and ethical codes for humankind. These codes are so important that adhering to them is a condition of entry into the Kingdom of God, or heaven. In every monotheistic system there are express statements that following the defined, revealed code of ethics provide the only way to guarantee either the favor of God or eternal existence with him. Some more liberal speculation permits that God has given all humankind the gift of conscience, which, when followed faithfully and whole-heartedly, will lead human beings on the path of the appropriate ethics—opening the door ever so slightly to the promised land for the honest but uninformed pagan. What I am driving at here is that the entire value system of each monotheistic religion is built on the concept of the absolute rightness of the God-given code of conduct. And yet, what do we find? We find that in each of these systems, the god is allowed to act in a way that would be completely abhorrent if done by a human. Stand next to a hospital bed where a young child lies taking her last pain-ridden breaths before dying of leukemia. Go to a village in central Mexico and see not one building standing and half of the population buried alive after a violent earthquake. Walk the desiccated waste of Burkina Faso or the southern Sudan and step over the sun-baked cadavers of thousands who have died of starvation brought about by drought. See a thalydomide baby now grotesquely grown. See a 747 falling ablaze to kill all four-hundred passengers on board. I guarantee you that, if anyone reading this were present at any one of these events, much less all of them, and at every other occasion of natural disaster or human violence where pain, anguish, or death were involved—if any of us knew what was to happen and had the power to stop it and did not, that man or woman would be hated, detested, an outcast to humanity. And yet, we have defined and worship a god who does just that; a god who is supposed to have given humanity a conscience, a love, to have somehow created humanity in his own image, turns out to have revealed to humanity a moral code—and will punish with eternal damnation anyone who does not hold to that code—which is totally at odds with his own conduct. Human beings must ask whether they can believe in and worship a god who cannot measure up to the moral standards that every person knows in his or her heart are right and good and just.

The modern theologian recognizes that it is time to reject this "god ethic"; it portrays a god who is just too embarrassing for even human beings, with all their limitations and foibles, to believe in. If God is to be personified, to be able to act, to have all power and knowledge—in other words, if God is what he has been traditionally defined to be in the monotheistic religions, we, his creation, turn out to be infinitely more moral than he is. I dwell on this point because I consider it to be one of the most dangerous of all monotheistic beliefs. If there is a "god ethic," one so foreign either to the moral codes thought to have been either revealed to humanity by God or to have been developed situationally by pagans, the "religious" person has the opportunity to appeal to and use the god ethic under the guise of divine guidance or spiritual inspiration. The "religious" person can act the way god is allowed to act—unethically, immorally, violently, unlovingly, unforgivingly in terms of human conduct— and claim that it is right because God told him or her to do so. We all know what Abraham was willing to do when convinced that he had spoken with his god; Kierkegaard saw Abraham's willingness to sacrifice his son as something quite profound: A teleological suspension of the ethical, he called it.

Inquisitions, pogroms, religious wars of conversion, mass martyrdoms such as those prompted by the Ayatollah, and the perilously immoral ravings of some of the religious right (God is against returning the Panama Canal to the Panamanians)—if you have trouble comprehending these just read the books that they read, not concentrating on how their god tells them to act but on how that god himself acts. From this perspective, their actions are not only understandable, they are inspired. To repeat an earlier sentiment, monotheism does not need a devil when it has such a god.

What does the future hold? I think that by now my position is apparent. The technical, scientific analyses of the "hard" data of monotheism has unquestionably undercut the literalness of the inerrant word. The theological analysis of the "soft" data has pushed the traditional portrayal of the monotheistic god to the point where that portrayal is almost ridiculous. To many, the god of monotheism is no longer tenable and must be redefined. I am not talking about the type of redefinition that might take place as the result of the much-heralded ecumenical movement with its interfaith dialogues. At best, this process is one that seeks out and focuses on common ground in belief and downplays or learns to live with the differences. This is not really a redefinition, although, if successful, it may eventually result in some truly radical developments as the areas of common ground become more deeply analyzed and appreciated while the other areas lose their importance due to general speculative inattention.

The real changes are taking place among those people who are completely reinterpreting the meaning and importance of the belief systems of monotheism. This is being done in a way that is very compatible with humanist sentiment: The general principle being used is that when belief and reason are truly at odds, belief must give way.

Belief is, or should be, concerned with Truth. One does not believe something known to be false. The word also implies uncertainty, for what is self-evident, or essentially impossible to question, is not a matter of belief. Belief is not inevitable, it is not simply compelled by what is given. Most of us are told what to believe when we are children, and we continue to hold these beliefs in a community of believers, so that they are an essential part of our self-understanding and self-definition. Threats to them, whether from the outside or from our own internal questioning, are easily and often perceived as threats to ourselves. This is why we rarely question their truth: The loss of them raises the uncomfortable—no, horrible—possibility of the loss of family and community, of everything in which we were embedded by the circumstances of our birth.

Thus, we protect the most fundemental of these beliefs at all costs: We are willing to reject our reason or risk our lives to see them survive. We wrap their truth in a garment of divine revelation guaranteed by God in the holy book; we make them sacred, and their attackers become heretics and sinners.

Obviously such a response is totally evasive. It puts the believer in the same position as the one that arises when one believes in miracles. One is essentially forced to hold that the loving, compassionate god had given the right beliefs, the truth, to a select group—usually one's own. Whatever those other groups claim to have, be they Christian, Jew or Muslim, it is not the word of God; that belongs only to our group. We are not the slightest bit concerned about why God did not give the ancestors of those other groups that same information that was given to our ancestors; and we don't care to speculate on why our god would create a world and reveal a truth in such a manner that one's access to it becomes nothing more than an accident of birth.

This is a highly implausible position, to say the least; but if one remembers the connection between belief, community, and self-definition, the fact that it is held is quite understandable. Submitting our beliefs to the closest critical scrutiny is truly a dangerous business, but it is apparent that it must be done. If our beliefs are true, the process will serve to intensify our understanding and appreciation of the Truth. If they are slightly misdirected or false, the process will help us find the truer or more truing path.

John Meagher, the great Canadian theologian, has developed a five-step method that one can use to test the worthiness of one's beliefs:

1. Ask yourself what value you attach to belief X, what you instinctively think it implies.

2. Look at belief X closely; does it really imply Y, what you are used to getting from it?

3. Is there any other way of arriving at Y without depending on X?

4. What would it cost to put belief X on hold, register it as doubtful, or simply accept it as a pious invention?

5. What would it cost to keep belief X?[1]

This was the method that was employed in our earlier discussion of miracles, free will, and evil; and one can see that it has powerful implications.

Faith is not belief. It is not an intellectual process. It is rather a condition of the whole person. It is that ineffable matrix within each of us that defines what and how we are prepared to actively receive and welcome the world around us. This receptivity is much deeper than understanding; it is the ground in which understanding takes root. It conditions all of the ways in which we appropriate reality, and thus conditions our becoming real. Faith is the condition by which we belong to the real, and it to us.

Each of us has the gift of faith. It is concomitant with the gift of human life. Insofar as the very humanity of existence is common, all of us share a mutual faith; yet insofar as we are individuals, are discrete physical, mental, and spiritual units of self-awareness and receptivity, our faiths—the character and quality of our readiness to accept, value, trust, and love whatever is—can be and are quite particular.

I think it right to say that the character of our faith is what defines our religion. The religious system we are willing to accept is the one that most suitably fits our faith. It is the one whose beliefs, practices, codes, and philosophy weave a personally comfortable fabric of possibilities for understanding all that is. Many people choose to limit the word "religion" to those systems that have a god. At this point, I do not, because I am not at all sure of what others mean when they use the word "god," and it is likely that the term means something very different to each of us. However, the way in which religion is understood should not affect my general argument.

I contend that no two believers' Christianity—or Islam, or whatever—are exactly alike. To some extent, each takes the received system and designs, alters, and emphasizes parts of it to provide such a fit. When the religion and the faith are so different as not to be reconcilable, some people will set that religion aside in favor of another or of the search for another that will provide the framework necessary for human actions and expression. Some others, however, give up completely or never truly engage in the search; they fall into a spiritual rigor mortis, acting out human existence in the deepest of anguish, incapable of or unaware of the possibility of setting their lives on a more truing course.

Religion is not faith. It is ideally the system that perfectly verbalizes and actualizes one's faith. It is the sound that is heard when the chord is struck: one is not independent of the other; they are not part of a greater whole, yet they are not the same. Religion is also not belief, although beliefs are required to express and define at any one moment how that religion attunes to the faith. Beliefs are provisional; they express how we are understanding the Truth at a given point in time. When we grasp that Truth in a different way, these beliefs cease to be useful, except as tracings of our own and all humankind's quest. When they become more than irrelevant, when honoring them actually conflicts with our faith as it is expressed through our religion, then they must be abandoned without remorse.

One might best understand this faith–belief division by looking at science. A set of observable facts—part of the experience of all humankind or all attending humankind—are concantenated in such a way as to give rise to or be explained by a general theory. This general theory leads to further observation of the facts, further information about those facts, predictions with regard to them, and, possibly, connection with other similarly devised theories into a grander theoretical system.

These scientific theories are nothing more than beliefs. We do not have the reality of evolution, of the expanding universe, of the big bang; we have the theory. Any time that new facts come into the equation, the theory stands the chance of losing its believability. Unfortunately, we have seen all too often that even for scientific theories, the comfort of the old can powerfully impede the acceptance of the new. Indeed, we can even see that the human desire for the security of the old has often prevented the scientific community from even investigating areas that appear to pose a threat to existing theories.

Yet, often the incontrovertability of some facts or the insight and courage of an investigator has brought about the rejection of one theory or belief in favor of another. All of this constant development, change, or replacement of scientific theory-beliefs, however, has not and does not challenge the faith that is at the root of the scientific system: there is an ordered reality; this order can be apprehended by man; the establishment of a finite series of temporally related events is sufficient to extrapolate the fact of an infinite cause and effect relationship. There are a number of such articles of scientific faith, and the Truth of these is completely independent of the theories that humanity develops for the purpose of better understanding this Truth.

Religious beings must be granted the same respect that science has. We do not ridicule science because a history of science is basically the study of the development, acceptance, prominence, attack, and rejection of one scientific theory after another. We do not ridicule Newton in the light of Einstein, Lamarck in the light of Darwin, or Rutherford in the light of Schroedinger; and we do not reject science because of the impermanence of its theories. We must allow belief the same flexibility as science has. As Einstein can derive relativity from the illogical axiom that the speed of light does not vary, so too religious believers can posit the inerrancy of the sacred text. As Mandelbrot's sets and Lorenz's attractors can find magnificent patterns in what are otherwise totally random mathematical solutions to nonlinear equations, so too believers should be allowed to find divine patterns behind natural processes and human activities. As Bohr can make the mutually exclusive wavelike and particlelike behavior be properties of one and the same light, so to God can be indescribable and personified in the same theology.

The scientific and the religious must be allowed the same flexibility of theory-belief, as long as people realize that their theories are not properties of reality and that their beliefs are not properties of God. They are, instead, properties of our interaction with reality.

I am not a lone voice calling in the wilderness on this. Many theologians from many denominations and religions have either expressly or tacitly come to the same understanding; and these people have begun to subject the belief systems of their various faiths to the closest scrutiny. Remembering what we said about the close link between belief and community, belief and social definition, many of these people have been vilified, banned from writing and teaching, excommunicated; but they are pressing ahead just the same, and their numbers and influence are growing significantly. Many have even found ways of staying in the system, of couching their thoughts in a manner that is radical enough so as to be provocative but subtle enough not to permit them to be officially branded as heretics or outcasts by the power structure. Others have broken brand new paths of understanding, of approaching the Truth, and have rejected outright whole segments of old beliefs; but as a result of their sheer numbers, they have been able to avoid official sanction.

For instance, female theologians have, to a great extent, totally rejected all patriarchal references in both Judaism and Christianity. Their religious communities have only begun to experience the superficial changes brought about by this movement: minor liturgical edits; female ministers and rabbis; removing gender bias from numerous biblical passages. Belief systems have as yet been affected only in minor ways; but once the box has been opened and the second, third, and fourth steps have been taken, there is a strong likelihood that a new concept of God will have evolved.

Naomi Goldenberg writes,

> In the new age of changes for our gods, Christ and Yahweh will no longer behave as egotistical, spoiled children in our psyches—they will no longer keep us from giving our attention to other members of the psychic families. Instead, Christ and Yahweh will be valuable images that maintain our ties with history. They will remind us of the patriarchal monotheism which we have outgrown but which we will need to remember. We should expect to treat the old gods as we treat the places of our childhood—as important places of our past which demand regular visits and recollection but where we can never live again.[2]

Rosemary Ruether, possibly the leading Catholic feminist theologian, believes that we must get rid of the parent image of God and become autonomous: "Patriarchal theology uses the parent image for God to prolong spiritual infantilism as virtue and to make autonomy and assertion of free will a sin." Even the attractive human person of Christ will no longer serve as a model of "religious personhood" for women because "the Christological symbols have been used to enforce male dominance." Women will "say that the very limitations of Christ as a male person must lead to the conclusion that he cannot represent redemptive personhood for them. That they must emancipate themselves from Jesus as redeemer and seek a new redemptive disclosure of God and of human possibility in female form."[3]

Liberation theology is having and will have immense effects. Currently it is a Catholic phenomenon of Central and South America, but the process is quickly influencing many of the Protestant denominations in this region, and its point of view is gaining many supporters in North America and Europe. The liberation theologians are seriously challenging old belief structures; they are redefining sin, salvation, the Kingdom of God, the importance of human actions. To the liberation theologian, God is redefined as being totally and completely involved with humanity and human existence, and, therefore, human experience becomes a fundamental dictum of theology. God becomes almost a partner in the process of growth and change to the point where God, too, can be thought to grow and change.[4]

Another interesting movement is the one taking place in China today. Once the scene of hotly contested conversion and baptism contests between European missionaries of all major Christian denominations, China became a wasteland for missionary work and religious growth for almost four decades. The Chinese government has now reopened the country to religious activity, but has done so in a very interesting fashion. The Christians can preach, open meeting places and seminaries, but they cannot engage in denominational bickering. They all must preach the same thing, or, if there are differences, they must be minor and no emphasis whatsoever may be placed on them; they are to be explained as different ways of understanding the same truth, each equally valid, none excluding any other. The Chinese call it the "Three-Self-Help Movement" or "Post-

Denominational" Christianity, and individuals and churches not adhering to it lose their license to operate. The long-term implications of this approach on the continuation of rigid denominational belief systems is evident; there will be a forced evolution of an essential Christianity that will likely have an impact far beyond the borders of China.

Of course, there are numerous individual voices challenging the most fundamental of monotheistic beliefs for Christians, from the virgin birth to the Trinity, from the resurrection to the divinity of Christ. Analyzing the biblical references and early historical developments in Christianity, they are finding that the grounds for many of the traditional Christian beliefs are not nearly as strong as was once supposed. As a result, they are calling for either the rejection of some of these, their reinterpretation, or a totally new understanding of their meaning.

The Bishop of Durham, holding the third ranking position in the Church of England, can say:

> It is simply not true that there is anywhere a church which is guaranteed to get it right under God. As there are no miracles which prove to everybody that God is around, so there is no church with authority which can settle decisively and definitely forever what God is like and what God wants. To claim this, or to behave as if this were so, is to present an impossible and unworthy picture of God . . . . For the records of all churches contain acts of inhumanity, declarations of stupidity and indications of triumphalism, arrogance and insensitivity which are a disgrace to God—or, indeed, to ordinary humanity.[5]

Jean Meagher, Canada's leading liberal Catholic theologian, says:

> A new humility is making its way into Christian understanding, in the fact of the chastening negative experience of lost confidence in the underpinnings of traditional apologetics and the enlightening positive experience of the evident richness and maturity of other religious paths . . . . Christianity can make use of the resources developed in the other religious traditions, which are not less wise or less authoritative or less revealed. Only false pride can disguise the historical truth that the Christian tradition has always borrowed from its neighbours . . . . But there is one important change of attitude still to be accomplished . . . . I suggest that the more appropriate disposition would be to acknowledge not that all major religions are fully mature, but that none of them is. The religions of the world, Christianity included, are at best at a stage of adolescence, and this new situation is a clear invitation to advance toward maturity.[6]

One can also find a demythologization of the Koran. Muhammed Abduh holds that Muslim belief should follow the natural order of things. It has no need, therefore, for belief in extraordinary or miraculous events. When a literal understanding of a text conflicts with reason, then reason is to prevail. Religion, says Abduh, is a friend of science; it stimulates science to investigate the data of the universe. It demands that people should act according to the laws of nature with strength of character and readiness for action.[7]

We can see what is emerging here. A reevaluation of the belief systems of our traditional great monotheistic religions—one based upon a greater confidence in the abilities and responsibilities of humanity and upon the almost polytheistic recognition of the situational usefulness of belief in approaching the Truth rather than being the Truth itself—has led theologians and philosophers to reconsider the old "God." The old divine attributes had made God the supreme exception to human experience; we grew and moved while God was perfect; we anguished and changed, whereas God was sublime and complete. Because of these vast differences, theologians would talk about God only to a point, and that was usually the point at which they could reasonably contend with the descriptions of God as revealed in their sacred texts. Past that point, they would retreat to the inscrutable nature of an indescribable God—that point was usually where those same revealed sources depicted a god who, in human perception, acted or was defined in terms contradictory to the preferred divine picture.

In the new theology, all reality is continuously undergoing modification and change. God is also part of this, and far from being unrelated to the physical world, God is conditional and is affected by everything that happens in the world. In the new theology, God's "absoluteness" is not the traditional final, unlimited, and unchangeable absoluteness. In this system, God is absolute because the divine experiencing is composed of the totality of all experience, and when these increase, God increases. Since the main quality of existence in this theology is experiencing in continuum, God is not the Unchangeable One but the ever more Becoming, ever more Related, ever more Involved One.

The god of the old theology was the total, efficient cause of everything, able to create anything, even out of nothing. In this theology, God has all *possibilities* in his vision (the new omniscience); God is the formal well-spring of all value (the new all-goodness); but does not have the power to force reality to this value. God's power is, instead, that of suasion—the power to lure, to attract the process of experience to the most valued possibility, but not the ability to compel it.

In this type of process theology, divine revelation is seen in the emergence of all the experience making up the world because this constitutes the concrete experience of God. Human achievement, therefore, is God's envisioning made concrete and is to be extolled and fostered. God's strength is now his vision of all possibilities; and his love is understood as the desire for a fuller and more intensive relationship. In the process system, the divine destiny is tied to humankind, tied to the fact that God needs what humankind can give.

The pattern I have outlined is obvious. Its inevitablity can be questioned, because any number of unforeseen and unpredictable micro-events could radically alter or redirect the seeming mega-religious trends. I think that honest-thinking secular humanists must investigate this pattern quite closely. Their classic anti-religious position is one that I believe is as mistaken about what religion and religious faith are as that of the religious establishments themselves. As religion and courageous religious thinkers place belief in a context that can be considered to be parallel to scientific theory (that is, it is the best way we have at the moment of understanding and explaining our current comprehension of the truth of physical reality), as these thinkers recast a definition of God away from the old fixed, complete, omnipotent, manipulative, patriarchal images to one that processes God and faith through a continuum of human experience, human worth, and human values—as all of these are taking place, secular humanists must see that their long-argued dangers, limitations, and human debasements of religion are not at all necessary concomitants to it.

The secular humanist must come to realize that some people's faith in God can be a healthy and full working partner of the humanistic faith in humanity. They must stop childishly attacking religion and religious faith itself and start attacking what is the true antagonist—those intolerant and outdated belief systems that have blocked and continue to block all humankind, believer, agnostic and atheistic alike, from faithfully pursuing the Truth.

## Notes

1. John Meagher, *Feast of Epiphany* (New York: Doubleday, 1990).

2. Naomi Goldenberg, *Changing of the Gods* (Boston: Beacon Press, 1979), pp. 83-84.

3. See Rosemary Ruether, *Sexism and God-Talk* (Boston: Beacon Press, 1983) and *To Change the World: Christology and Cultural Criticism* (New York: Crossword, 1981).

4. One need only to read the foundation text of liberation theology, Gustavo Gutierrez, *A Theology of Liberation* (Maryknoll, N.Y.: Orbis, 1973) to see the critical changes in traditional theology espoused by this school.

5. David Jenkins, *God, Miracle and the Church of England* (London: SCM Press Ltd, 1987), p. 7.

6. Meagher, op. cit.

7. Cited in D. M. Donaldson, *Studies in Muslim Ethics* (London: Methuen, 1963), p. 251.

# Three Dimensions of Religion

## Joe E. Barnhart
### (United States)

It is tempting to load one's definition of religion with one's own advanced conclusions. Mr. Thwackum, the provincial parson in Henry Fielding's *Tom Jones*,
declares: "When I mention religion I mean the Christian religion; and not only
the Christian religion, but the Protestant religion; and not only the Protestant
religion, but the Church of England." A contemporary Calvinist, Gordon Clark,
promises to spare his readers the "whirlpool of equivocal disputation" if they
will only accept his definition in terms of the articles of the Westminster Con-
fession.[1] At the other end of the continuum is Salomon Reinach's definition
of religion as "a sum of scruples which impede the free exercise of our faculties."[2]
The *American Heritage Dictionary,* by defining religion arbitrarily in terms of
the supernatural, eliminates Theravada Buddhism, whose atheistic perspective
tends to regard gods, demons, and ghosts not as supernatural beings, but as
personifications of human desires, anxieties, fears, and ignorance.[3]

In the attempt to be fair to the traditional religions, some scholars have
sought an unequivocal definition in etymology. The Latin *religare* ("being bound")
and *relegere* ("gather together") are prime contenders. This is a fruitful approach,
and an exceptional scholar can do much with it despite its serious limitations
and vagueness.

Too much has been demanded of a single definition of religion. The greater
the depth of the definition, the more restricted its scope. In order to reduce
self-serving arbitrariness and blatant prejudice in advancing a single loaded definition of religion, I propose three kinds: (1) preliminary definition, (2) reportive
definition, and (3) ideal definition.

The preliminary definition of religion sacrifices depth to provide breadth
and scope. Scope is essential in order to prevent various acknowledged traditional religions from being arbitrarily excluded from the arena of study. To
rule out Theravada Buddhism or any other religion that does not emphasize
the supernatural is argument by fiat rather than reason. The preliminary defini-

tion of religion does not raise the question of the truth or falsity of any religion's claims. Rather, its function is to mark off the territory in which inquiry and study are to be carried out.

It is the crucial mistake to presume that all religions are going in the same direction. It is more likely that they are coming from the same general problem, which I call *core finitude*. The preliminary definition of religion focuses on this universal problem or concern. Human individuals and groups are religious in a preliminary way if they are concerned or preoccupied with the finitude of themselves or their identity group. Historically, the resolutions offered are astoundingly diverse and can in no significant way be harmonized except to say that they are dealing with the roughly common concern of core finitude. Religious traditions over the centuries have struggled with the problem of death because few phenomena can equal death in creating in the species a sense of finitude. The traditions differ greatly in the way they handle death and other manifestations of finitude.

Core finitude can be sensed in at least three dimensions of human experience: (1) the cognitive or intellectual, (2) the moral, and (3) the emotional.

In the *cognitive* dimension we experience the shock of ignorance and doubt as well as the anomalies that our inherited cognitive system cannot satisfactorily explain. In Western culture, science is perpetually generating doubts and intellectual tremors, if not quakes, that remind us of our finitude. Far from curing the species of this sense of finitude (which is the *universal* religious problem), science guarantees that it will not only continue, but intensify. Science does not offer fixed intellectual certitude, but rather upsets the mind with new doubts and new vistas previously never dreamed of and never explored. It reveals to us the abyss of human ignorance.

In the *moral* dimension of human experience, the gap between one's ethical norms and one's behavior often generates a sense of finitude, that is, limitation and frailty. Guilt and shame are symptoms of the chasm between what is and what we think ought to be. One religious tradition has taken this empirical fact and created from it a doctrine of original sin. Another tradition has developed the rival theory of original and inevitable conflict. Whatever scheme is used to explain the gap, all religious traditions recognize the gap between the *is* and the *ought*.

The third dimension in which core finitude manifests itself is the *emotional* dimension. We feel the impact of the loss of our loved ones. We suffer emotionally the shocks of disaster and turbulence, and we feel the sting of a thousand slings and arrows. To be alive and to watch our plans and dreams unravel before us is to quake as the muscles and glands of the body agitate and emote in the presence of defeat. Many traditional religions have provided rituals for grief suffered in defeat and ceremonies for rejoicing in the hour of triumph and victory. Some traditions purport to call in the gods; other traditions call in dead ancestors to join them in these rituals; one tradition does not profess to invoke the presence of dead ancestors, but rather to invoke the words and examples that live on after the ancestors themselves have perished. Each faith works out its own emotional bonds and attachments to those fellow mortals who have gone before them and to those who will follow them in the future.

With good reason, some scholars emphasize the etymological definition of religion as the bond or tie that holds together the community. This binding factor can be better understood if viewed against the background of the core finitude that community members suffer intellectually, morally, and emotionally. Individuals are better able to absorb the shock of finitude if it is shared by the community. I suggest that what appears to be a primitive herding instinct in the bonding factor is better understood by viewing human beings as social creatures who suffer excessively if they must endure their finitude in solitude.

This point, however, should not make us blind to the fact that once a socio-political community evolves and more or less solidifies, it takes on a momentum and structure of its own. In doing so, it sometimes not only fails to deal success-fully with the individual's sense of finitude, but actually exacerbates and intensifies it. The sociologist Emile Durkheim failed to note carefully this phenomenon, but it can be easily witnessed in those traditions that intensify the dread of death as a means of recruiting converts and servants for their own ends.

Again, the preliminary definition of religion (as concern with core finitude) provides breadth and scope at the expense of depth. The second kind of definition, the *reportive* definition, opens the door to depth. On this new plane of inquiry, the student of religion seeks to report accurately and sensitively the diverse ways in which the traditions have sought to deal with the numerous manifestations of finitude in at least the cognitive, moral, and emotional dimensions. Astounding diversity prevails at this level, and the duty of the student of religion is to report the intricate details of the traditions in the terms and categories of the believers themselves. This is required by the canons of fairness and accuracy. Further-more, on this plane, it is the solemn duty of the researcher to report what a particular religious tradition means to the insiders or believers. (Its meanings in other possible contexts can be explored at still another level.) The sociologist of religion Max Weber emphasized this requirement of internal meaning under the heading of *Verstehen*.[4]

The third kind of definition of religion may be called the *ideal* definition; or more accurately, it is the expanded definition of what the researcher regards as the ideal responses to the sense of core finitude in all its dimensions. It is at this level of inquiry that questions of truth and falsity are consciously raised. The *comparative* and critical study of religion begins implicitly at the repor-tive level, but at the third level it becomes explicit. It is here that traditions and their claims are scrutinized and evaluated. Scrutiny is made more profound the more it is informed by the second level, where religious traditions are stud-ied in the context of their meaning to insiders and believers.

At the third level, the question is often raised, "Who understands a particular religious tradition better—the insider or the outsider?" Much fruitless energy has been spent in defending each side. I submit that understanding will increase for both insiders and outsiders if they share their research and insights with one another. Indeed, every student of religion is both insider and outsider. To be an insider of Sunnism is to be an outsider to Mahayana Buddhism. Ideally, the student of religion tries to take both the *role* of insider and the *role* of outsider. To do this takes years of training and study as well as discipline.

Objectivity requires taking both roles in the effort to better understand any given religion. Objectivity does not require the scholar, however, to refrain from making judgments and evaluations. Indeed, the whole point of objectivity is to help insure that judgments and evaluations will come forth and that they will be informed. Objectivity does not require scholars to deceive themselves by thinking they can divest themselves of all biases in the study of religion. It is self-contradictory to speak of a neutral viewpoint. An open mind is not a blank mind. Scholars always bring their biases with them, but in the process of inquiry, they are often forced to revise them or in some cases to exchange them for what they hope will be more fruitful biases that have been corrected and improved by criticism and information.

My own bias or position is that naturalistic, nontheistic, process metaphysics and humanistic ethics approximate the ideal way to respond to the religious problem or concern of core finitude. Naturalism concludes that the claims of absolute triumph over all human finitude either in this life or in a putative afterlife are delusions. In the evolutionary process many species have perished; there is no guarantee that any one species will continue endlessly. The moral challenge, therefore, is to enjoy the possibilities that are at hand, to share them with others, and to overcome any feeling of resentment at not having an existence that extends into infinity.

The naturalistic and humanistic framework is still in the process of maturing. Questions of personal meaning, right and wrong, hope and despair, joy and sorrow will continue to be raised and answered in concrete situations. The growth of profound ethical humanism among theists like Charles Hartshorne and others is encouraging to nontheists like myself, who wish to build bridges of cooperative endeavor while maintaining pluralism of thought. John Dewey, the great philosopher of naturalism and instrumentalism, has stated brilliantly a response to finitude that I think many humanists, both theistic and nontheistic, could embrace:

> We who now live are parts of a humanity that has interacted with nature. The things in civilization we most prize are not of ourselves. They exist by grace of the doings and sufferings of the continuous human community in which we are a link. Ours is the responsibility of conserving, transmitting, rectifying, and expanding the heritage of values we have received that those who come after us may receive it more solid and secure, more widely accessible, and more generously shared than we have received it.[5]

This analysis, I believe, throws some light on the debate between secular humanists and religious humanists; each group is responding to the universal sense of finitude. The secular humanists do not deny that they are dealing with the problem of finitude with which traditional religions have wrestled for centuries. The uniqueness of secular humanism lies in its insistence that its responses to core finitude place no stock in the claims of supernaturalism. I count myself among those secular humanists who oppose traditional religions' predilection for magic and miracles, which cut the tie between human actions and their consequences.

At the same time, I am sympathetic with those religious humanists who, after leaving behind the lust for magic, understand nevertheless the need to cultivate emotional enrichment and inspiration among human beings. Secular humanism tends to emphasize the cognitive role of debunking flim-flam and exposing the excessive claims of those who seek to gain immunity from critical analysis by traveling under the flag of "spirituality." Religious humanism, it seems to me, stresses the need for constructive and uplifting responses that help individuals to face their dark moments of despair and to celebrate the moments of triumph and enjoyment. As a secular humanist and rational hedonist, I can only applaud the creative and compassionate efforts of the religious humanists, so long as they do not forget the hard victories that the secularists have won in many areas, particularly of the intellect and morality.

## Notes

1. Clark, Gordon, *Religion, Reason and Revelation* (Philadelphia: Presbyterian and Reformed Publishing Co., 1961), p. 24.

2. Cited in E. S. Brightman, *A Philosophy of Religion* (Englewood Cliffs, N.J.: Prentice-Hall, Inc., 1940), p. 16.

3. See Robert C. Lester, *Theravada Buddhism in Southeast Asia* (Ann Arbor, Mich.: University of Michigan Press, 1973), p. 38.

4. See Marcello Truzzi, ed., *Verstenhen: Subjective Understanding in the Social Sciences* (Reading, Mass.: Addison-Wesley Publishing Co., 1974).

5. John Dewey, *A Common Faith* (New Haven, Conn.: Yale University Press, 1934), p. 87.

# IX.

# Bringing Up Children/
# Moral Education

# Pleading for an Ethical Approach

## Lydia Blontrock
### (Belgium)

We stand on the threshold of the twenty-first century. It is time to draw up the balance sheet of this century, which has been the scene of so much racism, so much violence, so much irreversible degradation of nature that doom-mongering has become the rule.

Humanism, however, refuses to play this game. For humanists the twentieth century is indeed a century of inhuman practices, but it is also the century of human rights, of democracy, and, last but not least, of secularization and emancipation—all processes that will continue, provided that we stay watchful of every restoration movement and other moral rearmament, and that, in the twenty-first century, we have as our absolute priorities attention to inhuman world problems such as hunger, war with the utmost sophisticated arms, and environmental pollution.

Scientific and technological developments will come about in the next century at a much faster pace. Such evolution often inspires fear; nevertheless, for humanists fear never served as a guideline for thinking and doing. Reasonability and emancipation will certainly do so.

New attainments do not necessarily lead to inhuman situations. On the contrary, they can be liberating and stimulating, under the express condition that people trust their own ethical ability.

It is our assignment to evaluate such problems as bioethics, euthanasia, genetic engineering, and so on, in the light of the pillars of humanism, self-determination, and commitment to others. When we evaluate, we humanists adopt an unprejudiced and rational attitude—we use reason, but also feelings and intuition. So we come to temporary value judgments, which of course will be replaced when better ones appear.

Concerning life and death, we consider as positive every movement from human dependency on so-called natural or fatalist events to conscious and well-considered choices. More self-determination brings about more freedom, more rationality, and more responsibility. Such an intentional control over nature and the upgrading of the quality of life are guarantees of more human dignity and more well being in autonomy.

It seems that people become conscious of a need for change when new developments have to be placed in the service of human beings and their environment. It is not too late. But not everyone agrees on method. Some preach turning back to nature; others, who point out the deterioration of the former values, aim for an ethical revival; still others fall back on old certitudes and firm tenets.

Humanists assert there is no reason to make a U-turn and hang on to the past for dear life. We have to face the future uninhibited and confident. This is possible only when we choose unambiguously an ethical attitude and give priority to humanist values over unscrupulous materialism and profit, to self-determination over extreme consumptivism, to commitment to our fellows and the whole of nature over egoism. That mentality exists—more than we can imagine. It is one of the tasks of humanists to give that potential aspiration form and content.

People have to learn not to avoid new problems, but on the contrary, to face them, and to do that from an ethical position. Progress has been too exclusively measured in terms of science, technology, and economy. Time and again the ethical component is omitted. It is the goal of humanism in the future to give expression to this concern and to clarify the humanist view of humanity and of the world all over again.

From our humanist principles of free thinking and free inquiry we have to learn to find new contents for humanist values, to develop new moral attitudes for new situations, and to look for new solutions to new moral problems. We must continue searching in an honest and creative way, without certitudes and without hold, but with the courage shown by so many humanists throughout the ages, convinced that it is possible—that it must be possible.

One of the main concerns of humanism is moral education. This is quite logical: Everyone who lives according to the principles of freethought and autonomous action based on reason and responsibility knows that children have to be educated toward that mentality. It doesn't come automatically.

So, there is agreement about the necessity of nonreligious moral education, but there is not always agreement about the precise nature of this education. Some humanist educators want to keep nonreligious moral education neutral so as to avoid any risk of indoctrination. Value-transfer, as it is done in religious moral education, is an example of this. It overemphasizes cognitive goals in its laudable pursuit of objectivity. But objectivity does not mean neutrality. That is why, in my opinion, it is wrong.

Indeed, moral education cannot be neutral: It always has to deal with values and attitudes. In the euphoria of the 1960s, when liberty and anti-authoritarianism were stressed, people let youngsters go their own way. Concerning morals, we have actually left them to fend for themselves. And, of course, it is true that children have a set of moral skills at their disposal, but these, like any other skills, need to be developed. If we do not guide children in some ways but leave moral development to the youngsters themselves, we cause moral underdevelopment.

Guiding has nothing to do with indoctrination, for indoctrination—the forcing of one's opinions and personal values upon another person—is the negation of the growth to autonomy. Indoctrination is not moral education; it is not education at all.

Some people are wary lest they fall into moralizing. Preaching belongs, they say, in religion, which prescribes a moral with its values about good and evil. This mentality makes some educators uneasy about the use of good examples in education.

Finally, some educators are afraid to start values education, because it demands a special didactical approach. A lesson based on cognitive goals gives more security. The teachers feel safe and don't have to give themselves away—nor do the pupils.

But there is no moral education without values education. There are, however, some fundamental questions. Lea Dasberg asks, "How many children grow up with an adequate system, explaining all things, based on the Bible or on the Communist Manifesto? Most of the children in the current Western world have the dubious privilege [of choosing for] themselves; but between what they may choose, they aren't told."

Is that what humanists do? What humanists have to do? Is it really a dubious privilege for children to be able to choose their own values? And is it necessary to tell them between which values they may choose?

First it is necessary to make a distinction between abstract ethical values that are universal and supra-individual, that is, the terminal values, and ethical values that are concrete and personal, that is, the instrumental values.

These abstract ethical values are actually humanist values and can be divided into two subsets: On the one hand we have self-determination, the right to give sense and meaning to one's own life, and on the other hand but inextricably bound with the former we have equivalence, social responsibility, commitment to others and to the whole of nature. We deliberately provide these values to the young.

To provide values is something quite different from value transfer, where values and rules are passed on with hardly any contribution from the young people themselves. To provide values, on the contrary, means making young people aware that they exist and teaching the experience of fundamental ethical values that will act as guides, as a frame of reference for each moral choice and for each moral attitude. But the content of these values, the filling in of the frame, the assessment, and the appreciation of personal values will be left to the young people themselves.

The teacher thus provides a valuable humanist frame of reference that will offer help and encouragement for the hard task of building up a personal value system, of giving one's life individual meaning.

It is clear that in this way youngsters, although quite free in their choices, are not abandoned to their fate. On the contrary, such an ethical framework, offered with warmth and authenticity, means a valuable moral hold for youngsters who in the unstable period between childhood and adulthood threaten to sink into an ethical and existential vacuum with all the serious problems it brings along. Humanist values are the cornerstones that young people will use as they see fit for building the "home" of their dreams. You cannot build a house on sand.

The providing of values must be linked with the whole education, so that every discussion is lifted to the ethical level. But in addition to this occasional approach, we need a systematic approach, certainly in courses on morals. This supposes theme-centered lessons as well as student-centered lessons, which will meet the existential questions of the students, and where there is room for their own values and feelings. Moreover, student-centered lessons make possible the integration of humanist values so that youngsters are able to develop harmonious personalities. That is why children must be granted a nonreligious education based on humanist values.

The privilege of youngsters to choose their own concrete values is not a dubious one, but to help them choose correctly we must provide the ethical, humanist values that all youngsters have a right to. The problem is, which methods and techniques can we use for student-centered lessons in values education?

Everyone knows the famous teaching strategies of Simon, Raths, Harmin, and others. They did very good work in the field of moral education and inspired many teachers. Nevertheless, in a way they neglected the social component. They overemphasized self-determination, which provoked the criticism that moral education leads to extreme value relativism and hyperindividualism, and does not take into account the feelings of others or of the "me" that grows within a person. In fact, such approaches do not stimulate youngsters to develop their own values, as they only have values clarification in mind.

Furthermore, these educators left the choice of values absolutely free. I think that the humanist teacher has the right to provide humanist values in such a way that "values" such as fascism and racism are not a possible choice. The teacher outlines certain limits.

We have also found inspiration in the Dutch authors Hermans and, most of all, Paul van der Plas, who focus their model lessons not only on the "me," but also on the "other" and on "together," so that not only self-determination but solidarity and responsibility are stimulated.

Every teacher who wants to do something about values education—and I hope humanist teachers do—has to include lessons of various types: lessons about values generally (found in poems, songs, newspapers, religions, culture), lessons about values clarification (my personal values, what are we worth), lessons about value development (my maxim, our proverb, I make a contract, I am worth what I want to be), and, finally, lessons providing humanist values such as peace, communication, and solidarity.

Only with such varied lessons can we stress the integration of new values with values clarification. Students become aware that they are responsible for the development of their values, old as well as new ones, and for fitting them into the frame of reference of humanist values. It is very important that students know what we aim for with these lessons and know that these lessons require a special approach.

We should try to teach students, through our words and deeds, about actively listening to one another, about authenticity and sincerity in speaking about one's own values, and about attention and respect for the values and feelings of others. If we take all this into account, we can make nonreligious moral education meaningful and valuable. It is hard work, but it is the only way to give nonreligious youngsters what they have a right to.

# Critical Issues in the Next Century

## Lisa Kuhmerker

### (United States)

We should think of elementary school as a primary vehicle for giving children experiences in reflective participatory democracy. School democracy at the secondary-school level is an idea that is gaining currency; genuine school democracy at the elementary-school level is primary—literally and figuratively.

This message has special relevance and urgency for secular humanists, who are concerned with the future of education and the implications of research and practice in sociomoral development. Parents and teachers all over the world want children to grow up to be kind and just, but in the minds—and curricula— of the majority, these goals are linked to religious education and teaching by precept. We must be able to show that secular education based on democratic principles fosters sociomoral and civic development in a way that far surpasses the traditional strategies used in conjunction with religious instruction.

No single aspect of education, even so critical a one as the opportunity for reflective participatory democracy, is a panacea. As adult participants in the critical events of our time, and as caregivers and educators of children who will grow into these roles in the coming years, we must plan and act simultaneously on a variety of levels. We must function on four levels: personal, local, national, and international.

Our skills and inclinations will influence the way we apportion our time among these priorities. There will be times in our life cycles when all or most of our time will be focused in one direction. There will be times when the full realization of our mutual interdependence will make us stretch to reach beyond our immediate concerns. Yet even during the times when our locus of activity is most narrowly conceived, we must keep in mind that survival on our planet requires human concern for justice and care on all four levels. We need to share this awareness and commitment with our children.

No matter how "favored" may be the status of the country in which we live, we are all vulnerable to nuclear holocaust. Similarly, the economies of the world are so intertwined that no national economy, no industry, and no individual family's security is truly or totally assured. Every technological advance brings with it the risks of misuse and the chaos of potential breakdown. To a greater or lesser degree, each sub-group or minority within a nation is in danger, because twentieth-century history has taught us that international public opinion will not—and perhaps cannot—protect us from prejudice and genocide.

What implications do these realities have for the nurturance and education of our children?

We owe our children honesty. If we are vulnerable in our interdependence, this is a reality we cannot deny through words or through silence. Yet the primary need is for children to develop trust in their caregivers, in themselves, and in the processes of interaction and conflict-resolution. This is not a new discovery. We know what children need; if children remain "in need," it is not for lack of our knowledge.

The cutting edge of educational research and practice in the coming years should be the most broadly conceived kind of civic education. This civic education should not be confused with history or with information about branches of government and electoral procedures. It should be genuine, guided reflective participatory democracy in the place and time all children are legally mandated to share: the school.

The secondary school is too late for this initiation into participatory democracy. On the one hand, the secondary school is often forced to try to undo the damage done by boredom and cynicism with school, and by the growing awareness among adolescents of the conflict between the rhetoric of society and the realities of life around them. What is more, adolescence is by its very nature a time of questioning, rebellion, and peer pressure.

Children can profit from the experience of mediating conflicts in democratic ways and from taking part in the governance structure of their schools from an early age. Children as young as six years of age can take part in the governance structure of the elementary school, if the issues are part of their everyday experience.

School-age is an optimal time for such experiences. It is a time when children have begun to understand and care about rules; when their basic ideas about fairness, care, and responsibility are shaped. It is a time when the need to belong, to have and keep friends, and to understand how the world of peers and adults works are powerful motivators for learning the social skills of taking perspective and resolving conflict.

Very few—if any—of today's adults attended elementary schools in which children had genuine decision-making power and responsibility for their social interaction, so most of us would find it difficult to initiate and sustain programs with such goals. But new research and technology make it possible to document such educational processes in action with the use of videotape, and to document student change through the application of developmental theory on assessment strategies.

Four kinds of school governance structures create the framework for reflective participatory democracy at the elementary school level. Regular classroom meetings form the core of the program. Delegates from each class form a student advisory council that meets at regular intervals with the principal of the school and reports back to the individual classrooms. "Fairness" or "Due Process" committees at various grade levels deal with infractions of the rules that have been arrived at by the school community. A system of charts, used from grade to grade in a cyclical way, teaches and reinforces concepts related to laws and human needs. The lines of communication from the tiniest first-grader to the ultimate authorities in the school structure are facilitated and protected in a variety of imaginative ways.

The ultimate effect is that the school governance structure and issues of fairness and friendship are the *explicit*—not the hidden—curriculum. An ad hoc international education commitee might well aim to collect and share information about school practices in countries that have the ethical and secular core that may help our children to cope with the uncertain future of the next century.

# Moral Education:
# Homo Sapiens or Homo Religiosus

Wendell W. Watters
(Canada)

If one were to make a list of the ten most powerful myths operating in Western society, at the top of that list would be the notion that religious indoctrination and religious affiliation contribute to or are positively correlated with moral behavior in human beings. So powerful is this myth that for many Christian god-talkers the word "moral" is synonymous with the word "religious."

I submit that this is not only one of the most powerful myths operating today but one that is most in need of critical examination. In fact, I would like to make a case for the opposite hypothesis, namely that indoctrination with Christian god-talk is incompatible with the psychological growth and moral development of human beings, individually and collectively; that, in effect, those Christians who do lead decent moral lives do so despite their religious indoctrination and because of the kind of human being they are innately and their critical and meaningful interactions with other human beings in early life.

Conversely, we must not forget that many, if not most, of the residents of our penal institutions come from Christian backgrounds of one sort of another. Is it possible that they really and truly believed it when the Sunday-school teacher, priest, or minister repeated—week after week—that they are innately evil creatures born into a state of original sin? If that is so, did they then gradually make their behavior conform to the self-concept they were encouraged to develop?

In the area of health promotion, Christian indoctrination, rather than having a healing effect on human beings, in fact promotes unnecessary suffering and illness-inducing behavior. Other behavioral scientists have come to similar conclusions. The behavioral scientist Albert Ellis even goes so far to state that the adherents of religion are emotionally disturbed—"usually neurotic but sometimes psychotic."[1]

I no longer divide illness into mental and physical illness, since such dichotomization, largely a hangover from Christian dualism, creates a great many problems throughout the field of health care. Whether one uses archaic terms like "body" and "soul" or more modern terms like "physical" and "mental," one is helping to keep alive the division of the indivisible human being into a "flesh" and a "spirit." Psychiatry's attempt to put the human Humpty Dumpty together again with terms like "psychosomatic" is having only limited success.

This mind/body dichotomy is frequently blamed—erroneously—on René Descartes. The fact is that when Descartes was born the Christian establishment had had fourteen centuries of indoctrination of the notion that the human being was cleft in twain; when Descartes was four years old an Italian philosopher, Giordano Bruno, was burned at the stake by the Inquisition for teaching a unitary view of reality and God. This event suggests a religious climate that may have had more than a little influence on Descartes's subsequent philosophical views regarding the body and mind.

Besides this destructive dualism there are many other pathogenic features of Christian doctrine, including the belief in original sin, Christ's sacrifice on the cross to save us from the consequences of our innate wickedness, the belief that Christ/God is the source of all our human strength/wisdom/goodness, and that such characteristics are present only in those human beings who grovel abjectly at the feet of this celestial worthy. Because of our innate evil and despite the fact that Christ's sacrifice was meant to redeem us, Christians still have it drummed into them that they are worthless creatures who must reject human supports, and prostrate themselves at the feet of the divine big daddy. They are encouraged to embrace suffering in emulation of Christ's suffering on the cross, this masochistic self-flagellation being a strategy for currying favor with a capricious, sadistic deity. If you think I exaggerate, I suggest you read or reread the book that is reputed to have had more influence in promoting Christianity than any other book save the Bible: *Imitation of Christ*, by the German ecclesiastic Thomas á Kempis. This book is full of exhortations to Christians to reject their fellow human creatures, to think of themselves as worse than nothing, to turn their backs on knowledge, and to suffer, suffer, suffer; not simply to endure suffering when it occurs, but to seek it as a means of storing up brownie points in heaven.

Central to all of this is the issue of guilt. Christianity is literally the house that guilt built. As George H. Smith put it in *Atheism: The Case Against God,* "Guilt, not love, is the fundamental emotion that Christianity seeks to induce—and this is symptomatic of a viciousness in Christianity that few people care to acknowledge."[2]

Behavioral scientists are not very knowledgeable about guilt; indeed, it has been subjected to very little critical study. One common myth about this painful affect is that the manipulation of another person's guilt is a useful and adaptive strategy for shaping or molding behavior. In fact, nothing could be farther from the truth.

Guilt may be a normally occurring emotion in human beings; however, in the interest of raising healthy children, it is not one that should be encouraged as a behavioral control strategy. At times, manipulating an individual's guilt may produce a seething conformity: The child obeys but is sullen and hostile. At other times, guilt has the opposite effect: It promotes an exaggeration of the behavior about which the individual is encouraged to feel guilty.

The mechanism works like this. If a child's guilt is stimulated by care-taking adults, it makes him or her feel that he or she is a bad or inadequate person. If these feelings are intense enough and prolonged enough, the child may escalate the unacceptable behavior, as if seeking more punishment to assuage that guilt. This guilt-punishment cycle may lead inexorably straight to the prison door. As development proceeds, the miscreant may come to wear this guilt on the sleeve— a badge of honor to neutralize the rage of those who are most harmed by the antisocial behavior. Many a chronic alcoholic, compulsive gambler, and child molester indulges in repeated orgies of verbal breast-beating, unaccompanied by any change in the antisocial behavior. Indeed, many of these destructive behaviors have been elevated to the respectable status of illnesses, and hordes of health-care professionals expend massive amounts of their own energy, and equally massive amounts of public money, helping such people change behavior that they have no real desire to change.

When it comes to the use of guilt in controlling the sheep in the flock, the founding fathers of Christianity developed most of their leverage in two areas of human life: sexuality and dysphoric affects (or emergency emotions), particularly anger. As for the use of sex, Rabbi Abraham Fineberg hit the nail on the head when he said, "The sex drive gave organized religion an opportunity to amass what was indisputably the greatest power ever lodged in human hands."[3] As a couple/sex therapist, every day I see the disastrous consequences of Christianity's use of the human sexual drive to fuel its policies on demographic aggression. No one can dispute the "success" of such policies, since Christianity now claims more adherents than any other religion. Indeed, we have not yet adequately documented the extent of human suffering caused by traditional Christian teachings about sexuality; damage that can never be hidden and will never be reversed by the many buckets of theological whitewash (or, if you prefer, hogwash) currently being applied to such teachings by liberal Christian theologians. Attitudes about sexuality derived from centuries of Christian influence have been driven deeply into our collective consciousness and into the structure of our institutions in ways that make it very difficult, if not impossible, for human beings to grow up with their sexuality integrated in a healthy manner with the rest of their personality. In fact, it is on the battlefield of sexuality that we find most of the wars between the "flesh" and the "spirit."

Another aspect of human experience that the Christian church has been able to use to satisfy its lust for power, another guilt button the god-talkers have consistently pushed to gain more control over human beings, is the area of dysphoric affects—notably sadness, grief, anxiety, and especially anger. One Christian cleric, naively thinking that Christianity could really be reformed, wrote in 1973 that "there seems to have been in the church a tendency to stifle the expression of real personal feelings (for instance, anger, ecstasy, despair, grief) and to encourage a constant 'neutral pleasantness' as the proper way to express oneself."[4] Thomas á Kempis is full of admonitions about the expression of real human feelings.

Christians always have been encouraged to believe that if they feel despair or anxiety, it means that their faith is weak, thus adding to the burden of guilt they are already carrying around like Atlas shouldering the world. They are encouraged to deny their essential humanity even more than they already were doing, and to grovel ever more abjectly at the foot of the cross.

One emergency affect—anger—reached the lofty status of one of the seven deadly sins, and for centuries the Christian approach to anger has shaped our social attitudes to this emotion, whether or not we are card-carrying Christians. Such attitudes are embedded deeply and widely in the social woodwork. I am reminded here of Emerson's statement to the effect that the name of Jesus Christ was not so much written as ploughed into the history of the Western world. Our collective social approach toward what is essentially a normal human emotion is illustrated in the advice given by one Christian psychologist who, reinforcing the view that experiencing negative emotions indicates a lack of trust in Divine Providence, suggests that the best way to deal with anger is to swim fifty yards, run a mile, or do thirty push-ups. He says nothing about trying to express the anger openly and directly to the person with whom one is angry in an attempt to resolve the underlying issue itself.

Freud, a declared atheist, in theorizing about anger (or "aggression," as he termed it), gave further reinforcement to Christian notions when he postulated the death instinct. This instinct, which he called Thanatos, was opposed to the life-promoting libidinal instinct Eros. Parenthetically, I am sure Freud would be whirling in his grave if he knew how many other aspects of his theory, especially those having to do with female sexuality, gender roles, and human reproduction, have been found to be reflections of Christian doctrine.

After twenty-five years working in the field of psychotherapy with individuals, couples, and families, I would say that problems in coping with anger are at the bottom of most individual emotional difficulties and relationship stresses. Because of deeply engrained social attitudes toward this emotion, we have not yet learned to deal with it adaptively but tend rather to defend excessively against it; nonetheless, it is usually expressed in covert destructive ways that increase relationship static. I wish I had a dollar for every couple that has told me—with pride, mind you—that they never fight or get angry at each other. These unfortunate people are paying for this unreal, inhuman equanimity with utterly joyless relationships.

Whether we are speaking of individual health, relationship health, or moral health, what is the actual mechanism involved? How does Christian indoctrination about anger contribute to self-destructive, violent, or other kinds of immoral behavior?

This is an oversimplified account of what happens in a society so highly imbued with Christian notions about anger. Anger is a normal human emotion, a response to frustration of one kind or another. At the best of times anger is an unpleasant emotion, one we would rather not feel. The general tendency is to train children from an early age to believe that they are bad, evil people for feeling this way, for not being able to suppress this unpleasant emotion and prevent it from emerging in the first place. I submit that this attitude generates intense conflict between what the child actually feels and what the child "should" feel in order to be accepted by the caretaking group. Such conflicts are intensified if a child witnesses angry or violent outbursts in the caretakers, who themselves have not been trained to deal with these feelings in an adaptive way. The child's confusion is compounded when such violent behavior is directed toward him or her by the very caretakers who have tried to train the child to suppress such emotions entirely.

Conflicts of this sort generate anxiety, which in its extreme form is a very unpleasant emotion indeed. To avoid this unpleasant affect, humans develop or learn that we psychiatrists call "defense mechanisms." These are simply attitudinal and behavioral responses designed to ward off the unacceptable feeling that gives rise to the anxiety. Thus to deal with the conflict between the real feeling and the prescribed feeling, the child may simply deny the unacceptable anger (hence the term "denial"). The child, unacceptably angry at mother, may vent the anger on a younger sibling or the family dog (a mechanism we call "displacement"). The child may bend over backward to prove that he or she is really not angry at mother and become over-attentive and solicitous (a mechanism we call "reaction formation"). Or the child may distort the reality of the situation and insist that it is not he or she who is angry at the mother, but rather the mother who is angry at the child (this we call "projection").

In performing the task of keeping unacceptable angry feelings out of awareness, an individual's defenses may work for some time. But under some circumstances these defenses break down, and the unacceptable feeling threatens to break through into awareness. This may produce the kind of symptoms that may take the individual to a doctor or even a psychiatrist, or it may contribute to relationship disharmony. At other times the breakthrough of the unwelcome emotion occurs in a manner that leads to overt antisocial violent behavior. If the individual believes that he or she is basically evil even to feel angry, when the feeling erupts from behind brittle defenses, it may be expressed in a form that confirms the Christian view of anger—a violent, destructive act. This explosion effect reinforces the impression that anger is a feeling that human beings should avoid at all costs—that it is indeed one of the seven deadly sins.

If, on the other hand, children are raised in an environment that enables them to learn that all of these feeings are natural and normal, an entirely different scenario may unfold. Under these circumstances we would see a clear distinction in the child between the feeling itself and the behavioral and verbal responses to that feeling. The child learns that anger does not mean a withdrawal of love. While encouraged to believe that he or she is not an evil person because of the anger, it is certainly made clear that some behaviors are acceptable when one feels angry and some are not. Learning the difference should be no problem. If the child is not encouraged to feel guilty in the presence of anger, learning becomes possible. It is not possible where the guilt-punishment cycle is the order of the day. As maturation proceeds, the child learns age-appropriate ways of dealing with such feelings. Since under such circumstances the child is not utilizing large amounts of energy in defending against feelings of anger, that energy can be used to develop such adaptive strategies for dealing with the affect. If the child learns to be at home with the feeling in this way, the tendency to be caught up in the guilt-punishment cycle is reduced and the risk of antisocial behavior diminishes.

Of course, the problem of dealing with anger alone does not explain all antisocial behavior. Other factors are certainly involved, and some stem from Christian indoctrination in other areas. Our purpose here is not to analyze immoral or antisocial behavior completely, but rather to demonstrate how one aspect of Christian indoctrination may contribute to the problem.

What does all of this have to do with education?

In various parts of Canada we have two public education systems; one for Roman Catholics and one for everyone else. In Ontario, the Roman Catholics recently won all-party approval for an extension of public funding to the end of grade thirteen, where it previously stopped at tenth grade. It is taken for granted that the children in the separate school system get as much Christian god-talk as the traffic will bear; what is most distressing is that even in the so-called public system, legislation in some provinces provides for Christian god-talk to take place in the schoolroom.

But getting rid of Christian god-talk in the classroom alone will not do much to eradicate the destructive impact of centuries of dominance of this religious influence.

As a society we are slowly coming to realize the contribution of Christian doctrine to our stunted, warped, antihuman attitudes toward sexuality. It is time we recognized that the impact of Christian teachings in many other areas has been equally devastating, and the task of designing educational programs to reverse and overcome these effects is formidable. In the area of teaching human-to-human communication and negotiation skills, we have made less progress than in the area of sex education. Indeed, we have not yet recognized that teaching children how to communicate and negotiate with one another should be more important than teaching them how to communicate with a computer or with a deity. No amount of religious indoctrination or computer training will help the growing child learn to be at home with emotions, to be comfortable in communicating with others, or to negotiate with others, especially in the presence of conflicting needs, aspirations, and priorities.

We should not dismiss the notion that our educational system could play a role in helping young people to learn communication and negotiation skills, particularly where angry feelings make such learning difficult. Much—if not most—of the work of psychotherapists, family therapists, and couple therapists consists of helping people to cope with anger; to give up maladaptive strategies for dealing with it, which are both self-destructive and destructive of relationships; and to develop more adaptive aways of coping with such feelings. If such maladaptive strategies can be modified through a therapeutic process in adult life, why not help children to learn adaptive strategies in the first place through an educational process?

For example, the teacher devises a scenario for role-playing in the group that will inevitably generate conflict and hence run the risk of making the children angry at one another. At a certain point, Johnny becomes angry at Suzy, decides he doesn't want to play any more, and starts to walk away. The teacher brings him back and a discussion ensues in which Johnny reveals that his parents always told him if he ever felt angry at anyone he should walk away, thereby communicating to him that he should be afraid of his anger and that he couldn't be expected to find acceptable ways of expressing it. Further discussions of the options open to Johnny may lead him to realize that he can acknowledge how he feels without walking away, and that he can keep the negotiation going until a satisfactory resolution of the conflict has been realized, with compromise on all sides. Other children may try to strike out physically or resort to manipulative tears under the influence of anger because of a lack of verbal skills for expressing this emotion in a nondestructive way.

This is a simplistic example, and programs of this sort could not be mounted without very close cooperation between the home and the school. Just as in the case of sex education, parent education is as vital as the education of the child. If the father is a violent man who strikes when angry or if the mother gives the father the silent treatment when she is angry at him, it would be difficult for the child to learn adaptive ways of handling anger. In other words, the parents would have to go back to school for the program to succeed for the child.

In our present God-centered world, it is a violation of all we know about human psychology to believe that people can be helped to lead moral lives by manipulating their guilt and fear in the way that Christianity does. In the human-centered world, the child would be encouraged to develop a sense of the importance of human-to-human interdependency in this global village of ours. Religions, with their emphasis on the God-human connection, inevitably work against the formation of strong human-to-human supports—not withstanding all of the hollow rhetoric about fellowship. Daily news headlines from Northern Ireland, India, and Lebanon tell us just how much fellowship religion actually promotes.

In a humanist orientation toward life, individuals would be prepared to take responsibilities for their moral choices. No more would people be able to justify oppressing other human beings as "doing the will of God" or explaining away antisocial behavior with "the devil made me do it."

In order for human beings to make the best moral choices possible, they must be well and accurately informed on all aspects of the issues on which they must make such choices. Since the Renaissance, Christianity has been the implacable foe of real learning, fighting science tooth and claw at every step of the way; even going so far as to establish Christian universities in order to keep as much control of the human mind as possible.

In a humanist educational approach, it is essential that religion in general and Christianity in particular becomes the subject of critical study—not religious indoctrination and not the reverential, uncritical examination of religion that comes under the rubric of comparative religion—but *critical* evaluation.

Many Christians worry about what takes place currently in the public schools, where they think their children are being filled with all manner of diabolical secular humanist propaganda; this is the argument they use to justify building their own schools. The truth is that most public schools try to teach children to think for themselves about most things, although few public schools encourage this very vigorously in the area of religion. Nonetheless, any child who is encouraged to think for himself or herself about anything is a loose canon to the fundamentalist Christians; hence, the need to build their own schools, where doctrinal straitjackets can be applied to youthful minds.

In reality, the public-school system should be doing the very job the fundamentalists accuse it of—helping children to think critically about religion just as they are encouraged to think critically about every other aspect of their lives. One teacher with the courage to do just that was recently thrown out of his job at a school in Prince Edward Island, which incidentally is the only province in Canada that does not have any abortion facilities. This teacher showed his students a documentary on Christian fundamentalism and then asked them to interview people on the role religion played in their lives. The furor was so intense and so immediate that the school board had him cancel the assignment and then suspended him. The mere act of asking people to use their native human intelligence to examine their religious beliefs and the real impact of those beliefs on their lives was too threatening for the good Christians of Prince Edward Island.

The humanist alternative will be alive and well only when religion can be examined critically in all schools—when the various myths can be explored, including the myth that religious affiliation promotes moral behavior. Other myths might also be examined: the myth that Christ died for us on the cross to save us from our sins; the myth that traditional Christian attitudes about sexuality and reproduction have anything whatsoever to do with the teachings of Jesus of Nazareth; the myth that God has reserved a place for us in heaven if we only accept what the Christian snake-oil salesmen tell us.

The more our children and grandchildren come to appreciate that the fate of the world is in human rather than divine hands, the more likely they are to get on with the task of forging the human-to-human links that must be forged if we human beings are to develop the problem-solving strategies that might save us from the extinction toward which god-talk is hurling us at a great rate.

## Notes

1. Albert Ellis, "Is Religion Pathological?" *Free Inquiry* 8 (2), Spring 1988, pp. 27–32.

2. George H. Smith, *Atheism: The Case Against God* (Buffalo, N.Y.: Prometheus Books, 1979), p. 304.

3. Abraham Feinberg, *Sex and the Pulpit* (Toronto: Metheun, 1981), p. 46.

4. William A. Miller, *Why Do Christians Break Down?* (Minneapolis, Minn.: Augsburg Publishing, 1973), p. 31.

# From Child to Citizen: The Role of Playing

## Anne-Marie Franchi
### (France)

Games, education, and some measure of public spirit are universal, yet at the same time they are specific to each society. But does playing contribute to the development of civic notions in children? Play and the spirit of play are probably as old as humankind, and I believe they do contribute to the healthy development of children in the areas of human rights, development of personality, social competence, socialization, and public spirit. *Rien ne va plus,* or no more playing, and *jouer le jue,* or playing the game, are also important factors in society.

Public spirit can be seen as the individual counterpart of human rights in terms of the responsibilities and duties expected of individuals in a given time and place. The moral conceptions of individuals are intricately and inextricably linked to the history of the societies in which they live; my moral conceptions, for instance, are tied to the history of Old Europe.

Public spirit, to me, is not a passive obedience to authority, but a conscious and active affiliation to one's community; not a xenophobic nationalism, but a well-defined and self-conscious identity; not a collective or individual selfishness, but a fraternity. The structured games we play in childhood can prepare us for the practice of public spirit. We learn to take our turn, to switch roles, to experience hierarchy, and to cooperate with other. We experience victory and defeat, conflict and mediation. We face imposed rules and roles in acceptance, transgression, and negotiation.

Game-playing, which is often at once spontaneous and methodical, helps children to develop an ordered conception of themselves and of the world around them. Games initiate into liberty, by the power of imagination.

Play is an important outlet that can free one from personal conflicts and difficulties by recreating any situation while also changing the ground rules. Symbolic games may have a therapeutic function. Often, they start with a conditional formula: "Let's pretend I'm a wolf," or "I'm going to rescue you from a sinking ship." Playing the wolf or the hero, you can be as strong and important as you wish. Symbolic games allow us to rebuild a previous, incompletely assimilated experience through a sort of experimental exorcism.

Playing and dreaming, though different, serve the same function: Both permit an apparent absurdity, yet in each everything is significant. Dreams play with the meaning, but the meaning is played in games. Playing is situated between the inner reality of the moment and the appreciation of the exterior reality, in the experiencing of probabilities. Unstructured, imaginative games are in a sense quasi-magic; there is no more time or space and no prohibitive constraints. Play that is not defined by a specific set of rules aids in the acquisition of social and communication skills and of mental organization.

Communication skills precede logic. The exchanges between infants and their parents or caregivers become, little by little, communication; communication is the first step toward social intelligence, which in normal development leads to the ability to resolve increasingly complex problems. The development of social competence is in large part assisted by early play-experiences, and is closely connected to repetition.

Socialization—a progressive relationship in a group defined by values, interests, models, laws, and institutions—leads to public spirit by enhancing self-knowledge, knowledge of others, recognition and respect of common rules, conscious solidarity, personal and collective responsibility, historical and current knowledge, active good will, critical thinking, respect of fundamental human rights, and a sense of community.

Every level of public spirit is connected with a level of game-playing, and the whole is connected with playing functions. Of course, play alone cannot lead to public spirit, but it can play a major role if it is integrated into a loving and caring education that respects human rights. If play leads to cooperative public spirit, why then do we encounter unpopular, deliquent, and marginal children? Why do so many adults become criminals, or simply uncivil and unconcerned people?

There are several reasons.

Unresolved troubles may find no outlet. Initiative games turn into mindless repetition, growing powerlessness, difficulty in communication, and, eventually, a terrible loneliness. War toys and violent games are often cited as having detrimental effects on impressionable minds, but we must remember playing functions and not confuse effect and motive.

American studies about unpopular children have found them to be less active in peer groups, to frequently ask for help from their elders, and to be less conscious of daily life. Being less socially competent will make it difficult for those children to find their own place. A lonely person is not necessarily painting like Van Gogh.

Conformism appears to be increasing in American society, and some researchers see it as an effective strategy for blending in and thus not being bothered. Of course, keeping to oneself is the antithesis of an active public spirit.

Perhaps the most important factor preventing children from developing through healthy play is that many of the world's children are victims. Some will be able to play, but some will not because they will grow up amid conflict, war, distress, neglect, abuse, illness, and famine. When a child can no longer play, his or her childhood is destroyed. Too many children are used like toys by adults. They become weapons that adults use against other adults; they become the tools of certain governments; they become scapegoats or sexual playthings. As humanists, our first order of business should be to act to prevent these kinds of abuses.

But what is to be done?

Education is the first step. We must understand and help—but to do that we must learn some things ourselves.

First, under good living conditions, children should not be shielded from risk and conflict. Second, we should preserve playing spaces—but that does not mean parking children in a play area or in front of television. Third, we must be wise with toys. Toys are only one possible part of a game; some very sophisticated toys make the player inactive, as if the game had been already played by someone else.

The United Nations' Declaration of Children's Rights states that all children have the right to play. The terminology and contents could be better, but this right is important even amid all of the world's other needs. We must show that that right is connected with all the other rights, for the whole of humanity.

I shall conclude with a quotation from the French poet Paul Fort:

*Si tous les gars du monde*  
*Si toutes les filles du monde*  
*pouvaient se donner la main,*  
*cela ferait autour du monde*  
*une grande ronde.*

If all the boys in the world  
If all the girls in the world  
were given the chance to rule  
they would make the world  
one big circle.

# X.

# Future Issues and Trends: Biomedical Ethics

# Living Longer, Growing Younger: The Ethics of Cloning and Other Life-Extension Technologies

## Carol Kahn
### (United States)

To develop an ethics for the future, we must know what the future holds in store for us. Certainly vast increases in life span will become possible, perhaps within the lifetime of many of us. But as with each new technology, questions and new ethical dilemmas will arise. As the bioethicist and humanist philosopher Joseph Fletcher writes, "New knowledge forces us uncomfortably to reappraise many things—family relations, life and death, male and female, good and evil, personal identity and integrity, parental ties, health and disease—nearly everything."[1]

Paul Segall, a gerontologist and visiting scientist at the University of California at Berkeley, has identified seven "life-extension sciences," areas of research that have been developed mainly for other purposes but that could be brought together to form a powerful multidisciplinary attack on the aging process and on death itself.

The first life-extension science is interventive gerontology—slowing, stopping, or reversing the aging process. More than fifty years ago, Clive McCay, a nutritionist at Cornell University, did a series of experiments that are considered a benchmark of research in gerontology. By cutting the caloric intake of laboratory rats to half of what they would normally eat, he got them to live 50 percent longer than rats allowed to eat all they wanted. In later studies of caloric restriction, some of the animals lived more than 1,800 days, which would be like a person living to the age of 150.

Some years ago, Segall began a series of experiments on laboratory rats based on McCay's work but modified along the lines developed by Richard Gordon, a former director of research at Monsanto. Rather than cut down on all the calories, he reduced a single essential amino acid, tryptophan. Such a diet could never be applied to humans, since lack of tryptophan could be deadly. In Segall's experiments, a number of the rats died, but a few survived to great old age. The diet also dramatically delayed reproductive aging. One female rat gave birth to a live pup when she was thirty-three months old and lived to be four years old, when 90 percent of her contemporaries had died by the age of three, a feat equivalent to an eighty-year-old woman having a baby and then living to raise it.

No one really knows why we age; there are many competing theories. The one favored by Segall is that aging is programmed in the brain. Selected populations of cells die off according to a program that begins during embryonic development. When the brain cells that make neurotransmitters die, that, in turn, causes other cells to die in a kind of cascade effect. The result is the decrements of old age and finally death.

This theory has enormous implications for antiaging strategies. If we could identify the cells that go out with age and replace them with either fetal cells or the products made by the cells that die off, we might be able to achieve partial rejuvenations. Several research teams are already using human fetal brain transplants in people with Parkinson's disease. Many researchers believe that fetal brain cells could be used to treat other conditions in which brain-cell destruction plays a role, such as Alzheimer's disease and stroke. And if the theory of selective cell death with age is true, then fetal cell implants might reverse aging itself.

The second life-extension science is suspended animation, the use of low temperature to slow down the body processes. There is a species of frog in the northern United States that actually freezes during the winter months. When the snow falls, it crawls under the leaf cover and one third of its body turns to ice. Then in the spring, the snow melts, the sun warms the frog and it comes to life. In 1982, a group of scientists found that at the time they start to freeze, these frogs produce the chemicals glucose or glycerol, which act as a cryoprotectant, a kind of biological antifreeze that protects their cells.

Segall and his colleagues have succeeded in chilling hamsters and dogs to very low temperatures and then reviving them. In one highly publicized experiment he removed a dog's blood, replaced it with a blood substitute, chilled the animal to 38 degrees Fahrenheit, and kept it at that temperature for fifteen minutes. At that point the dog was essentially dead, its heart stilled, its blood in the refrigerator. Segall then reversed the procedure, replacing the blood substitute with the animal's blood and warming it back up again. The dog revived fully and is still alive and well two years later.

The use of chilled blood substitution could revolutionize medicine and surgery. For instance, there are indications from other animal experiments that it might be possible to keep someone at the ice point—the temperature at which water starts to freeze—for up to eight hours. In the recent Johns Hopkins operation on Siamese twins who were joined at the head, the doctors had to race against the clock, running over the one-hour safety limit by ten minutes, with results yet to be determined. Imagine if they could have had eight hours. Blood substitutes could be used in certain dangerous operations where one slip of the knife can mean that a patient bleeds to death, or in bypass surgery, where patients may require up to thirty pints of transfused blood. It would also mean not having to rely on transfused blood, which might carry undetected infectious agents. In cancer, surgeons could drench an affected organ with antitumor drugs while the rest of the body was maintained at the freezing point, protecting it from the toxic effects of the chemotherapy. This technique could also be used after death to preserve the body until the best possible use of its organs for transplantation could be determined.

The most developed of the life-extension sciences are organ transplantation and artificial organs. For more than two decades now, people whose hearts or kidneys could no longer sustain life have been given second, and in some cases, even third reprieves from the death sentence that hung over them. The success of transplanted organs is mainly due to a remarkable drug, cyclosporin A, which suppresses the immune-rejection response. The very success of the organ transplantation program has led to a second problem: Where will the organs come from? One response has been to develop artificial organs, which at present are poor substitutes for human ones. The artificial heart program, which was plagued with problems in the first go-round, has just been given the green light to develop a fully implantable synthetic heart. Bionic lungs, livers, eyes, ears, glands, blood, uteruses, and even brain-assist devices are all on the drawing board.

But in Segall's view, artificial and transplanted human organs are only a stopgap until the fifth life-extension science, cloning, is available. Cloning is the use of asexual reproduction to produce an individual that is a genetic duplicate of the individual from which it is derived. The clone begins with a cell taken from some part of the body other than the testicles or ovaries. The nucleus of the cell, which contains the chromosomes, is then removed and placed into an egg cell that has been emptied of its own nucleus. The egg now contains only the genetic information from the individual who donated the body cell, and when it develops it will be a clone of that individual.

Segall's idea is to use this technology to create *body clones* that could be used as spare parts. First an embryo would be cloned from a somatic cell (any cell that is not an an egg or sperm) and then, when the embryo is six weeks of age, the collection of primitive cells called the telencephalon, the forerunner of the higher brain, would be removed and frozen. In this way, the clone would never be allowed to develop the one thing that makes us human—our brains. Indeed, it would never become a sentient being. It would then be grown to term in a surrogate uterus of some kind, either in a closely related species such as a chimp, or in a human uterus that was removed during a hysterectomy and maintained by organ-preservation techniques, or in a womb made of synthetic materials.

Once it was delivered by Caesarian section, it would be grown to appropriate size by intravenous feeding and hormone injections. At this point it would be the equivalent of a brain-dead organ donor. Since the clone would have exactly the same genetic makeup as the cell donor, all its parts—from the facial features to its vital organs—would be identical to the donor's. The use of cloned cells, tissues, and organs would allow nearly every part of the body that has been damaged by disease, age, or accident to be replaced with no possibility of rejection. Even the cells of the telencephalon that had earlier been set aside and frozen could be thawed and used as brain-cell transplants the way fetal cells are now. Cloning would make total age reversal a reality, allowing your old worn-out body to be replaced, inside and out, by your youthful self.

Is cloning possible? Until a few years ago, the possibility seemed unlikely. Although it had been done with frogs in 1962, except for one unrepeatable experiment no one had ever succeeded in doing it in a mammal. Then in 1986, to everyone's great surprise, Steen Willadsen, a Danish researcher working in England, announced the successful cloning of three lambs. He and others then went on to clone bulls and cows. In the case of the farm animals, the cells used to create the clones were taken from embryos in the very early stages of development. But if cloning is to be used for medical purposes, it will be necessary to clone cells taken from adults, which has not yet been successfully accomplished even in frogs. However, I have interviewed many of the leading cloners, including Willadsen, who is now with a high-tech agricultural company in Calgary, Canada. They all agreed that the techniques now exist for cloning human embryos and that cloning from adult cells is a distinct possibility in the future.

The sixth life-extension science is resuscitation—bringing people back from the dead. I spoke with the world leader in resuscitation, Peter Safar, director of the Resuscitation Research Center at the University of Pittsburgh. Using techniques that Safar helped to develop, two people have been fully revived after twenty minutes of clinical death, which is defined as a prolonged state of pulselessness. He believes that the "five-minute limit," which clinicians have long considered the outside margin for resuscitation, is no longer accurate. By the year 2000, he predicts, revival after twenty minutes will be routine. This will be done by hooking a person up to a heart-lung machine to control the circulation and delivering resuscitation drugs like the ones now being tested in worldwide clinical trials coordinated by Safar. The addition of lowered temperatures should make it possible to extend the period of revival after death to an hour or more or to keep a person on ice until resuscitation can be carried out.

Closely tied to resuscitation is the seventh life-extension science, regeneration. Whereas resuscitation is aimed at bringing the dead back to life, regeneration is directed at creating new life at the cellular level. The first medical use of regeneration has already begun with the use of growth factors. These are hormonelike substances in the human body that stimulate or guide the development of new cells. Blood growth factors have been used to generate red and white blood cells in patients with AIDS, anemia, and cancer. Skin growth factors grow skin in the laboratory and have halved the time it takes wounds to heal. So far about thirty growth factors have been discovered and almost all of them are being explored for their healing potential. Even the brain and spinal cord, long believed to be incapable of growth and repair, are being made to regenerate. In one extraordinary series of experiments on cats whose spines had been completely severed, researchers in Ottawa and Boston were able to get 8 percent of the spinal fibers to grow back across the severed area. While the animals still had no function in their lower bodies, the investigators were able to transmit electrical signals across the severed spines into the brain. This kind of nerve regeneration, says Jack de la Torre, the Canadian researcher who carried out the work, may one day allow paralyzed people to walk again, Alzheimer patients to regain their memories, and people with brain damage caused by aging, disease, or the removal of cerebral tumors to have their mental and physical functions restored.

The ultimate application of the life-extension sciences is cryonics, or freezing people at death until it becomes possible to revive them in the future. This science incorporates all the others. It combines suspended animation; resuscitation; cloned body parts; the surgical techniques of organ transplantation and artificial organs; the antiaging drugs of interventive gerontology; and, in cases where one elects to keep only one's brain and replace it with an entirely new body, the brain–spine reconnection of regeneration technology. With reversible cryonics, human beings would achieve near immortality.

Cryonics is the most futuristic application of all the life-extension sciences and the one that will take the longest to develop, though progress is being made. The techniques for freezing people and protecting their bodies against ice damage are constantly improving. At the same time, researchers are able to bring back animals from lower and lower temperatures. In his latest experiments, Segall has brought frozen hamsters to minus 20 degrees centigrade (minus 4 degrees Fahrenheit) and kept them at that temperature overnight. Although he has not been able to revive them, he did get some electrical activity in the heart, indicating that a number of the heart cells were still intact. And then there is the experiment in nature that is successfully repeated every winter when the north-country frogs freeze and revive again in the spring. If we could learn the secrets of the frogs, the burial ground of the twenty-first century might consist of cryocapsules for storing frozen bodies, accompanied by liquid nitrogen tanks.

This, then, may be the future that awaits us. Don Yarborough, a former candidate for governor of Texas who has done much to promote life-extension research, has a saying: "You cannot go into the twenty-first century with the morality of the sixteenth century." And I believe that to be the case. As a journalist, I feel that my first responsibility is to bring the advances of medical technology to people's attention and let them make up their own minds. The future is already happening. So, as ethical humanists, what should our response be?

The first question one might ask is, Is life extension desirable? Among the things that people have said when asked about this are: "Life is long enough"; "Life would get boring"; "Death is a part of life"; "It goes against nature"; "Will God get mad?" Many people would disagree with these assessments. Joseph Fletcher writes, "If any act or policy is the wisest as measured by human need and well-being, then it's *positively* good, *positively* the right thing to do."[2] It is well within the humanist tradition to relieve human suffering. Nothing in the entire world creates or has created more suffering over the centuries than disease and old age. My mother died of cancer at the age of fifty, and my father had a debilitating stroke, which left him almost quadriplegic with only 80 percent use of his left arm. To promote activities that would allow us to prevent or alleviate this kind of suffering and to live truly functional lives for as long as humanly possible seems to me most ethical and humane.

If you can agree that life extension is a desirable and ethical goal, then the next question is, what about the means by which it will be carried out? Are these ethical? Humanists maintain that the restraints on human happiness have to come from man, not from God. In other words, the means employed should not harm others or violate our common sense of humanity.

So where does that leave us with respect to using brain-absent clones for spare-parts replacement? Even if the goal is a worthy one, should an individual be allowed to pursue it if the means required grossly offend our sensibilities? What if the means involve removing the higher brain of a fetus so that it never develops into a thinking, feeling individual? Or gestating this brainless baby in the womb of a chimpanzee and then dismembering it in order to harvest its parts for transplantation?

These are not questions for which there are easy answers, but there are precedents. In the United States and in many other countries, abortion on demand has been legalized because it is generally believed that the woman's right to choose not to have a child takes precedence over the fetus's right to be born. Again, it is the promotion of human happiness and well-being that is at stake. The fetus is regarded, at least in the early and middle stages of gestational life, as something less than a fully functional human being, and unless one believes that the fetus has an immortal soul that is being destroyed, no other conclusion is logical.

Human fetal cells are now being used in Mexico and Sweden to treat Parkinson's disease. Though the practice has been stopped in the United States, anencephalic babies that lack a higher brain continue to be used in West Germany as organ donors; the courts have ruled that the anencephalic fetus has never been alive despite the presence of a heartbeat, and therefore pregnancy involving a brain-absent fetus can be terminated at any stage. In a report in the *New England Journal of Medicine,* however, the medical team that performed the West German operations registered their objections to "relaxing the protection of fetuses or newborns with anomalies less devastating than anencephaly and also to offering any financial gains for parents who might allow their anencephalic infants to be born as organ donors."[3]

One may argue that the difference between harvesting a body clone and using the tissues of an aborted fetus or the organs of an anencephalic baby is that in the latter instances, the fetus was not conceived for the sole purpose of using its spare parts. But the body clone is exactly the same as the anencephalic infant or the early fetus in that no sentient being is being harmed in the process. As I mentioned earlier, the cells destined to become the higher brain of the clone are removed very early in fetal life, before they have differentiated into actual brain cells. In this way the clone develops into a brainless body and is nothing more than a collection of living cells, tissues, and organs. It has no consciousness to guide its actions or provide an identity. It cannot feel pain, think, experience, have an emotion, or sense its environment. On an evolutionary scale, it is lower than fish. And, significantly, body clones would do away with the fears expressed by the German doctors and others that mothers might sell their fetuses or anencephalic babies for spare parts. Since the purpose of a body clone is to provide rejection-free parts, it can only do this for the person from which it was derived. The clone would not have this value for any other individual.

We must also consider what we would giving up by not going forward with such research. A few years ago my twenty-six-year-old nephew, a wonderful young newlywed, died after a harrowing battle with leukemia. A cloned bone-marrow transplant would have saved his life. During a scientific meeting recently, I was talking to two researchers about the possibility of body clones. One was appalled by the idea and said it should be stopped at all costs. The other said, "I had a kidney transplant. If I could have had the choice of a cloned kidney, I would have taken it." Today, in order to keep a transplanted organ from being rejected, patients must take drugs that interfere with immune function and in some cases even cause an AIDS-like syndrome in which the body is unable to ward off opportunistic infections.

Cloning would also solve another increasingly vexing problem of transplantation—the supply of available organs. Right now the majority of people in need of a transplant die before a suitable organ becomes available. The suffering of those with organ disease is immense and terrible to behold. Anyone who has ever seen someone they love waste away from cancer or has experienced the loss of function of some part of his or her body knows how just how inhuman that is. The question we have to ask is, which is more inhuman—creating a brain-absent clone for the purpose of harvesting spare parts, or purposely refraining from using the technology when it becomes available, allowing the individual to suffer and die instead?

Another potentially explosive issue raised by radical advances in life extension is: Who would benefit from it? Would it be only for the wealthy? Would the gap between the haves and have-nots become an abyss in which those who have wealth and power would become close to immortal while those who are poor would lead lives that were not only wretched but short? Right now it is a fact of life that the rich enjoy much better health care and lead longer lives. But we have seen that medical breakthroughs eventually are made available to virtually all strata of society. Antibiotics are now in use everywhere and smallpox has been wiped off the face of the earth. Life expectancy has risen all over the world, even in the poorest societies. And it is a given that once a technology becomes mass-produced, its price drops precipitously. Indeed, there are indications that cloning would not be all that expensive. Willadsen is trying to get the cost of cloning a cow down to $3,000—far less than most medical procedures, and one-third the price of many new cars. And with mass production, costs could dip even further. Of course, there is expense of storing the clone in liquid nitrogen and having transplant operations performed, but this would still be far lower than today's chemotherapy treatments and anti-rejection drugs. In the long run, cloning would be a cheap way to save lives.

Even the cost of cryonics, which is paid for today with insurance policies that run about a dollar a day for someone twenty-five years old, will become much lower as the machines that are required to put a body into suspension are produced on assembly lines. As with everything else, choices will have to be made and people will have to decide whether they will forego certain luxuries today in order to have longer lives tomorrow.

Another major problem is what we will do with all the people that may result from a longevity revolution such as I have described. Of course, birth control would be essential, but we are already approaching zero population growth in many parts of the industrialized world. In fact, in some countries, such as Romania, the government is worried about underpopulation. Also, Segall's experiments in interventive gerontology show that the reproductive life of the animal is extended. If this holds true for humans, a woman might choose to hold off having a child until she is eighty years old. Moreover, many areas of the world are currently uninhabited. Canada is one of the largest land masses in the world and has a population of just twenty-two million. In the future we may learn to make this and other areas, including the deserts, the mountaintops, and the ice caps suitable for habitation by large numbers of people. And of course, we have our rockets aimed at the stars. But how are we going to get there?

We are going to get there through cloning, cryonics, and suspended animation. We are going to need all these things if we are going to have life extension, and we will need life extension if we are going to travel vast distances into space. Life extension will make possible space migration and space migration in turn will solve the overpopulation problem brought about by life extension. Maybe you think this is science fiction, but I like to think it will happen. Maybe our human destiny in the twenty-first century is to not only extend our own lives, but to extend life itself beyond the confines of the earth.

## Notes

1. Joseph Fletcher, *The Ethics of Genetic Control* (Buffalo, N.Y.: Prometheus Books, 1988), p. 17.

2. Ibid., p. 31.

3. Wolfgang Holzgrove, et al. "Kidney Transplantation from Anencephalic Donors," *New England Journal of Medicine,* Vol. 36, No. 17, April 23, 1987.

# Prospective Wisdom and Euthanasia

## Marvin Kohl

### (United States)

The next century should provide us with greater mastery over nature, especially in matters of life and death. The question is, How wise will this mastery be and why is it so difficult to make wise decisions about the practice of euthanasia?

It would be possible to argue (and, I think, with much justice) that our mastery will not be very wise and that this failure will be largely due to the geriatric nature of wisdom. As long as humankind was unable by means of the arts of understanding and practice to know how to live well until old age, it was natural to conclude that one cannot be wise until the golden years, if at all. And it is possible that the cultivation of this belief, the belief that wisdom requires the experience of vast amounts of life and only flourishes in its last seasons, gave human beings courage and confidence, thereby enabling them to carry the burdens of old age more successfully. But one could hardly seriously contend that this is an adequate explanation of the nature of wisdom.

I suggest that wisdom is a deep understanding of how to live well; that full wisdom is worthy of being loved or at least rationally pursued because it combines excellence in theoretical matters and excellence in actual living; that exceptional intelligence is not limited to the geriatric passages of life; and, finally, that prospective wisdom is more valuable than retrospective wisdom even though it is, in an important sense, more difficult to obtain.

Let me begin with the last point. To have retrospective or geriatric wisdom is to understand how to live well after the fact. In contrast, to have prospective wisdom is to understand how to live well before the challenge of actually doing so. It is to understand how to live a relatively good life (or a good life-passage) before experiencing the vicissitude of that human condition. And if the point of the game we call life is not merely to *understand* how to live well or how to play the game after it is essentially over, but to *actually* live well, then prospective wisdom clearly is the more valuable of the two.

We may be reminded that it is easy to see the past and difficult to foresee the future. Indeed, this is true. But it is one thing to urge that it is generally easier to see and to understand the past; it is another to claim that it is impossible to intelligently foresee the future and that wisdom is limited to those who have lived a long life, say a life of eighty years or so. Revulsion against the latter proposition is, I believe, a tribute to the fact that men and women of sufficient understanding accept a vital part of what I call a Greek prospective view of wisdom, namely, that life is governed by certain rules and, to the degree one understands and courageously implements these rules, one can live a wiser and happier life.

To be more specific, wisdom is generally considered to be the way a certain kind of knowledge and understanding is held and actually used. We typically distinguish between the person who knows only about knowledge and the person who lives wisely because he or she has a mastery of a certain kind of knowledge and has successfully implemented that knowledge. Therefore, a thoughtful individual may know what the important things in life and the limits of human power generally are, but may have neither the will nor sufficient control over his or her own life to be able to actually live wisely. For example, an individual may know or at least believe that it is important to die without unnecessary pain or suffering, yet may lack the strength of heart to do what has to be done to accomplish that end. Again, many individuals may understand that it is undesirable to continue living when their lives, or the lives of others, have been irreparably blasted by accident of disease. Yet they may lack the courage to recommend and support the practice of active voluntary euthanasia.

Similarly, a person may have species-bound and idiosyncratic knowledge about the important things in life and may not be able to rank them or decide what must be given up when one cannot "have it all." By way of illustration, consider the case of a person who considers it important not to have a society kill or allow the killing of the innocent, but finds it equally important to be loving and merciful. Such an individual knows what his or her values or idiosyncratic interests are, but cannot rank these values and act decisively because these conflating values are held to be equally important. This illustration may arouse protest. But when examined the reaction against it will turn out to be because it is difficult to face up to the truth that it is one thing to know what one's values and interests are, and another to know how to rank them or to give up one of a set of conflicting beliefs, thereby preventing intelligent action.

Wisdom is the "science" of understanding how to live well. It seems to require knowledge about, or a capacious understanding of, relevant aspects of nature (universal factors), the important things in human life (species-bound factors), the important things in an individual's life (idiosyncratic factors), and knowledge about what can and cannot be done. But wisdom is a matter of degree. At its fullest, it requires the highest degree of knowledge as well as its successful implementation. At its fullest it requires relevant knowledge about the nature of proximate and ultimate reality, how human beings are organized and behave, the idiosyncratic facts about oneself (including need-like correlate interests and what one wants out of life) as well as an understanding of what can and cannot be done. The latter is often referred to as the Greek pension for limits, the belief that in order to live well one also has to understand, in a sense, what one does not know and the limits of self—what one morally and physically can and cannot do.

Elsewhere I suggest that it is extraordinarily difficult to have full wisdom about matters of life and death.[1] I also suggest that we can describe some of the things a partially or moderately wise person knows about death.

First, death exists and places an important limit on every individual life. This means not only that we will all die but that we should not waste time with trifles or confuse the urgent with the important. "The significance of death," John Kekes writes, "is not merely that it puts an end to one's projects, but also that one's projects should be selected in the light of the knowledge that this will happen."[2]

Second, a moderately wise person knows that life is precious and that, except in certain special circumstances, it is a benefit to its possessor. Correspondingly, he or she knows that death is usually an evil and that it may be rational to fear and intelligently act to prevent accidental and other forms of unnecessary death. Insofar as one can establish such a thing, wise people understand that human life is worth protecting, worth preserving, and generally worth living to its end. They also understand that one can be happy with a life that is far from ideal and that being abnormal, handicapped, disadvantaged, or disabled does not necessarily mean that one cannot lead a relatively full, busy, and contented life. Similarly, they seem to understand that a life that is, on balance, unhappy is not necessarily an empty one. Exiting from an unhappy life is, therefore, one thing; exiting from an irreversibly meaningless existence is another.

Life itself—that is to say, bare subsistence—is not in itself valuable. What gives life value is not its mere existence but its *quality*. Those who have partially mastered knowledge about death and dying further distinguish between a life completely devoid of quality, one almost devoid of quality, and one just tipped on the negative side of the scale. Under the influence of what may broadly be called a quality-of-life point of view, they urge that sanity and wisdom consist not in the pursuit of life but in the pursuit of a quality life, and that where a life is irreparably blasted by the most loathsome forms of disease and degradation, it may be desirable to cease to exist. Despite the great variety of justifications offered, quality-of-life advocates basically agree that suicide and voluntary euthanasia are sometimes excusable, permissible, virtuous, or obligatory. Indeed, the quality-of-life group might well be called "Promethean," since it is hostile to the idea of just letting nature take its course and insists that humanity should consciously and intelligently control its own destiny. The essence of the quality-of-life position is that we are not being wise (to say nothing about being humane) when we do *not* distinguish between and actively respect differences, especially radical differences, in life quality. When an adult correctly judges his or her own life to be irreparably devoid or almost devoid of quality and wants to die, it is difficult to understand why wisdom would prohibit it. In fact, when such judgments are correctly made, when someone is allowed to die or to take his or her own life because he or she truly would be better off dead, it is difficult to understand why that gentle peace is not enjoined by wisdom.

A critic may wish to remind us that the controversy concerning euthanasia is acute and long-standing. Philosophers and others have expended enormous energy deliberating the wisdom of morally permitting the deliberate death of innocent human beings. This being the case it is not so difficult, a critic might argue, to understand why voluntary euthanasia is not enjoined by wisdom: because it is not the morally correct thing to do. Or one may additionally claim that the pursuit of wisdom is not worthy of our energies if otherwise rational beings cannot be persuaded by its commands.

The fundamental trouble with this objection is that it concludes that something is wrong with our analysis of euthanasia, or that wisdom is not worthy of our high regard simply because there is disagreement about what ought or ought not to be done in certain circumstances. It completely sidesteps the question of alternative theories of wisdom and the importance of distinguishing between prospective and retrospective, partial and full wisdom. For example, in the book of Job there appear to be at least two theories of wisdom: The first is that wisdom is associated with God in creation, that to be wise is to know all that God knows, and that this cosmic wisdom is accessible to human beings; the second is that, since this wisdom is accessible only to God and is not to be found in the land of the living, we have to accept a lesser wisdom, we have to accept God as an ultimate mystery and simply have faith in his creation and his laws as interpeted by proper religious authority.[3] From either point of view one might consistently (but not convincingly) argue that one knows that God wants to prohibit the killing of the innocent. For how do we know, strictly speaking, what God wants us to do? And if this knowledge is not directly available, why assume that it is indirectly available? Why assume that a particular religious authority knows what God wants us to do, especially when religious authorities differ so when it comes to judgments about such topics as voluntary euthanasia?

This, however, does not fully reply to the critic's claim that voluntary euthanasia is not enjoined by wisdom because it is not the morally correct thing to do.[4] But a justification for the inclusion of this particular theory (or group of related moral theories) in a theory of wisdom would of course amount to a deeper analysis of the nature of prospective wisdom, and so is beyond the scope of this paper.

Yet it should be recognized that if numbers and diversity count, then one can add at least three other theories to my own ideal utilitarian support of certain aspects of euthanasia. As James Rachels observes, the morality of euthanasia—in the central case of the terminal patient who wants to be killed—is supported by such diverse ethical precepts as the principle of utility, Kant's categorical imperative, and the golden rule.[5] Perhaps more important, the theory of prospective wisdom here outlined is not a closed theory. It is devoted to opening and enlarging the ways of what is best in humankind. As John Dewey wrote, "A true wisdom, devoted to the latter task, discovers in thoughtful observation and experiment the method of administering the unfinished process of existence so that frail goods shall be substantiated, secure goods be extended, and the precarious promises of good that haunt experienced things be more liberally fulfilled."⁶ And in the case of the wisdom of voluntary euthanasia, the frail good in question is that of being humane.

While this reply makes the situation look more complex than in fact it is, it cannot be denied that being humane occupies a peculiar position in any vigorous theory of wisdom. It requires special treatment and at least a paper to itself.

## Notes

1. "Wisdom, Death, and the Quality of Life," *Free Inquiry* 8(3), Summer 1988, p. 19.

2. John Kekes, "Wisdom," *American Philosophical Quarterly* 20:3 (1983), p. 280.

3. For some intriguing discussions of conflating conceptions of wisdom in the Old Testament, see James Wood, *Wisdom Literature* (London: Gerald Duckworth, 1967), pp. 41–71; and James L. Crenshaw, *Studies in Ancient Israelite Wisdom* (New York: Ktav, 1976).

4. For a fuller discussion of this problem, see *The Morality of Killing* (London: Peter Owen and New York: Humanities Press, 1974), and Marvin Kohl, ed., *Beneficent Euthanasia* (Buffalo, N.Y.: Prometheus Books, 1975).

5. James Rachels, "Euthanasia," in *Matters of Life and Death*, 2nd Edition, edited by Tom Regan (New York: Random House), pp. 35–76.

6. John Dewey, *Experience and Nature* (New York: W. W. Norton, 1925, 1929), pp. 760–777.

# Humanism in Medicine

## Richard Taylor
### (United States)

The philosophical problems spawned by technological advances in medicine are sometimes bizarre. One thinks, for example, of the questions of parenthood raised by a woman who recently gave birth to triplets resulting from *in vitro* fertilization, the ova for these having been provided by her own daughter. Or consider the problems presented by a mother who offered to donate the organs of the living unborn child she was carrying, this child having been discovered to be a victim of spina bifida and thus to have no significant promise of a future of its own. Situations more or less like these are now of common occurrences in medicine. The news media seize upon them for their inherent interest, while clergymen, philosophers, and physicians render their varying verdicts on how we should think about them. These verdicts, often delivered with an authoritative tone of finality and sometimes inconsistent with one another, sometimes do more harm than good in the long run, precisely because of how they are arrived at; namely, by the application of preexisting rules rather than by a consideration of human needs.

It is common to suppose that all the ethical problems in medicine result from technological advances—techniques for fertilizing ova in a dish, for detecting serious fetal defects, for sustaining life in the terminally ill, for transplanting vital living tissues, and so on. And of course it is obvious that ethical problems do arise from medical technology. But that is only one source. Another, which is rarely questioned and indeed almost never noticed, is the practice within Western culture of resolving all ethical issues by the application of rules of morality. It is assumed that this simply means to ask whether a given practice is or is not morally allowable. If some time-honored principle forbids it, then it is deemed wrong, and that is the end of the matter. This, for example, is the basis for the opposition to the abortion of a fetus. That act, it is correctly noted, is the taking of an innocent human life. And therefore it is, by definition, murder. And murder, no one doubts, violates a moral principle or command that is as old as civilization. It is, accordingly, wrong, whatever the circumstances, and no considerations of convenience or cost can make it otherwise.

The approach to ethical problems through the application of moral rules is the product of the Judeo-Christian tradition, which originally represented moral obligation as obedience to God's will, as expressed, for example, in biblical commandments. Such an approach to ethics was accordingly quite foreign to the ancient Greeks. Plato and others did, to be sure, speak of principles of justice, but these were thought of as ideals, not as rules for the determination of moral right and wrong. Indeed, the ideas of moral right and wrong, as we think of them, were quite unknown to the philosophers of antiquity. One finds no hint of them in Aristotle's ethical writings, for example. Instead, the Greeks thought of ethics as concerned with virtue, and virtues were always thought of as qualities of people, not of actions.

Today philosphical moralists still think of moral obligation as adherence to moral rule or principle, even though virtually all of them have abandoned the quaint notion that these rules were at some time past delivered to man by God. Ethics, it is assumed, has to do with moral right and wrong. And the distinction between moral right and wrong is the distinction between what is and what is not permitted by moral rule or principle. Find, then, the rules applicable to a given course of action, and you will be able to say whether that course of action is or is not morally permissible. Whenever a group of moralists tries to resolve a question of ethics, whether in medicine or not, they simply assume themselves to be searching for some applicable rule of ethics, and this is true whether these moralists are clergymen, philosophers, physicians, or whatever. They do not ask themselves whether that is the correct approach to a problem. They simply presuppose that it is. And when they hit upon such a rule that they can agree on, they consider their inquiry completed, often with little regard to the implications that their "solution" might have for human well-being.

The one exception to this approach is the moralist whose position is that of situation ethics. This moralist asks not what some inherited rule of ethics might permit or forbid, but rather, what course of action is most likely, in a given situation, to promote human well-being. Naturally, the course of action suggested by such an approach will differ from one situation to another, as the factors bearing on human well-being change, and as the rules applicable to some will not work for others.

This approach to the resolution of ethical questions is widely viewed with deep suspicion. It is thought to provide an excuse for ethical compromise, a means of defending courses of action that moral principle does not permit. Yet it should be fairly obvious to anyone who thinks about it that the most time-honored rules of morality, such as those forbidding homicide, theft, adultery, the inflicting of injury upon one person for the benefit of another, and so on, were all invented to promote peace and safety, or the advancement of human well-being—the very thing that is central to the method of the situationist. These rules were then ascribed to a divine source in order to vest them with authority, that is, to provide an incentive to obey. But if this is so, then human well-being is the ultimate basis of morality after all, and reason would require that, instead of compromising human benefit in order to preserve fidelity to moral principle, it is the rules themselves that should be modified or, indeed, abandoned altogether when they militate against our well-being. Such an approach does not, to be sure, enable one to determine, in a given situation, what the "morally right" course of action might be, but that is no loss. What is gained, an appreciation of human needs and how best to fulfill them, is vastly more worthwhile.

To understand the very great differences between these two approaches to ethics, consider the following situations that are fairly typical of those that arise in medicine.

1. A comotose patient develops a severely swollen testicle. Should surgery be undertaken in the hope of relieving that condition?

2. An infant is born so severely brain-damaged as to have a life expectancy of perhaps two years, filled with physical pain to the infant, psychic suffering to her family, and astronomical monetary expenditures. Should her healthy vital organs be removed in order to save another infant who might thereby enjoy a long and fulfilling life?

3. A patient's Parkinson's disease can be arrested by the transplantation of very young living brain tissue. May such tissue be taken from an aborted fetus?

To answer "yes" to any of these questions is to violate some well-established moral principle. The first asks whether a patient's right to informed consent to surgery should be honored, the second whether it is all right to kill one person in order to improve the life of another, and the third whether the bodily parts of someone deliberately destroyed might be used for someone else's benefit, and perhaps even be sold for that purpose.

It is not hard to see that negative answers to all these questions are yielded by the application of familiar moral principles, and even someone who, like myself, has liberated himself from the tyranny of such principles finds questions like these discomforting.

If, however, one views such situations as these not in terms of what is "right" or "wrong," but rather in terms of human well-being, then every one of these questions receives an affirmative answer.

Thus, surgeons will not concern themselves about informed consent if they can instead address themselves confidently to the needs of comatose patients, nor need they worry that an established principle of medical practice is thus violated.

Or consider our far more difficult second example, involving the killing of one human being for the benefit of another. This surely flies in the face of moral principle, and moralists are thus apt to feel the negative answer to the question forced upon them. No one, they are likely to say, no matter how pitiful his or her condition may be, may be sacrificed just to enhance another's life, however promising. And of course in general that is true, just out of considerations of human well-being alone. But when an infant's condition is hopeless and its life promises to be brief and filled with suffering that will carry over to the parents and others, and when, moreover, the life of another might be made long and fulfilling by the procedure here contemplated, then we are dealing with a situation unlike anything for which the rule of morality was intended. This situation arose recently when a couple in California learned that the child they were expecting was thus hopelessly afflicted. They were advised that some other child could be made whole and given the promise of a fulfilling life through the sacrifice of theirs. This news to some extent replaced their despair with rejoicing—at which point, of course, the moralists stepped in with their time-honored moral principles, the effect of which was to destroy the rejoicing of this couple and, of course, restore hopelessness to whatever child might have benefited. The defective fetus turned out to be stillborn, however— and the problem was thereby "solved," presumably in a manner satisfactory to all, since no difficult decision then had to be made. But such an outcome can hardly be viewed as satisfactory with respect to the child, forever unknown, whose hope for a fulfilling life was thereby demolished.

Finally, in terms of our third example, it has quite recently been discovered that the victims of Parkinson's disease, a malady hitherto thought irreversible, might improve through transplantation of young brain tissue. And of course such tissue exists in abundance in the thousands of fetuses that are routinely and legally aborted. Yet such use of fetal tissue has aroused a storm of protest simply on moral grounds. No one, I think, could be so intellectually obtuse as to suggest that human well-being would be advanced by the sheer discarding of such precious tissue, in case it should turn out that a dreadful disease could be alleviated by putting it to use. But to the traditional moralist what counts is what is morally permissible as determined by principle, rather than what might be beneficial to this person or that.

From what little has been said it can be seen that, until this humanistic approach is substituted for the moralistic one that we have inherited from a religious tradition, the problems of medical ethics are apt to become worse. This follows from the fact that today's medical technology is constantly creating unprecedented situations to which it is not merely idle, but pernicious, to try applying rules of morality that arose from more commonplace situations. Consider the woman who, acting as surrogate for her own daughter, gave birth to triplets generated from her daughter's ova and fertilized in vitro by the daughter's husband's sperm. Whose name should be entered by the obstetrical hospital as the mother of these children? Was this woman, as the newspapers had it, somehow the mother of her own grandchildren? And what shall we say of a woman who, exercising her constitutional right to an abortion, offers the organs of her as yet unaborted fetus for medical experimentation? Should she be entitled to reimbursement for this?

The impulsive, almost automatic response to such questions is to try to think of what would be "right" or "wrong," to draw analogies to familiar situations in which the answer has already long been established, imagining that the problems are thus "resolved." But of course they are more often than not just made worse by that approach. Thus, with respect to the illustration just offered, someone is sure to ask why an affirmative answer would not justify, by analogy, hiring women to become pregnant so that we might buy up their aborted fetuses or, going a step further, buy up their full-term infants just in order to dismantle them for their parts. But that approach is not the road to moral enlightenment—it is the road to darkness. We shall not shed light on such problems until we abandon the moralistic approach, which is at bottom the approach of religion, in favor of the humanistic one, which asks, simply, what course of action is most likely to promote the greatest amount of human well-being.

One final comment is needed. It is widely believed that the approach of situation ethics is simplistic or, worse, that it provides convenient and easy answers. The very opposite is true. Situation ethics is frightfully difficult, because it requires one to actually think instead of rendering moral judgments based on time-honored principles—something that even unthinking and unreflective people find fairly easy to do. Accordingly, it is the moralistic approach, which rests upon little more than the mindless application of rules, that is easy—and, in the long run, dreadfully destructive.

# The Right to Voluntary Euthanasia

## Jan Glastra van Loon
### (Netherlands)

Euthanasia is a highly emotional as well as a highly controversial subject. It is therefore a subject frequently excluded from rational discussion. However, it is also a subject that humanists cannot and should not ignore.

One of the most important human rights is the individual's right to self-determination, by which I mean the right of all persons to shape and organize their own existence while respecting the right of others to do the same.

The choice between the continuation of one's life or the ending of it is inextricably connected with this right to self-determination. All individuals must be allowed to decide for themselves about their own life or death. The right to voluntary euthanasia that cannot be placed in anyone else's hands. There should, therefore, be legal provisions granting and protecting the right to make this decision about one's own life and concerning the assistance of those who have freely and unequivocally expressed the wish to end their lives.

Medical technology has made it possible to continue life longer than ever before, but sometimes this is done in such a way that the individual concerned finds it undesirable. For example, a ninety-five-year-old woman in a hospital bed at a nursing home in the Dutch town of Purmerend was in a medically hopeless situation. Her life had lost all flavor, all meaning. At her urgent and repeated request, her general physician, after consultation with another doctor, ended his patient's life. The doctor's plea of "force majeur," meaning that the situation put "intolerable pressure on [his] conscience," was accepted by the court in the Hague. The doctor was acquitted.

This is an example of Dutch jurisprudence in a case of voluntary euthanasia. All the necessary criteria of carefulness had been fulfilled. All concerned were satisfied—first and foremost, the patient. It is not an exceptional case.

An important distinction must be made between voluntary euthanasia and the ending of medical treatment. The latter—and likewise, the omission of medical treatment at the request of the patient—fall outside the scope of euthanasia. Certain forms of ending medical treatment are sometimes called euthanasia, though strictly speaking they are not. For example, the decision not to apply resuscitation and/or articial-respiration techniques in an acutely life-threatening case is not voluntary euthanasia. Nor is the nonapplication or discontinuation of medical treatment at the request of the patient. Every patient has the right to refuse medical treatment. If nonapplication or discontinuation of treatment causes death, this does not make it a case of euthanasia. It is a case of natural death.

A clear and workable definition of euthanasia is necessary to frame proper legislation and procedure: *Euthanasia is a deliberate life-ending act by anyone other than the person involved, at the latter's request.* Euthanasia means that patients who are incurably ill may be given treatment on their own request in order to end suffering. The essential difference here is that there is a conscious wish to die. A patient who, when competent, has expressed this wish should have the best help possible. Leaving patients who are incurably ill to their own devices is an act of cruelty.

In the Netherlands, views on euthanasia differ from those in most other countries. Dutch doctors have been in the forefront of international medical organizations concerning discussions on voluntary euthanasia. Together with their colleagues from the Scandinavian countries and the United Kingdom, they take a comparatively liberal attitude toward the practice.

Despite Holland's more open attitude in this regard, voluntary euthanasia has not been legalized; indeed, the penal code contains a number of articles that forbid euthanasia. Taking a person's life by request is punishable with a maximum of twelve years' imprisonment. Assisting a suicide is punishable with a maxiumum of nine months' imprisonment. A person who fails to come to the rescue when someone is in mortal danger can be punished with three months' imprisonment plus a fine. Although voluntary euthanasia is not legally allowed, there have been some trials in which the courts have spelled out guidelines under which a physician can go unpunished in a case of active voluntary euthanasia.

The following conditions that must be fulfilled have emerged from this Dutch jurisprudence:

1. There must be clear evidence of an enduring and well-considered request to put an end to life. This is the most essential of all conditions.

2. The patient must show a thorough understanding of the situation based on adequate information.

3. The patient must be experiencing unbearable suffering in an irreversible situation.

4. There must be an absence of reasonable alternatives that are acceptable to the patient.

5. Voluntary euthanasia is to be applied only by a qualified physician after consultation of a second physician.

6. Due care must be taken by the physician in reviewing and verifying the conditions as well as in performing the act of euthanasia itself.[1]

Thus, according to the Dutch jurisprudence, in certain circumstances and under certain conditions, euthanasia, if practiced by a physician applying proper and verifiable procedures, is permissible.

Recently a Private Member's Bill on euthanasia was introduced in the Dutch Parliament. The bill says that patients whose suffering has become unbearable may be put out of their misery by a doctor, stipulating conditions that guarantee that euthanasia will take place only at the express request of the patient involved. An important point is that the patient's physician has to consult a colleague in order to establish that the patient is in an incurable state and that he or she wishes to end life of his or her own free will.

Again, great emphasis is put on the free will of the patient. If these criteria are met euthanasia will not be punishable.

The present government is of the opionion that euthanasia should, with some exceptions, remain a criminal act on the criminal code. One exception would be to allow euthanasia when a patient is already dying and the physician in charge considers the inevitable end to be near. Here the patient's wishes are taken into account only insofar as certain objective criteria regarding the condition of health are met. In actual fact, this means that doctors, rather than their patients, must make vital decisions. Thus, the criteria are only seemingly objective, as the decisions made by doctors can conceal subjective elements and will therefore be less instead of more verifiable than those made according to the wish of the patient.

In fact, regardless of the laws of various nations, euthanasia does occur regularly throughout the world. The everyday practice requires clear legislation. Without such legislation the patient and the doctor have to face unacceptable uncertainties. The patient doesn't know whom to approach regarding the issue, and the doctor does not know how to legally respond to a request for euthanasia.

Legal provisions have an advantage over jurisprudence in that such insecurities are more clearly taken away. Morever, legal practice formed via jurisprudential development will require much time, and it may be many more years before the needed clarity will be achieved. In the meantime, various institutions (hospitals, homes for the elderly, nursing homes) in which patients often raise questions regarding euthanasia have already begun to draw up staff procedures on how to answer such questions. These questions are still too often evaded or not answered at all. Rapid changes in medical technology tend to crush the patients' right to self-determination. With a clear practice and legislation, individuals will find clear answers to their questions about voluntary euthanasia.

An individual's choice between life and death is part of the right to self-determination, and the artificial continuation of life is not always desirable. The quality of life can be more important than its duration.

Internationally there is, by and large, a desire to keep silent about euthanasia. "Life" and the preservation of life are the central theme. Under the influence of Christian beliefs, the premature termination of life usually is not a permissible subject for discussion. Voluntary euthanasia is seen by its adversaries as an act aimed at deliberately causing the death of a patient, and thus as being directly in conflict with medical ethics. The humanist viewpoint is that it is up to the individual—and no one else—to determine the quality of his or her own life and the desirability of its continuation.

Euthanasia raises some fundamental questions: The freedom to decide upon one's own way of living and dying becomes a matter of principle when one finds oneself in a vulnerable and dependent position. At the same time people are not always able to make clear decisions when they are sick and suffering.

Prolonged medical treatment can sometimes hamper rather than assist us in deciding how we will face our own life; it can hamper our accepting the inevitable and our departing in a dignified way. This seems to be the problem behind the problem of euthanasia: How does the medical profession regain the art and ethics by which a patient's clear and freely expressed wish to end his or her life, rather than the physician's overwhelming expertise and ability to prolong it, is the principle according to which the doctor's actions are decided.

How do we establish in our societies that an individual undergoing medical treatment remains a *person* with an inalienable right to determine his or her life and therefore also to discontinue it, and that such an individual may never be considered a mere object of a physician's care and responsibility, however great the doctor's competence and abilities?

There are no easy answers to these problems. On the contrary, there are only difficult cases that will always be with us.

But that should not stop us from being clear about our principles, from striving for legislation that provides maximum clarity in most cases and that thereby best secures the individual's right of self-determination by guaranteeing the medical help and assistance to which he or she is entitled, while also protecting his or her life against interference by others. At this moment, even more important than solutions is lifting the taboo on the subject so that reasonably rational discussion of it may become possible.

Death may be a problem, but it may be an even greater problem when it is denied.

## Note

1. These seven criteria are taken from a speech by Ph. R. Sutorius, Attorney at Law, Arnhem, the Netherlands.

# Ethical Concerns About Aging and the Aged

## Ruth Bennett
### (United States)

Aging is a burning issue due to worldwide demographics. Gerontologists call this the demographic imperative. Throughout the world the aged population—that is, those sixty-five and older—is the fastest growing age group. Within that category, those eighty-five and over comprise the fastest growing subgroup. We can now keep alive the very old and frail longer than has ever been true in history.

Though this sounds great to most of us, it has many implications, not the least of which is the cost to society. This has become a hot political issue in the United States and elsewhere, but the growth of the population of aged need not be linked to the costs issue. This linkage tells more about our current thinking than it does about the issue. Thus far, the general public seems totally unaware of issues of aging and, if they are aware at all, they behave as though these issues will go away. But they will not go away and, indeed, things may get worse.

Most people—the aged included—seem unaware that they can have a say in framing issues and making decisions. In fact, most of what determines life expectancy for the majority of people—that is, whether we have an aging population of considerable size and how well that population lives—is based upon decisions that are sociopolitical in nature. That is, we as a society ultimately decide who should live and who should die and when. Society decides how to use its resources. A simple example is the preparation for and declaration of war. Once a country has decided to use most of its resources for waging war, many things follow, including the probability that those countries that have experienced war often are not as healthy and long-lived as those that have not.

Most public-health issues are sociopolitical in nature, though today many people seem to believe that health and long life are biologically determined.

Without societal or sociopolitical intervention, the fact that most humans are programmed to live to around a hundred years of age means very little, especially in societies too poor to feed most of their people. More people everywhere are living to extreme old age and this, to a greater or lesser extent, is decided by states of societal consensus that we can all influence. Thus, numbers alone, both now and in the future, should help the elderly to influence states of consensus.

But today, many of the elderly do not know how to exert a powerful influence on political issues. Those who wish to affect the political process or the social climate on their own behalf but do not have the expertise to do so can employ younger people to act as their advocates. But this may not always continue to be the case; younger people may not want for their own future the things that elderly people want now, and also, elderly people may become sufficiently knowledgeable and sufficiently integrated into society so that they will not need to buy the expertise of younger people. This latter alternative is seen as desirable up to a point by many gerontologists. However, since we all plan to age, we all should have some say over societal decision-making affecting the aged. There are many reasons why the current group of older people generally have had little say about events that are occurring in their own lives.

1. Isolation. Many aged are socially isolated from the mainstream of society rather than socially integrated. As of 1987, almost one-third of the aged lived alone; most of the rest lived with elderly spouses, but even these pairs may be isolated. Five percent are segregated in institutions, and who knows how many are ghettoized in segregated housing or communities for the elderly. Such isolation may mean that they can exert very little influence over states of societal consensus. They are often isolated due to factors beyond their control, such as frailty, forced retirement, lack of education, personality traits, and so on. In many ways what happens to the aged is similar to what happens to racial minorities and other powerless groups. There is a question about what they will do. Will they further segregate or ghettoize themselves, isolate themselves individually, work only with other elderly, or seek allies with whom to work? These are tough decisions and slow processes. Since it is hoped that all of us will be elderly, we can and should work to influence the isolation-integration process.

2. The feminization of aging. Most of the aged (two-thirds of those over sixty-five; three-quarters of those over seventy-five) are women, and this reduces their influence. Their natural allies may be their caregivers—usually middle-aged women—but they too have very little influence. This may be true worldwide. Relatively few women are powerful political or even social leaders. Many women have resources but do not control their use, so they cannot advocate for the elderly as well as their numbers might lead us to believe.

3. Other vulnerabilities. Many aged are poor, frail, and fearful, which keeps them from working, lobbying, or advocating on their own behalf.

4. Ageism. Many elderly feel as though they are invisible. To reduce ageism requires massive efforts in prejudice reduction. This may happen as more of

us realize we're growing older, but it is a real and hard-to-change part of our youth-oriented cultural climate. Related to ageism are cost-cutting or tax-cutting themes and the medicalization of many human services, which may in turn increase their cost to society.

These cultural themes cannot be easily changed, and we probably need to learn how to live with them and work with and/or around them.

Living to old age should fill one with pride, not guilt. This country should be proud to have so many older people, but it does not seem to be. We hear much about costs and little about pride. Pride about aging and about the size of our aging population will require major alterations in our attitude. I'm not sure that this can or will happen. The elderly have to want this and work for it, as do many of the rest of us.

Aging issues that must be addressed by all groups include the following:

1. We must learn to see the benefits of an aging population. Very little has been said about the positive side of aging or about what the aged bring to the family, the community, the city in which they reside. Much more research is needed to determine the positive contributions made by the elderly. I believe that communities are in serious trouble without the aged or when the aged are badly integrated, although today there are no sociobiological data to support this point. From my observations, young people become seriously demoralized when they see that after a lifetime of work, the elderly are not respected or are treated miserably. "What's the point?" they may well ask. Furthermore, I will go out on a limb and suggest that much of the problem-behavior among the young may be explained on the basis of what they may view as the pointlessness of life and in anticipation of their lot at the end of the line.

2. Whose job is it to care for the aging? Middle-aged people—women in particular—seem to be torn between two sets of conflicting and equally salient role expectations. Should they use their scarce resources to support their children or to help their aging parents and maybe grandparents? While they are being tormented by these conflicts, middle-aged women are being encouraged, or perhaps, forced to go back to work or school. No wonder we're hearing about midlife crises. Can these crises be resolved by each person, one at a time, or do they cry out for social solutions? Pluralistic ignorance should not be so prevalent in such a tension-laden arena. There is much policy talk nowadays about "returning" the care of the aged to families—it is said that family supports, informal supports, natural support networks should replace the formal service system. But it is difficult to see how the demographic sociocultural picture can lend itself to strengthening informal supports.

Demographically, the United States is experiencing a declining birth rate and an increasing number of older persons, with the most rapidly growing sector over the age of seventy-five. Thus, fewer younger people are available to work and to care for elders. And, since more women are entering the labor force than ever before, they are no longer available for caretaker roles. Our social climate encourages women to work; there are very few intact nuclear families, let alone extended families in today's society. The job comes first: geographic and social mobility are highly valued, even by the older persons who are abandoned as their offspring move on.

Furthermore, our cultural climate encourages the negative stereotyping of the aged by young and old alike. There is little desire to consider their problems high priority.

Despite this, a 1977 GAO survey conducted in Cleveland found that 70 percent of caretaking was done by relatives, mainly spouses. And a 1986 National Center for Health Statistics (NCHS) report found that nationwide, most caregiving is done by daughters and daughters-in-law, 12 percent of whom leave their jobs to do this caregiving (as compared with only 5 percent of sons). Research done in New York, Cleveland, and Los Angeles has found that many families plan to provide care until they are stressed by the deteriorating condition of the older person. Nonrelated caretakers are not as stressed. Many families and nonrelated caretakers shoulder immense burdens for as long as they can. Often they decide to institutionalize because there is no alternative. A well worked-out alternative delivery system including home care, day care, transportation, respite care, and a variety of nontraditional services would allow more families to keep older persons at home. However, this will not cut costs even with the most sophisticated types of case management.

However, I believe that changes in the types and manner of long-term-care service delivery will occur, if only because of education. At present the most educated population group in the United States is entering old age. This group may make greater demands for and will probably utilize services. Moreover, they may demand improvements in the quality of life in general. And this will not be cheap.

3. Isolation versus integration of the aged. More and more old people with or even without resources may be so discouraged by intergenerational tension that they may continue to segregate themselves into "retirement communities" to escape the fray. I believe this represents a great loss to each community, the overall effects of which have not as yet been felt. Survey results consistently indicate that morale is highest among the elderly who are living in age-segregated as opposed to age-integrated settings. What does this mean for all of us? Can any segregation be good? We have just come out from under a century-long battle to desegregate the races and the sexes. Will we have to fight another battle to desegregate the generations?

Age divisions may well replace class divisions on the political and social scene unless there is a conscious effort to stop this process. Older people may not wish to support schools with their taxes; younger people may not wish to support Social Security. Against a backdrop of ageism, it is not hard to tell who will win. However, as the aged grow increasingly numerous and better educated, they will constitute a mighty political and social force. And we will not be able to ignore them, as we often do children, because the aged can vote.

We cannot afford to think of these problems of "them versus us," and this requires that a great deal of information be available to politicians, professionals, and laypersons alike. We cannot continue to make political and social decisions as if each age group exists in a vacuum. Now that we know that 70 percent of all persons born today are expected to grow old, decision-making at all levels should expand to include choices and alternatives that make sense over an entire lifetime.

More lifestyle options should be available that can be sustained or tolerated by the community to span a lifetime. People need support, help, and education at all ages. We shouldn't stop helping people when they turn eighteen and start again when they turn sixty-five. Not all of us can be counted on to build a resource network to last a lifetime; many networks may be fragile throughout the lifespan and may need regular shoring up. One is not a failure at age forty-five if a fragile network falls apart; these networks disintegrate for all sorts of reasons. For example, the average age of widowhood in the United States is fifty-six. Political and social entities are worthless if people of all ages and stages of life cannot count on support and sustenance within them.

England, Sweden, and France seem to have learned a bit more than we have about how to shore up natural or informal systems such as communities, parishes, and families. In the United States, we still seem to be in the business of inventing ways to break up, rather than shore up, these informal systems.

4. Gerontological education on a societywide basis. Learning how to be an old person may be something each of us has to do quite early in life. It may not come naturally at this point in our history, especially when few have role models of successful aging. Aging on a large scale is a new phenomenon on the world scene, and everyone may need to learn about aging and the aged in order to live with the process. It's here to stay, I assure you, and it beats the alternative.

The following groups need to learn about aging in a big hurry:

• Older people themselves, who seem to be having a terrible time of it, to judge from findings on depression, suicide, demoralization, and related attitudes. Twenty-five percent of all suicides are among the elderly, although they make up only 12 percent of the population.

• Grandparents and grandchildren. Grandparenting can be fun and good for everyone if one learns how to do it well. But how many know how? Studies show there is very little interaction between grandparents and grandchildren.

• Young families. Family relations may be better if older people are involved. But how many know how to prepare for this or do it well? Extended families may have to be reinvented.

• Neighbors, who can constitute an important support group if they wish to do so.

• Politicians and policymakers, for the obvious reason that their decisions affect all of us.

• Those in all of the helping professions.

I believe our cultural themes will need to be changed in order for all of us to change our attitudes and to adjust to aging. Caring is something we do quite naturally; we need only to extend the notion to cover the lifespan, that is, we must encourage intergenerational friendships. New professions of a caring nature will arise that require humanistic and interdisciplinary skills—these will include case managers, case coordinators, long-term-care planners, family therapists, and so forth. Today, cost-benefit research seems to be in vogue. We know that a growing aging population will be costly, but the benefits are as yet unclear, and a different approach to research is needed.

Answers would be forthcoming if more humanistic studies were conducted. Yet the trend against humanistic research continues. Humanistic studies would concentrate on such subjects as discovering and evaluating different methods for reducing ageism and isolation; more experimentation with innovative psychosoial programs, both in and out of institutions; experimentation with methods for reducing the strains and burdens of middle-aged persons; and experimentation with less totalistic institutions. Such research should be encouraged, because what is good for the aged will ultimately be good for all of us.

# AIDS and the Twenty-First Century

## Mathilde Krim
### (United States)

It is a tall order for a humble biologist to be asked to offer thoughts on the twenty-first century. I will do it from the personal perspective of one who has long observed with some bewilderment—as all native Europeans do—American culture and institutions. I will also do it from the standpoint of one who has been immersed, over the past eight years, in the study of AIDS.

Because this global natural calamity magnifies society's imperfections, it will challenge our institutions everywhere and have a significant impact on human life in the next century.

Let us first consider what AIDS is, reflecting on where such an epidemic fits into the general scheme of things, biological and human; how it could happen; what we know about it; and what we ought to do.

Epidemics do occur; the great plague killed a quarter of the European population in the fifteenth century, and the influenza epidemic of 1918 killed some twenty million people worldwide, including a half-million in the United States alone.

Epidemics happen because the evolution of all living forms is continuously fueled by small genetic variations that result from slight mistakes in the complex processes of genetic replication. Mutations also occur in the genetic material of microorganisms and viruses, causing new strains to arise occasionally that have either lesser or greater disease-causing potential. Thus the AIDS virus naturally evolved from a preexisting nonpathogenic human virus or from one of the many viruses that infect nonhuman primates and become capable, through a series of genetic changes, of infecting human cells.

The first case of AIDS in the United States, recently diagnosed retrospectively from hospital records and frozen tissues, occurred in 1969. Sporadic but unrecognized cases occurred in the 1970s on both coasts of the United States and in Central Africa. Suddenly, in 1981, close to a hundred previously healthy young American men became ill with a condition characterized by profound immunosuppression and symptoms of various "opportunistic diseases," infections and cancers not seen in immunologically healthy people. Many of these patients were homosexual, which pointed to the possibility that they shared a common underlying disorder. Their condition was named Acquired Immune Deficiency Syndrome, or AIDS, and was reported to the Centers for Disease Control because it appeared to be new, serious, and rapidly spreading.

Starting in 1982, and with certainty in 1983, the surveillance system instituted by the Centers for Disease Control revealed that, although certain groups— gay men, intraveneous drug users, and hemophiliacs—were stricken by AIDS more often than others, the condition was not necessarily linked to gender, sexual orientation, age, race, or socioeconomic status. Cases had also occurred among blood-transfusion recipients of both sexes and any age, among women who were the sexual partners of men with AIDS, and among their newborns.

By putting these facts together, we knew as early as 1983 that AIDS was a venereal disease caused by a blood-borne infectious agent. This conclusion immediately suggested—at least to biologists—that anyone could acquire AIDS if exposed to its etiological agent through sex or blood. This was soon confirmed by reports from Central Africa and the Caribbean region that showed that, in those areas, AIDS was transmitted mainly heterosexually and afflicted men and women in equal numbers, as well as a large proportion of their infants. By 1983, the number of AIDS cases was doubling each year, everywhere.

The lack of appropriate response to this evidence on the part of our society in general, and the Reagan Administration in particular, has been astounding and appalling.

U.S. federal health authorities adopted and maintained a "wait and see" attitude. Those few of us who expressed apprehension were called "alarmists." The Centers for Disease Control persisted in issuing reports, without explanatory comments for the lay public, which listed AIDS cases by "risk group." This continually emphasized their higher incidence in the United States among gay men and intravenous drug users. The public misinterpreted this to mean that merely being a gay man or a drug user *caused* AIDS, and it adopted a moralistic stance that amounted to blaming those afflicted for their misfortune.

I realized then, with a good deal of astonishment, that our society believes that being homosexual is an indulgence deliberately chosen in defiance of prevailing norms. Because of this view, homosexual behavior is commonly seen as immoral and is equated with sin in religious parlance. The same is believed to be true of addiction. Most people do not understand and therefore do not believe that, once acquired, habituation to a drug causes new physiological needs which, unless fullfilled by the intake of that particular drug, lead to overwhelming craving, disease, and even death. The public does not believe that the true addict has no choice. Because homosexuality and addiction are seen as willful choices of self-destructive behavior, they are considered immoral or sinful.

It is often said that misfortune that befalls sinners is just retribution. The regrettable corollary to such a statement is that "moral behavior" protects from disease. This, in turn, rationalizes denial of risk as well as self-righteous indifference to the plight of others.

This response to the suffering and death of thousands of human beings proved not only absurd, but fateful. For the bigoted beliefs that so few denounced as wrong, for failing to see that AIDS is a plague on everyone's house, for failing to be our brothers' keepers, we are now paying, and we will all pay an increasingly heavy price.

Indeed, biomedical research has shed light on a good many things since 1983. We now know that AIDS is the terminal stage of a viral infection caused by the Human Immunodeficiency Virus, or HIV. We also know that, once acquired, HIV is acquired for life; it is a retrovirus, one that permanently integrates its genetic blueprint into the human genetic material. We know that HIV elicits a complete and effective immune response, but that this response becomes inefficient in the long run because HIV infects and progressively destroys crucial immunoregulatory cells, the T4 cells found lacking in people with AIDS. This virus, therefore, also renders the people it infects infectious to others for the duration of their lives.

We know that HIV is a virus that can destroy two organ systems without which life cannot be sustained: the immune system and the nervous system. We know that it is a virus that causes disease only after a long incubation period and is therefore usually transmitted among unsuspecting, apparently healthy adults, and to their unborn children. We know that most, if not all, people infected with HIV will become fatally ill within eight to fifteen years. We know that this virus, whose spread has now been virtually arrested in the gay community, will—like many other infectious agents—continue to spread mainly among the poor, the naive, the sad, and the ignorant, those who are also fertile ground for the drug culture and its shooting galleries.

We know that, in the United States alone, 1 to 1.5 million people are already infected with HIV and will die of AIDS unless effective treatments are developed and used rapidly. We know that throughout the world five to ten million people are already infected who will quite surely die of AIDS, and we know that the infection is spreading virtually unabated.

On the basis of eight years of experience with thousands of people infected with HIV or AIDS, studied in hospitals and among their families, and on the basis of thorough epidemiological and laboratory studies, we know that HIV is *not* transmitted through casual human contact, but only as the result of circumstances under human control. Thus the presence of AIDS or HIV infection does *not* require a change in human interactions other than the most intimate ones. Those who are not infected can protect themselves through exercising prudence in intimate behavior. For those already infected, modern biological sciences and clinical research offer definite hope, and they are the only hope.

AIDS will cause an enormous burden of disease and suffering everywhere before this century is over. It will be politically and economically destabilizing to the Third World. It will force all Western countries, and this country in particular, to rethink the national agenda and restructure many institutions. It will also force us to defend our value system in the face of considerable fear, enduring prejudice, and economic pressures. This will spawn some ill-conceived schemes purported to protect the public health, which would not only fail to do so but would threaten everyone's civil liberties.

We now stand at the threshold of such a time.

Our national agenda should long ago have included, and from now on *must* include, three components to be promoted at the highest level of national leadership:

1. A program of intensive biomedical and social-sciences research to develop effective treatments and a preventive vaccine.

2. An intensive planning and development effort for a cost-effective, diversified, and humane system of medical care, including drug-rehabilitation treatment. Either the financial burden must be justly spread among public and private resources, or a system of universal national health insurance must be created.

3. An intensive, sustained, and consistent educational effort aimed at slowing the spread of HIV infection, including the enactment of federal anti-discrimination laws for the protection of HIV-infected people and those who care for them. Laws must also be passed for the equal protection of homosexuals, who do not enjoy full civil rights in the United States; fear of AIDS now provides a good excuse for discrimination based on plain old homophobia.

President Reagan's response to the clear recommendations of his own appointed Commission was reluctant and weak. In particular, he failed to act on the cornerstone of the Commission's report—namely, the demand for strong federal anti-discrimination legislation to protect HIV-infected people.

So this is where we stand today: knowing a lot, capable of a lot, but still unprepared to face over the coming years a mounting tide of suffering and death that, in kind and size, will be unlike anything recent centuries have seen. Enduring prejudice, unwarranted fears, and economic pressures can endanger painstakingly earned civil liberties and the very values on which our legal and political systems are built. AIDS, it has been said, endangers rationality, solidarity, and liberty. It does, but only to the extent that we let it do so, only to the extent that our response to the epidemic is irrational, or becomes punitive and coercive.

In view of all of this, what is likely to happen?

On the campaign trail, George Bush promised that his administration would propose federal anti-discrimination legislation to protect HIV-infected people. Whether this becomes a reality, of course, remains to be seen.

Our society will have to learn to live with AIDS. The number of sick will create an enormous burden on all existing medical-care facilities, both those privately and publicly supported. The quality of health care for everyone will suffer. Many will go neglected and even untreated.

The private insurance industry will protect itself by successfully avoiding covering people at risk of AIDS, which will leave many more millions without health insurance. But soon these unprotected people will be our loved ones, our friends, and our children. An uproar of indignation will rise that will amount to an irresistible call for a form of national health insurance.

Thousands of babies will be born with AIDS each year in the United States. Their placement in foster homes or adoptive families will be increasingly difficult. The present rules governing child placement will have to be bent. Gay couples will become acceptable as foster or adoptive parents, and group homes will be created. This is quietly happening already.

As legal protections for people at risk of contacting HIV infection increase and remedies that can delay the onset of AIDS are developed, people will increasingly avail themselves of testing methods and, if infected, will be treated and will refrain from having children. Conventional marriage will have less appeal for them and living arrangements will become more diverse, more often and more openly involving same-sex couples or group living. The rest of society will have to tolerate these arrangements and in fact welcome them, because they will become a necessity in coping with the epidemic and in curbing its spread.

Ensuring the birth of healthy children will cost personal sacrifices: Premarital heterosexual relations will have to be curbed. The health rationale for doing this will be so obvious that moralizing by established religions will become irrelevant. Children will be fewer and more precious. This, in time, will create political pressure for better health-care and educational systems, which we need today and cannot do without in the next century.

A variety of health-care institutions will spring up over the next ten years. They will be too little and too late for many, but still, as we reach the twenty-first century, the present glaring gap between the fee for primary care by a physician and acute care in a hospital will progressively narrow. Home health-care services, day-care hospitals and homes, and long-term residential-care institutions and hospices will be available to the elderly and to all those suffering from chronic diseases. All wealthy nations will move along these lines.

In the Third World, particularly in Africa, AIDS will more than decimate populations and ravage the ranks of the most productive people. This will have profound demographic consequences: The total population will actually decrease in Central Africa. The mass migration to urban centers may stop, because village life will be safer, if poorer. Treatments with costly drugs will not be available in Africa. The gulf between the developed and the developing world, between the rich and the poor, will deepen, at a terrible psychological and political cost.

Western societies will have to face the reality that international cooperation and assistance will be necessary for their own protection. The scope and cost of vaccination programs needed to eradicate AIDS worldwide will make those of smallpox eradication pale in comparison.

The economic burden of national and international AIDS-related programs will force even the wealthiest nations to reexamine their priorities. It is to be hoped that these nations will realize in time for most of their people that, when allied with HIV-infection, poverty, ignorance, and prejudice are possibly the worst threats to democracy, to civilization, and to humankind itself. The resources to deal with AIDS and to save this planet from ecological catastrophe will require a fundamental reallocation of resources away from armaments and toward investments for mere survival.

I believe that such changes and reallocations will occur under irresistible pressures caused by the parallel horrors of AIDS and environmental decay.

Therefore, I see a twenty-first century bearing the scars of terrible wounds, emerging from a period of great suffering and anguish, of political turmoil and economic upheaval, having learned to invest in scientific ingenuity, reaping the fruits of biological revolution, respecting life and human diversity, caring for its children, and protecting human survival and the environment on a global scale. Many battles will have been lost. Life will not be easy. Tensions will still abound, but AIDS will have had a major sobering effect.

AIDS will have been a great equalizer; it will have taught us about our common humanity and about how fragile life and civilization are.

Confidence in this scenario exists in the scientific community because scientists trust the powers of the modern medical sciences. AIDS, they believe, can now be conquered within a time that is very short from the historical perspective. The resources that can be put to the service of science in developed countries—as soon as the political will to do this exists—are sufficient for the task.

The only enduring and justified anguish I and many others have is that technological and scientific victories not be earned at the cost of the ethical framework of civilization. In order to protect our value system, it is important that the voices of all humanists—and I use the word here in its broadest sense—be heard loud and clear. Each of us has to do our share in the fight against AIDS, so that not only our lives but also our culture, our values, our laws, and our ethics can survive it.

Only enlightened compassion and the respect for justice and for human beings, together with the biomedical sciences, can ensure a healthy and honorable way of life for future generations.

# XI.

# The Future of the Humanist Movement

# On the Human Right to Self-Determination

## Rob Tielman

### (Netherlands)

There is a well-known story of a little boy who saved the Netherlands by putting his finger in a leaking dike. Only a foreigner could invent such a story,
for to know Holland is to understand that this land below sea level has survived not by the simple solutions of a single individual, but by centuries of
human cooperation. In this human-made country, people are very much aware
of human freedom and responsibility. So it is not surprising that the Netherlands is the most secularized society in the free world; nor is it surprising that
the humanist movement in the Netherlands is one of the strongest in the world:
half of the Dutch are atheists or agnostics, and 25 percent identify themselves
as humanists. Humanists have had and continue to have an important impact
on Dutch society and its acceptance of the right to self-determination.

The constitution of the Netherlands, ratified in 1982, is one of the most modern in the world. Article 1 formulates the principle of nondiscrimination. It recognizes no exceptions for public institutions, but grants private institutions—a church,
for instance—the freedom to discriminate against women, homosexuals, and
unmarried couples, as they are free to abandon the institution any time they choose
to do so. This example of discrimination management is perfect for illustrating
the implementation of the right to self-determination. In many countries the debate
is over the tension between freedom and equality. Freedom often is interpreted
as the right to discriminate against others, whereas equality implies the right not
to be discriminated against. This dilemma only can be solved by a principle higher
than freedom or equality. This higher principle is self-determination.

Self-determination means the right to give meaning and shape to one's own
life, so long as others are not harmed by one's decisions. If certain adults choose
to be part of an institution that discriminates against them, they should not
try to implement state legislation against the institution unless it is one in which
we all must participate. This implies, of course, that there should be a clear

separation of state and church. Individuals have the right to seek to apply anti-discrimination laws to those public institutions or individuals that are impossible to avoid, such as schools, police, hospitals, and so on. Under the Dutch Constitution, a discriminating institution cannot be subsidized by the government. Those who wish to discriminate are free to do so, as long as they do not harm people who don't want to be part of that institution. In other words, no woman, homosexual, or unmarried couple is forced to be part of a church that discriminates against these groups.

Another illustration of the application of self-determination is the way in which the Constitution guarantees the rights to privacy and to the integrity of the body. No medical treatment can be forcibly applied without the informed consent of the patient, unless lack of treatment would constitute a danger to public health. This makes it illegal to force people to take HIV/AIDS antibody tests, since the virus is transmitted between consenting adults only when partners engage in what they know to be risky practices. No distinction is made between "guilty" and "innocent" victims, because everyone is responsible for the risks he or she takes.

Better than the concepts of freedom and equality, the principle of self-determination is able to settle tensions between individuals and groups. It is understandable that the Dutch developed the principle of self-determination as the leading philosophy behind their constitution. The Netherlands has a long tradition of dealing with religious, ethnic, and other minorities, and most Dutch people are aware that they themselves belong to at least one of these minority groups. If everyone considers himself or herself to be part of a minority, then everyone is more sensitive to defend the rights of other minorities. Awareness of the need for minority protection is a guarantee for a real pluralistic democracy.

Learning from the Dutch experience, what role can the humanist movement play in building a humane and democratic world community? Humanism maintains that human beings are free and responsible to give meaning and shape to their own lives. The force of the humanist movement is not to attack religions, but to create a positive alternative to fundamentalism. Humanism guides people in such a way that they may become as free and responsible as is possible. Humanism isn't vague; it is concrete and applicable in daily life.

The international, national, and local humanist movements do not only reflect upon ethical principles; they implement those principles in daily life in a nondogmatic way. In the Netherlands we educate young people in humanist philosophies and life-styles. We counsel people as they try to create their own lives and find solutions to the problems with which they are confronted. We present our ideas to the general public through the media. We are responsible for the training of humanist professionals. We have created bridges between the humanist movement and other movements directed toward self-determination, such as the women's, peace, gay and lesbian, human rights, and environmental movements. We are developing coalitions that work against the attacks of fundamentalists, and for the separation of state and church. The humanist movement is a source of inspiration; it stimulates the awareness that we are all responsible for improving our own quality of life and that of all other human beings by giving meaning to life and creating a more humane world.

At times we all feel like the little boy with his finger in the dike, trying to save our own world using the limited resources we have. But it is important to remember that we are not isolated or completely dependent upon higher authorities. We all have the capacity to give meaning and shape to our own lives, to cooperate with other responsible human beings, and, by doing so, to develop a world community in which everyone will find life worth living.

# Does Humanism Have a Future?

## Levi Fragell

### (Norway)

On a flight to New York last year I was seated beside a "typical" modern, professional young man. He sat skimming through one magazine after another about computers, then proceeded to *Time, Newsweek,* the *New Yorker,* and the *Economist.*

In the meantime I had opened my issue of the American *Humanist* magazine, and my neighbor sent curious glances my way.

"I've never seen that one before," he said.

"Haven't you?" I asked. "This is published by the American Humanist Association."

"I don't know very much about the humanists," my fellow traveler said. "You know, in the United States there are so many different groups."

"You may have heard of Corliss Lamont," I offered, "the humanist philosopher from New York."

"I think I've heard his name . . ."

"How about Paul Kurtz? He is often on television talking about paranormal phenomena."

"Something about astrology? Sorry, I've been in Europe since September."

"Bertrand Russell was a humanist," I said. This was my last card.

"Really? I wrote a thesis on Bertrand Russell," said the computer-whiz, "but I never knew that."

I don't tell this story because it is funny, but because it is sad.

The young man beside me was not a Christian. His father was a Presbyterian and his mother a Catholic, but he himself had no religion.

He might have been a humanist, but he wouldn't know. He might even have become a member of one of the humanist groups, but he didn't know that we existed.

And there are millions of people in exactly the same position.

The twentieth century is the first period in history when a significant number of people have called themselves "nonreligious." The *World Christian Encyclopaedia* states that in 1900 only 0.2 percent of the world's population was nonreligious, whereas by 1975 the percentage had risen to twenty.

This may be one of the most important cultural and social changes of our time (though the figure has climbed in part because entire nations now consider themselves "atheist"). No one can deny that only parts of the European and American populations today hold religious beliefs, or that the Western world a hundred years ago was almost completely Christian.

Such extensive changes in values and attitudes during just a couple of generations have caused turbulence and confusion, affecting people's personal lives, family traditions, ethical attitudes, and existential emotions. In the search for a new basis many have turned to political dogmatism, paranormal escapism, and nihilistic hedonism.

Where does humanism stand in this picture?

Humanism, which introduced itself as The Alternative more than fifty years ago, is at the close of this century almost nonexistent in the world arena. The only nation in the world where as much as 1 percent of the population are organized humanists is Norway, a very small country on the outskirts of civilization.

Many people call themselves humanists without being active members of a humanist organization. But passive sympathy does not write books, change laws, create alternative ceremonies, or offer counseling.

In 1965, when UNESCO published a book on the life-stances of the world, the editor included a chapter on modern humanism, written by the honorable British humanist Harold Blackham. Would this have been done today? I doubt it. Organized humanism at the end of the twentieth century is struggling for survival. This is an unpleasant truth, but we must face it—and we must do something about it.

In my younger days I owned a small public-relations agency, marketing products and services. Once I was asked to promote a new product in the Norwegian market, a combination vacuum cleaner–carpet beater. The problem was, it could not be called a vacuum cleaner—no one would buy a vacuum cleaner like that. And it could not be called a carpet beater—who needed a carpet beater with such inappropriate dimensions?

The product was excellent—useful and time-saving—and was sold by a company of the best reputation. But because the producer was not able to tell us exactly what it was, it sold close to nothing in Norway and soon vanished from the market.

The international failure of humanism is due to more than one factor, but beyond doubt a major problem is that most national humanist organizations have failed to give humanism a family name. It is not a religion and it is not a philosophy. It may be a little bit of both, but what *is* it?

Many humanists get the creeps when I mention that humanist organizations are limited by the same laws of communication as are the producers of household appliances. The idea of using commercial persuasive techniques to promote humanism is rather disgusting to me. But humanists don't use any techniques at all. They just speak to one another—a little bit louder than before, I must admit, but that is only because age has reduced their hearing abilities.

A couple of years ago, the International Humanist and Ethical Union appointed me the leader of their Committee for Development and Growth. I asked,"What are we to develop and grow—a religion, a philosophy, a world-view, a moral conviction?"

Paul Kurtz has taken this challenge seriously and invented a new expression: *eupraxophy.* Time will tell whether this word will be accepted and used.

The British Humanist Association has also given this basic policy question thorough consideration, with Harry Stopes-Roe as the driving force. He has come up with the expression *life-stance,* which is gaining increasing recognition in the United Kingdom. I believe that during the past couple of years this term has been adopted to some extent in humanist circles in the United States, as well as in other English-speaking countries.

But even worse than the family-name confusion is that most humanists don't even use the first name properly.

A rather substantial number of members of the International Humanist and Ethical Union do not call themselves humanists at all, but freethinkers, rationalists, atheists, or Unitarians. And those who use the term *humanist* often add the flourish of an adjective such as *secular, ethical, naturalistic, scientific,* or *religious.* As a life-stance, humanism should be written with eight letters, and nothing more.

A movement without an identity isn't really a movement, and is not at all a *cohesive* movement.

In 1979 I was asked by the board of IHEU to write a program for membership recruitment. At that time I was executive director of the Norwegian Humanist Association, which had raised its membership from 1,500 in 1976—when we started our recruitment activities—to 5,000 in 1979. I was told that such a rapid growth had never been heard of in the IHEU. Since then, my program has been distributed all over the world; a lot of discussions have been taking place, working parties have been arranged, and local schemes have been worked out. But as far as I know, the Norwegian Humanist Association is the only humanist organization that has increased its membership remarkably since 1979. We thought that we might have reached the roof with our 5,000 members; but today the membership is 35,000, and we continue to grow steadily, gaining 3,000 new members each year.

The population of Norway is 4 million; the population of the United States is 250 million. Given the same growth rate, the United States by now would have had 2.5 million organized humanists—and 250,000 new members a year.

I do not wish to discourage the American humanists, but, on the contrary, to point out the potential of humanist organizations. Of course there are enormous differences between our countries, but we are living in the same world, and this world is getting smaller and more homogeneous all the time.

Why haven't the national humanist organizations grown during the past few years, even though they have realized the need for growth and discussed strategies for achieving it?

There are three reasons.

First, there is something basically wrong with the international identity of humanism, including that it lacks a generally accepted, common name and has not made clear what it is—a religion, a philosophy, or a life-stance.

Second, the discussions about growth still circulate around the question: Is growth really that important? Isn't quality more important than quantity? Let me answer that question: Of course quality is more important than quantity. But there is nothing wrong with the quality of humanism. There *is* something wrong with the quantity.

We don't recruit new members by improving humanism. History gives no evidence to the assumption that the best life-stances automatically attract very many people, and it clearly proves that the most inhuman, suppressive, inconsistent, and unreasonable organizations can penetrate and dominate whole continents.

Third, even extensive studying of recruitment strategies has not led to actual growth because studies and discussions do not recruit a single person.

Most humanist leaders complain that it is difficult—almost impossible—to get new people involved.

The truth is that it is not very difficult at all. I don't know one humanist who wouldn't be able to provide one new member during one day's efforts. Most of us would do it within an hour, and quite a few would do it with a five-minute telephone call.

The real problem is that humanists are not willing to give active recruitment their personal priority, not even for one hour of their lives, not to speak of a full day. They want to write articles, lecture, go to meetings, read books. Unlike members of other organizations—such as those for religion, politics, civil rights, nature preservation, feminism, and peace—humanists find it unsuitable to hand out leaflets on the street-corners. Arranging a demonstration at the neighborhood shopping center would be more disgraceful than being caught shoplifting in the same place.

The future of organized humanism is not a question of ideology. It is a question of strategy.

# Overcoming Humanism's Weaknesses

## Corliss Lamont

### (United States)

If the twenty-first century is to be a proper improvement on the twentieth century, humanism must grow in strength and influence; for a stronger and more influential humanism will help to build a better and more peaceful world community. Two main points seem to be weakening the humanist movement today.

The first is that humanist organizations, humanist individuals, and the humanist movement in general are tending to neglect basic humanist principles by stressing the ethical, social, economic, and international activities of humanism. We seem to be neglecting the basic humanist principles of rejecting the supernatural, denial of belief in God and immortality, and the teaching of science, the scientific method, and reason as the cues to joyful living.

We must be vocal in our rejection of religious faith in divine guidance and in our support of reason and the scientific method for the solutions to human problems. I suspect that the main reasons for these omissions are a hesitation to offend religious people, and a desire to maintain general "respectability." The result is to turn humanism into a mere ethical philosophy. Humanism becomes humanitarianism.

Especially important is the denial of immortality. Way back in 1935 I wrote a book entitled *The Illusion of Immortality*. I became interested in this question when I was still in college, in the early 1920s, primarily because my father's sister was convinced that she was a spiritualist, and she kept bringing me messages from the "beyond." On my twenty-first birthday, my dead cousin Joe supposedly sent me a poem. I shall always remember its profound first line: "Corliss, thou art a man today." I was skeptical of all this business and decided I must determine whether or not there was personal survival after death. I soon concluded that there was not.

It is important to note that humanist neglect of basic principles is taking place in countries other than the United States. For instance, the noted Indian humanist, V. M. Tarkunde, has written, "I would define humanism as consisting of a philosophy and an attitude of mind which gives primacy to men and women as individuals and recognizes their right to live in freedom and dignity." Tarkunde's article proceeds in this same general vein, as do many others currently being written by prominent humanists. This kind of definition summarizes in an ethical sense what humanism stands for; but it is seriously deficient because it makes no mention whatsoever of humanism's opposition to religious supernaturalism.

All of the other fine causes that proceed under humanist auspices are extremely important and, in general, extremely well done. But we must stress in equal measure the teaching of science and the rejection of the supernatural.

During the Reagan years we learned that our president was making appointments and decisions according to his astrological forecast. It is scandalous that a president of the United States, the alleged leader of our people, should be relying on a mad supernatural thing like astrology. And yet there are probably at least two million believers in astrology in the United States.

This is why it is so important to teach the scientific method as a humanist doctrine. We have our work cut out for us in this regard.

The second problem plaguing today's humanist movement is that the American people are not at all well educated as to the meaning of humanism— which leads me to comment on the ongoing controversy within the humanist ranks as to whether naturalistic humanism is a philosophy or a religion.

Ever since I joined the American Humanist Association I have been arguing about this matter, and have firmly upheld the position that humanism is a philosophy or a way of life. In 1935 I wrote an article entitled "The Racket of Religious Redefinition," in which I noted that people can make anything a religion if they consider it their greatest life commitment, be it sex, sports, music, or poetry. The brilliant American philosopher Morris Cohen once said, "The real religion of the American people is baseball." Well, why not?

We must stop this business of wrangling over the semantic meaning of these terms; at the age of eighty-six, I have fought this battle for fifty years. I am tired of it. Those who wish to call themselves religious humanists may freely do so; but I and others will call humanism a philosophy. By dropping this whole irritating matter we shall save a lot of time and energy that could be better spent on other humanist issues and work. Religious humanists and nonreligious humanists cooperate on other matters and will continue to do so in the future; so let us just agree to disagree on this small point, accept everyone into our compassionate arms, and try to further this great system of thinking.

Finally, we must work toward a new global ethics based frankly on the humanist view that tells all humanity that we must center our endeavors in the here and now and not bind ethical conduct to the hope of immortality and a providential god. We are concerned with life before death, not after death.

All hail to humanist progress in the twenty-first century!

# Of Humanism and Goo

## William F. Schulz

### (United States)

The connections between Unitarian Universalism and humanism run long and deep. Indeed, the 1933 Humanist Manifesto, so critical to the formation of contemporary humanism in the United States, was largely the creation of Unitarian ministers like Edwin Wilson and Raymond Bragg.

The skepticism captured so eloquently in that Manifesto has been an integral part of the Unitarian Universalist vocabulary for more than fifty years. Leon Birkhead, for example, who signed the Manifesto when he was the minister of a Unitarian Universalist church in Kansas City, Missouri, once attended a prayer meeting called by the orthodox ministers of that city to petition God to alleviate a terrible drought that was plaguing the midwestern states. The Reverend Mr. Birkhead had thought to bring with him one article that his orthodox colleagues had forgotten: an umbrella. "I take it I am the only member of the clergy," he told a reporter, "who has any faith."

And so, while not all Unitarian Universalists would call themselves humanists, the humanist commitments to reason and science, to the promotion of universal peace and human rights, have shaped latter-day Unitarian Universalism more decisively than any other philosophy or school of thought.

But how do we create far more humanists in the world than we have today? In North America the number of people who explicitly identify themselves as humanists is infinitesimal. I reject the common claim that, steeped as it is in a religious heritage, the United States is not fertile ground for a nontheistic faith. A recent Gallup Poll indicated that 92 percent of the American people believe in God; but that means that well over 20 million people say they do not. This number is a far cry from the number of Americans affiliated with a humanist organization or with the Unitarian Universalist Association (UUA).

Why, then, the dearth of people on this continent—for neither Canada nor Mexico are hotbeds of humanism either—willing to identify themselves explicitly with our perspective?

It has something to do with the observation made by the poet Wallace Stevens when he said, "The truth, my friend. Ah, yes, the truth depends upon a walk around a lake."

One of the differences between religion and science is the posture that each takes toward truth. For science, the discovery of that which is true about the world is the raison d'etre for all of its endeavor. Scientists may well debate their moral responsibility regarding the way in which the truth they obtain is applied, but it is the truth itself that claims their first fealty.

Religion, on the other hand, while not indifferent to truth, cares for it only as a vehicle to something more, to something like Salvation or Enlightenment. Religion's first job is not to disclose the truth but rather to inspire us and sustain us in the face of life's agony and complexity. Jesus said, "I am the Way, the Truth, and the Life," but notice that he claimed *first* to be the Way.

This distinction corresponds roughly to one of my favorite sociological axioms, namely, that the world can be divided between the partisans of prickle and the partisans of goo. The partisans of prickle are the hard-headed ones among us, the pragmatists, realists, and rationalists, who snarl at daffodils and snicker at kittens. The partisans of goo, on the other hand, are our fuzzy-headed mystics and befuddled poets for whom a balanced checkbook is the mark of a miracle.

Throughout its history, humanism has cast its lot primarily with the partisans of prickle. Without delving into the complex question as to whether or not humanism is a form of religion, I would say that on balance humanism has shown itself to be more sympathetic to science and its search for truth than to religion and its quest for inspiration.

In part this is because so much foolishness and hatred have been rent upon the world in the name of religion. So much foolishness that Erasmus could report having been shown by a priest a vial allegedly containing milk from the left breast of the *Virgin* Mary. So much hatred that the early church found itself in need of a saint—Saint Praxedes—whose unique calling was to mop up the blood of the Christian martyrs once they had lost their heads.

Humanism has quite rightly sought to disassociate itself from such antics and in their place to introduce a new way of being in the world, a way in which the human and the natural become the focus of true respect and glory, a way in which a global ethics takes precedence over parochial ones, a way in which truth is more valued than fantasy.

All of these are admirable goals, and humanism has been relentless in their pursuit. They are goals that wide numbers of people share. Why then have so few identified themselves as humanists? I suggest that it is in good measure because humanism has a tendency to forget that prickles alone are not enough to satisfy the human heart and that not all gooery is foolishness.

Our humanist blind spot has been not unlike that of the great mathematician, Charles Babbage. Upon reading Alfred, Lord Tennyson's poem, "A Vision of Sin" for the first time, Babbage wrote the poet as follows:

Dear Sir: In your otherwise splendid poem there is a line which reads, "Every moment dies a man/every moment one is born." It must be obvious that if this were true the population of the world would be at a standstill when in fact the rate of birth is slightly in excess of that of death. I suggest therefore that in the next edition of your poem, you have it read: "Every moment dies a man/Every moment 1 1/6th is born." Strictly speaking, this is still not correct. The actual number is a decimal so long I cannot get it into a line but I believe that 1 1/6th is accurate enough for poetry.

But the fact is that most of human life—or at least human life as most humans actually live it—is not based on close calculation and apodictic certainty, but on things like poetry, metaphor, intuition, speculation, ritual, hunches, and, yes, faith.

Indeed, a phenomenological approach to science itself reveals that science too is indebted to metaphor, intuition, and faith just as surely—if in a different context—as is religion. Our knowledge of the brain confirms that fully half of that remarkable instrument is dedicated to an appreciation of the aesthetic, affective, nonlinear elements of creation.

It may well be true that there simply are no definitive answers to life's most pressing questions—questions like, "Why is there something rather than nothing?" "Is there meaning to life?" "Why do bad things happen to good people?" "Why must I and all I love perish from the earth?" There may well be no definitive answers, and the reasonable thing may be to dismiss the questions as meaningless; but the fact is that most of us *live* those questions every day of our lives. It is a rare person who would use his or her last breath on earth as the Jesuit grammarian Dominique Bouhours did when, turning to his friends gathered round, he said, "I am about to—or, I am going to—die; either expression is grammatically correct."

We do not lead our daily lives by the strict rules of logic. We lead them by hunches and intuition, imagination, and faith. Thus humanism has two options: Either it can rail against this fundamental fact and take as its calling the encouragement of a more rational, linear, prickly mind set among the citizens of the world, or it can recognize that, valuable as rationalism is to avoid vials of virgin's milk and the blood of martyrs, the insights of the rational must be supplemented and extended by a touch of goo, by majesty and metaphor, art, poetry, and imagination. When Van Gogh was asked why he painted so many self-portraits, he replied, "Because I am seeking a deeper resemblance than the photograph."

The poet Ntosake Shange, author of *for colored girls who have considered suicide/when the rainbow is enuf,* tells of a very simple experience that transformed her life: "I was driving home after a class one day, when suddenly I saw a huge rainbow over Oakland. I realized that we [black women] could survive if we decide that we have as much right and as much purpose for being here as the air and the mountains do."[1]

All the philosophical arguments for human rights, important as they are to make, cannot possibly touch as many hearts or change as many minds as

Shange's simple image can.

But that's not all, for I contend that a cultivated imagination is itself a moral imperative; for without it how can we possibly muster the moral fervor to break out of the cocoons of our parochialism and envision a global ethics?

Not a single one of us has ever experienced a *true* world community. Globalism requires that we imagine one—not just think about it, but allow its implications and its flavors, its meaning and its marvel to course over us. To reject the root metaphor that the stranger is an enemy requires the boldest leap of faith; it requires that we remember that at one time we too were strangers in the land of Egypt. If we can remember that, imagine that, *feel* that deep in our hearts, then a world community is within our reach; for then and only then, says the novelist Cynthia Ozick, "Those who have no pain can imagine [what it is to be like] those who suffer. Those at the center can imagine those outside. The strong can imagine what it is to be weak. And we strangers can imagine that the hearts of other strangers are familiar ones."[2]

I believe that one reason humanism has remained of modest size is because it has tended to dismiss as unintelligible those urgent existential questions that have no easy answers; it has tended to shy away from affect and feeling for fear that they are little more than masks of nonsense; and it has neglected ritual and celebration in favor of the utilitarian and pragmatic.

Mine is no call for mysticism or for magic, but for a humanism with a poetic touch, for a humanism with a heart. Mine is a call to recognize that for the vast majority of the world, awe is a more compelling passion than argument. I want us to put wonder, mystery, passion, and poetry at the service of a resplendent humanism. Richard Selzer, a surgeon, writes:

> I stand by the bed where a young woman lies. Her face is postoperative, her mouth twisted in palsy, clownish. The surgeon had followed with religious fervor the curve of her flesh; I promise you that. Nonetheless, to remove the tumor in her cheek, I had had to cut the little nerve. Her young husband is in the room and together they seem to dwell in the evening lamplight, isolated from me, private. Who are they, I ask myself, he and this wry-mouth I have made who gaze at and touch each other so lovingly, greedily.
>
> The young woman speaks. "Will my mouth always be like this?" she asks. "Yes," I say. "It is because the nerve was cut." The young woman nods and is silent. But the young man speaks. "I like it," he says. "It is kind of cute."
>
> All at once I know who he is. I understand and I lower my gaze. One is not bold in an encounter with a god. Unmindful of my presence, he bends to kiss her crooked mouth and I am so close I can see how he twists his own lips to accommodate to hers, to show her that their kiss still works.
>
> I remember that the gods appeared in ancient Greece as mortals and I bow my head and let the wonder in.[3]

In the last analysis my plea is very simple. I believe that the petty little orthodoxies of the world have no monopoly on passion or wonder, affect or inspiration. In the last analysis my plea is very simple: for a humanism that lets the wonder in; for a humanism that finds even in a crooked mouth the evidence of glory.

## Notes

1. Quoted in Carol Christ, *Diving Deep and Surfacing* (Boston, Mass.: Beacon Press, 1980), p. 99.
2. Cynthia Ozick, "The Moral Necessity of Metaphor," *Harper's,* May 1987, p. 68.
3. Richard Selzer, *Mortal Lessons* (New York: Simon & Schuster, 1976).

# Summation of the
# Tenth World Humanist Congress

## Howard B. Radest
### (United States)

Each of us attends a different congress even while we join to share our ideals and commitments. So, too, with our meetings in Buffalo during a very hot and dry summer week in 1988. As I've tried to do at other congresses, I look for a metaphor that catches my experience. Reflecting on it, this congress might be recalled as a circus. So much went on in so many places all at once—speeches, discussion groups, dinners, classes of the Humanist Institute, meetings of the Humanist Academy, of *Free Inquiry,* of the American Ethical Union, of the Canadian Humanist Association, of the North American Committee for Humanism, of the International Association of Counselors, Leaders, and Educators. The hustle and bustle was certainly entertaining, yet all of it just could not be taken in by any one of us. Or I think of the congress as a bazaar, where humanists from more than forty countries showed their wares and sampled the wares of others. Above all, this congress, like all the others, was a place for talk—some of it exciting, much of it worthwhile, and all of it serious.

I must complain of our seriousness. Too easily, we humanists turn the serious into the ponderous and miss the delicious quality of the human comedy. A part of me regretted the absence of some modern-day Aristophanes or Erasmus or Rabelais. True, Steve Allen shared his comedic genius with us and Roger Greeley delivered the incisive satire of Robert Ingersoll. But these experiences and others like them—biographies of humanist hereos and heroines for example—were set aside at formal dinners, thus confirming our sobriety by showing that we separate entertainment from reality and ceremony from the important stuff of humanist life. The eighteenth century in all its radical puritanism is still very much with us.

I heard the voices of absent friends. Too few of us recalled Jaap Van Praag of Holland, the founding chair of the IHEU who served us so well for more than twenty years. Sidney Scheuer of the United States and Lucien DeConinck of Belgium were gone from among us. Harold Blackham of England could not attend, nor could Justice Tarkunde of India. I realized how much older we have grown since our founding congress in Amsterdam in 1952. I became aware, deeply aware, that in the years to come the list of those absent will be longer—and our memories will be dimmed unless we find a way to keep memory alive, to keep our history vivid.

There were striking moments: the music of the Buffalo Philharmonic on the opening day, the passionate call for more "people of color" by William Jones. I missed the voices of the young and the noises of children. Yes, we spoke of families, but if we mean it, then future Congresses—Brussels in 1990 and Amsterdam in 1992—should provide opportunity and place for these. Humanist gatherings cannot merely be occasions where we hear and argue the prose of men and women speaking a familiar script.

And we were reminded of our causes; most of all, of the urgent need to defend human rights everywhere. Organized by the IHEU Commissoner for Human Rights and his team of volunteers—present and active in Buffalo—the work goes on in the East and in the West, at the United Nations and the Council of Europe, in Geneva and Paris and New York. Subtle and not so subtle human-rights violations occur in schools and courts and neighborhoods. Discrimination against those with different lifestyles grows more serious. The rights of conscience are by no means secured anywhere.

Whenever humanists gather, there is passionate talk, and this congress was no exception; the passions were, as usual, abundant, giving lie to the notion that humanists are unemotional, and that rationality must leave us cold. Two classical themes of humanist debate tell the story, for me, and for all our effort to look forward: the place of religion and the place of science.

A certain tone of stridency set the mood, joined to a delusional certainty of definition. So, listening carefully, I heard partisans pro and con claim that "Religion is . . . " and then complete the sentence variously with terms like "necessary," "benificent," "human," or "superstitious," "false," "authoritarian," and so on. But in our anxiety to make points against an opponent we simply did not capture the richness and complexity of human experience; nor could we finally put to rest the question of whether humanism is or is not a religion. Clearly, for some it is and for some it is not, and the debate, no matter how passionate the humanist believer or nonbeliever, will not be resolved. The attempt to legislate an answer cannot help but fail, and the effort to impose one cannot help but destroy.

To be sure, there are real differences among us and real oppositions out there. Ironically, just as we were meeting with our thousand-plus participants, many thousands were meeting just a few miles away at a Billy Graham Crusade. But he, at least, offers a relatively subdued and humane evangelical Christianity. To his right are angrier, more vicious, and less charitable others. Fundamentalism is visible everywhere, bringing with it a subversion of democratic freedoms, of toleration, and of community. The joining of politics and religion is surely a danger to human dignity and even to life itself, whether in the Middle East, the United States, Ireland, Iran, or India. But that calls for a much more refined analysis and strategy from us, and it does not help at all when humanists, like their neighbors, yield to the fundamentalist temptation.

That temptation, the mood revealed in our oversimplifications of religious questions, showed itself too in the attempt to legislate what science is, as if science were one thing, entire and whole. This ignorance of what scientists are up to when doing science in all its complexity leads much too quickly to humanist idolatry. And I could not help but recall that Einstein spoke of *heilige curiöstitat,* and Spinoza of the *amor intellecus dei,* and that a modern critic, Jacques Barzun, rightly called science "the glorious entertainment." In short, science is not simply a pathway to power, and not simply the way to some single "truth." Its glory is in its openness, in the invitation to join in the search, the discovery, the insight, and in making as objective as possible the reasons for holding a particular truth. Fortunately, science also has its own myths, its own story-telling capacity for interpreting the world and all that is in it. For humanists, the better part would be to appreciate the sciences as well as to understand them. And we are most misguided when we try to turn the sciences into "science" and then into a counter-ideology. Yet, that is the attempt among us. At the same time, too many of us are simply ignorant of what has developed in the sciences since the eighteenth century. And, ironically, there are humanists who, despite our traditions, now reject science by confusing it with the horrors of an abused technology.

The debate about religion and science might be trivial—after all, humanists engage in many debates where the moves are almost as predictable and as programmed as a classical ballet—but did it not reveal symptoms most serious? We are not immune to the pressures of a world that wants quick answers, un-equivocal solutions to hard problems, and simplified rallying cries. We all enjoy the call to battle and we all are comforted when we have a known enemy. That is the psychological and political background for the temptation to erect our own humanist fundamentalism, to rush to the joys of ideological warfare, and to mask authoritarian motives with the claim of one truth, one faith.

Countervailing voices were heard at the congress, to be sure, but for me the important and useful tone was not to be found so much in direct refutation but in calls for a legitimate humanist pluralism and for the importance of invit-ing and hearing the many voices of humanism; so too the need to invite to humanism the poet's voice and the musician's voice, and the voice of the genera-tions young and not so young to which we scarcely attend. The voices of women were much more audible in 1988 than in 1968 or 1952, and yet it was not enough. The voices of people of color from the many places in the world that we hardly know still are not heard among us. Voices from the worlds of politics and business and labor have yet to join with those from the academy, the clinic, the professions. In this regard, it was good that for the first time there were voices from the Soviet Union and from China. But we need more, and we need to do more.

Our announced theme was "Humanism in the Twenty-First Century." And we no doubt made a start in that direction—looking anew at problems of aging and of medicine and of education, at political complexities particularly problematic for the democratic spirit, at the need to direct humanism toward a richer and more rounded way of life or life-style (or, for some, religion), and at the need for greater clarity and vigor in knowing what humanism is and what it can achieve for persons and communities. But it was only a start; ironically and inevitably, each congress is only a start.

If we are to move toward the twenty-first century, then we must learn to orchestrate much more effectively than we have yet learned to do the riches and varieties of human experience. Surely, humanists begin with the notion that "nothing human is alien to me." That announces a commitment to orchestration as the mission of humanism. How shall we bring together the fascinating diversity of human beings in community while avoiding uncritical sentimentality on the one side and the idoltry of fundamentalism on the other?

For a humanist's biography, embedding humanism in personal life and as a way of living remains a perennial task. Not far behind is making that way of living tangible in action, in the conduct of life, as a message to others of humanism's rewards and possibilities. There can be no substitute for the efforts and energies of the individual humanist. We must do it ourselves, *for* ourselves, or it will not be done. Beyond the benefit to our own lives, we thus exhibit the legitimacy and verify the validity of humanism by repeated and multiple examples. Or, to put it another way, we will win the humanist argument by what we do and demonstrate, not just by how we formulate propositions.

That said, we still need to be far more responsible to reason and intellect than we have been. It is sad, indeed, that a movement born in the Enlightenment by and large is still trapped in outdated and impoverished scientific ideas, and has not contributed significantly enough to the evolution of democratic society in a corporate culture. With the ending of each congress, we are clearer than before about the task ahead, and this tenth congress was no exception. As humanists, we cannot turn our backs on reason, freedom, or community. But, we are now some two-hundred years beyond the American and French revolutions. In order to bring humanism into the twenty-first century, we still need to confess our roots in the eighteenth; but we must acknowledge at the same time the need to reconstruct its values. The Tenth Humanist World Congress was, if nothing else, a revelation of that agenda.

# A Declaration of Interdependence:
# A New Global Ethics

## Preamble

There is a compelling need to define and proclaim a new global ethics for humankind.

It is dramatically clear today that our earth is made up of interdependent nation-states and that whatever happens on one part of the planet affects all the rest. Whenever human rights are violated, all of humanity suffers. The basic premise of this global ethics is that each of us has a stake in developing a universal moral awareness, each of us has a responsibility to the world community at large.

## I. The Need for a Global Moral Consensus

We who endorse this declaration begin with the conviction that every human person is equal in dignity and value. We wish to encourage the development of free, democratic, and pluralistic institutions that promise individuals opportunities to pursue their personal goals, express their talents, and realize their unique visions of a humane life.

We wish to maximize human freedom, the autonomy of the individual, and personal creativity. We believe in mitigating human suffering and in ensuring positive social conditions so that all people will have the opportunity to achieve happiness and the fullness of life. We do not defend unbridled license; rather, we encourage moral growth and the highest reaches of human discovery and achievement.

The world is divided into diverse ethnic and national communities; each of us has specific moral obligations incumbent on his or her role in these communities. There are, however, basic moral decencies that are commonly recognized as binding in virtually all civilized communities of the world. These ethical principles embody the collective heritage of humankind. They have been tested in the crucible of human experience by their consequences for human good. They include the need to be truthful; to keep our promises; to be sincere, honest, loyal, and dependable; to act with good will; to forbear from injuring other persons or their property; to be beneficent, compassionate, and fair; to show gratitude; to be just, tolerant, and cooperative; and to use peaceful methods to negotiate differences.

These ethical principles have all too often been applied selectively only to the members of a cohesive group—whether tribal, ethnic, national, racial, or religious. Moreover, competition among groups has often engendered animosity and hatred. *It is time that we clearly enunciate these ethical principles so that they may be extended toward all members of the human family living on this planet.*

The great religions of the past have often preached universal brotherhood. Unfortunately, intolerant or divisive faiths have made this moral ideal almost impossible to implement. Narrow parochial doctrines of salvation have made it difficult for those outside particular denominations to be fully entitled to moral consideration from those within. Secular political ideologies have likewise asserted the universality of their ideals, yet they have often resorted to force to impose their views on those who differ with them.

In recent centuries nation-states have emerged, each a law unto itself, each exercising ultimate sovereignty over those living within their defined territorial boundaries. For a long time national self-determination was considered progressive, for it liberated ethnic groups from foreign domination. With the decline of colonialism, new countries have come into being—there are now more than 150 nation-states. National governments can play constructive roles in maintaining a system of law and order and can encourage economic prosperity and cultural development within their own boundaries. They can help to achieve conditions of harmony and enrichment for the people living under their jurisdiction.

Regrettably, however, many nation-states have violated the rights of their citizens, or they have resorted to violence to achieve their national purposes: The bloody wars of history demonstrate that the "rule of the jungle" often prevails on national and international levels. For there does not as yet exist a body of world law, universally recognized and respected by all countries of the globe and supported by the force of law on a transnational level.

Economic rivalries between nation-states, regional blocs, and multinational corporations dominate the world scene. National budgets, taxation, trade, commerce, and fiscal and economic-development policies are made in haughty isolation, without concern for their effect on the global community.

Fortunately, there have been efforts at economic and political regional cooperation. There have been pacts and treaties between countries and regions. Rules of civilized behavior have emerged to govern these interactions, recognizing mutual interests. Unfortunately, they do not go far enough. The negative consequences of nationalistic chauvinism have been vividly demonstrated: Balance-of-power politics and economic exploitation, racial strife and religious bigotry, hatred and violence.

There is an urgent need to develop new political, economic, cultural, and social institutions that will make possible the peaceful coexistence and cooperation of the various regions of the globe. Before this can be fully achieved, however, it is essential that we reach a genuine worldwide ethical consensus that recognizes our responsibilities and duties to the world community.

## II. Human Rights

The beginnings of a new global ethics are now evident. Universal declarations of human rights enunciate the rights of *all* human beings. We strongly support these declarations. We hereby reaffirm the following:

1. All persons are born equal in dignity and value.

2. All persons are entitled to rights and freedoms without discrimination based upon sex, race, language, religion, politics, creed, national or social origin, property, or birth.

3. The right to personal security and self-protection.

4. The fundamental right to personal liberty. This includes: (*a*) freedom from involuntary servitude or slavery, (*b*) freedom from harassment, (*c*) freedom of thought and conscience, (*d*) freedom of speech and expression, and (*e*) moral freedom to express one's values and pursue one's lifestyle so long as it does not harm others or prevent others from exercising their rights.

5. The right to privacy, which means that the rights of others should be respected regarding: (*a*) confidentiality, (*b*) the control of one's own body, (*c*) sexual preference and orientation, (*d*) life-stance, (*e*) reproductive freedom, (*f*) birth control, (*g*) health care based on informed consent, and (*h*) the desire to die with dignity.

6. The right to intellectual and cultural freedom, including (*a*) the freedom to inquire and to engage in research, (*b*) the right to adequate education, (*c*) the right to cultural enrichment, and (*d*) the right to publish and express one's views.

7. The right to adequate health care.

8. Freedom from want, which means that society should guarantee (*a*) the right to work, (*b*) the satisfaction of basic needs when individuals are unable to provide for themselves, (*c*) care for the elderly, (*d*) care for the handicapped, and (*e*) the right to adequate leisure and relaxation.

9. Economic freedom, including (*a*) the right to own property, (*b*) the right to organize, and (*c*) protection from fraud.

10. Moral equality, which entails equal opportunity and equal access.

11. Equal protection under the law, which is vital in a free society: (*a*) the right to a fair trial, (*b*) the right to protection from arbitrary arrest or unusual punishment, and (*c*) the right to humane treatment.

12. The right to democratic participation in government, which includes a full range of civil liberties: (*a*) the right to vote, (*b*) the legal right of opposition,

(*c*) the right of assembly and association, and (*d*) the right to hold religious beliefs or not to hold such beliefs.

13. The rights of marriage and the family: (*a*) the right to marry or cohabit, (*b*) the right to divorce, (*c*) family planning, (*d*) the right to bear and raise children, and (*e*) child care.

14. The right of children to be protected from abuse and physical or cultural deprivation.


## III. Human Responsibilities

Concomitant with the recognition of universal rights is the obligation of individuals to develop moral responsibilities. Individuals have responsibilities to themselves—to their health care, their economic well-being, and their intellectual and moral growth. A person has a basic duty to become all that he or she is capable of being, to fully realize his or her talents and capabilities.

Individuals also have responsibilities to others: Parents have the responsibility to bring up their children and provide them with food, shelter, love, education, and cultural enrichment. Children have concomitant duties to discharge in regard to their parents, to love, honor, and support them, and to help care for them when they are sick or elderly. Two individuals who have freely entered into marriage or cohabitation have duties to each other so long as the relationship is viable. Moral devotion does not depend solely on blood-ties, but extends to those with whom one has developed ties of friendship. Similarly, we also have moral responsibilities to others in the smaller communities in which we have everyday relationships: teacher and student, shopkeeper and customer, doctor and patient, factory worker and consumer, and so on. There are also duties and obligations that we as citizens have to the towns and nation-states in which we live and work.

Last but not least is the need to recognize that each of us has responsibilities to the world community, for each of us is (*a*) a member of the human species, (*b*) a resident of the planet earth, and (*c*) an integral part of the world community.

It would be appropriate for the citizens of each nation or region of the world to add the following affirmation to their pledges of loyalty:

> I pledge allegiance to the world community, of which we are all a part. I recognize that all persons are equal in dignity and value. I defend human rights and cherish human freedom. I vow to honor and protect the global ecology for ourselves and for generations yet unborn.


## IV. The Ethics of the World Community

Humanism, we believe, can play a significant role in helping to foster the development of a genuine world community. We recommend the following for consideration.

1. Moral codes that prevail today are often rooted in ancient parochial and tribal loyalties. Absolutistic moral systems emerged from the values of the rural and nomadic societies of the past; they provide little useful guidance for our post-modern world. We need to draw on the best moral wisdom of the past, but we also need to develop a new, revisionary ethics that employs rational methods of inquiry appropriate to the world of the future, an ethics that respects the dignity and freedom of each person but that also expresses a larger concern for humanity as a whole. *The basic imperative faced by humankind today is the need to develop a worldwide ethical awareness of our mutual interdependence and a willingness to modify time-hardened attitudes that prevent such a consensus.*

2. Science and technology continue to advance rapidly, providing new ways to reduce famine, poverty, and disease and to improve the standards of living for all members of the human family. The great imperative is to extend the benefits of the scientific revolution to every person on earth. We need to guard against the population explosion, the destruction of the environment, and the reckless use of technology. We disagree with those fearful voices seeking to censor science and thus limit future discoveries that could can have great benefits for humankind. Biogenetic and neurobiological engineering hold enormous promise; yet such research is extremely controversial. New reproductive technology calls for new legal and ethical thinking to protect the rights of the people involved and avoid commercial exploitation. Critics warn that we might be opening a Pandora's box. Proponents reply that although we must be alert to possible abuses, each new scientific advance in history has had its prophets of doom.

The frontiers of space exploration continue to beckon humankind. We have hurled satellites to the moon, to the planets, and even beyond our solar system. Scientists tell us that it is technologically feasible to build space colonies and to mine other planets. The possible adventures in space that await us are truly Promethean in dimension. Computers and other electronic media facilitate instantaneous communication to all corners of the planet. Yet in many countries the mass media or organs of propaganda often abdicate their responsibilities by feeding the public a diet of banalities.

*We face a common challenge to develop scientific education on a global scale and an appreciation for critical intelligence and reason as a way to solve human problems and enhance human welfare.*

3. The awesome danger of thermonuclear war is held in check only by the fear of "mutually assured destruction." Fortunately, the great powers have entered into an era of negotiation for the reduction of nuclear arms, which is welcomed by men and women of good will. Still, these negotiations are no substitute for a broader diplomacy that promotes more fundamental understanding and cooperation. We have not yet learned how to control warfare, for there does not exist any supernational sovereignty with sufficient power to keep the peace between nation-states. We submit that it is imperative that such a sovereignty be created. The United Nations has made valiant attempts to develop transnational political institutions—but so far with limited success. We recognize that in this

quest for a world community, we will need to guard against the emergence of an all-powerful nondemocratic global state. We believe, however, that *it is necessary to create on a global scale new democratic and pluralistic institutions that protect the rights and freedoms of all people.* As a first step, humankind needs to establish a system of world law and to endow the World Court with enough moral force that its jurisdiction is recognized as binding by all the nation-states of the world.

4. The disparities in economic wealth between various portions of the globe widen. Economic development in the Third World is now virtually stagnant. Massive debts to foreign banks, runaway inflation, and uncontrolled population growth place a heavy burden on fragile economies and threaten to bankrupt the world's monetary system. We believe, however, that the more affluent nations have a moral obligation to increase technological and economic assistance so that their less developed neighbors may become more self-sufficient. We need to work out some equitable forms of taxation on a worldwide basis to help make this a reality.

5. Economic relations today are such that many corporations are multinational in scope, and some of these have been successful in promoting intercultural tolerance. All regions of the globe—socialist and nonsocialist alike—are dependent upon the continued flow of world trade to survive. Interest rates, deficits, capital investments, currency and stock-market fluctuations, commodity prices, and import quotas in any one nation can influence trade on a global scale. The loss of industries in some countries and the consequent rise in unemployment are a direct function of the ability to be productive and to compete effectively for international markets.

The governments of the separate nations nevertheless continue to prepare their budgets in haughty isolation and primarily in terms of national self-interest. Full-scale cooperation among countries is still limited, and competitive rivalries rule the day. *A new global economic system based on economic cooperation and international solidarity needs to emerge.*

6. The vitality of democratic societies over authoritarian or totalitarian regimes has been vividly demonstrated. Democratic institutions make possible higher standards of living and provide more opportunities for creativity and freedom than their alternatives. Genuine political democracy still eludes much of the world; unfortunately, many countries are ruled by dictatorial or authoritarian elites that deny their citizens basic human rights. *We need to firmly defend the ideals of political democracy on a worldwide basis, and to encourage the further extensions of democracy.*

7. Each of the regions of the world cherishes its own historical ethnic traditions and wishes to preserve its national identity. We should appreciate the richness and diversity of cultures and the values of pluralism and polyethnicity. Yet *we urgently need to enlarge our common ground. We should encourage the intermingling of peoples* in every way we can. Continuing scientific, artistic, and cultural exchanges are vital. The right to travel across national borders should be defended as a human right. Intermarriage can help unify the world more solidly than can conventional politics, and those who intermarry should not be

considered the pariahs of society but rather harbingers of the new world of tomorrow.

8. We all inhabit the same globe; we have a vital stake in helping to preserve its ecology. The contamination of the atmosphere, damage to the ozone layer, deforestation, the pollution of the oceans, the increase in acid rain, the greenhouse effect, and the destruction of other species on this planet adversely affect us all. *We urge the establishment of an international environmental monitoring agency, and recommend the development of appropriate standards for the disposal of industrial waste and for the control of toxic emissions.* The time has come to sound the alarm before the global ecological system deteriorates further. *We have a clear duty to future generations to curtail excessive population growth, to maintain a healthy environment, and to preserve the earth's precious resources.*

The overriding need is to develop a new global ethics—one that seeks to preserve and enhance individual human freedom and emphasizes our commitment to the world community. Although we must recognize our obligations and responsibilities to the local communities, states, and nations of which we are citizens, we also need to develop a new sense of identity with the planetary society of the future.

As we approach the twenty-first century, we need to ask: How can we work cooperatively to create a peaceful and prosperous world where combating national allegiances are transcended? How can we confer dignity upon all human beings? How can we build a genuine world community?

We who endorse this declaration dedicate ourselves to the realization of its enduring ideals. Although we may not agree with every provision of this statement, we support its overall purpose and call upon other men and women of good will to join us in the furthering its noble aims.

**A Declaration of Interdependence: A New Global Ethics** has been endorsed by the Board of Directors of the International Humanist and Ethical Union and the Tenth World Congress of the International Humanist and Ethical Union, meeting July 30 to August 4, 1988 at the State University of New York at Buffalo. It has been signed by the following Humanist Laureates of the Academy of Humanism:

**Isaac Asimov,** author
**Mario Bunge,** Professor of Philosophy, McGill University
**Bonnie Bullough,** Dean of Nursing, State University of New York at Buffalo
**Vern Bullough,** Dean of Natural and Social Sciences, State University of New York College at Buffalo
**José Delgado,** Professor, Center for Neurological Research, University of Madrid
**Herbert Hauptman,** Nobel Laureate; Professor of Biophysical Science, State University of New York at Buffalo
**Paul Kurtz,** Drafter of the Declaration of Interdependence; Professor of Philosophy, State University of New York at Buffalo

**Gerald Larue,** Chairman, Center for the Scientific Examination of Religion; Professor Emeritus, University of Southern California
**Jean-Claude Pecker,** Professor of Astrophysics, Collége de France
**Max Rood,** Professor of Law and Former Minister of Justice of Holland
**Svetozar Stojanović,** Professor of Philosophy, University of Belgrade

# Contributors

**Gina Allen** is the author of many books and articles, and is a humanist counselor in San Francisco.

**Elizabeth Rice Allgeier** is professor of psychology at Bowling Green State University.

**Oldrich Andrysek** is legal adviser for the Human Rights Commission of the International Humanist and Ethical Union.

**Joe E. Barnhart** is professor of philosophy at the University of North Texas in Denton. He has written numerous articles and books on religion, including *Jim and Tammy, The Billy Graham Religion,* and *The Study of Religion and Its Meaning.*

**Renate Bauer** is secretary of the Bund Freireligioser Gemeinden Deutschland, and a member of the Board of Directors of the International Humanist and Ethical Union.

The late **Paul H. Beattie** was president of the Fellowship of Religious Humanists and co-editor of the magazine *Religious Humanism.* He was a minister of the First Unitarian Church in Pittsburgh.

**Ruth Bennett** is professor and director of the Graduate Education Division of Geriatrics and Gerontology at Columbia University.

**Lydia Blontrock** is chair of the Humanistisch Verbond Belgie.

**Noel Brown** is director of the United Nations Environmental Program.

**Vern L. Bullough** is dean of natural and social sciences and a distinguished professor at the State University of New York College at Buffalo. He is the author or editor of more than twenty books on history, sexology, neurology, and other fields.

**Mario Bunge** is Frothingham Professor of Foundations and Philosophy of Science at McGill University in Montreal, Quebec, and a member of the Academy of Humanism. He is the author of many books and articles on theoretical physics, the philosophy of science, metaphysics, and science policy.

**Rodrigo Carazo** is president of the University of Peace and former president of Costa Rica.

**Tad S. Clements** is Emeritus Professor of Philosophy at the State University of New York College at Brockport.

**John Corcoran** is professor of philosophy at the State University of New York at Buffalo.

**José M. R. Delgado** is director of the Centro de Estudios Neurobiologicos in Madrid, Spain, and a member of the Academy of Humanism. His publications deal mainly with electrical and chemical control of the brain.

**Edd Doerr** is executive director of Americans for Religious Liberty, and vice-president of the American Humanist Association.

**Fang Fu Ruan** is professor of medical sociology at Beijing Medical University.

**Levi Fragell** is executive director of Human-Etisk Forbund i Norge and copresi-dent of the International Humanist and Ethical Union.

**Anne-Marie Franchi** is the vice president of the Ligue Française de l'Enseigne-ment et de l'Education Permanente. The league is the largest association of teachers and parents in France.

**Betty Friedan** is an author and the founder of the National Organization for Women (NOW).

**Victor Garadja** is director of the Institute for Scientific Atheism in Moscow.

**Herbert Hauptman** is a Nobel Laureate and professor of biophysical science at the State University of New York at Buffalo.

**Randel Helms** is associate professor of English at the University of Arizona. He is the author of *Gospel Fictions* and numerous articles on literature, psychology, and biblical studies.

**Robert L. Holmes** is professor of philosophy at the University of Rochester.

**R. A. Jahagirdar** is a justice on the Supreme Court of India.

**Carol Kahn** is a feature writer for *Omni* magazine and the author of two books on life extension: *Living Longer, Growing Younger* (with Paul Segall), and *Beyond the Helix: DNA and the Quest for Longevity.*

**Marvin Kohl** is professor of philosophy at the State University of New York College at Fredonia and the author of *Beneficent Euthanasia, The Morality of Killing,* and other books and articles.

**Mathilde Krim** is an associate research scientist at St. Luke's Roosevelt Hos-pital Center and College of Physicians and Surgeons, Columbia University, and a founding chair and director of the American Foundation for AIDS Research.

**Lisa Kuhmerker** is a visiting scholar at the Harvard Graduate School of Edu-cation and on the adjunct faculty of the Boston University Department of Education. She is the publisher and editor of the *Moral Education Forum.*

**Paul Kurtz** is professor of philosophy at the State University of New York at Buffalo, editor of *Free Inquiry* magazine and copresident of the Inter-national Humanist and Ethical Union. He is the author of *Eupraxophy, Forbidden Fruit,* and *The Transcendental Temptation* among other books.

**Corliss Lamont** is a retired philosophy lecturer at Columbia University and Honorary President of the American Humanist Association. He is the au-thor of *The Philosophy of Humanism.*

**Gerald A. Larue** is President Emeritus of the National Hemlock Society and is Emeritus Professor of Religion, Archaeology, and Biblical Studies and adjunct professor of gerontology at the University of Southern California at Los Angeles.

**Lin Zixin** is a writer and editor-in-chief of *Science and Technology Daily*, the first newspaper to report the Chinese student rebellion of 1989.

**Mario Mendez-Acosta** is an attorney and television news commentator in Mexico City, and chairman of the Mexico Skeptics.

**Lester W. Milbrath** is professor of political science at the State University of New York at Buffalo.

**Frank T. Miosi** is professor of Egyptology at the University of Toronto and supervisor of the Ontario Ministry of Colleges and Universities.

**John Money** is professor of medical psychology and pediatrics and Emeritus Director of the Psychonormal Research Unit at the Johns Hopkins University and Hospital. He is the author of *The Destroying Angel, Venuses Penuses, Vandalized Lovemaps,* and other works.

**Henry Morgentaler** is a medical doctor and president of the Humanist Association of Canada. He has been active for more than twenty years in the struggle to humanize Canada's abortion law.

**Johan Nordenfelt** is director of Publications and World Disarmament at the United Nations.

**Indumati Parikh** is a medical doctor and president of the Radical Humanist Association.

**Jean-Claude Pecker** is professor of astrophysics at the Collège de France and a member of the French Academy of Science.

**John F. Priest** is professor of religion at Florida State University.

**Armin Rieser** is professor of hydrology at the University of Bonn and president of the Bund Freireligioser Gemeinden Deutschland.

**Howard Radest** is director of the Ethical Culture Schools and dean of the Humanist Institute. He is former executive director of the American Ethical Union.

**William F. Schulz** is president of the Unitarian-Universalist Association.

**Matthew Ies Spetter** is associate professor of social psychology at the Peace Studies Institute of Manhattan College and leader of the Riverdale Society for Ethical Culture.

**Svetozar Stojanović** is professor of philosophy at the University of Belgrade, and author of *Between Ideals and Reality, In Search of Democracy in Socialism,* and *From Marxism and Bolshevism to Gorbachev's "Perestroika."*

**Harry Stopes-Roe** is professor of philosophy at the University of Birmingham.

**Hope N. Tawiah** is director of the Rational Centre in Ghana.

**Richard Taylor** is Professor Emeritus of Philosophy at Union College and a member of the Academy of Humanism. He is the author of *Freedom, Anarchy and the Law* and many other works.

**Rob Tielman** is professor of sociology at the University of Utrecht and copresident of the International Humanist and Ethical Union.

**Victor Timofeyer** is deputy director of the Institute for Scientific Atheism in Moscow.

**Jan Glastra van Loon** is the Commissioner for Human Rights of the International Humanist and Ethical Union and a member of the Dutch Parliament.

**Wendell W. Watters** is professor of psychiatry at McMaster University in Hamilton, Ontario.